The Selection of Politicians in Times of Crisis

Selecting candidates for elections is a major goal of political parties and a major function of political regimes in democratic systems. With the negative effects of the economic crisis being seen to translate into changes in voting patterns, and citizens using elections to punish parties in government for their roles in economic mismanagement or lack of response to the global economic crisis, a broad examination is required.

This book is presented as the first comparative study of the effects of the political crisis on candidate selection covering a large number of countries. Using an integrated framework and unified strategy, it examines how new relevant political actors are implementing participative ways of candidate selection; whether they are being innovative in their political environments; and the extent to which traditionally mainstream parties are changing selection procedures to permit more open and inclusive mechanisms as part of internal, or intra-party, democracy. The book illuminates these issues through empirically-driven chapters explaining changes in the way candidates for parliaments are selected in countries where new parties have emerged and consolidated, or where traditional mainstream parties have adopted new mechanisms of selection, affecting (if not challenging) traditional politics. Additionally, therefore, this work will serve as a response to some current debates in the discipline on the consequences of the democratization of party life, relating political participation and representation.

This text will be of key interest to scholars and students of political parties, organizational change, social and political elites and more broadly to the fields of comparative politics and sociology.

Xavier Coller is Professor of Sociology at the Universidad Pablo de Olavide in Seville, Spain.

Guillermo Cordero is Assistant Professor of Political Science at the Universidad Autónoma de Madrid, Spain.

Antonio M. Jaime-Castillo is Associate Professor of Sociology at the Universidad de Málaga, Spain.

Routledge Research on Social and Political Elites
Series Editors: Keith Dowding and Patrick Dumont,
Australian National University, Australia.

Who are the elites that run the world? This series of books analyses who the elites are, how they rise and fall, the networks in which they operate and the effects they have on our lives.

The Selection of Politicians in Times of Crisis

Edited by Xavier Coller,
Guillermo Cordero, and
Antonio M. Jaime-Castillo

Routledge
Taylor & Francis Group

LONDON AND NEW YORK

First published 2018
by Routledge
2 Park Square, Milton Park, Abingdon, Oxon OX14 4RN

and by Routledge
711 Third Avenue, New York, NY 10017

Routledge is an imprint of the Taylor & Francis Group, an informa business

© 2018 selection and editorial matter, Xavier Coller, Guillermo Cordero, and Antonio M. Jaime-Castillo; individual chapters, the contributors

British Library Cataloguing-in-Publication Data
A catalogue record for this book is available from the British Library

Library of Congress Cataloguing-in-Publication Data
A catalog record for this book has been requested

ISBN: 978-1-138-89521-8 (hbk)
ISBN: 978-1-315-17957-5 (ebk)

Typeset in Times New Roman
by Apex CoVantage, LLC

Contents

Figures

Tables

Contributors

Editors

Xavier Coller is professor of sociology at the Universidad Pablo de Olavide (Seville, Spain) and holds a PhD in Sociology (Yale University). He has taught in several universities in Europe and the US and has been visiting fellow at Warwick University, University of California (Berkeley), Yale, Harvard, Georgetown, Montpellier 1, and Libera Università Internazionale degli Studi Sociali. He was the Seventh Prince of Asturias Chair, Georgetown University (2005–07). He has authored over a hundred works on political sociology, social theories, research methods, collective identities, political elites, and complex organizations. He is the winner of several international awards, among them the 2003 Sussman Dissertation Award (Yale University), and an honourable mention in the 2003 Seymour Martin Lipset Award (Princeton University).

Guillermo Cordero is assistant professor of political science at the Universidad Autónoma de Madrid (Spain). Previously, he held postdoctoral teaching and research positions at the Universitat Pompeu Fabra in Barcelona and pre-doctoral research positions at the Center for Advanced Studies in the Social Sciences (CEACS, Juan March Institute) in Madrid. He has been visiting fellow at the University of Essex, the University of Michigan, the Université de Montréal and the University of California, Berkeley. He holds a MA in Democracy and Government as well as a PhD in Political Science. His main areas of interest include political attitudes, electoral behaviour and the selection of political elites in Europe. His most recent research on these topics has been published in *Acta Politica*, the *American Behavioral Scientist*, the *Canadian Journal of Political Science*, *Parliamentary Affairs*, *South European Society and Politics*, and *West European Politics*, among others.

Antonio M. Jaime-Castillo is associate professor of sociology at the Universidad de Málaga (Spain). He has been Visiting Scholar at the Norwegian Social Science Data Services (University of Bergen), the Zentral Archiv (University of Cologne) and the Workshop in Political Theory and Policy Analysis (University of Indiana). His research interests include welfare attitudes, inequality, political sociology and quantitative methods of comparative research. His work has been published in journals such as the *American Behavioral Scientist, European Sociological Review, Journal of European Social Policy, International Political Science Review, Social Forces* and *Social Science Research,* among others.

Contributors

Mélany Barragán, holds a PhD from the University of Salamanca and is a member of the project Latin American Parliamentary Elites. She focuses her research on elites and political careers, comparative politics, selection, leadership, methodology and comparative politics and has attended multiple conferences, such as IPSA, ECPR or ALACIP. She has conducted fieldwork in El Salvador, Honduras, Panama, Costa Rica, Ecuador and Uruguay. She has been visiting scholar at Goethe University (Germany), and University of Pittsburgh (USA). Currently, she is working on political careers in federal systems and Latin American former presidents.

Asbel Bohigues is a PhD candidate of the University of Salamanca and member of the project Latin American Parliamentary Elites. His research focus is on parliamentary elites, political parties, and the quality and varieties of democracy in Latin America. He has conducted fieldwork in Venezuela, Bolivia and Uruguay. His last publication is "El control democrático de la agenda: implementando la democracia directa", in *Política y Democracia: anversos y reversos,* by Manuel Alcántara, Mario Serrafero and E. Martín Cuesta (Buenos Aires: L&D 2016).

Patricia Craig is a political sociologist and currently Dean for international and professional experience and senior lecturer at Yale-NUS College in Singapore, a liberal arts institution jointly founded by Yale University and the National University of Singapore. She is formerly the Executive Director of the Center for European Studies at Harvard. Her work focuses on party politics and institutions, as well as on the globalization of higher education.

Klaus Detterbeck is professor at the University of Education Schwäbisch Gmünd (Germany). His areas of expertise are party politics, federalism and European integration. He has been co-convenor of the ECPR Standing Group on Federalism and Regionalism. Among his most recent publications are *Parties and civil society in federal systems* with Wolfgang Renzsch (Oxford UP 2015), *Multilevel party politics in Western Europe* (Palgrave Macmillan 2012), *Parteien und Parteiensystem* (UVK Verlag 2011), and *Föderalismus in Deutschland* with Wolfgang Renzsch and Stefan Schieren (Oldenbourg Verlag 2010).

Gunnar Helgi Kristinsson is professor in political science at the University of Iceland. He has published widely on several aspects of Icelandic politics in international journals such as the European Journal of Political Research, Party Politics, Scandinavian Political Studies and West European Politics as well as book chapters with major international publishers. His main fields of research include political parties, the politics of the executive, public policy and public administration. He is founding editor of the Icelandic Review of Politics and Administration and has served for long periods as chair of the Institute of Public Administration and Politics and the Department of Political Science at the University of Iceland.

Vít Hloušek is professor of the Department of International Relations and European Studies, Faculty of Social Studies, Masaryk University, Czech Republic. He graduated in History and Political Science at the Faculty of Arts and Faculty of Social Studies, Masaryk University (1995–2000). In 2000–2003 he took his PhD degree in Political Science at the Faculty of Social Studies, Masaryk University, and he became Professor in 2015. He has been involved in the International Institute of Political Science since 2012 (working there prior to this between 2002 and 2007). He also teaches at the Department of International Relations and European Studies at the Faculty of Social Studies, Masaryk University. His research interests include comparative political science (especially comparisons of political and party systems of European countries), contemporary history and issues concerning the genesis and development of modern mass politics in Central Europe. He teaches comparative political science and modern European political history. He has authored a number of articles in scholarly journals and books, edited several volumes, and written monographs such as *Origin, Ideology and Transformation of Political Parties. East-Central and Western Europe Compared* (with L. Kopeček, Ashgate 2010) and *Party Systems in East Central Europe* (with L. Cabada and P. Jurek, Lexington Books 2014).

Marcelo Jenny is a professor at the University of Innsbruck. Previously he was a postdoctoral researcher and member of the Austrian National Election Study (AUTNES). He holds degrees in political science from the Universities of Vienna and Mannheim. His research interests and publications span the topics of democratic representation, legislative politics, candidate selection, campaigning and electoral behaviour. His most recent co-authored publication appearing in Electoral Studies shows how legislative candidates use their party's manifesto in an election campaign.

Manina Kakepaki has been a researcher at the National Centre for Social Research (EKKE) since 2010 and has participated in more than 20 national and international research projects, including QUING, Intune and ESS. She has studied in Athens (Bachelor's Degree, PhD) and Essex (MA Political Behaviour) and was a postdoctoral Fellow at the University of Athens researching gender differences in political values and attitudes. Her current research interests concern aspects of youth political socialization, political participation and elite representation. Her latest work is an edited volume on the social and political characteristics of Greek parliamentarians from 1996 to 2015 (EKKE-Papazisis 2016). She is on the editorial board of the *Greek Review of Social Research*.

Lubomír Kopeček is professor of the Department of Political Science, Faculty of Social Studies, Masaryk University, Czech Republic. He is a graduate in Political Science, History and Law at Masaryk University, Lubomír Kopeček focuses on party and political systems in European countries, theories of democracy, and Czech politics. He has been teaching at the Department of Political Science, Faculty of Social Studies, Masaryk University since 2001 and in 2012 became involved in the International Institute of Political Science. He has authored (or co-authored) several books and dozens of articles in political science journals, both at home and abroad, and has been principal investigator on several grant projects. His most important publications include the monograph, *Origin, Ideology and Transformation of Political Parties. East-Central and Western Europe Compared* (with V. Hloušek, Ashgate 2010).

Joy Langston is professor of political science at CIDE in Mexico City. She earned a master's degree and doctorate in political science from Duke University, and has published in the *Journal of Politics, Comparative Political Studies, Comparative Politics*, and *Legislative Studies Quarterly*. Her research interests include campaigning, legislatures, candidate selection, and other aspects of party behaviour and organization.

Marco Lisi is an assistant professor in the Department of Political Studies, Nova University of Lisbon and researcher at IPRI. His research interests focus on political parties, electoral behaviour, democratic theory, political representation and election campaigns. He published several articles in national and international journals such as *International Political Science Review, Comparative European Politics* and *South European Society & Politics*. His latest books are *Party Change, Recent Democracies and Portugal: Comparative Perspectives* (Lexington 2015) and *Political Representation in Times of Bailout: Evidence from Greece and Portugal* (co-authored with André Freire, Ioannis Andreadis and José Manuel Leite Viegas, Routledge 2016).

Eva H. Önnudóttir is an associate professor in political science at the University of Iceland since 2015. She defended her PhD project, 'The Nature and Outcome of representation' at the CDSS/University of Mannheim in July 2015. She has published papers in West-European Politics, Party Politics and Icelandic Review of Politics & Administration. Eva H. Önnudóttir is a member of the Icelandic National Election Study (ICENES), the True European Voter (TEV) project, the Comparative Candidate Surveys (CCS) and the Comparative Study of Electoral Systems (CSES).

Theresa Reidy is a lecturer in the Department of Government at University College Cork, Ireland, where her teaching and research interests lie in the areas of electoral behaviour and public finance. Theresa has been co-editor of Irish Political Studies since 2012 and is Vice President of the Political Studies Association on Ireland (PSAI). She has held visiting teaching and research positions in Germany and Canada. Theresa has convened a large number of conferences, including the annual conference of the PSAI in

2006 and 2015, and many events focused on political reform and elections. She has given expert evidence to parliamentary committees and the Constitutional Convention and is a regular contributor to national and international radio and the print media.

Marion Reiser is professor of political science at the Friedrich-Schiller-University Jena (Germany) and holds a PhD (University of Goettingen) and a Habilitation (University of Frankfurt) in Political Science. Previously she has been professor at Leuphana University Lueneburg, and held postdoctoral teaching and research positions at the universities of Frankfurt, Hamburg and Halle (Saale) and has been visiting fellow at the universities of Copenhagen, Birmingham and Oslo. Her main areas of interest include political parties, political elites, political sociology, and local politics.

Stefano Rombi is a postdoctoral fellow at the University of Cagliari. He teaches Political Science at DISSI – Department of Social Sciences and Institutions, University of Cagliari. His main research interests include quality of democracy, elections, and candidate and leadership selection. He is member of Candidate and Leader Selection, the standing group of the Italian Political Science Association, and of the editorial board of Quaderni dell'Osservatorio Elettorale. He has published articles in academic journals including Contemporary Italian Politics, Italian Political Science Review and Quaderni di Scienza Politica. He has authored, co-authored, and co-edited books on electoral accountability and candidate selection, including *L'accountability dei governi democratici* (Carocci 2014).

Antonella Seddone is a postdoctoral fellow at ESPOL – the European School of Political and Social Sciences, Université Catholique de Lille. She teaches also at DCPS – Department of Cultures, Politics and Society, University of Turin. Her research interests are focused on political parties, primary elections and political communication. She is co-convenor of Candidate and Leader Selection, standing group of the Italian Political Science Association. She is also a member of the executive committee of the PSA's Italian Politics Specialist Group (IPSG). She has published several articles in academic journals including Acta Politica, Italian Political Science Review, Modern Italy, Journal of Modern Italian Studies. Recently she co-edited *Party Primaries in Comparative Perspective* (Ashgate 2015).

Audrey Vandeleene has been a postdoctoral research fellow at the Institute of Political Science Louvain-Europe (ISPOLE), Université catholique de Louvain (Belgium) and at Lund University (Sweden) from January 2017 onwards. She defended her doctoral thesis in 2016. Her doctoral work handled a comparative qualitative and quantitative analysis of candidate selection processes in Belgian political parties. Her research interests cover party politics, candidate selection, intra-party democracy, electoral systems and women in politics. She has published in *Representation* and *American Behavioral Scientist*. She is one of the two managers of the *Belgian Candidate Survey* in 2014.

Lieven De Winter is senior professor at the Institute of Political Science Louvain-Europe, Université Catholique de Louvain (Belgium). He wrote his PhD on the Belgian Legislator at the European University Institute. He has published widely on electoral behaviour, parties, parliaments, cabinets, political elites, and regionalism, mainly from a European comparative perspective. He coordinated the Belgian Candidate Survey of 2007, 2010, and 2014, and currently is editing a comparative volume (with Hermann Schmitt and Rune Karlsen) on the basis of the CCS data.

1 Economic crisis and the selection of candidates

Xavier Coller, Guillermo Cordero and Antonio M. Jaime-Castillo

Selecting candidates for legislative elections is a major goal of political parties and one of the most relevant services parties pay to the functioning of democracies. It is a critical factor affecting a wide range of elements, such as the MPs' profiles and their behaviour (Gauja and Cross, 2015; Coller, et al., 2018), party cohesion and discipline in parliaments (Cordero and Coller, 2015), internal distribution of power (Gallagher et al., 2001; Hopkin, 2001), the voting behaviour of selectors (Cross and Blais, 2012), or the stability of governments and institutions (Hazan and Rahat, 2010). Consequently, selection has an impact on the quality of democracy – those who are selected for an electoral list and end up having a seat in parliaments, make decisions that have an impact on citizens' quality of life, and therefore affects the relationship between politics and citizens. All parties follow some sort of mechanism (rudimentary or sophisticated, more or less detailed in parties' by-laws) to select their legislative candidates. In this book, we follow Hazan and Rahat (2010, 4) when they define "candidate selection methods" as "the nonstandardized and predominantly unregimented particular party mechanisms by which political parties choose their candidates for general [or regional, local, supranational] elections. The result of this process is the designation of a candidate, or list of candidates, as *the* candidate(s) of the party".

Questions and goals: crisis, selection of candidates and descriptive representation

With the Great Recession in the background as intervening variable, this book explores answers to three basic questions – Are the new parties that have emerged during the crisis implementing open and inclusive ways of selecting legislative candidates? Have these "new" selection mechanisms been incorporated by mainstream parties in a "contagion" effect? Are the new selection practices producing changes in the social structure of parliaments? The book tries to answer these questions by empirically exploring a number of cases affected differently by the Great Recession.

The growing interest on the study of intra-party democracy (IPD) focused mainly on the selection of leaders, and the scrutiny of how parties select their legislative candidates (see Chapter 2), both qualify Gallagher and Marsh's (1988) perception that candidate selection may be considered "the secret garden of politics". There are a number of studies using macro variables to explain variation in the selection of candidates (see Shomer, 2010). However, since parties implement different mechanisms of selection following mainly informal procedures beyond party by-laws (Ranney, 1981; Gallagher and Marsh, 1988; Katz, 2001; Fujimura, 2012), we still know little about the real factors beyond selection (Cordero, et al., 2016), rendering this crucial activity as an almost "secret garden" or "obscure" function (Hazan and Rahat, 2010, 6) that takes place inside parties. The number of studies exploring, from an empirical perspective, how the selection of candidates operates is somehow limited and covers a small number of cases (Coller et al., 2016). Therefore, the concerns of Hazan and Rahat (2010, 13) may still hold: "The lack of cross-national empirical studies is, thus, the Achilles' heel of any attempt to make further progress". This is so, especially, if we take into account that candidate selection mechanisms may change, especially under turbulent political environments fostered by the economic crisis. The political derivations of the crisis, the growing demands for more participation, the emergence of new sociopolitical actors, and the reaction of citizens towards traditional politicians and their parties may have changed the way parties select candidates. This is the idea that prompts the exploration covered in this book.

The deep and long economic crisis has impacted countries in a variety of ways and with different intensity. The North-South divide (with the incorporation of Ireland and Iceland as Northern deviant cases) has left a deep mark and emerges as a relevant factor explaining a number of political effects. The crisis has had important political implications.[1] One of the first consequences analysed by the literature has been a growing volatility and abstention (Lewis-Beck and Nadcau, 2012; Magalhães, 2014). The negative effects of the economic crisis soon translated into voting patterns, with citizens using elections to punish parties in government for their roles in economic mismanagement or lack of response to the global economic crisis. However, this important political consequence was only the beginning of the story. As the economic crisis deepened across countries, affecting a wide range of citizens, the levels of political distrust and alienation also increased dramatically. As the literature has demonstrated (Armingeon and Guthmann, 2013; Torcal, 2014, 2016; Muro and Vidal, 2017), the inability of traditional actors to solve the crisis eroded satisfaction and trust in the parties and the political system (Papadopoulos, 2013), creating the conditions for a political crisis. This political crisis has led to the emergence of new political actors (or the strengthening of old, irrelevant ones) in different parts of the world (Cordero and Simón, 2015), the subsequent reorganization of party systems along the lines of new cleavages like the establishment vs. anti-establishment (Morlino and Raniolo, 2017) or the "old" vs. "new" politics, and the introduction or consolidation of changes in the functioning of traditionally mainstream parties.

Following this basic assumption, for the purposes of this book we chose to study countries that were differently affected by the Great Recession. There are countries where the crisis hit hard and new actors emerged, or in which not entirely new but small parties gained electoral strength, alone or in alliance, or became new mainstream parties. Examples are Italy (Five Stars Movement), Czech Republic (ANO Party, Public Affaires), Spain (Podemos and Ciudadanos), Ireland (Social Democrats, Anti-Austerity Alliance – People Before Profit), Greece (SYRIZA, Golden Dawn), Iceland (Reform, Bright Future, Pirate Party) and some countries in Latin America. The counter case here is Portugal and somehow Mexico, and chapters 13 and 12 explain the reasons.[2] In Central-Eastern European countries, new entrepreneurial parties (Kopecek, 2016) emerged, gaining prominent positions in several party systems (Czech Republic, with TOP 09, Public Affairs or Dawn of Direct Democracy, or Poland, with Modern or Solidarity Poland, or Hungary with LMP, not covered in this book). In some other cases, the crisis was not felt so strongly but new parties appeared as well in the political scenario, such as in Germany (Alternative für Deutschland, Pirate Party), Austria (NEOS, Pirate Party, List Pilz and Team Stronach). Belgium and the US are the negative cases here, as explained in chapters 4 and 15.

At first sight, there are reasons to believe that the Great Recession plus demands for more participation have produced different political outputs in terms of party changes, and implementation of IPD mechanisms is one of them. However, changes in political parties do not fully have their origins in the recent past. Over the last decades, decreasing political participation and partisanship has been a matter of concern for the social sciences and certainly an organizational problem for the parties themselves (van Biezen et al., 2012). The democratization of the internal life of political parties has been seen as a solution by a large number of politicians and social scientists (Katz and Cross, 2013, 173). In fact, a common trend towards the democratization in the selection of candidates and party leaders has been shown by the literature (Rahat and Hazan, 2007; Cross and Blais, 2012; Sandri et al., 2015).

Although the democratization of the internal life of parties is not new, the recent political crisis may have challenged the traditional functioning of parties provoking what organizational sociologists name "adaptation to the environment". Several social movements have emerged in the world since 2008, such as the "Indignant Citizen Movement", the "Direct Democracy Now!", "Real Democracy Now", the "Occupy" movements, or more locally, the "umbrella revolution" in Hong-Kong or "Hart boven Hard" and "Tout Autre Chose" in Belgium, contesting the negative effects of the crisis and most of them demanding open avenues of participation in politics (Della Porta and Mattonia, 2014).[3] As a response to this wide demand, some parties have implemented more open mechanisms for participation, including democratization of the selection of their elites. This response is not only a consequence of the emergence of new social movements but also an attempt to recover the electoral support lost throughout this crisis and before (Katz and Cross, 2013, 173), and is contingent upon pressures from the environment. Adaptation may be beneficial for the survival of the party in a changing environment but inevitably generates unexpected consequences (Hazan and Rahat, 2010) and tensions inside, since resistance to change is a given in any organization.

Emerging parties linked to some of these social movements (such as Podemos, Anti-Austerity Alliance – People Before Profit, the Pirate Party and others studied in this book) were born to give voice to those who did not feel represented by the mainstream parties, especially where these movements were based on horizontalization in their decision-making processes. Thus, the emergence of these new actors and the reaction of mainstream parties concerning candidate selection may be analyzed as part of the trend towards democratization already pointed out by the literature (Sandri et al., 2015; Hazan and Rahat, 2010; Hopkin, 2001; Kenig et al., 2015). New political and social movements may be changing the way candidates are selected to be part of an electoral list and, thus, obtain a seat in parliament. Opening up candidate selection may be a key step towards more inclusive ways of participation, although the extent to which "old" and "new" politics are confronted in this matter is yet to be seen. Shedding light on this issue is one of the main goals of the book.

Although there are relevant contributions to the democratization of parties, these are not recent enough to reflect the possible changes in political parties since the Great Recession. This is the case of the inspiring work of Hazan and Rahat (2010), whose analytical framework is liberally applied in the study of candidate selection in this book, especially centralization (Where does selection takes place?) and inclusiveness (Who selects?), dimensions developed as well in an earlier work (Rahat and Hazan, 2001). Other influential works, such as that of Cross and Katz (2013a), does not offer a case-by-case perspective that analyses the specificities of each case and pays limited attention to the mimetic effects innovative candidate selection may have over mainstream traditional parties. Additionally, one of the most recent and interesting contributions to the field, Cross and Pilet (2014), is devoted to the selection of party leaders, but not of candidates, and as Kenig et al. (2015) remind us, there are substantial differences among them. Lastly, Sandri et al. (2015) also do not cover the recent effects of the Great Recession on changes in candidate selection. However, the success of these books is an indicator of the interest awakened in social sciences in the internal democratization of the mechanisms of candidate selection.

As argued before, in the context of the Great Recession, some changes are expected in the way that traditional and new parties drive their candidate selection, although countries' specificities may show different patterns and outputs, as we will see in the chapters of this book. Consequently, the first question we ask is whether these new relevant political actors, for whom the promotion of internal democracy is in many cases embedded in their DNA, are really implementing participative or inclusive ways of candidate selection and how they are (or are not) being innovative in their specific political environments. It seems that innovation is common amongst populist parties in Latin America, PAN in Mexico, somehow in Podemos and Ciudadanos in Spain, Five Star Movement in Italy, NEOS and Pirates Party in Austria, and some parties in Iceland and Ireland. However, innovation does not seem to be common amongst new parties in the Czech Republic because of their entrepreneurial nature, Syriza (Greece) or ÖVP (Austria) which are in power and making attempts to centralize candidate selection.

There are different factors that explain variations in the forms of candidate selection. Lundell (2004) finds that region and party size are relevant so that small parties may be more decentralized while large parties may need more central-ized mechanisms. This is qualified if we introduce the political structure of the state so that multilevel polities present incentives (different levels of elections) for parties to decentralize authority and selection (Cordero et al., 2016). However, the case of Spain (chapter 14) partially qualifies this statement. Also, Shomer (2014) finds that, contrary to previous considerations, electoral systems and ways of candidate selection are not causally related, discarding as well other factors like ideology, party size, or type of democratic regime (see also Bermúdez and Cordero, 2017). As indicated, regions are important and Rahat (2007) shows that Nordic countries tend to follow more decentralized patterns of candidate selec-tion. However, as will be seen in some chapters of this book, the cases of Five Star movement (Italy), Podemos (Spain) and somehow Syriza (Greece) challenge this finding, although the case of Iceland provides support for it. The explanation to this challenge hinges on the concept of "organizational learning" (Cyert and March, 1963). Political parties, *qua* organizations, learn from the environment and from other experiences. Therefore, what in 2007 was valid may be revised ten years later. Consequently, the second question we try to answer in this book is whether we can observe the effects of organizational learning: parties which somehow emulate others and change their ways of candidate selection. The next section theorizes the "emulation" or "contagion" process.

Paying attention to mainstream traditional parties and new actors alike, we are able to explore empirically the extent to which isomorphic pressures alter the balance of inclusiveness and centralization in the selection of candidates in a given party system. In this sense, we try to go beyond Cross and Blais (2012), who conclude that electoral defeat or mimetism are the basic drivers of change, especially in small, new and leftist parties, showing how large and conservative (and, yes, new) parties also introduce changes in candidate selection. We also try to go beyond Pilet and Cross (2014), whose conclusion, based on explaining that country and system-level factors (electoral defeat or years in the opposi-tion), explains changes in how more inclusive methods are implemented to select leaders. Keeping in mind that leadership selection is not candidate selection, we will show that sometimes parties react by increasing centralization, reduc-ing inclusiveness and affecting internal democracy, in large part due to electoral expectations (if success is expected, the party may want to have control over who becomes a candidate), the newness of the party (control over the nomination list prevents further defection and party switching), or the fact that they have been in power for a while and need to control who is getting into the lists. Some-times, IPD practices form part of the political culture of a particular party system, although new parties do not want to resort to them or even try to reverse IPD as party elites attempt to regain control over the formation of electoral lists. Risks of defection or party switching; the need to have a "harmonious" (not multivocal) parliamentary group; the need to have a disciplined parliamentary group while in government; conveying an image of robustness; reducing risks of rebellion: all of these are motives behind the reversing of trends towards decentralization and inclusiveness.

At some point, social scientists have to ask whether IPD practices affect something else in the internal life of a party *qua* organization. Katz and Cross (2013, 175) rightly set up the question: "Is the primary concern with producing candidate pools that are inclusive and generally representative of the electorate or with decentralized and participatory selection process regardless of the outcomes they produce?" The third question this book tries to answer is whether changes in candidate selection have contributed to a better or more accurate descriptive, demographic or microcosmic representation (Norris and Lovenduski, 1995, 94). This book helps to assess whether the trend towards a more diverse and heterogeneous parliamentary elite identified by the literature (Best and Cotta, 2000; Cotta and Best, 2007) holds and has intensified with changes in the methods of selection. The general expectation is that more inclusive ways of selection will produce a more accurate descriptive representation, although the reverse may also be true (Rahat and Hazan, 2001).[4]

This book aims at answering this set of three questions by putting together empirically-driven chapters explaining changes in the way candidates for parliaments are selected in countries where new parties have emerged and consolidated, or where traditional mainstream parties have adopted new mechanisms of selection affecting (if not challenging) traditional politics. Countercases are also explored so that the reader can evaluate whether country-specific factors can explain the variance.

Innovations in organizations and politics

Intra-Party Democracy (IPD) is a set of practices promoting the participation of members (affiliates, sympathizers, voters) in internal organizational processes, mainly the selection of party leaders and candidates for elections at different territorial levels.[5] As such, it has a number of virtues and problems that Cross and Katz (2013b), Katz and Cross (2013) and Hazan and Rahat (2010) deal with conveniently. Beyond virtues and problems, IPD practices may be considered an organizational innovation insofar as they add something new to the internal routines and structure of parties adopting them. Furthermore, they may imply a change in the culture of the organization. For instance, IPD may require changes in the by-laws, special organs or committees devoted to organize, regulate, and monitor the implementation of IPD practices and their results; by inducing participation following the one man one vote (OMOV) principle, they may undermine old forms of doing politics where some groups had power to select candidates. They thus contribute to a change in the organizational culture. Ultimately, they may have an effect on electoral results (although the evidence is not clear and robust, as Ramiro (2016) shows) but especially in the social profile of MPs, creating more diversity.

The most fruitful school in the social sciences studying innovations in organizations is the New Institutionalism (DiMaggio and Powell, 1991). According to this school, organizations strive for legitimacy in their organizational field and end up having similar characteristics, a process that has been called "isomorphism". An organizational field is composed of all organizations with structural relationships between them, including rivals and competitors. Incorporating innovations is one way of appearing as an organization that has done what it is supposed to do to avoid the risk of appearing negligent or irrational (Meyer and Rowan, 1983, 31), but not necessarily as one willing to solve a detected problem. Organizations may incorporate innovations to gain legitimacy even if they do not address the problem the innovation is supposed to solve. Decoupling problems and solutions has been observed in some of the cases analyzed here.

Incorporating innovations follows three stages (Tolbert and Zucker, 1996).[6] The first one is called "habitualization": an innovation appears in the organizational field as a solution to a problem. IPD practices may be considered a solution to the problem of growing demands for participation (especially during and after the crisis, as chapter 2 suggests) or even as a solution for internal disputes among factions, as chapter 11 on Latin America suggests. Its success depends on a number of factors: decision-makers sharing both cognitive frameworks[7] (Weick, 1979) and beliefs favouring innovations, a window of opportunity to change internal rules, the will to overcome internal resistances,[8] or external factors such as electoral defeats (as in some cases in Belgium and Greece, studied in chapters 4 and 7) or expectations of electoral growth (as in Italy or Spain, in chapters 10 and 14).

The second stage is that of "objectification", which means that the innovation is perceived as adequate for the problem and is adopted by other organizations. A growing consensus that the innovation is good is based on its positive results and some degree of theorization indicating that it would be useful for similar organizations. Diffusion of IPD practices spread among parties in a regional or national setting (as the cases of Italy or Spain illustrate in their respective chapters), but given the globalization process, international settings for mimetism should not be discarded, as is shown in the cases of Latin America (chapter 11) and partially in Mexico (chapter 12).

The third stage is that of "sedimentation" which takes place when the innovation is taken for granted and spreads in the organizational field without being much questioned. At this point, there is a decoupling between the problem that provoked the innovation and the innovation itself, which takes on a life of its own. IPD may be understood as a legitimated repertoire of practices that may be incorporated to the life of a party to meet the dominant *zeitgeist* and seeking external legitimacy but not because the party has an internal problem or experiences a wide demand for participation. This is what the case of Iceland shows (see chapter 8) – new parties did not challenge IPD mechanisms that were already operating in their organizational fields but adopted them and went even further. This is also evident in the case of Ireland (chapter 9), where IPD practices were already in motion once the new parties emerged. It may be that where in a particular setting there exists a repertoire of IPD practices operating to select candidates and a political culture prone to using them, the incentives to adapt to the environment are much higher than the costs of initiating exclusive and centralized selection of candidates.

IPD practices in candidate selection may be considered an organizational innovation that, once introduced in a party, may generate what DiMagio and Powell

(1991) call structural isomorphism: organizations tend to look alike once some sorts of IPD mechanisms have been incorporated with variations due to country, ideology, party traditions, electoral systems, and the like. There are three factors behind isomorphism. Firstly, the State with its norms and regulations may force political actors to behave in a particular way, generating "coercive" isomorphism. This is what happens when the State regulates the presence of, say, women in electoral lists (see the cases, for instance, of Greece and Spain). Secondly, but not so much in political markets, professionals (and their organizations and business schools) transfer different practices (innovations) across organizations; this is what has been called "normative" isomorphism. Thirdly, competitors and rivals try to emulate others (especially successful ones) through "mimetic" isomorphism.[9]

Without discarding coercive isomorphism,[10] which sets the rules of the game in countries like Germany (chapter 6) and the US (at the State level, chapter 15), it is reasonable to think that mimetic rather than normative isomorphism takes place in the political market of some party systems, as Pasquino and Valbruzzi (2016) suggest in the case of Italy. IPD practices are there in the organizational market and ready for newcomers to use although implementation and functioning are not free of tensions (Scarrow et al., 2002). They may be seen as a successful solution to a perceived problem or widespread demand and once successfully incorporated into a party, others may follow, although with some "controlled" variations (see the case of PP in Spain (chapter 14) or, to some extent, ND in Greece (chapter 7).[11] The consequence of these processes is the spread of IPD practices in different parties and at different speeds, and detailed case analysis carried out in this book may explain why they succeed or do not exist. In the end, as the chapter on Latin America suggests, adopting IPD practices in a context of political disaffection is a way of rebuilding legitimacy in the political system. However, the case of Iceland shows that when IPD is the common currency, in the context of the Great Recession newcomers may want to go further (chapter 8). Or, as the case of Ireland shows (chapter 9), with IPD practices available, most newcomers do not follow suit for internal reasons (lack of resources in party building, or lack of a consolidated structure, mainly). The case of Mexico (chapter 12) shows as well that opening candidate selection may be reversed or not an option thanks to protective institutions and the role played by leaders' interpretation of the political environment.

Analysing IPD practices in candidate selection leads to a critical paradox: often parties are considered the basic pillars of the functioning of democracies without being internally democratic, especially in what selecting their leaders and candidates is concerned. Without going further, the iron law of oligarchy coined in 1911 by Robert Michels (1962) explains this paradox. However, IPD practices may challenge Michels' law insofar as rank and file members end up having a say in the internal life of their parties, most especially in the selection of their leaders and candidates. The cases studied in this book leave a mixed conclusion. Certainly, wherever IPD practices have been implemented, affiliates have somehow participated even when there have been tensions in the implementation of

IPD (see, for instance, the case of Podemos in Spain, chapter 14). This does not disprove Michels' law, although it does qualify it, introducing a counterbalance to oligarchic tendencies inside parties. However, there are cases where it seems that Michels is still at least partially right and his thesis alive, as shown in some chapters of this book.

There are negative cases in which IPD practices do not advance and are even reversed. In Belgium, for instance, it seems that a combination of the relatively low impact of the crisis, compared to other countries, with the lack of transformation of protest movements into parties and the balkanization of the party system left little room for new parties to emerge; and the existing ones adapted their candidate selection methods according to electoral failures, (expected) successes, or the need for professionalization, but generally speaking followed trends toward centralization and exclusiveness (see chapter 4). Portugal, despite the harsh financial crisis and austerity policies implemented, and despite citizen protests, did not witness the appearance of new relevant political actors, and the traditional ones (except the Socialist Party and due to an internal crisis) did not change anything in their candidate selection methods. Nor in Ireland, except in one case, did new parties use available IPD methods to select candidates, due to the lack of resources and weak organizational structure, The Czech Republic is a clear case in which new parties have emerged but their entrepreneurial nature is at odds with IPD practices, as is the case of Team Stronach in Austria. In Greece, open lists and preferential voting may be seen as rendering IPD practices less attractive or unnecessary but the point is that a party like Syriza, whose DNA has IPD practices embedded, moved towards a more centrally coordinated candidate selection, like the one used by the rival ND. Holding power, as the PAN shows in the case of Mexico, may lead parties to reverse or reduce the extent of more inclusive selection practices, proving Michels right.

In most chapters, authors have been able to provide data on the social profile of MPs to explore the idea that new selection methods or even new parties emerged during the crisis (or old parties becoming mainstream ones) could bring parliaments more social diversity. Indeed, this seems to be the case of some parties such as M5S, Podemos or Syriza. However, the general trend is not uniform and there are different patterns that cannot be entirely explained by the presence of new parties. Regarding female representation in parliaments, in Austria, Greece, Ireland and Portugal some parties (but not all) increased the number of female representatives. And the crisis brought about some ideological congruence between citizens and representatives in the case of Iceland. Beyond these cases, the impact of changes in selection procedures in the social profile of MPs seems to be still limited at the country level.

Plan of the book

This book contributes to a number of areas in the social sciences. First of all, it develops debates in the field of organizational change where political parties are the forgotten organizations. From the new institutionalism point of view, pressures coming from the environment (in the form of regulations, or of competitive or, more rarely, normative nature) may lead parties to introduce changes producing organizational isomorphism of coercive, mimetic or (very rarely in politics) normative nature. However, party traditions, structures of power and windows of opportunity generated by the electoral system may foster internal resistances or multiply the avenues for implementing changes in the selection of candidates.

Throughout the chapters of the book we explore the idea that "IPD in candidate selection is perceived in terms of an inclusive participatory process and a representative outcome" (Rahat, 2013, 137). And this in two respects. First, beyond international calls for the implementation of IPD measures (Cross and Katz, 2013b, 2), we need to know whether new political actors abide by these calls and whether they create a more horizontal and democratic selection of candidates, although the prospects for it, following Rahat's (2013) framework (inclusive, fair, free, competitive), are reduced. Furthermore, this book assesses the extent to which old mainstream parties adjust as well to calls for IPD in candidate selection and explore the reasons for its implementation. Second, new, more inclusive and perhaps decentralized patterns of candidate selection may lead towards a political elite that reflects better the social structure of a given society in terms of descriptive representation.

Chapter 2 analyses how the political crises in most of the countries included in this book had an impact on the way candidates are selected, reviewing critically the "democratizing effect" of candidate selection in intraparty politics. The chapter focuses on the Great Recession and how it has generated a legitimation crisis, leaving old parties facing demands for more participation and opening a window of opportunity for new parties to emerge with new demands. Analyzing the interdependencies of economic and political crisis, Detterbeck emphasizes party vulnerability and lack of trust from citizens, which generates discontent but also a challenge for organizational reaction. Democratizing how parties select their candidates is such a reaction. However, making electorates more inclusive affects different aspects of party politics that are analyzed in the chapter: participation, competitiveness, representation, responsiveness, and electoral rewards.

In Austria, the economic crisis was softer than in other countries, although discontent with traditional parties (mainly the SPÖ, social democratic, and the ÖVP, conservative) was ample and evident in different elections, as Jenny reports in Chapter 3. Changes in the selection of candidates can be explained by electoral defeats or expected victories mediated by party size, ideology and election timing. Furthermore, multiple tiers in the electoral system makes parties approach the selection of candidates in a different way both among and inside parties. Bottom up (ÖVP) or top down approaches (NEOS, Pirates Party) show a mix of mechanisms for candidate selection.

Chapter 4 analyzes the negative case of Belgium since, contrary to other countries, Belgium has not seen the emergence of new parties channelling the discontent of the crisis and, contrary to a general trend, the younger parties have implemented more exclusive and centralized ways of candidate selection.

Furthermore, rather than being a case of mimetic isomorphism, Vandeleene and De Winter show that traditional parties have not changed either the way they operate, avoiding thus the general trend towards IPD practices. Belgium, like the Czech Republic and Portugal, in some respects are negative cases.

The case of the Czech Republic studied in chapter 5 shows that new parties do not fit in the general trend of expansion of IPD practices because of their entrepreneurial nature. Contrary, more centralization is seen in the selection of candidates, perhaps, as in one of the cases analyzed in Belgium (N-VA), because of the newness of the organizations, expected electoral growth and the need to control who gets into the electoral lists. Furthermore, Hloušek and Kopeček show that, with the exception of ČSSD, the traditional, established parties did not feel the need to open the selection of candidates to the rank and file members of their parties. A sort of reverse mimetic isomorphism may have taken place here since the political newcomers did not challenge traditional organizational practices.

Germany is one of those cases where previous innovations (such as gender quota) have spread out in the party system, although internal democracy is the effect of coercive mimetism: the State mandates, for obvious historical reasons, that parties use democratic principles to select their leaders and candidates, be it in the form of primaries or party delegates. As Reiser suggests in chapter 6, the stable party system of Germany combined with an attenuated crisis has left little room for new parties to emerge with the exception of Alternative for Germany (AfD), which has gained momentum to the point of entering regional chambers and getting 94 seats (13%) in the Bundestag in the 2017 elections (making it the third party after CDU and SPD). Given the institutional setting, little innovation is expected and AfD has established inclusive and decentralized ways of selecting candidates but with some violations of the rule concerning the procedures (fairness, transparency and freedom of choice for candidate selection), as reported by Reiser. Perhaps, for this reason, AfD MPs are slightly different from the rest (especially in gender) and score lower in the descriptive representation of Germany. No mimetism is reported there but on the contrary, traditional parties (CDU, CSU, SPD), had more inclusive selectorates until 2009, when the tendency stopped, although smaller parties (Greens, the Left Party and the Liberals) combined more inclusive selectorates with some party delegates as the setting for selecting candidates.

Greece is one of those countries where the crisis and subsequent austerity measures hit its citizens hardest, with many protests and demonstrations channelled by two old parties which acquired new relevance (Syriza and Golden Dawn) while traditional parties suffered electorally, especially the Socialists. Kakekapi shows in chapter 7 that although IPD practices are embedded in Syriza's DNA, the rapid electoral growth shown in the polls enables the party leadership to gain control over nominations for electoral lists. On the contrary, conservative Nea Demokratia, facing electoral defeat and leadership change, although it kept exclusive control over electoral lists, introduced a (very) basic innovation, namely, a participatory mechanism consisting of an online registration system where individuals can offer themselves to become candidates. Open lists and preferential voting may explain a low interest in IPD practices for selecting candidates, although some changes in the social profile of MPs can be observed.

Chapter 8 reports the very particular case of Iceland where parties already implemented IPD mechanisms before the Great Recession and so, Kristinsson and Önnudóttir argue, there was no need to channel demands for more participation. However, new parties emerged amidst anti-establishment sentiments and looked for more radical ways of participation, such as direct democracy or even highly personalized ways of representing constituencies while not questioning primaries as such. Sometimes, IPD practices may involve the deinstitutionalization of parties according to a known thesis put forward by Hazan and Rahat (2010). This means that IPD could have an effect on representation, competitiveness inside the party, responsiveness, and participation. While this may be part of the negative consequences of IPD, the chapter on Iceland shows that this is not the case and that IPD mechanisms, out of the question for newcomers in politics in Iceland, can have positive effects for democracy as a regime, at least in small settings,

Also in Ireland, as reported by Reidy in chapter 9, parties have been familiar with IPD practices and have extensively used them following the OMOV principle since, at least, the end of the eighties. The crisis helped some parties to emerge, channelling the discontent of a country that, together with the south of Europe, was hit hard by the crisis. These new parties followed two different strategies, according to the ideological divide. On the one hand, the far left alliance (in fact, a coalition of old parties) followed inclusive and moderately decentralized systems of candidate selection. However, the rest of the new parties used exclusive and national (centralized) ways of candidate selection, mainly interviews with prospective candidates. Lack of clear organizational structures and funds explains the situation. In any case, the new parties, as in other countries, introduced larger social diversity in parliament.

Italy is perhaps the best natural scenario to analyse the spread of IPD practices since, as Seddone and Rombi suggest in chapter 10, the Italian party system has seen a routinisation of primaries in several ideological families. The economic crisis there spread protests and indignation that a former comedian channelled through a brand new party (M5S) that implemented innovative ways of selecting candidates using information and communication technologies, including the internet, similar to the case of NEOS in Austria. These inclusive methods for candidate selection led other parties to incorporate more open primaries and this had an effect on the type of MPs selected.

Latin America has experienced a number of changes in candidate selection, as reported by Barragán and Bohigues in chapter 11. The countries analyzed have seen the emergence of new parties with new methods of selection involving some IPD practices in part because they are in their DNA (usually populist of the left) and in part as a solution to the perceived problem of political disaffection and internal infighting. In the absence of state regulations, party-specific factors explain the adoption of IPD practices which, although they have promoted more social diversity among MPs, do not eliminates the traditional profile found in most democracies – male, middle aged, with high education credentials.

Mexico appears as a country in which the economic crisis generates demands for change and participation, but mainstream parties, as Langston shows in chapter 12, are isolating themselves thanks to protective institutions and the role of strong leadership, which control nominations for candidates in a variety of ways. This applies broadly to the three main parties, although, while the PRI stands as a party that is closed to IPD practices and the PRD moved towards reduced participation, the PAN followed its history of inclusive and decentralized nominations although with some tendencies towards centralization explained by officials holding power for over a decade.

Chapter 13 teaches an interesting lesson – besides the crisis, its deep impact on Portuguese society and the protests that were organized, the party system remained almost intact. This means that no relevant new actors appeared in the political scenario. Furthermore, traditional parties, apart from suffering some internal crises, have not changed their candidate selection methods, although they have incorporated a new feature as a reaction to citizen protests: as Lisi demonstrates, parties have enrolled in their electoral lists more candidates with strong civic links, assuring a deeper and stronger connection between parliamentary politics and society and thus slightly changing the social profile of MPs.

Spain is a case similar to others in which the economic crisis combined with corruption scandals eroded the legitimacy of institutions and political trust, fostering protests that were channelled mainly by two new parties (Podemos and Ciudadanos). The constitution mandates the internal democratic functioning of parties although, like mainstream parties in Germany, the mechanism mostly used to select leaders (and also legislative candidates) was party conventions and delegates, and party committees. Although primaries had been established in parties of the left to select their leaders in the late 1990s, the newcomers introduced some innovations and new technologies. However, candidate selection was not without tensions. In Podemos, Jaime-Castillo, Coller and Cordero report in chapter 14 attempts of the party leadership to control the selection process while in Ciudadanos there is a tendency to revert inclusiveness and decentralization to prevent MPs switching party and to acquire more control over potential candidates. The newness of the parties and their large size (both newcomers have been quite successful in obtaining seats at national, regional and local elections) may explain the situation. The newcomers have introduced some degree of diversity in the descriptive representation of chambers (more Podemos than Ciudadanos, which behave as mainstream parties), although they are adding to a trend initiated by mainstream parties rather than introducing significant variations.

The US is a case that brings together a number of features that make the selection of candidates a special feature of the political system. Primaries are regulated at the state level and, although there have been protests over the negative effects of the Great Recession, the lack of real alternatives to the two mainstream parties has led to what Craig calls "insurgencies" in chapter 15. Insurgent groups (i.e. The Tea Party) try to gain access to nominations and control the selection of candidates, finding a powerful ally in the "donors consortium", which has an effect on who gets selected in each party. Polarization of politics in the US, Craig argues, combined with insurgent movements and the donor consortium factor, has provoked a growing distance between representatives and the median voter.

Finally, the last chapter establishes a comparison among the countries included in the book, paying attention to commonalities and differences. There, Cordero, Jaime-Castillo and Coller summarize the findings of the book, focusing on the different political responses to the selection of candidates in the context of the political derivatives of the economic crisis and a growing demand for participation.

Acknowledgements

We wish to thank the following people for their help in the creation of this book. Fernando Ramírez de Luis helped to homogenize the bibliographic references. Manuel Jiménez read the introduction and made relevant suggestions. Some of these chapters originated in a panel held at the 23rd International Conference of Europeanists, entitled "Resilient Europe?", organized by the Council for European Studies at Philadelphia in April 2016. We thank the participants in this panel for their contributions and participation. Especial thanks are given to the authors of the volume, who reacted positively to most of the comments made by the editors in the three rounds of revisions. It has been a pleasure to be able to count on this group of highly committed scholars.

On a personal note, Xavier Coller would like to thank Paula Queraltó and Lucas Coller Queraltó for bringing him joy and understanding the demands a professional task like editing a book like this poses on our private lives. Antonio M. Jaime-Castillo would like to thank Paula Penalva and Emma Jaime Penalva for being there every step of the way. Guillermo Cordero would like to thank Eduard Bonaclocha for his personal and unconditional support.

Notes

1 See Bosco and Verney (2012), Kriesi (2014), Bermeo and Bartels (2014), Freire et al. (2014), Morlino and Raniolo (2017).
2 See also Fishman (2017) and Fishman and Everson (2016).
3 In some respects, the "insurgencies" disputing control over the mainstream US parties (chapter 15) could be considered as the functional equivalent of these social movements.
4 But see as well Ashe *et al.* (2010) for contrary evidence, and Gauja and Cross (2015) for a qualification on shared authority when selecting candidates.
5 See Geissel and Newton (2012) for a discussion of some of these mechanisms, such as deliberation or direct democracy.
6 See, however, Askarany (2005), who, following Rogers (1983), makes the diffusion of innovations contingent upon the nature of the innovation, the social system, and the attributes of adopters.
7 A common definition of reality, incorporating demands posed to the party or even avoiding protective institutions like in the case of Mexico explained in chapter 12.
8 For instance, as the case of Belgium shows in chapter 4, younger newer parties are more willing to introduce changes in the selection of candidates than old, traditional ones.
9 See Hazan and Voerman (2006).

10 In some countries like in Spain (article 6 of the constitution, see chapter 14) or Portugal (article 51.5 of the constitution) mandates that parties have to operate internally applying democratic principles. In some others like Romania (art 16 of the law on Political Parties), Germany (arts. 6–15 of the Law On Political Parties of 1967, and art. 21 of the Federal Election Law of 1956, see chapter 6) or Finland (Political Parties Act, although Finland is an exception in Scandinavian countries) there are legal provisions as Mersel (2006) and Sundberg (1997) indicate. See Gauja (2010) and Van Biezen and Romée Piccio (2013) for general overviews. However, while courts (and the general public we might add) demand that parties pursue democratic ends and abide by the rules of democracy, less attention is paid to the internal democratic organization and practices of the party.

11 A similar "innovation" may be the introduction of gender quotas, for which Davidson-Schmich (2010) found a limited "contagion" effect in the case of Germany (no contagion at all in the recent case of the AfD as can be seen in chapter 6) as Verge (2012) and Santana et al. (2016) did for the case of Spain.

Bibliography

Armingeon, K., and Guthmann, K. (2013). Democracy in crisis? The declining support for national democracy in European countries, 2007–2011. *European Journal of Political Research*, n/a–n/a. doi:10.1111/1475–6765.12046.

Ashe, J., Campbell, R., Childs, S. et al. (2010). Stand by your man. *British Politics* 5, pp. 455–480.

Askarany, D. (2005). Diffusion of innovations in organizations. In Khosrow-Pour, M. (Ed.), *Encyclopedia of information science and technology*. USA: IDEA Group Publishing, pp. 853–856. doi:10.2139/ssrn.1370753

Bermeo, N., and Bartels, L. (2014). Mass politics in tough times. In Bartels, L. and Bermeo, N. (Eds.), *Mass politics in tough times. Opinions, votes and protest in the great recession*. Oxford: Oxford University Press, pp. 1–39.

Bermúdez, S., and Cordero, G. (2017). Who is recruiting our crew? Contextual determinants of MPs selection. *Acta Politica* 52 (3), pp. 265–285.

Best, H., and Cotta, M. (Eds.). (2000). *Parliament representatives in Europe 1848–2000. Legislative recruitment and careers in Eleven European countries*. Oxford: Oxford University Press.

Bosco, A., and Verney, S. (2012). Electoral epidemic: The political cost of economic crisis in Southern Europe, 2010–11. *South European Society and Politics* 17 (2), pp. 129–154.

Coller, X., Cordero, G., and Jaime, A. M. (Eds.). (2016). Candidate selection in multilevel democracies: America vs. Europe. *American Behavioral Scientist* 60 (7), pp. 773–908. Retrieved from http://abs.sagepub.com/content/60/7?etoc

Coller, X., Jaime, A. M., and Mota, F. (Eds.). (2018). *Political power in Spain: The multiple divides between politicians and citizens*. London: Palgrave Macmillan.

Cordero, G., and Coller, X. (2015). Candidate selection and party discipline. *Parliamentary Affairs* 68 (7), pp. 592–615.

Cordero, G., Jaime, A. M., and Coller, X. (2016). Selecting candidates in multilevel democracies. In Coller, X., Cordero, G. and Jaime, A. M. (Eds.), "Candidate Selection in Multilevel Democracies: America vs. Europe", *American Behavioral Scientist*, 60 (7), pp. 773–780 (published first online February 18th, 2016. doi:10.1177/0002764216632818)

Cordero, G., and Simón, P. (2016). Economic crisis and support for democracy in Europe. *West European Politics* 39 (2), pp. 305–325.

Cotta, M., and Best, H. (Eds.). (2007). *Democratic representation in Europe. Diversity, change, and convergence.* Oxford: Oxford University Press.

Cross, W., and Pilet, J-B. (Eds.). (2015). *The politics of party leadership. A cross-national perspective.* Oxford: Oxford University Press.

Cross, W., and Gauja, A. (2014). Designing candidate selection methods: Exploring diversity in Australian political parties. *Australian Journal of Political Science* 49 (1), pp. 22–39.

Cross, W. P., and Blais, A. (2012). Who selects the party leader? *Party Politics* 18 (2), pp. 127–150.

Cross, W. P., and Katz, R. S. (2013a). *The challenges of intra-party democracy.* Oxford: Oxford University Press.

Cross, W. P., and Katz, R. S. (2013b). The challenges of intra-party democracy. In Cross, W. P. and Katz, R. S. (Ed.), *The challenges of intra-party democracy.* Oxford: Oxford University Press, pp. 1–10.

Cyert, R. M., and March, J. (1963). *A behavioral theory of the firm.* Englewoods Cliffs, NJ: Prentice Hall.

Davidson-Schmich, L. (2010). Gender quota compliance and contagion in the 2009 Bundestag election. *German Politics and Society* 28 (3), pp. 133–155.

Della Porta, D., and Mattonia, A. (2014). *Spreading protest: Social movements in times of crisis.* London: ECPR.

DiMaggio, P., and Powell, W. W. (1991). The Iron Cage Revisited: Institutional Isomorphism and Collective Rationality. In Powell, W. W. and DiMaggio, P. (Eds.), *The new institutionalism in organizational analysis.* Chicago: Chicago University Press, pp. 63–82.

Fishman, R. M. (2017), "How Civil Society Matters in Democratization: Setting the Boundaries of Post-Transition Political Inclusion", *Journal of Comparative Politics*, 49 (3), pp: 391–409.

Fishman, R. M. and D. W. Everson (2016), "Mechanisms of Social Movement Success: Conversation, Displacement and Disruption". *Revista Internacional de Sociología*, 74 (4): e045. doi: http://dx.doi.org/10.3989/ris.2016.74.4.045

Freire, A., Lisi. A., Andreadis, I., and Leite Viegas, J. M. (2014). Political representation in bailed-out Southern Europe: Greece and Portugal compared. *South European Society and Politics* 19 (4), pp. 413–433.

Fujimura, N. (2012). Electoral incentives, party discipline, and legislative organization: Manipulating legislative committees to win elections and maintain party unity. *European Political Science Review* 4 (2), pp. 147–175.

Gallagher, M., Laver, M., and Mair, P. (2001). *Representative government in modern Europe.* Boston: McGraw-Hill.

Gallagher, M., and Marsh, M. (1988). *Candidate selection in comparative perspective: The secret garden of politics.* London: Sage.

Gauja, A. (2010). *Political parties and elections: Legislating for representative democracy.* London: Routledge.

Gauja, A., and Cross, W. (2015). Research note: The influence of party candidate selection methods on candidate diversity. *Representation* 51 (3), pp. 287–298.

Geissel, B., and Newton, K. (2012). *Evaluating democratic innovations. Curing the democratic Malaise?* Abingdon: Routledge.

Harmel, R. (1981). Environment and party decentralization: A cross national analysis. *Comparative Political Studies* 14, pp. 75–99.

Hazan, R. Y., and Rahat, G. (2010). *Democracy within parties: Candidate selection methods and their political consequences.* Oxford: Oxford University Press.

Hazan, R., and Voerman, G. (2006). Electoral systems and candidate selection. *Acta Politica* 41, pp. 146–162.

Hopkin, J. (2001). Bringing the members back in? Democratizing candidate selection in Britain and Spain. *Party Politics* 7, pp. 343–361.

Katz, R. S. (2001). The problem of candidate selection and models of party democracy. *Party Politics* 7, pp. 277–296.

Katz, R. S., and Cross, W. P. (2013). Problematizing intraparty democracy. In Cross, W. P. and Katz, R. S. (Ed.), *The challenges of intra-party democracy*. Oxford: Oxford University Press, pp. 170–176.

Kenig, O., Cross, W., Pruysers, S., and Rahat, G. (2015). Party primaries: Towards a definition and typology. *Representation* 51 (2), pp. 147–160.

Kenig, O., Cross, W., Pruysers, S., and Rahat, G. (2015). Party primaries: Towards a definition and typology. *Representation* 51 (2), pp. 147–160.

Kenig, O., Rahat, G., and Hazan, R. (2015). Leadership selection versus candidate selection: Similarities and differences. In Sandri, G., Seddone, A. and Venturino, F. (Eds.), *Party primaries in comparative perspective*. Surrey, UK: Ashgate, pp. 21–40.

Kopecek, L. (2016). I'm paying, so I decide. *East European Politics and Societies* 30 (4), pp. 725–749.

Kriesi, H. (2014). The political consequences of the economic crisis in Europe: Electoral punishment and popular protest. In Bartels, L. and Bermeo, N. (Eds.), *Mass politics in tough times. Opinions, votes and protest in the great recession*. Oxford: Oxford University Press, pp. 518–522.

Lewis-Beck, M. S., and Nadeau, R. (2012). PIGS or not? Economic voting in Southern Europe'. *Electoral Studies* 31 (3), pp. 472–477.

Lundell, K. (2004). Determinants of candidate selection – the degree of centralization in comparative perspective. *Party Politics* 10, pp. 25–47.

Magalhães, P. C. (2014). Introduction – financial crisis, austerity, and electoral politics. *Journal of Elections, Public Opinion and Parties* 24 (2), pp. 125–133.

Mersel, Y. (2006). The dissolution of political parties: The problem of internal democracy. *International Journal of Constitutional Law* 4 (1), pp. 84–113. doi:10.1093/icon/moi053

Meyer, J. and Rowan, B. (1983). Institutionalized organizations: Formal structures as myth and ceremony. In Meyer, J. W. and Scott, W. R (Eds.), *Organizational Environments: Ritual and Rationality*, Beverly Hills, CA: Sage, pp. 21–44.

Michels, R. (1962 [1915]). *Political parties. A sociological study of the oligarchical tendencies of modern democracy*. New York: Free Press.

Morlino, L., and Raniolo, F. (2017). *The impact of the economic crisis on South European democracies*. Basingstoke: Palgrave Macmillan.

Muro, D., and Vidal, G. (2017). Political mistrust in southern Europe since the Great Recession. *Mediterranean Politics* 22 (2), pp. 197–217.

Norris, P., and Lovenduski, J. (1995). *Political recruitment. Gender, race and class in the British Parliament*. New York: Cambridge University Press.

Papadopoulos, Y. (2013). *Democracy in crisis? Politics, governance and policy*. London: Palgrave Macmillan.

Pasquino, G., and Valbruzzi, M. (2016). Primary elections between fortuna and virtù. *Contemporary Italian Politics* 8 (1), pp. 3–11.

Pilet, J.B and Cross, W.P. (2014), *The selection of political party leaders in contemporary parliamentary democracies*. London: Routledge.

Rahat, G. (2007). Candidate selection: The choice before the choice. *Journal of Democracy* 18 (1), pp. 157–170.

Rahat, G. (2013). What is democratic candidate selection? In Cross, W. P. and Katz, R. S. (Eds.), *The challenges of intra-party democracy*. Oxford: Oxford University Press, pp. 136–149.

Rahat, G., and Hazan, R. (2001). Candidate selection methods: An analytical framework. *Party Politics* 7, pp. 297–322.

Rahat, G., and Hazan, R. (2007). Participation in party primaries: Increase in quantity, decrease in quality. In Zittel, T. and Fuchs, D. (Eds.), *Participatory democracy and political participation. Can participatory engineering bring citizens back in?* London: Routledge, ECPR Studies in European Political Science Series, pp. 57–72.

Ramiro, L. (2016). Effects of party primaries on electoral performance. The Spanish Socialist primaries in local elections. *Party Politics* 22 (1), pp. 125–136.

Ranney, A. (1981). Candidate selection. In Butler, D. (Eds.), *Democracy at the polls: A comparative study of competitive national elections*. Washington: American Enterprise Institute for Public Policy Research, pp. 75–106.

Rogers, E. M. (1983). *Diffusion of innovations*. New York: Free Press.

Sandri, G., Seddone, A., and Venturino, F. (Eds.). (2015). *Party primaries in comparative perspective*. Surrey: Ashgate-Routledge.

Santana, A., Aguilar, S., and Coller, X. (2016). Who leads and who lags behind? Women MPs in the Spanish regional Parliaments. *Revista Internacional de Sociología* 74 (2): e033. doi: 10.3989/ris.2016.74.2.033

Scarrow, S. E., Webb, P., and Farrell, D. M. (2002). From social integration to electoral contestation. In Dalton, R. J. and Wattenberg, M. P. (Eds.), *Parties without partisans: Political change in advanced industrial democracies*. Oxford: Oxford University Press, pp. 343–361.

Shomer, Y. (2014). What affects candidate selection processes? A cross-national examination. *Party Politics* 20 (4), pp. 533–546.

Sundberg, J. (1997). Compulsory party democracy: Finland as a deviant case in Scandinavia. *Party Politics* 3 (1), pp. 97–117.

Tolbert, P. S and Zucker, L. G. (1996). The institutionalization of institutional theory. In Clegg, S. Hardy, C. and Nord, W. R. (Eds.), *Handbook of organization studies*. Thousand Oaks: Sage, pp. 175–190.

Torcal, M. (2014). The decline of political trust in Spain and Portugal: Economic performance or political responsiveness? *American Behavioral Scientist* 58 (12), pp. 1542–1567 (First published online May 2014, doi: 10.1177/0002764214534662).

Torcal, M. (2016). Political trust in Western and Southern Europe. In Zmerli, S. and Van der Meer, T. (Eds.), *Handbook on political trust*. Cheltenham, UK: Edward Elgar Publishing, pp. 418–439.

Van Biezen, I., Mair, P., and Pogunntke, T. (2012). Going, going, . . . gone? The decline of party membership in contemporary Europe. *European Journal of Political Research* 51 (1), pp. 24–56.

Van Biezen, I., and Romée Piccio, D. (2013). Shaping intra-party democracy: On the legal regulation of internal party organizations. In Cross, W. P. and Katz, R. S. (Eds.), *The challenges of intra-party democracy*. Oxford: Oxford University Press, pp. 27–48.

Verge, T. (2012). Institutionalising gender equality in Spain: From party quotas to electoral gender quotas. *West European Politics* 35 (2), pp. 395–414.

Weick, K. E. (1979). *The social psychology of organizing*. New York: Random House.

Young, L., and Cross, W. (2002). The rise of plebiscitary democracy in Canadian political parties. *Party Politics* 8 (6), pp. 673–699.

2 Political crisis and its effect on candidate selection

Klaus Detterbeck

Introduction

Among the various internal processes within political parties, there is arguably lit-tle that has been studied more intensively than candidate selection. There are two main reasons for this strong interest among party scholars. First, studying candi-date selection allows insights into a crucial step in the recruitment of the political elite. Across the modern democracies, nearly all members of parliament and most members of government are chosen from the pool of personnel that intra-party selectors have created. In many places, party nomination for a "safe" seat or list position is equivalent to obtaining the public mandate (Gallagher, 1988; Hazan and Rahat, 2006).

Second, studying candidate selection can tell a lot about internal power balances between party levels as well as between party leaders, party activists and ordinary members. Nomination processes are a vital part of internal party democracy (or the lack of it). Accordingly, the degree of centralization with respect to the locus of selection, the instruments of central party intervention and the inclusiveness of participation have become standard parameters of analysis in candidate selection (Bille, 2001; Cross and Katz, 2013).

There is also a direct link between candidate selection and the debates on party change which have dominated the field for some decades now. In accounts which established an evolution of party types over time, the mechanisms of candidate selection have been among the main indicators for changing power relations within parties (Kirchheimer, 1966; Katz and Mair, 1995). The current academic debate has become fascinated by the fact that an increasing number of parties have opened internal decision-making processes beyond parliamentary groupings or delegate conventions to include all party members, or even voters.

Party primaries have been used mainly in the fields of candidate and leader-ship selection (see Sandri, et al., 2015). The effects of more inclusive selector-ates on factors like leadership qualities, political representation, membership activism, internal power balances, party cohesion, parliamentary behaviour and electoral performances has attracted much academic interest in recent years (Galderisi and Lyons, 2001; Sivaelis and Morgenstern, 2008; Hazan and Rahat, 2010; Scarrow and Gezgor, 2010; Pilet and Cross, 2014; Cordero and Coller, 2015; Cordero, et al, 2016).

Party scholars interpret the effects of membership ballots on intra-party democracy in quite different ways. While some see the empowerment of ordinary members as a manipulative attempt by the party elite to circumvent the more critical mid-level activists in delegate conventions, others find evidence for party renewal in a more participatory mode (for the debate, see Detterbeck, 2013, 271–273). The US model of open primaries, mandatory in a majority of US states by law, and now spreading to other places, such as France or Italy, has mostly been interpreted as taking control out of the hands of party agents and strengthening the role of individual candidates (Ware, 2002; Sandri et al., 2015).

However this may be, most researchers would agree that the drive towards more inclusive methods has been motivated by weakening voter loyalties and shrinking membership figures. The decline of party identification and the erosion of popular trust in parties have led parties in a state of vulnerability leaving them unclear about their prospects of organizational survival (Mair, 1997; Dalton, 2004; Poguntke et al., 2015). In attempts to win back popular support, parties strove towards more open internal procedures. Not surprisingly then, electoral setbacks have often been seen as the main trigger of party modernization (Cross and Blais, 2012). Hence, there is arguably a link between internal party democratization and party vulnerability.

In this volume, we are studying the political implications of the Great Recession in the Americas and Europe. Among these implications is a growing gap between the established parties and sections of society, in particular groups directly affected by the crisis or fearing losing out in the longer term (Bartels and Bermeo, 2014). This has been particularly pronounced in cases where populist forces from either the left or the right have attacked the elitist style of the mainstream parties (Müller, 2016). In continental Europe, right-wing political challengers such as the French Front National or the Austrian FPÖ have become serious contenders for political power, while in Southern Europe new parties on the left prospered, most notably the Greek Syriza (Mudde, 2010; Stavrakakis, and Katsambekis, 2014). In Latin America, radical leftist governments in Venezuela, Bolivia and Ecuador have sought to combine strong executive leadership with mass mobilization and popular participation in political decision-making (Mainwaring, 2006; Ellner, 2012). In the US, the surprise victory of Donald Trump in the 2016 presidential elections has dramatically shown the extent to which many voters feel alienated from the established political forces (Sides et al., 2017).

More generally, party systems in many Western democracies have changed significantly within a few years. There has been an increase in party system fragmentation and polarization as new parties have emerged and smaller parties, often with a less middle of the road policy agenda, have gained electoral strength at the expense of the more moderate "old" parties (Casal Bertoa and Weber, 2016). As a consequence, parliamentary majorities have become more fragile and government formation a much more difficult task (Kriesi, 2012; Kriesi, and Pappas, 2015).

The main argument here is that these repercussions of the recent economic crisis have tapped into an ongoing process of parties losing touch with society. This is not something which is completely new. Since the 1970s, a profound crisis of democratic legitimacy has been debated from quite different political and academic angles (see Crozier et al., 1975; Habermas, 1975; Mouffe, 2000; Crouch, 2004). However, the Great Recession has intensified the pressure on political parties to cope with popular dissatisfaction. This chapter seeks to develop this argument in more detail. It begins with some general reflections on the nature of political crises. Next, we will try to use these perspectives to develop a conceptual argument on how the economic crisis has exacerbated parties' legitimacy crisis. We will then look at the changing methods of candidate selection and their impact on democratic quality. The conclusion will link this debate to party crisis.

The nature of political crises

Crises are defined by the key elements of threat, urgency and uncertainty (Rosenthal et al., 1989, 10). In a crisis, social systems prove unable to tackle specific challenges that potentially violate the core functions or values of that system – ranging from public security to democratic legitimacy – with routine mechanisms. What has worked so far is no longer effective as the environment has changed significantly in a moment of shock. The threat is perceived to be particularly serious if there is a sense of immediacy. Action needs to be taken in order to prevent a breakdown of the social system. Yet, decision-making in a state of crisis is surrounded by a lack of precise information about the causes and consequences of the threat as well as about the effects of the various options available (Boin and t´Hart, 2006).

Crises are therefore open processes. The famous Kennedy *bon mot* that the Chinese word for crisis represents danger and opportunity simultaneously may not be fully correct linguistically but captures the vital point of choice. At critical junctures, things may change for the better or lead to disaster. Much depends on the strategies and decisions chosen by the actors. They may take the right steps to stop the danger, for example by introducing reforms to the system, and demonstrate resilience by bouncing back after a crisis. But they may also fail by ignoring threats and suppressing warning voices, or by simply going the wrong way (Deutsch, 1963). This also points to the contested nature of crises. In most cases, the public perception of threat, trust in political authorities and the politicized interpretation of a given situation will decide on whether problems are seen as matters of routine business or as crisis phenomena (Boin and t´Hart, 2006, 48).

As will be shown in the next section in more detail, there are close interdependencies between economic and political crises. More precisely, the erosion of trust and legitimacy which has to do with social and political change more generally has weakened the capacities of political actors to cope with challenges arising from economic difficulties. Crises cross boundaries. Problems arising in one place or sector have the potential to cause trouble somewhere else. Crises can travel across place and cross geographical borders (e.g., epidemics); they can infect other sectors and jump functional boundaries (e.g., from financial markets to industrial systems); and they may even have long-term effects and transcend time boundaries (e.g., terrorism and the 9/11 crisis). As there are many linkages between social systems, functional and geographical spread can move crises in unforeseen directions and multiply their damage potential (Boin, 2009).

Crisis management has been described as something akin to an "impossible job" for political leaders (Hargrove and Glidewell, 1990). Leaders are held accountable for decisions in situations which remain unclear, in which there is pressure from the media and the public and in which there is only limited time to evaluate the problem and coordinate action. Yet, despite restricted capacities for controlling the process, leaders will have to engage in a series of political activities in order to frame the crisis. This involves preparing contingency plans for adverse events in advance, making sense of an evolving crisis, taking hard choices on trade-offs, learning under pressure and, finally, offering a convincing explanation which can generate political support and legitimacy (Boin, 2009).

The success of these framing activities will determine whether leaders can survive periods of crisis or even enhance their standing within their political community. While crises can threaten the basis of organizational power and call into question the leadership qualities of the dominant elites, effective troubleshooting may boost the popularity of political leaders. Investing scarce resources in reform activities may thus be seen as a rational response on the part of strategic actors. The more a situation is perceived to constitute a crisis, the more likely it is that priority is given to resolve the issue (Dutton, 1986). Crises provide policy entrepreneurs with windows of opportunities for reforming institutional structures and public policies (Kingdon, 1984; Boin and t´Hart, 2003).

However, complex organizations, such as parties, are confronted with the problem of escalatory dynamics in crises. The intricate structures of complex social systems not only hamper hierarchical control over the entire body, they also increase their vulnerability for disturbances. The coupling of the system´s component parts may lead to a rapid proliferation of problems and errors that finally produce a threat with devastating potential. In the lead up to a crisis, smaller failures (or pathogens) may combine and transform into disruptive forces (Boin and t´Hart, 2006, 46–47). Crisis approaches thus stress the inability of complex social systems to deal with escalating disturbances to routine activities.

Political crisis, party vulnerability and democratic legitimacy

How can we now apply these considerations to party politics and candidate selection? A useful starting point is the concept of party vulnerability, which Peter Mair (1997, 31–40) has defined as key to understanding party change. Starting from the empirical evidence of generally increasing levels of electoral volatility over the last decades, Mair has argued that the organizational hold of parties on society has loosened for a variety of reasons, some of them induced by social change, others by the catch-all strategies of parties. As a result of the weakening of party alignments, the organizational fortunes of individual parties have become more fragile. With the embeddedness of parties in society eroding, parties turned to the state in their search for organizational resources and political legitimacy. Governing the state increasingly replaced representing society (see also Katz and Mair, 1995; Mair, 2005).

In the terminology of the crisis literature, the main threat to the role of political parties in representative democracies has been their relative failure to maintain strong linkages with society. In some respects, parties could ward off the danger by exploiting state resources and by concentrating their efforts on parliamentary and governmental tasks. In other respects, however, parties remained vulnerable and threatened. Party legitimacy became more precarious. Citizens increasingly began to see parties as remote organizations which no longer pursued the interests of specific segments of society or represented the democratic will of the people. Anti-party sentiment rose from the decline in political trust. People dissatisfied with political institutions often expressed doubts about the capacity of parties to understand their interests and problems (Dalton, 2006, 260–267).

The Great Recession has amplified popular discontent with political parties. Economic recession and the Eurozone sovereign debt crisis have created an enormous amount of grievances which people expressed in electoral punishment and popular protest. In many countries affected by the economic crisis, the adoption of austerity measures, imposed by international institutions or the national government, has triggered protest mobilization (Kriesi, 2012). In this sense, the economic crisis brought immediate urgency – another defining element of crises – to the problem of party vulnerability.

The dramatic social consequences of the crisis in countries like Greece, Portugal and Spain, and the fear of many citizens elsewhere, eventually seemed to prove for many people that their mistrust in the elitist ways of parties was highly appropriate. From their point of view, governments staffed by party politicians cared about many things like the reduction of state debts, solidarity among EU member states or the survival of banks but certainly not about the interests of ordinary people. The appeal of the populist message in distinguishing between the "pure people" and the "corrupt elite" is exactly what has rung a bell with many dissatisfied citizens (Mudde, 2007; Müller, 2016).

So, here is what we may describe as the dynamic escalation of a party crisis in democratic legitimacy. While parties have found it harder to connect with society for quite some time now, they could still rely on their important functions with respect to elections, parliaments and governments. They may have neither been loved nor trusted as much as they would have liked but still parties were indispensable for running the state. The delivery of public goods, such as welfare and security, provided for an output legitimacy that increasingly supplemented and partly replaced the input legitimacy derived from representation (see Scharpf, 1999). With the recent economic crisis, however, both pillars of party legitimacy became threatened. In terms of input legitimacy, the fragility of party alignments became even more visible than already apparent. In terms of output legitimacy, the obvious limited partisan control of national policy-making in transnational political environments further undermined faith in party government (Mair, 2008).

In this sense, the legitimacy crisis of parties is now in full swing. The threat is no longer simply about declining party memberships and volatile electorates.

It is also about the privileged role of parties in state institutions and the level of popular trust in representative democracy. Smaller failures in party performances have combined and transformed themselves into disruptive forces. Therefore, for their own sake, parties have to find new and better answers to societal mistrust. In now turning to candidate selection, we focus on one specific aspect of party organizational modernization which may form part of such an answer.

Changes in candidate selection methods

The democratization of candidate selection can be interpreted as response to the legitimacy crisis. Democratization refers to the widening of party selection bodies which decide over the nomination of parliamentary candidates. Parties seek to renew linkages with social groups and to regain political trust by opening their internal procedures. By bringing party members back in, parties can implement more inclusive ways of political participation and combat the impression of an elitist closure of internal party processes. Closing the gap between party leaders and party members (or even voters, in case of open primaries) has become particularly relevant in times of crisis. The more people turn away from parties, the more parties are threatened with failure.

Seen through the lenses of crises approaches, democratization is an instrument of crisis management for securing organizational survival. There is considerable empirical evidence that the adoption of more inclusive selectorates has been a widespread but not universal phenomenon across Western democracies over the last few decades. Membership ballots have been introduced by parties in countries as diverse as Argentina, Belgium, Canada, Finland, Germany, Honduras, Israel, Mexico, the Netherlands, and the United Kingdom (Bille, 2001; DeLuca, M., Jones, M. P., and Tula, M. I., 2002; Langston, 2006; Hazan and Rahat, 2010; Cordero et al., 2016).

In explaining differences in the trend towards more inclusive methods of candidate selection, the three-level approach developed by Barnea and Rahat (2007) has proved to be analytically fruitful. In their distinction, the more long-term social and political trends at the level of political systems, such as democratization and personalization, would point to a general development towards stronger involvement of party members across the place. At the second level of party systems, the structures and dynamics of party competition would explain differences in the timing of party reforms, according to factors like electoral defeat and mimetic isomorphism. Finally, at the intra-party level, organizational structures, power struggles and factional interests would account for the non-simultaneous occurrence of democratization within individual parties.

In order to assess the consequences of more inclusive selection methods, party scholars have identified a number of dimensions for empirical analysis, including participation, competitiveness, representation and responsiveness (for an overview, see Rahat and Kenig, 2011). While the final verdict is still out, there are serious questions on the effects of direct democracy within parties on democratic quality. With respect to participation, the increase in the numbers of people involved in candidate selection, may come at the price of a selectorate which is less strongly involved in party affairs and thus less knowledgeable than smaller party conventions. To some extent, it seems that parties are trading quantity for quality (Hazan and Rahat, 2010). Looking at the internal mobilization effects of party primaries, however, a more positive interpretation seems also feasible. Membership ballots may draw a larger number of activists closer to their party. Mid-level elites can employ an additional instrument of having a voice next to the more traditional forms of internal participation (Detterbeck, 2013, 280–282).

There is also an interesting debate on the effects of primaries on intra-party competitiveness. Comparing candidate selection methods, Rahat, Hazan and Katz (2008) have found that incumbents faced fewer successful challenges in membership primaries than in delegate conventions. Open primaries for US congressional candidates seem to be particularly safe for incumbents given their advantages in media attention and campaign budgets (Maisel and Stone, 2001). Kenig's comparative study on leadership selection (2009) concluded that while there are more candidates running in primaries than in other formats, the contests become somewhat less tight and are often won by a clear front-runner. Pilet and Cross (2014, 234) basically confirm these results: "More inclusive selectorates attract more candidates, but do not necessarily produce more competitive races". Competitiveness seems to be connected to the ill fortune of a party, or probably more to its solidity in calm periods, with parties in opposition or parties just having lost an election being more likely to see a contested intra-party struggle (ibid).

More inclusive candidate selection methods also raise the question of representation. Party members constituting a large and rather uncoordinated crowd may be less helpful in producing balanced candidate lists that encompass all relevant groups in society than smaller party conventions or even central party nomination committees (Rahat et al., 2008). Demographic representation seems to be harder to accomplish with wider selectorates. However, the issue is settled neither empirically nor conceptually, as there are cases where primaries have not worked against groups like women and as parties use complex selection methods with shared authority between different groups of selectors (Ashe et al., 2010; Gauja and Cross, 2015). Moreover, the general shrinking of party size has arguably led to a demographically more balanced membership (except for age) whose empowerment may be beneficial for disadvantaged groups (Scarrow and Gezgor, 2010).

In a similar vein, the influence of selection methods on the behaviour of members of parliament is far from clear. Some would argue that primaries strengthen a more individualistic form of behaviour as MPs become less dependent on party hierarchies. Again, the US example is often cited in this respect. The highly inclusive and decentralized US primaries have been associated with relatively low levels of cohesion in parliamentary groups (see Ware, 2002). Non-party actors, such as the media and interest groups, would gain importance for the reselection of incumbents. Politicians would thus shift responsiveness in this direction. As a consequence, party cohesion may decline with agents losing a clear and cohesive principal (Rahat, 2009). Others, following the idea of party stratarchy, would deny that such a close relationship between the methods of candidate selection and policy-making in the parliamentary sphere exists. They would point to the mechanisms of hierarchy and specialization in parliamentary groups for solving potential problems in party unity arising from the dynamics of democratization (Carty, 2004; Bolleyer, 2012). In a similar vein, scholars have demonstrated that party cohesion in more decentralized and inclusive parliamentary groups can arise from deliberative processes (Cordero and Coller, 2015). Finally, ideological differences between party families may account for variations in party cohesion (Close, 2016).

Looking at the consequences of more inclusive methods of selection, we may also ask whether there is an electoral reward of democratization. Do parties with primaries have better results? Presumably, most parties expect competitive advantages from such organizational reforms, in particular in the wake of electoral setbacks (Cross and Blais, 2012). However, measuring the electoral effects of membership ballots is notoriously difficult. Given the fact that many factors will contribute to a positive or negative development of vote shares, any attempt to isolate the effect of selection methods on electoral behaviour has to be treated with caution. The limited available empirical data suggests a mild electoral bonus of party primaries. Parties seem to do a little better if they are giving their members a say. The most likely explanation here is that primaries are making more brisk the mobilization of party supporters. They may take on a more active role in electoral campaigns on the ground and also turn out in higher numbers in general elections (Carey and Enten, 2011; Indridason and Kristinsson, 2012; Detterbeck, 2013; Ramiro, 2013).

Conclusion

The political implications of the Great Recession have served to intensify the legitimacy crisis that has troubled political parties for quite some time. The escalatory dynamics of crises have added urgency and uncertainty to the threat of party vulnerability. The established parties constituting the core of party systems have been weakened further, both in their attempts to maintain strong organizational social linkages and in their capacity to provide for policy solutions that find public support across all segments of society. To the extent that party politics fails to generate pluralist consensus, it may indeed be that party democracy is prevented from functioning effectively or enjoying full legitimacy (Mair, 2008, 230).

Crises spell danger but they also provide opportunities. The literature on party change shows that parties have responded in strategic ways to the crisis of vulnerability. The democratization of candidate selection is among the responses. As I have argued above, there are still many open questions concerning the effects of more inclusive methods of selection on intra-party democracy. This volume adds to our knowledge of how internal democratization has changed power balances within political parties. To conclude, let us sketch out two such possible effects, taking into account the political repercussions of the recent economic crisis.

First, the arrival of new parties which mobilized for more direct democracy in politics has put additional pressure on the established parties to open their internal proceedings. We may expect more parties in more countries to adopt more inclusive methods of candidate and leadership selection. The success of new parties, or the strengthening of formerly small parties, and the subsequent changes in party systems they bring can thus be seen as drivers of democratic change. To be sure, there may be serious doubts on the democratic quality of some of these parties, both on the political right and the political left. We may also ask whether these parties are actually doing internally what they are preaching as anti-elitist cure for democratic renewal. To name just one example, the use of online primaries for selecting candidates in the case of the Italian Five Star Movement, a truly innovative method, has been strongly orchestrated by the party leadership (see Mosca et al., 2015). Still, the electoral success of anti-elitist parties most certainly signals that there is public demand for stronger political participation. Again, the chapters of this volume will tell us more about the extent to which new political actors are actually implementing internal party democracy.

Second, and following from the first point, the further escalation of the legitimacy crisis has the potential finally to yield truly open processes within established parties. While the emphasis on the manipulative potential of party primaries for securing additional leeway to the party elites in the cartel party literature may have been far-fetched right from the start, the strong gate-keeping role that party leadership groups exercised in keeping processes of internal party democracy under their control has repeatedly been demonstrated (Katz and Mair, 1995; Hazan and Rahat, 2010; Sandri et al., 2015). Party primaries contain elements of uncertainty about outcomes, and it is for this reason that so far party elites have been rather hesitant in making more extensive use of competitive membership ballots (Detterbeck, 2013). This period may well now be over. The stronger pressure on political parties to democratize their internal proceedings can unleash dynamics under which we see more open contests in terms of competitiveness and more representative outcomes in terms of a more socially heterogeneous political elite. In this sense, political crisis – which I have described here as a crisis of legitimacy worsened by the effects of the Great Recession – may have been the starting point of real change within mainstream parties. Or, to put it in more lyrical terms, crisis has been the midwife of stronger internal party democracy.

References

Ashe, J., Campbell, R., Childs, S., and Evans, E. (2010). "Stand by your man": Women's political recruitment at the 2010 UK general election. *British Politics* 5 (4), pp. 455–480.

Barnea, S., and Rahat, G. (2007). Reforming candidate selection methods: A three-level approach. *Party Politics* 13 (3), pp. 260–274.

Bartels, L., and Bermeo, N. (Eds.). (2014). *Mass politics in tough times. Opinions, votes and protest in the great recession.* Oxford: Oxford University Press.

Bille, L. (2001). Democratizing a democratic procedure: myth or reality? Candidate selection in Western European parties, 1960–1990. *Party Politics* 7 (3), pp. 363–380.

Boin, A. (2009). The new world of crises and crisis management: implications for policy-making and research. *Review of Policy Research* 26 (4), pp. 367–377.

Boin, A., and t´Hart, P. (2003). Public leadership in times of crisis: mission impossible? *Public Administration Review* 63 (5), pp. 544–553.

Boin, A., and t´Hart, P. (2006). The crisis approach. In Rodriguez, H., Quarantelli, E., and Dynes, R. (Eds.), *Handbook of disaster research*. Wiesbaden: Springer VS, pp. 42–54.

Bolleyer, N. (2012). New party organization in Western Europe: of party hierarchies, stratarchies and federations. *Party Politics* 18 (3), pp. 315–336.

Carey, J. M., and Enten, H. J. (2011). Primary elections. In Colomer, J. M. (Ed.), *Personal representation. The neglected dimension of electoral systems*. Colchester: ECPR Press, pp. 81–98.

Carty, R. K. (2004). Parties as franchise systems: The stratarchical organizational imperative. *Party Politics* 10 (1), pp. 5–24.

Casal Bertoa, F., and Weber, T. (2016). *Restrained change: party systems in times of economic crisis*. Paper presented at the Annual Conference on Elections. Public Opinion and Parties (EPOP), University of Kent, United Kingdom, September 2016.

Close, C. (2016). Parliamentary party loyalty and party family: The missing link? *Party Politics*, Online first: http://journals.sagepub.com/doi/pdf/10.1177/1354068816655562

Cordero, G., and Coller, X. (2015). Cohesion and candidate selection in parliamentary groups. *Parliamentary Affairs* 68 (3), pp. 592–615.

Cordero, G., Jaime-Castillo, A. M., and Coller, X. (2016). Selecting candidates in multilevel democracies. *American Behavioral Scientist* 60 (7), pp. 773–780.

Cross, W., and Blais, A. (2012). Who selects the leaders? *Party Politics* 18 (2), pp. 127–150.

Cross, W., and Katz, R. S. (Eds.). (2013). *The Challenges of Intra-Party Democracy*. Oxford: Oxford University Press.

Crouch, C. (2004). *Post-Democracy*. Cambridge: Polity Press.

Crozier, M. J., Huntingtion, S. P., and Watanuki, J. (1975). *The crisis of democracy. Report on the governability of democracies to the Trilateral Commission*. New York: New York University Press.

Dalton, R. J. (2004). *Democratic challenges, democratic choices: the erosion of political support in advanced industrial democracies*. Oxford: Oxford University Press.

Dalton, R. J. (2006). *Citizen politics. Public opinion and political parties in advanced industrial democracies*. Washington: CQ Press.

De Luca, M., Jones, M. P., and Tula, M. I. (2002). Back rooms or ballot boxes? Candidate nomination in Argentina. *Comparative Political Studies* 35 (4), pp. 413–436.

Detterbeck, K. (2013). The rare event of choice. Party primaries in German Land parties. *German Politics* 22 (3), pp. 270–287.

Deutsch, K. W. (1963). *The nerves of government. Models of political communication and control*. New York: Free Press.

Dutton, J. (1986). The processing of crisis and non-crisis strategic issues. *Journal of Management Studies* 23 (5), pp. 501–517.

Ellner. S. (2012). The distinguishing features of Latin America´s new left in power. The Chávez, Morales, and Correa governments. *Latin American Perspectives* 39 (1), pp. 96–114.

Galderisi, P. F., Ezra, M., and Lyons, M. (Eds.). (2001). *Congressional Primaries and the Politics of Representation*. Lanham: Rowmann and Littlefield.

Gallagher, M. (1988). Introduction. In Gallagher, M., and Marsh, M. (Eds.), *Candidate selection in comparative perspective. The secret garden of politics*. London: Sage, pp. 1–19.

Gauja, A., and Cross, W. (2015). The influence of party candidate selection methods on candidate diversity. *Journal of Representation* 51 (3), pp. 287–298.

Habermas, J. (1975). *Legitimation crisis*. Boston: Beacon Press.

Hargrove, E., and Glidewell, J. (Eds.). (1990). *Impossible Jobs in Public Management.* Lawrence: Kansas University Press.

Hazan, R. Y., and Rahat, G. (2006). Candidate selection: Methods and consequences. In Katz, R. S., and Crotty, W. (Eds.), *Handbook of Party Politics.* Sage: London, pp. 109–121.

Hazan, R. Y., and Rahat; G. (2010). *Democracy within parties. Candidate selection methods and their political consequences.* Oxford: Oxford University Press.

Indridason, I. H., and Kristinsson, G. H. (2012). Primary consequences. The effects of candidate selection through party primaries in Iceland. *Party Politics* 21 (4), pp. 565–576.

Katz, R. S., and Mair, P. (1995). Changing models of party organizations and party democracy: the emergence of the cartel party. *Party Politics* 1 (1), pp. 5–28.

Kenig, O. (2009). Democratizing of party leadership selection: do wider selectorates produce more competitive contests? *Electoral Studies* 28 (2), pp. 240–247.

Kingdon, J. (1984). *Agendas, Alternatives and Public Policy.* Boston: Little Brown.

Kirchheimer, O. (1966). The transformation of Western European party systems. In La Palombara, J., and Weiner, M. (Eds.), *Political Parties and Political Development.* Princeton, NJ: Princeton University Press, pp. 177–200.

Kriesi, H. (2012). The political consequences of the financial and economic crisis in Europe: electoral punishment and popular protest. *Swiss Political Science Review* 18 (4), pp. 518–522.

Kriesi, H., and Pappas, T. S. (Eds.). (2015). *European populism in the shadow of the great recession.* Colchester: ECPR Press.

Langston, J. (2006). The changing party of the institutional revolution. Electoral competition and decentralized candidate selection. *Party Politics* 12 (3), pp. 395–413.

Mainwaring, S. (2006). The crisis of representation in the Andes. *Journal of Democracy* 17 (3), pp. 13–27.

Mair, P. (1997). *Party system change. Approaches and interpretations.* Oxford: Clarendon.

Mair, P. (2005). *Democracy beyond parties* (Working Paper 2005–6). University of California, Irvine: Center for the Study of Democracy.

Mair, P. (2008). The challenge to party government. *West European Politics* 31 (1–2), pp. 211–234.

Maisel, S. L., and Stone, W. J. (2001). Primary elections as a deterrence to candidacy for the U.S. House of Representatives. In Galderisi, P. F., Ezra, M., and Lyons, M. (Eds.) (2001). *Congressional Primaries and the Politics of Representation.* Lanham: Rowmann and Littlefield, pp. 29–47.

Mosca, L., Vaccari, C., and Valeriani, A. (2015). How to select citizen candidates: the Movimento 5 Stelle online primaries and their implications. In De Petris, A., and Poguntke, T. (Eds.), *Anti-party parties in Germany and Italy. Protest movements and parliamentary democracy.* Rome: Luiss University Press, pp. 165–192.

Mouffe, C. (2000). *The democratic paradox.* London: Verso.

Mudde, C. (2007). *Populist radical right parties in Europe.* Cambridge: Cambridge University Press.

Mudde, C. (2010). The populist radical right: A pathological normalcy. *West European Politics* 33 (6), pp. 1167–1186.

Mudde, C. (2013). Three decades of populist radical right parties in Europe: So what? The 2012 Stein Rokkan lecture. *European Journal of Political Research* 52 (1), pp. 1–19.

Müller, J.-W. (2016). *What is populism?* Baltimore: University of Pennsylvania Press.

Perrot, C. (1999). *Normal accidents. Living with high risk technologies.* Princeton: Princeton University Press.

Pilet, J.-B., and Cross, W. (2014). The selection of party leaders in comparative perspective. In Pilet, J.-B. and Cross, W. (Eds.), *The selection of political party leaders in contemporary parliamentary democracies. A comparative study*. London: Routledge, pp. 222–239.

Poguntke, T., Rossteutscher, S., Schmitt-Beck, R., and Zmerli, S. (Eds.) (2015). *Citizenship and democracy in an era of crisis. Essays in honour of Jan W. van Deth*. London: Routledge.

Rahat, G. (2009). Which candidate selection method is the most democratic? *Government and Opposition* 44 (1), pp. 68–90.

Rahat, G., Hazan, R. Y., and Katz, R. S. (2008). Democracy and political parties: on the uneasy relationship between participation, competition and representation. *Party Politics* 14 (6), pp. 663–683.

Rahat, G., and Kenig, O. (2011). Leadership selection and candidate selection: similarities and differences. Paper presented at the ECPR Joint Sessions of Workshops, University of St. Gallen, Switzerland, April 2011.

Ramiro, L. (2013). Effects of party primaries on electoral performance. The Spanish Socialist primaries in local elections. *Party Politics* 22 (1), pp. 125–136.

Rosenthal, U., Charles, M., and t'Hart, P. (1989). Introducing coping with crises. In Rosenthal, U., Charles, M., and t'Hart, P. (Eds.), *Coping with crises. The management of disasters, riots and terrorism*. Springfield: Charles C. Thomas.

Sandri, G., Seddone, A., and Venturino, F. (2015). *Party primaries in comparative perspective*. Farnham: Ashgate.

Scarrow, S. E., and Gezgor, B. (2010). Declining membership, changing members? European political party members in a new era. *Party Politics* 16 (6), pp. 823–843.

Scharpf, F. W. (1999). *Governing in Europe: Effective and democratic?* New York: Oxford University Press.

Siavelis, P. M., and Morgenstern, S. (Eds.). (2008). *Pathways to power: Political recruitment and candidate selection in Latin America*. University Park: Pennsylvania State University Press.

Sides, J., Tesler, M., and Vavreck, L. (2017). How trump lost and won. *Journal of Democracy* 28 (2), pp. 34–44.

Stavrakakis, Y., and Katsambekis, G. (2014). Left-wing populism in the European periphery: The case of Syriza. *Journal of Political Ideologies* 19 (2), pp. 119–142.

Ware, A. (2002). *The American direct primary*. Cambridge: Cambridge University Press.

3 Austria

Tradition and innovation in legislative candidate selection

Marcelo Jenny

Introduction

The theoretical framework guiding this edited volume starts off with a severe economic crisis as the causal trigger for the formation of new parties that challenged the party system leading to the defeat of old parties in elections. Some of these newcomer parties bring with them new ways of selecting their candidates. Searching to reverse their losses, old parties study these innovations and critically evaluate their own procedures; some adopt reforms. Based on a trend postulated by the literature, new parties designing and old parties reforming their candidate selection procedures will exhibit a move towards greater internal party democracy.

Austrian parties are extreme cases in this framework. More specifically, they are "extreme-on-the-independent-variable" cases (Seawright, 2016, 502), as they sit at the low end of the economic crisis scale. While Austria endured the 2008 banking crisis, the Eurozone debt crisis and worldwide recession, it suffered arguably the least among the eleven Eurozone countries and the larger circle of European Union member states. If a probable cause is weak, hypothesized effects should be small or rare. Yet, major innovations and reforms of existing candidate selection procedures can be observed among Austrian parties, which means rival explanations require consideration.

Economic crisis is seen as the penultimate cause, but the direct causal arrow to the reform of candidate selection procedures starts with an electoral defeat. There are many ways for parties to lose elections, which is not the topic of this chapter. It suffices to say that electoral defeat is a probable reason for parties to reform or consider seriously their candidate selection procedures (Müller, Plasser and Ulram, 2004; Barnea and Rahat, 2007). For new parties candidate selection procedures are not a consequence, but perhaps a probable cause of their electoral success.

I will look at Austria's electoral system as providing a structural incentive and actual party size or expected electoral size of new parties as a variable that influence in combination *how* new parties designed, and old parties reformed, their candidate selection procedures. Among countries using a proportional electoral system for legislative elections several have more than one tier or layer of electoral districts in which votes are transformed into seats (Golder, 2005). How multiple tiers in proportional electoral systems produce intra-party variation in candidate selection procedures has not received much scholarly attention yet, compared to the study of countries with mixed member-electoral systems, and I will devote some space to a neglected dimension in multi-tier electoral systems: whether a party approaches the issue of candidate selection from a top down – from national lists to regional lists – or from a bottom up perspective. I will show that candidate selection procedures of the largest parties in terms of members and votes follow a bottom up perspective. The procedures of small parties, which most new parties are at the beginning, follow a top down perspective in which ranking the candidates on the national list takes centre stage and putting candidates on regional lists is only an afterthought.

Increasing the share of women in parliament to parity, or at least nearer to it, has been a long-standing goal of women's organisations. Some parties set numerical goals for female parliamentary representation in their statutes and introduced quotas for their candidate selection processes already decades ago (Steininger, 2000, 2006; Niederkofler, 2013), but the share of women in parliament has remained in the low thirties in percentage terms (e.g. Jenny, 2017). During the period studied women's organisations in the Social Democratic Party (SPÖ) and the People's Party (ÖVP) pushed hard for further changes to and stricter implementation of party rules and I will show the effects on the candidate lists in the latest elections.

Data and methods

The chapter covers candidate selection procedures in Austrian parties from the outbreak of the economic crisis in 2008 to the most recent changes introduced before the parliamentary elections of October 2017. It draws on several data sources: candidate lists and election results, national party statutes and Land party statutes, media reports, candidate surveys (Eder, Jenny and Müller, 2015, Müller, Eder and Jenny, 2016), and several interviews with party functionaries and active and former Members of Parliament. The parties are covered in differing detail. Attention is given primarily to parties where changes can be observed and to parties representing new types or introducing new elements to the topic of candidate selection. Among the latter or new parties running in 2013 I will include NEOS – The New Austria (founded in October 2012), Team Stronach (founded in September 2012) and the Pirates Party (founded already in July 2006), among the new parties running in 2017 the List Pilz, a split-off from the Greens in parliament, that brought disaster to the latter in the elections of 2017.

The next section describes the economic and political background, followed by an analysis of the electoral system from the perspective of candidate selection, and a description of and the observed changes to the candidate selection procedures of old and new, large and small parties.

Economic and political background

A fortnight after the bankruptcy of the US bank Lehman Brothers, Austria held national legislative elections on 29 September 2008. They had been called three months before due to the break-up of the coalition between the Social Democratic Party (SPÖ) and the People's Party (ÖVP) after only two years in office. Since then two additional legislative elections took place in September 2013 and October 2017, the latter again prematurely due to a coalition break-up between the same parties.

Public finances suffered a blow from the banking crisis and recession. Carinthia, one of the nine Länder, was on the brink of bankruptcy because of the collapse of its most important regional bank and the federal government had to come to the rescue (Valla, 2015). Yet, unlike citizens in most other European countries, Austrians were only indirectly affected by the economic crisis. While the previously excellent unemployment figures rose to a post-war high (Tridico, 2013), poverty indicators remained stable throughout the period (Statistik Austria, 2017). The country exhibited one of the best macroeconomic performances among Eurozone member states (Picek, 2017) and the federal government's budgetary counter-reaction was relatively small (Armingeon, 2012).

Discontent with established parties, however, was widespread, fuelled by scandals, quarrels in the government coalition and a perception of stagnancy and blocked reform (Aichholzer et al., 2014). Suffering most from the voters' discontent in the elections of 2008 and 2013 were the two traditional government parties, the Social Democratic Party (SPÖ) and the christian-democratic People's Party (ÖVP), while the Greens to the left and new and old opposition parties to the right such as the Freedom Party (FPÖ), Team Stronach and NEOS did well in 2013. The Alliance for the Future of Austria (BZÖ), a FPÖ split-off created by its former leader Jörg Haider in 2005, suffered too, because it was deeply involved in the bankruptcy of the Carinthian bank *Hypo Alpe Adria* and in other instances of corruption or mismanagement by leading party members. In the premature elections of 2017 gridlock in the coalition between SPÖ and ÖVP was again a major topic. A second major theme was the many repercussions from the refugees crisis of 2015 on immigration and integration, especially of Muslims. Both government parties initiated changes to their candidate selection procedures, most notably in the case of the ÖVP. Candidate selection for the 2017 election also contributed to the negative events that split the Greens into two parties, resulting in the demise of the former parliamentary party and a successful parliamentary entry for the renegade list.

The relationship between the electoral system and candidate selection procedures

Political scientists have repeatedly hypothesized systematic relationships between institutions, such as the territorial organization of a state or type of electoral system and candidate selection procedures (e.g. Lundell, 2004;, Hazan and Voerman, 2006; Hazan and Rahat, 2010; Shomer, 2014; Bermudez and Cordero, 2017). Shomer concluded in her large-scale cross-national study that "territorial organization and regional patterns are among the chief factors accounting for variation in selection processes across parties. Parties competing in unitary systems will tend to adopt more centralized and exclusive selection processes, whereas parties under federal countries will adopt more inclusive and decentralized selection mechanisms", and that "factors such as ideology and party size do not seem to systematically influence candidate selection processes" (Shomer, 2014, 543). Austria is a federal country with parties of varying size adhering to different ideologies. According to this study the latter characteristics should not matter and we should candidate selection procedures to be similar across parties. All of them should be rather inclusive and decentralized.

Yet Hazan and Rahat (2010, 50) found with respect to the Israeli case "high variance within the same party system". This indicates that some electoral systems do not have enough structural power to shape party rules. Its incentives are too weak to influence how a party designs its candidate selection procedure.

Where does the Austrian case fit in? Is its electoral system a 'strong' or 'weak' institution? In this section I will attempt to show that it influences the shape of candidate selection procedures as large and small parties take its effects into account.

A three-tier electoral system

Since 1992 elections to the National Council, the lower house of parliament, employ a three-tier proportional electoral system (Müller, 2005). Apportionment of seats to constituencies and transformation of votes into seats is highly proportional, despite a four percent entry threshold at the national level. Seat allocation is logically connected across the tiers in a bottom-up process. Initially there were 43 regional districts; after territorial reform in Styria ahead of the 2013 elections it changed to 39. Almost all regional districts created by the 1992 reform were new geographic entities made from adjacent administrative districts from the same Land. They remain unfamiliar to many voters and the party organisations of established parties are still structured by the territorial layers of municipalities, administrative districts, Länder and national level (Müller, 1992, 1994).

Party candidacy

A party requires support signatures from three current members of the National Council or from a number of citizens to stand in an election. Running nationwide requires 2,600 signatures. Candidate lists for the Land and the nested regional districts together constitute the Land list proposal (*Landeswahlvorschlag*). It has to arrive not later than 58 days before the day of the election and the national district candidate list (*Bundeswahlvorschlag*) 48 days before to allow time for printing the ballot papers. These deadlines drastically curtail the time available for selecting candidates in premature elections.

In 1995, the coalition between SPÖ and ÖVP broke up after one year. All parties except for the Greens drew heavily from the candidate lists presented in the previous election. Within a year both ÖVP and SPÖ changed from their most inclusive candidate selection ever, the party primaries held in 1994 (Leitner and Mertens, 1995; Nick, 1995), to highly exclusive candidate selection by national and Land party executives. In 2008 the ÖVP ended the coalition with the SPÖ on

7 July after two years in office. New elections were scheduled for 28 September, 83 days after the break-up. Parties had to create 53 candidate lists for the 43 regional districts, 9 Land districts plus one nationwide district within a month. Again, they recruited many candidates who had already run in the 2006 elections. The elections of 2013 in contrast were scheduled at the end of a legislative term. Parties had enough time to implement selection procedures as stipulated by their statutes and re-candidacy rates were lower.

Seat allocation

In the regional districts and Land districts the number of seats won by a party are based on the Hare quota calculated separately for each Land. The party's total number of seats is calculated by another quota, the 183-largest number produced by the D'Hondt method, applied to its nationwide number of votes. Seats won in nested regional districts are deducted from the number of seats calculated for the Land district, the remaining ones are allocated to Land district candidates. The seats remaining after deducting the lower tier seats from the total number are allocated to national district candidates. Only parties who pass the 4 percent national threshold or win a regional district seat can participate in the second and third tier seat allocation.

Since 1992 eight legislative elections have been held under this electoral system. Figure 3.1 is a ternary plot (Cox, 2004) showing the shares of seats a party won in each tier. The FPÖ seat distribution in 2013 is labelled for easier reading: the party won 40 percent of its seats in regional districts (indicated by an arrow pointing horizontally to the left side of the triangle), 40 percent in Land districts (arrow sloping up to the right) and 20 percent in the national district (arrow sloping down to the right).

The graph shows SPÖ and ÖVP always in an upper right location as they obtained more than half of their seats in regional districts and less than twenty percent in the national district. The FPÖ results are spread widely over the area of the triangle. The Greens and the other parties are almost always located on the bottom scale as they had no regional district seats, Land district seats varying from 40 to above 80 percent, and national district seats constituting the remainder of the parliamentary party. By contrast, in the ÖVP in 2002 three-quarters of the MPs came from regional districts, a bit more than 15 percent from Land districts and less than 10 percent from the nationwide district.

The composition of a parliamentary party and the relative weight of the tiers it draws its MPs from, is determined by party size. Figure 3.2 shows the bivariate patterns for the eight legislative elections held since the current electoral system came into force. The three scatterplots corresponding to the three tiers show how seat shares change with increasing party size.

Small parties, from barely passing the entry threshold to about ten percent of the votes, obtain no seats in regional districts, most of their seats in Land districts and the remainder in the national district. A regional district seat would require an extraordinarily high geographic concentration of votes. A small party has twice

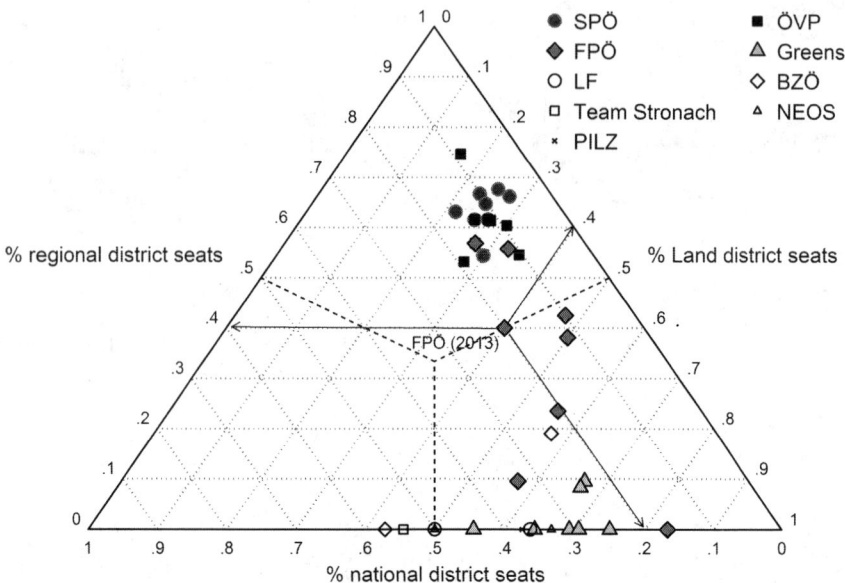

Figure 3.1 Parties' share of seats in electoral system's three tiers (1994–2017)

Source: Own calculations based on Ministry of the Interior's official seat allocation results of national legislative elections, available at www.bmi.gv.at/412/Nationalratswahlen/.

Note: Marker position indicates the fraction of seats a party obtained in regional districts (first) tier, Land districts (second) tier and national district (third) tier.

(BZÖ in 2006, Team Stronach in 2013) won more national than Land district seats. Any party with more than 25 percent of the votes consists mostly of regional district MPs. National district MPs are a small minority in the parliamentary party.

The number of national district seats won per party has ranged from a minimum of three to a maximum of ten; the median is six seats. Due to the larger number of districts at the Land and regional tier, only a top or immediately below the top position is a safe or probable seat. Calculating the border between safe and probable seats is difficult, however, as fulfilling the seat quota at one of the lower levels deducts a seat from the higher levels. To increase chances a candidate can run on one list per tier, which sometimes results in two or even three parallel seats claims. Depending on the seat chosen a party can then 'recalibrate' the composition of its parliamentary party group to grant a faction's wish or increase the share of women in parliament.

As we have seen party size is an important moderator of intra-party power in this electoral system. Unless a national party leadership has control over the subnational lists it faces a variable situation, contingent on the outcome of the election. Of course, electoral success bestows authority to a party leader which can override the regionalising effect of the seat allocation process. A great electoral victory in the premature elections of 2002, initiated by ÖVP party leader

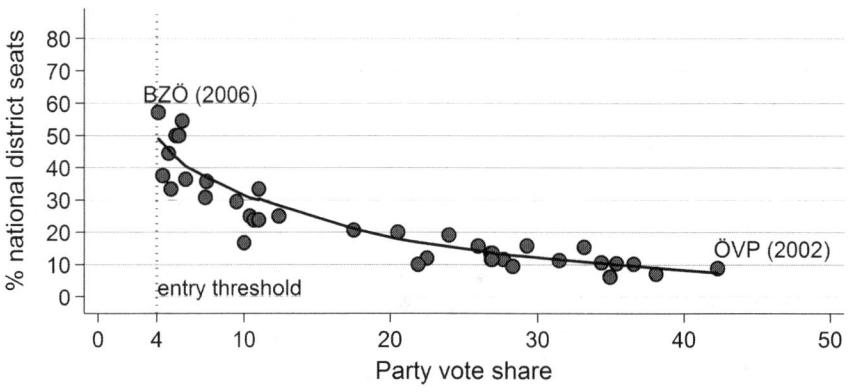

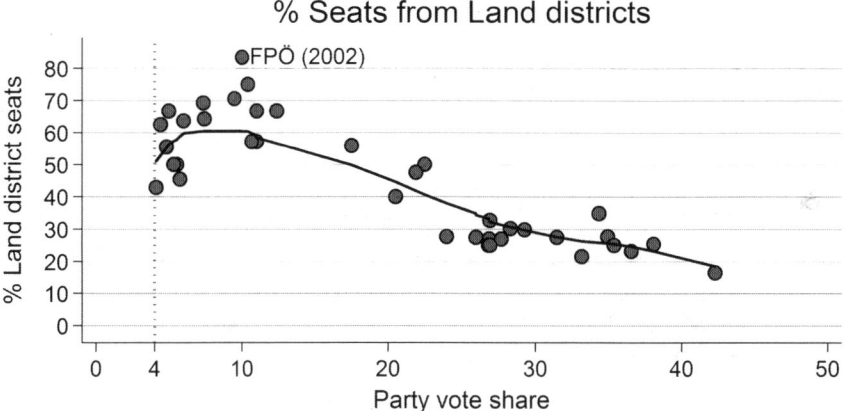

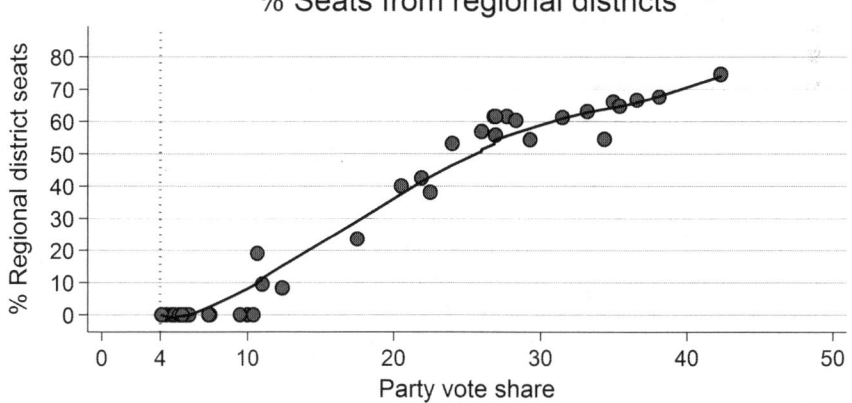

Figure 3.2 Composition of the parliamentary party and party size (1994–2017)

Source: Own calculations based on Ministry of the Interior's official seat allocation results of national legislative elections, available at www.bmi.gv.at/412/Nationalratswahlen/.

Note: Scatterplots of party's share of valid votes and of seats obtained in each tier with lowess curves added.

Wolfgang Schüssel, endowed him with tremendous intra-party authority (Ennser-Jedenastik and Müller, 2015), even though less than ten percent of the MPs were from the party's national list over which he had most control. The ÖVP Land party organisations traditionally nominate the candidates for the lower two tiers and thus control the majority of the party's safe seats, which has been frequently bemoaned by party leaders and reformers (Neisser and Plasser, 1992; Müller and Plasser, 2004). There is not much parachuting (Pedersen et al., 2007) of nationally prominent politicians to regional district lists (Müller et al., 2001, 110–117), but ministers from SPÖ and ÖVP have often taken top positions in Land districts.

From the effects shown in Figure 3.2 we can hypothesise that small and large parties will differ in their attention to candidate list creation for the tiers. It should be either set up as a bottom up or as a top down process. Small parties decide on the national candidate list first and on lower lists later. As they win no seats there, they should not bother a lot about the candidate lists for regional districts. Large parties in terms of votes, but even more so in terms of members, will follow the order of the seat allocation process and manufacture candidate lists by proceeding from the regional to the national level.

Personalisation of the electoral system

Though preferential voting has existed from the beginning (Müller, 2005), Austria is among the countries where personalisation of the electoral system has increased in recent decades (Renwick and Pilet, 2016). When the current three-tier system was introduced preferential voting was available only for the lower two tiers and quite ineffective. It was extended for the 2013 elections to the national tier and thresholds for winning a seat by jumping to the top of a party's candidate list were set at 7 percent of the party votes in the national district and lowered to the still high levels of 10 percent in a Land district and 14 percent in a regional district. In 2013 a single MP from the People's Party won her seat due to preferential votes (Aichholzer et al., 2014, 28–29; Jenny and Müller, 2014) and the evaluation from 10 years earlier still held: "intra-party candidate selection remains much more decisive than the general election for parliamentary representation" (Müller, 2003, 228–229). The ÖVP however, voluntarily lowered the thresholds for its candidates by half for the 2017 elections and some Land party organisations adopted intra-party seat allocation based on the candidates' ranking in terms of preference votes. The lower hurdles produced changes on the party's lists. In line with the expectations about party size, candidates from small parties have paid less attention to personalised campaigning for preference votes in regional districts than candidates from large parties (Eder, Jenny and Müller, 2015).

Candidate selection procedures

This section provides an overview of the procedures used by various parties. It covers instances of reforms in old parties and innovations introduced by new parties. Apart from eligibility requirements for candidates – citizenship and minimum age of 18 years – no public regulation of the candidate selection process exists (Müller, 2003, 226). In designing a candidate selection procedure parties are free. Party statutes of Austrian parties may include criteria for eligibility and re-candidacy, quotas in support of female candidates or informal quotas for policy specialists that the national party wants represented in its parliamentary group; or the statutes may decide on the admissibility of non-party members as candidates.

Table 3.1 provides indicators of party size and summarizes candidate selection at the three tiers. Party membership statistics and best electoral results are from the period covered. Candidate selection procedures are taken from national and Land party statutes. The parties are arranged along the left-right ideological dimension based on candidates' self-placement (Eder, Jenny and Müller, 2015; Müller, Eder and Jenny, 2016).

The *SPÖ* has had a long-running intra-party debate over a decades-old unfulfilled commitment in the party statute to not only have 40 percent women on its candidate lists, but more importantly achieve a share of 40 percent women in the parliamentary party (Niederkofler, 2013). The actual share of Social Democratic women MPs has never been much above 30 percent (e.g. Jenny, 2017). In 2010 the party added a gender zipper system to the party statute, which some Land parties implemented only loosely for the 2013 elections. The party tightened the rules in 2014 and the national party executive was granted the right to veto lower level candidate lists whose composition poses an obstacle to reaching a 40 percent share of female MPs. The SPÖ party statutes mention ad hoc regional district assemblies made up of delegates from administrative district parties that create the regional district lists. The Land district list is created by the Land party executive. All candidate lists have to be ratified by a wider national party body.

According to its pre-2015 party statute the *ÖVP* national party executive has to issue a guidance (*Vorwahlregulativ*) for local and administrative district party chapters on how to propose and select candidates and for the Land party how to create the regional district lists. Creation of the Land district list was left to Land party statutes. The national party leader had to propose the composition and candidate ranking of the national district list, which was then ratified by the national party executive. After several electoral defeats and the departure of three party leaders within a short period (Ennser-Jedenastik and Müller, 2015), the next party leader Reinhold Mitterlehner presided over a party reform in 2015. It brought a new party programme and a new organisation statute (Rois, 2016; Maier, 2016). The ÖVP has a decades-old unfulfilled commitment in the party statute that one third of the parliamentary party should be women. The new organization statute stated that candidate selection should enable the party "to achieve a preferably balanced proportion of women and men in all bodies". It ordered gender zipper lists for the national and the Land district lists, but exempted the regional district lists. The new party statute also allows Land parties to weigh preferential vote results much more strongly in intra-party seat allocation. Some Land parties have turned to reordering the list after the election based on the number of preference votes won, a popular idea among party members (Maier, 2016, 117).

Table 3.1 Party size and party selectorates (2008–2017)

	Greens	SPÖ	Pirates Party	ÖVP	NEOS	Team Stronach	BZÖ	FPÖ
Party size								
Party members	7,000	180,000	<100	600,000	2,700	350	>10,000	60,000
Best election result	12.4	29.3	0.8	31.5	5.3	5.7	10.7	26.0
Party selectorates								
Regional district lists	Party members and non-members at Land party convention	Party delegates at regional district convention and wider national party executive	based on result of Land party primary	Regional party delegates	based on result of Land party primary	Land party executive	Land party leader and Land party executive	Land party executive and national party executive
Land district list	Party members and non-members at Land party convention	wider Land party executive and wider national party executive	Party primary	Land party executive	3 body open party primary	Land party executive	Land party leader and Land party executive	Land party executive and national party executive
National district list	Party delegates at national party convention	wider national party executive	Party primary	National party executive → Party leader (2017)	3 body open party primary	National party executive	National Party leader	national party executive
Old or new party	Old	Old	New	Old	New	New	Old	Old
Rules changed	No	Yes	No	Yes	No	No	No	No

Sources: Based on national party statutes and Land party statutes. Data on party members statistics taken from ORF.at (2014, 2017), derStandard.at (2008), Pirates Party (2017).

Notes: The SPÖ introduced a gender zipper system for candidate lists in 2010, the ÖVP followed in 2015.

Party leader Mitterlehner resigned in May 2017, exasperated by the intra-party debate on when he would step aside for the party's rising star, Foreign Minister Sebastian Kurz, who was expected to end the coalition with the SPÖ and lead the party into premature elections. Kurz, however, presented the party with a list of conditions for assuming the office. He demanded greater powers, including over candidate selection (Bonavida and Ettinger, 2017), which the party quickly conceded, and the party statute was amended again. The party leader now creates the national district list and may enlist non-party members as candidates. Kurz filled the top positions on the national list with personally chosen non-party members and had a hand in the selection of some top candidates of Land districts. Another important change is that the gender zipper system now applies to all tiers, which means that male ministers and MPs lost many safe seat positions. The greater weight given to preferential votes at the same time provided them with a realistic chance to jump to the top of the list through a personal vote.

The *FPÖ* traditionally ratifies its candidate lists through decisions of party executives. Past conflicts between the national party leadership and some Land parties have led to changes in the national and Land statutes endowing the national party with a veto right against a Land party's decisions (Luther, 2006, 2011). The national party executive creates the national candidate list. The Land party executive collects proposals from lower party chapters and sets the ranking of candidate on the lists for the regional districts and the Land district, but these lists still require the consent of the national party executive. In case of disagreements the national executive cannot add candidates to a list, but it can strike out candidates or reorder them and has therefore veto power over access to parliament. Candidates must be party members; exceptions require the consent of the Land or national party executive.

The *Alliance for the Future of Austria* is a split-off from the FPÖ created by the latter's former party leader Jörg Haider in 2005. Its candidate selection procedures have been on the exclusive end of the scale. The party leader had the right to create the national candidate list. The party failed the entry threshold in 2013 and did not run in 2017.

For a long time the *Greens* were proud of their transparent intra-party democracy with candidate selection by party conventions. Land party conventions are attended by party member (and open to non-members), the national party convention by party delegates. These events where candidates competed for each top list position in separate contests have often been suspenseful and unpredictable. Prominent MPs repeatedly failed to obtain renomination. In the national party convention in spring 2017 the party's best known and most senior MP, Peter Pilz, lost a vote for a safe seat on the national list against the youngest, and more popular, MP Julian Schmid. Pilz declared his resignation from politics at the convention, but shortly afterwards he presented a new party whose candidates were recruited through personal networks. His party *List Pilz* passed the threshold with 4.4 percent of the votes while the Greens dropped from 13.5 percent in 2013 to 3.8 percent in 2017. In their post-election dissection of mistakes, some Green Party functionaries criticised the party's candidate selection procedure.

Team Stronach was founded by Austro-Canadian billionaire Frank Stronach in 2012 and, according to him, will dissolve again by the end of 2017. Stronach emphasised economic liberalism and right-wing populism, without the anti-immigrant stance of FPÖ and BZÖ (Aichhorn et al., 2014). Party organisation was minimal and membership numbers were low, making Team Stronach an example of a business firm party (Hopkins and Paolucci, 1999; Mazzoleni and Voerman, 2017). The party executive consisted of the party leader, a deputy party leader and a finance officer. The first deputy party leader was a former personal assistant of the party leader. According to the party statute the party executive creates the national district list. Land party executives are responsible for the other lists, but the national party executive had a veto right. The national party statute does not mention the regional tier.

NEOS (The New Austria) was founded in 2012 and ran in the 2013 elections on a joint platform with a liberal student party and the older liberal party, Liberal Forum. NEOS introduced an innovative system of internet-based candidate selection that combines three separate selection bodies: citizens, the party executive and party members voting in successive order on the candidates (Jenny, 2016). The candidate selection procedure follows a top-down approach. Candidate lists for regional districts in 2017 were created from the subset of candidates living there and their ranking copied from the Land district list. The party has emphasised the innovativeness, transparency and inclusiveness of its candidate selection procedure in its campaigning. It has at the same time acted pragmatically and put candidates on the national list who did not undergo its selection procedure. In 2013 safe list were given to top candidates from its alliance partner, Liberal Forum. In 2017 it provided a safe list position for 'super candidate' Irmgard Griss, who had finished in third place in the first round of the Austrian presidential elections of 2016. Griss brought a valuable personal vote and had been also courted by ÖVP party leader Kurz.

The Austrian *Pirates Party* was formed in 2006 as an offspring of the international Pirate Party umbrella organisation. It collected enough support signatures to run in the legislative elections of 2013. The Pirates Party propagates "grassroots democracy" through internet-based procedures for voting and candidate selection ("liquid democracy") and NEOS took inspiration from the Pirates Party. According to the party statute the national party congress created the national candidate list through elections and the Land party organisations decided on the candidate lists for the Land and regional districts. Only paid-up members may vote and stand as a candidate. Candidate selection was via a closed primary, after a hearing of each candidate at a party congress in February 2013. The vote was repeated a few months later to increase the party's low share of women on the list. Candidates on the Land district list were added to regional districts list based on where they lived. The party at the time of the 2013 elections basically consisted of three active Land party organizations with about 100 paid-up members (Pirates Party, 2017). The Pirates Party is led by a collective: the national party executive. It won 0.8 percent of the votes in 2013 and did not run in 2017.

Female representation and list positions on candidate lists

Ahead of the 2017 election the women's organisations of the government parties, SPÖ and ÖVP, unsuccessfully lobbied their respective party leaderships to introduce a legal gender quota for parliament, However, as described in the previous section, both parties exhibited a greater sensibility for the representation of women in parliament. Table 3.2 shows that the share of female candidates increased from 35.5 percent in 2008 to almost 40 percent in 2017. Parties straddle the left-right dimension on this indicator with leftist parties exhibiting a higher share of women on the lists than rightist parties.

The gender position index in the lower part of the table measures gender representation in top list positions, i.e. where the safe and winnable seats are located. As we have seen, the range of safe seats per tier varies with party size but systematic comparison takes precedence here. To calculate the gender index value for the top 6 positions on national district lists I have assigned points in reverse

Table 3.2 Gender and top list positions (2008–2017)

	Greens	PILZ	SPÖ	ÖVP	NEOS	Team Str.	FPÖ	BZÖ	Total
2008									
Candidates	591	–	710	687	–	–	640	490	4,080
% women	50.1	–	42.3	36.7	–	–	18.1	23.7	35.5
2013									
Candidates	904	–	657	635	149	223	636	331	3,946
% women	45.9	–	47.6	37.5	23.5	23.3	20.4	30.2	36.2
2017									
Candidates	547	137	674	677	346	–	640	–	3,963
% women	53.2	36.5	48.5	48.3	26.6	–	23.8	–	39.7
Gender position index									
2008									
Top 6 national	33	–	43	43	–	–	24	10	
Ø Top 4 Land	73	–	37	41	–	–	24	14	
Ø Top 2 Regional	51	–	34	24	–	–	15	16	
2013									
Top 6 national	62	–	52	38	48	43	33	29	
Ø Top 4 Land	57	–	41	38	30	22	24	17	
Ø Top 2 Regional	54	–	32	27	19	24	18	21	
2017									
Top 6 national	48	43	43	43	48	–	19	–	
Ø Top 4 Land	60	47	47	51	42	–	19	–	
Ø Top 2 Regional	53	36	49	44	36	–	17	–	

Source: Own calculations based on Federal Ministry of the Interior's official candidate lists for legislative elections of 2008, 2013 and 2017.

Notes: The last column is based on all candidates (from 14 parties) who stood for office in 2008, 2013 (14) and 2017 (16). Index values for the Land and regional tier are district means.

order, ranging from six points for a woman listed first to one point for a woman in sixth place. Male candidates score no points. Points are then added up by party and divided by the maximum number of points of an all-female list. This creates an index ranging from 0 points for a men-only list to 100 points for a women-only list. Index values below 50 indicate that there are more male than female candidates or in case of equal numbers, that men have the better list positions. Index values above 50 indicate more and better list positions for women. The index values shown for the Land tier and the regional tier are mean values across districts.

The index shows the strong list positions of women in the Green Party and their weak representation at the top of lists in the FPÖ and the BZÖ. The Greens were the only party where women occupied the top list positions slightly more often than men. The SPÖ had a 'gender-neutral' index value for the national district list in 2013, as the national party leadership placed women in safe seats to compensate for the low number of female MPs elected in regional districts. The effects of the zipper lists enforced by the SPÖ and ÖVP in 2017 are more visible in the latter. Projections indicate that the SPÖ will for the first time fulfil its quota of 40 percent female MPs. The ÖVP will also get a higher share of female MPs, but the new intra-party rules for preferential vote results dampen the increase. Several male MPs did better than non-incumbent female candidates who were listed ahead of them.

NEOS propagates gender equality (Johann, Jenny and Kritzinger, 2016), but its share of female MPs was the lowest of all parties in the last term, partly because it had miscalculated the districts in which it would get a seat (and because a female MP won a seat in the European Parliament elections). An attempt to increase its share of female MPs in 2017 can be clearly seen. The low gender index values for the FPÖ went down further from 2008 to 2017. Overall, the share of female MPs in the parliament is likely to be close to where it stood last term as the Greens, the party with the highest number of female MPs, dropped out of parliament.

Conclusions

The chapter has shown the variety of candidate selection procedures employed by Austrian parties. The innovations and reforms in candidate selection procedures observed in this country cannot be ascribed to the European economic crisis. Austria weathered the crisis better than most European countries. However, the framework's intermediate variable, electoral defeat, remains the most likely explanation of why established parties have reformed their candidate selection procedures.

I have pointed to parties' pragmatic considerations when they have to draw up lists of candidates. In premature elections parties are repeatedly confronted by a lack of time. Candidate selection procedures with a high level of party democracy require more time; exclusive and centralised decision-making by small party bodies can be a relative advantage in such situations. I have argued that the complex three-tier electoral system, in combination with actual or expected party size, exert an influence on how parties devise or execute their candidate selection procedures. Depending on their size in terms of voters, parties focus on different tiers. Small parties, which also tend to have few local party chapters, tend to follow a top-down approach. They pay most attention to the creation of the candidate list for the national district and for Länder districts. For them the three-tier system effectively folds into a two-tier system. The largest (and also the oldest) Austrian parties in terms of voters and party members take a bottom-up approach. Their party statutes provide more detail on list development and creation at the regional district level and below. Large parties also pay more attention to the impact of seats shifting between tiers from one election to the next, as a quota can be narrowly missed or reached.

The new parties founded during the period studied exhibit a range of different party types, from the business firm party of Team Stronach to the Pirates Party as an internet-based party. NEOS and the List Pilz have both claimed that they were created by citizen initiative and even the 'New ÖVP' led by Kurz has laid claim to the 'movement' label. The candidate selection of these new parties does not exhibit a uniform trend towards greater internal party democracy.

Reforms of candidate-selection procedures by established parties have not wholeheartedly embraced more intra-party democracy, as the example of the ÖVP shows. Its new party leader Kurz chose to increase the party's appeal to new voter groups by filling the national list with non-members, which he exclusively selected for their personal qualities. The Greens have often touted their high level of intra-party democracy, but they split in 2017 when cliques and ideological tendencies fought in the candidate selection process ahead of the elections.

In the last section I have documented the increasing importance of gender representation in several but not all parties. It was most prominent and visible in the effective implementation of gender zipper systems by the SPÖ and ÖVP in the 2017 election. The latter, however, combined it with lower hurdles for list changes through preferential votes, which weakened the gender zipper system's effect on actual seat allocation.

Primary sources

The primary sources consist of national and Land party statutes, in various revisions, of SPÖ, ÖVP, FPÖ, Greens, BZÖ, Team Stronach, NEOS, Pirates Party and List Pilz. Additionally, background interviews with party functionaries, former and active Members of Parliament from several parties were conducted which provided valuable guidance for reading the party statutes.

References

Aichholzer J., Kritzinger, S., Jenny, M., Müller, W. C., Schönbach, K., and Vonbun, R. (2014). Die Ausgangslage: In: Kritzinger, S., Müller, W. C. and Schönbach K. (Eds.), *Die Nationalratswahl 2013: Wie Parteien, Medien und Wählerschaft zusammenwirken*. Vienna: Böhlau Verlag, pp. 9–38.

Armingeon, K. (2012). The politics of fiscal responses to the crisis of 2008–2009. *Governance* 25(4), pp. 543–565.

Barnea, S., and Rahat, G. (2007). Reforming candidate selection methods. *Party Politics* 13 (3), pp. 375–394.

Bermúdez, S., and Cordero, G. (2017). Who is recruiting our crew? Contextual determinants of MPs selection. *Acta Politica* 52 (3), pp. 265–285.

Bonavide, I., and Ettinger, K. (2017, May 14). Die ÖVP gibt Sebastian Kurz alle Macht. *Die Presse*. Retrieved from http://diepresse.com/home/innenpolitik/5217803/Die-OeVP-gibt-Sebastian-Kurz-alle-Macht

Cordero, G., Castillo, A. M., and Coller, X. (2016). Selecting candidates in multilevel democracies. *American Behavioral Scientist* 60 (7), pp. 773–780.

Cox, N. J. (2004). Speaking stata: Graphing categorical and compositional data. *Stata Journal* 4 (2), pp. 190–215.

derStandard.at (2008). *Wieviele Mitglieder haben die österreichischen Parteien jeweils?* (2008, October 31). Retrieved from http://derstandard.at/1224776617579/Wieviele-Mitglieder-haben-die-oesterreichischen-Parteien-jeweils.

Eder, N., Jenny, M., and Müller, W. C. (2015). Winning over voters or fighting party Comrades: Personalized constituency campaigning in Austria. *Electoral Studies* 39 (3), pp. 316–328.

Ennser-Jedenastik, L., and Müller, W. C. (2015). Intra-party democracy, political performance and the survival of party leaders. *Party Politics* 21 (6), pp. 930–943.

Golder, M. (2005). Democratic electoral systems around the world, 1946–2000. *Electoral Studies* 24 (1), pp. 103–121.

Hazan, R. Y., and Rahat, G. (2010). *Democracy within parties: Candidate selection methods and their political consequences*. Oxford: Oxford University Press.

Hazan, R. Y., and Voerman, G. (2006). Electoral systems and candidate selection. *Acta Politica* 41 (2), pp 146–162.

Hopkin, J., and Paolucci, C. (1999). The business firm model of party organisation: Cases from Spain and Italy. *European Journal of Political Research* 35 (3), pp. 307–339. doi:10.1111/1475-6765.00451

Jenny, M. (2016). *Innovative candidate selection as an electoral campaign nonus: The internet-based curial primaries of NEOS*. Paper prepared for the 23rd Annual Conference of the Council of European Studies, Philadelphia.

Jenny, M. (2017). Austria. *European Journal of Political Research Political Data Yearbook*, 56 (1), pp. 1–10.

Jenny, M., and Müller, W. C. (2014). Das Wahlergebnis. In Kritzinger, S., Müller, W. C. and Schönbach K. (Eds.), *Die Nationalratswahl 2013: Wie Parteien, Medien und Wählerschaft zusammenwirken*. Vienna: Böhlau Verlag, pp. 215–230.

Johann, D., Jenny, M., and Kritzinger, S. (2016). Mehr Wettbewerb bei Österreichs Wahlen? Die neue Partei NEOS und ihre engsten Konkurrenten. *Zeitschrift für Parlamentsfragen* 47 (4), pp. 814–830. Retrieved from www.nomos-elibrary.de/10.5771/0340-1758-2016-4/

Leitner, L., and Mertens, Ch. (1995). Die Vorwahlen der österreichischen Volkspartei zur Nationalratswahl 1994: Analysen und Reformvorschläge. *Österreichisches Jahrbuch für Politik 1994*, pp. 199–218.

Lundell, K. (2004). Determinants of candidate selection: The degree of centralization in comparative perspective. *Party Politics* 10 (1), pp. 25–47.

Luther, K. R. (2006). In. Dachs, H., Gerlich, P., Gottweis, H., Horner, F., Kramer, H., Lauber V., Müller, W. C. and Tálos, E. (Eds.), *Handbuch des politischen Systems Österreichs: Die Zweite Republik*. Vienna: Manz, pp. 364–388.

Luther, K. R. (2011). Of goals and own goals: A case study of right-wing populist party strategy for and during incumbency. *Party Politics* 17 (4), pp. 453–470.

Maier, G. (2016). "Evolution Volkspartei" – die Bewegung zur Weiterentwicklung der ÖVP: Ein gelungener parteipolitischer Drahtseilakt. *Österreichisches Jahrbuch für Politik 2015*. Vienna: Böhlau Verlag, pp. 109–124.

Mazzoleni, O., and Voerman, G. (2017). Memberless parties: Beyond the business-firm party model? *Party Politics* 23 (6), pp. 783–792.

Müller, W. C. (1992). Austria (1945–1990). In Katz, R. S. and Mair, P. (Eds.), *Party organizations: A data handbook on party organization in Western democracies, 1960–90*. London: Sage, pp. 21–120.

Müller, W. C. (1994). The development of Austrian Party Organizations. In Katz, R. and Mair, P. (Eds.). *How parties organize: Change and adaptation in party organizations in Western democracies*. London: SAGE Publications, pp. 51–79

Müller, W. C. (2003). Austria: Imperfect Parliamentarism but Fully-fledged Party Democracy. In Strom, K., Bergman, T. and Müller, W. C. (Eds.), *Delegation and accountability in parliamentary democracies*. Oxford: Oxford University Press, pp. 221–252.

Müller, W. C. (2005). Austria: a complex electoral system with subtle effects. In Gallagher, M. and Mitchell, P. (Eds.), *The politics of electoral systems*. Oxford: Oxford University Press, pp. 397–416.

Müller, W. C., Eder, N., and Jenny, M. (2016). *AUTNES candidate survey 2013: Public use version 2.1*. Vienna: University of Vienna.

Müller, W. C., Jenny, M., Dolezal, M., Steininger, B., Philipp, W. and Westphal, S. (2001). *Die österreichischen Abgeordneten: Individuelle Präferenzen und politisches Verhalten*. Vienna: WUV Universitätsverlag.

Müller, W. C, Plasser, F., and Ulram, P. A. (2004). Party Responses to the Erosion of Voter Loyalties in Austria. In Mair, P., Müller, W. C. and Plasser, F. (Eds.), *Political parties and electoral change: Party responses to electoral markets*. London: Sage, pp. 145–178.

Neisser, H., and Plasser, F. (Eds.) (1992). *Vorwahlen und Kandidatennominierung im internationalen Vergleich*. Vienna: Signum Verlag.

Nick, R. (1995). Die Wahl vor der Wahl: Kandidatennominierung und Vorwahlen. In Müller, W. C., Plasser, F., and Ulram, P. A. (Eds.), *Wählerverhalten und Parteienwettbewerb: Analysen zur Nationalratswahl 1994*. Vienna: Signum Verlag, pp. 67–118.

Niederkofler, H. (2013). Von der Hälfte des Himmels, oder: Die Geduld der Frauen ist die Macht der Männer. Geschlechterdemokratie und Quotendiskussion in der SPÖ. In Mesner, M., and Niederkofler, H. (Eds.), *Johanna Dohnal: Ein politisches Lesebuch*. Vienna: Mandelbaum Verlag, pp. 89–106.

ORF.at (2014, November 24). *Basis bricht weg*. Retrieved from http://orf.at/stories/2254885/2254886/

ORF.at (2017, July 17). *Zwischen Nutzen und Idealen*. Retrieved from http://orf.at/stories/2399160/2399159

Pedersen, M. J., Kjaer, U., and Eliassen, K. (2007). The geographical dimension of parliamentary recruitment: among native sons and parachutists. In: Cotta, M. and Best, H. (Eds.), Oxford: Oxford University Press, pp. 160–190.

Picek, O. (2017). *The "Magic Square" of economic policy measured by a macroeconomic performance index*. New School for Social Research Working Paper 02/2017, New York.

Pirates Party. (2017). *Party membership statistics*. Retrieved from www.piratenpartei.at/partei/transparenz/

Renwick, A., and Pilet, J. (2016). *Faces on the ballot: The personalization of electoral systems in Europe*. Oxford: Oxford University Press.

Rois, Ch. (2016). Der Weg zum neuen ÖVP-Grundsatzprogramm und Organisationsstatut: "Evolution Volkspartei" aus der Perspektive der Organisationsentwicklung. *Österreichisches Jahrbuch für Politik 2015*. Vienna: Böhlau Verlag, pp. 95–108.

Seawright, J. (2016). The case for selecting cases that are deviant or extreme on the independent variable. *Sociological Methods and Research* 45 (3), pp. 493–525.

Shomer, Y. (2014). What affects candidate selection processes? A cross-national examination. *Party Politics* 20 (4), pp. 533–546.

Statistik Austria. (2017). *Armut und Soziale Eingliederung.* Retrieved from www.statistik.at/web_de/statistiken/menschen_und_gesellschaft/soziales/armut_und_soziale_eingliederung/index.html

Steininger, B. (2000). Representation of women in the Austrian political system 1945–1998: From a token female politician towards an equal ratio. *Women and Politics* 21 (2), pp. 81–106.

Steininger, B. (2006). Frauen im Regierungssystem, 2006. In. Dachs, H., Gerlich, P., Gottweis, H., Horner, F., Kramer, H., Lauber V., Müller, W. C. and Tálos, E. (Eds.), *Handbuch des politischen Systems Österreichs: Die Zweite Republik.* Vienna: Manz, pp. 286–303.

Tridico, P. (2013). The impact of the economic crisis on EU labour markets: A comparative perspective. *International Labour Review* 152 (2), pp. 175–190.

Ucakar, K. (1985). *Demokratie und Wahlrecht in Österreich: zur Entwicklung von politischer Partizipation und staatlicher Legitimationspolitik.* Vienna: Verlag für Gesellschaftskritik.

Valla, N. (2015). State guarantees and defeasance structures. In Allen, F., Carletti, E. and Gray, J. (Eds.), *The new financial architecture in the Eurozone.* Florence: European University Institute, pp. 43–54.

4   The curious stability of candidate selection methods in Belgium in times of crisis

Audrey Vandeleene and Lieven De Winter

Introduction

Political crises are said to affect the political system deeply, and the party system in particular. Crises trigger the emergence of new political organisations and/or force existing organisations to reshape their political platforms or their working methods, for instance in the way they select the candidates running for office. This chapter studies Belgium as a negative case of the impact of political crisis on candidate selection habits. This does not, however, mean that nothing changed in Belgium after the crisis. But the modifications were not substantial nor did they head towards the recurring trend of intra-party democratization (Cross et al., 2016). Although one might expect that the political crisis would have triggered the emergence of new parties – and together with them innovative forms of candidate selection – this was not the case. No genuine anti-austerity parties with alternative selection methods emerged, nor did mainstream parties alter their modes of selection in favour of more inclusiveness.

This piece seeks to answer the following question: "why did the crisis not cause significant changes to the way political parties select their candidates?" We first uncover the emergence of new political actors in the Belgian consociational political arena, often defined as "non-traditional" parties. We discuss to what extent they can be really considered as the type of new political actors that typically would have emerged during the crisis period. We test the hypothesis that the newer actors would be likely to implement more inclusive candidate selection methods compared to older traditional political parties. We focus on four main post-pillarization actors in Belgium: the Greens, who already won their first seats in the 1980s but broke through only in the beginning of the 1990s; the New Flemish Alliance, a right-wing nationalist party that arose in 2001 and became Flemish market leader in 2010; and the most recent successful newcomer, the Workers' Party, which managed to enter Parliament only in 2014. However, none of these novel parties introduced very inclusive selection methods, rather the contrary. This chapter shows that they have tended to select their candidates in more exclusive (and centralised) ways over the years, displaying a contradictory trend to most of the other cases presented in this volume.

Our second objective is to investigate how mainstream – older – political parties behave where intra-party democratisation is concerned. Do they open up their selection procedures even though their new competitors do not? We explore the changes over time in candidate selection processes, in the level of inclusiveness and of centralisation of the selectorates, for the three traditional Belgian party families, i.e. the socialists, the Christian-democrats and the liberals – with the aim of understanding which factors prompted changes and what objectives these changes pursued.

The chapter unfolds as follows. We start by briefly reviewing the literature on the changes in candidate selection with a specific focus on the Belgian case. We then present the variety of data sources used. The subsequent section is divided into two main parts: the first explores candidate selection in the newcomers to the party system; the second focuses on the mainstream parties. We discuss the reasons why Belgium may be a "negative case" in the last section.

Theoretical and contextual background

In Belgium, the selection (almost) makes the election (Cross, 2008). Voters can hardly affect the names of the elected candidates since practically everything is predetermined within the party spheres at the time of candidate selection because of the semi-open (often called 'semi-closed' (Vandeleene et al., 2016)) nature of the electoral system. A very small number of candidates manage to bypass a candidate placed higher on the list (André et al., 2017). At the last federal elections in 2014, only six candidates (4%) were elected "out of list order" (Vandeleene et al., 2016). We thus need to understand how Belgian parties draft their electoral lists in order to understand parliamentary recruitment.

Empirical works on candidate selection have arisen *en masse* mostly since the seminal study of Hazan and Rahat (2010). In the Belgian case, Dewachter (1967) and Obler (1974) paved the way, followed by De Winter (1980, 1988) – but few scholars have scrutinised candidate selection in this country before the last decade (Put and Maddens, 2011; van Haute and Pilet, 2007; Vandeleene, 2014, 2016). This chapter relies on the two most studied dimensions developed by Hazan and Rahat (2010): the degrees of centralisation and of inclusiveness of the selectorates. We also refer to the degree of complexity of the procedures: the procedure is "assorted" (as labelled by Hazan and Rahat) when different selectorates select the candidates, or when different rules apply for certain types of candidates (most often the heads of list and/or the candidates on the so-called realistic positions, i.e. "all those positions that are seen at least as winnable before the elections" (Hazan and Rahat, 2010, 14).

The frequency of assorted methods among Belgian parties stems from the features of its electoral system. The Belgian system is proportional, which is said to encourage the centralisation of procedures (Gallagher and Marsh, 1988; Matland and Studlar, 1996). This holds true for most Belgian parties. The party's size – the number of candidates per party per constituency – is also critical in the determination of the procedures (Hazan and Voerman, 2006). The low party size in most Belgian constituencies, together with the high fragmentation of the party system – there are about six parties likely to win a seat in each constituency – imply that candidate selection really matters only for the first list positions. This is thought to stimulate parties to pay particular attention to a few number of safe seats and to allow decentralised selectorates licence to determine the candidates which fill the lists.

The increase in the effective number of parties coupled with the relative safe-ness of most seats despite changes to the geography of the constituencies and to the preference vote system[1] leads to a situation where we expect newcomer and traditional parties to behave differently regarding candidate selection. The tradi-tional parties used to organise a member poll at a time (until the end of the 1960s) where they were hardly challenged by newcomers in their electoral success. This culture of opening candidate selection to the whole membership is expected to fade as soon as the party's size declines because of the strategic need to control the choice of the MPs-to-be. On the other hand, newcomers are expected to act ration-ally and thus, with a similarly low party size, they may consider it not worthwhile to involve a large number of selectors.

Data

Candidate selection processes are investigated using a variety of data resources. First, we researched party statutes and official documents. Our analysis is based on several versions of party official rules in order to grasp the evolution of can-didate selection practices over time. We also consulted other party documents, for instance documents containing specific regulations on the selection processes.

However, as most party organisations are based on non-written practices that may differ from the formal stipulations, we unearthed these through interviews with party officials in the run-up to the 2014 elections. The interviewees com-prised the parties' national political secretaries, plus, in some parties, other party leaders. Political secretaries occupy a crucial position in the party organisation, being the party's administrative head, the right hand of the party president who is the actual political leader.

Finally, this chapter relies on data from large-N surveys conducted among can-didates for the 2007 (federal), 2010 (federal) and 2014 (regional and federal) elec-tions. This kind of information retrieved from the candidates reflects their views on their own selection process. The Belgian Candidate Survey (BCS) is a written post-electoral survey that takes place within the framework of the international network CCS (Comparative Candidate Survey).[2]

Our longitudinal analyses indicate that generally the selection methods in Belgian traditional parties have not changed much in recent years – unlike in newcomer parties. The following section reviews changes and consistencies in candidate selection in four non-traditional parties and in three traditional party families.

Selection in newcomer parties

Since no relevant new party arose out of the 2008 crisis, we focus on the most recent newcomers (Ecolo and Groen, the New Flemish Alliance, and the Workers' Party) that are not inheritors of the 19th century Belgian configuration of cleavages, like the traditional families (Lipset and Rokkan, 1967). We seek to uncover whether these new parties organise their candidate selection in a more inclusive way than the traditional parties.

The Greens: towards less direct democracy

The green parties in Belgium are peculiar in that they did not emerge from former state-wide party families but were created independently from each other. However, they now have the strongest ties in the Belgian party system (Wavreille and Pilet, 2016). Both parties were exponents of the post-materialist New Social Movements and transformed into real political parties in the late seventies. Over time they won several electoral victories but also suffered heavy defeats, from the acquisition of their first parliamentary seats in 1981 and first participation in government in 1999 to their major loss in 2003 (Hooghe and Rihoux, 2000). They both participated again in a government in 2009 but at the 2014 elections Ecolo lost badly, while Groen managed to maintain its support. The Greens' hectic electoral and governmental journey pushed them to review their internal organisation in order to moderate the party's ups and downs, and this also affected their candidate selection processes.

Ecolo used to respect its founding principles of direct democracy: all candidates were selected through a one-by-one decision-making process within a members' assembly. This process was very transparent in that all aspirants were publicly known. However, it led to some intense intra-party struggles that were considered harmful for party cohesion. From the 2007 general elections onwards, the party decided to adopt a multistage procedure whereby a draft list would be presented to a members' assembly. As underlined by an interviewee, the system was changed from direct to indirect democracy due to highly aggressive debates during the "polls": "Some polls have left traces for long".

In the new system, the list committee acts as a third actor which effectively manages a form of preselection by preparing a list proposal for the realistic positions. For the other candidates, a campaign board (party leaders at the decentralised level) was in charge with the proposal. These bodies have a "facilitator-preparer" role, while the general assembly holds the "final decision-maker" role by only deciding on the final list as a whole. In the (unlikely) case of non-ratification by the assembly after several rounds, a poll is organised, i.e. a member vote for each individual list position, as the party used to do before 2007. But this has never taken place in recent years. The federation council (an assembly of delegates at the national level) also holds an evocation right and could thus invalidate all lists but in practice never does.

The changes in the rules imply that the selectorates who really decide are now quite exclusive. Nevertheless, this exclusiveness is counterbalanced by the inclusiveness of the selectorates approving the list. The decision to considerably reduce the size of the selectorates was intended to smooth the process and thus counter the divisive consequence of inclusive procedures (Wichowsky and Niebler, 2010). A second justification is more strategic. The involvement of a small selectorate allows the party leadership to better control the outcome of the process. An interviewee highlighted that the leadership's main concern was "to do politics in the next 4 or 5 years to come", so their interest lies in forming a coherent parliamentary group for the legislative term that will start right after the elections. The new system is indeed safer for leaders since they are able to influence the choice of the eligible candidates and, in so doing, to determine the composition of the future parliamentary group: "We have an interest in having deputies and senators who hold water, who are strong and able to carry all themes". Empowering the list committee rather than giving a free hand to a general assembly provides stronger guarantees to implement the party leadership's strategy.

The Flemish counterpart, Groen, has used since 2007 an assorted process where candidates for the realistic positions are selected following a different process to that used for other candidates. The MPs-to-be are selected by a rather exclusive committee gathering national party leaders and decentralised representatives. The constituency members' congress then approves their choice. The remaining candidates are selected by a decentralised committee with the approval of the exclusive national party board. The Flemish Greens have therefore abandoned the principle of direct democracy, but the members can still exert an impact on the most important names. If they were to refuse the proposal, a position-by-position member vote would be organised. Over time, the degree of centralisation has increased. The party national headquarters has participated (again) in the selection since 2007, immediately after Groen's major electoral beating.

Groen does not give the rank-and-file a voice in the process regarding the *non-realistic* positions – which shows in the BCS figures (see Table 4.2). Only a third of Groen's candidates declared that they were selected by party members, against two-thirds for Ecolo. Groen would tend to consider that there are first and second zone candidates, the latter not being worth an inclusive selectorate. The rationale to justify the exclusiveness and centralisation of the realistic positions' selectorates is similar to Ecolo. As an interviewee acknowledged, the requirements are less important for candidates for non-realistic positions.

> "Those people who have a chance to enter the Parliament have to pass through a stronger screening. They really have a talk [with the selectors], almost a job interview. [. . .] The other people on the list also have a talk with the committee but that's not so tough."

The Belgian Greens – previously known as organisations with amateur-activist traits – have evolved towards stabilised structures with professional-activist traits,

Table 4.1 Degree of centralisation of the selection procedures, by party, by year (in %)

	Decentralised		2014			Centralised		2014		
	2007	2010	Initiative	Concret.	Decision	2007	2010	Initiative	Concret.	Decision
Ecolo	75.0	75.0	89.2	92.2	97.3	22.2	16.7	10.8	7.8	2.7
Groen	66.6	76.6	80.2	75.0	85.4	28.9	23.3	19.8	25.0	14.6
N-VA	42.9	82.0	78.0	77.5	51.4	50.0	18.0	22.0	22.5	48.6
PTB/PvdA	/	/	84.2	81.1	79.7	/	/	15.8	18.9	20.3
PS	72.5	83.7	82.7	81.3	77.5	25.0	16.3	17.3	18.8	22.5
sp.a	65.0	80.9	75.3	81.4	76.0	35.0	14.9	24.7	18.6	24.0
cdH	40.5	42.3	81.5	82.1	71.2	56.8	53.8	18.5	17.9	28.8
CD&V	64.6	81.3	85.6	84.2	85.3	33.3	15.6	14.4	15.8	14.7
MR	54.6	59.6	80.0	75.6	66.7	45.5	36.2	20.0	24.4	33.3
Open VLD	59.3	70.5	82.9	86.2	79.8	35.2	29.5	17.1	13.8	79.8

Source: BCS, 2007, 2010, 2014

Table 4.2 Degree of inclusiveness of the selection procedures, by party, by year (in %)

	Party members					A party delegate conference					Party leadership				
	2007	2010	2014			2007	2010	2014			2007	2010	2014		
			Initiative	Concret.	Decision			Initiative	Concret.	Decision			Initiative	Concret.	Decision
Ecolo	69.4	61.1	24.3	13.5	63.3	8.3	13.9	7.3	7.6	2.0	13.9	16.7	68.4	78.9	34.7
Groen	31.1	37.9	7.0	5.7	33.2	6.7	3.4	6.4	5.7	4.3	44.4	48.3	86.6	88.6	62.6
N-VA	21.4	41.0	7.0	0.0	1.7	14.3	6.0	10.5	7.1	9.5	35.7	44.0	82.5	92.9	88.8
PTB/PvdA	/	/	25.0	10.5	11.2	/	/	13.6	23.5	9.0	/	/	61.4	66.1	79.8
PS	20.0	19.1	14.4	9.2	18.4	22.5	25.5	7.2	2.3	4.9	55.0	55.3	78.4	88.5	76.7
sp.a	2.4	9.1	10.7	4.3	16.0	2.4	4.5	10.7	5.1	10.7	92.7	84.1	78.6	90.6	73.3
cdH	27.8	32.1	19.5	7.0	8.4	0.0	3.6	8.1	5.3	0.0	69.4	60.7	72.4	87.7	91.6
CD&V	18.8	22.2	8.6	1.5	11.0	0.0	0.0	5.7	7.6	2.1	68.8	74.6	85.7	90.9	86.9
MR	11.4	16.0	11.6	5.5	9.9	0.0	6.0	4.2	1.1	1.8	81.8	74.0	84.2	93.4	88.3
Open VLD	15.1	18.6	6.7	4.0	18.2	1.9	7.0	2.9	7.0	7.3	66.0	69.8	90.4	89.0	74.5

Source: BCS 2007, 2010, 2014

with the aim of facilitating their internal functioning and/or their strategy (Rihoux and Frankland, 2008). This change is exemplified in the involvement of list committees to draft the lists *before* the grass roots members could have a say. They apply some form of 'plebiscitary intra-party democracy' where members approve a pre-cooked decision, and have abandoned the 'assembly-based intra-party democracy' model (Poguntke et al., 2016). This trend goes in the opposite direction to what is usually known as the process of intra-party democratisation (Sandri et al., 2015). Ecolo and Groen emerged in the 1980s with extremely participatory forms of candidate selection and were, during their first decades of existence, quite resistant to the professionalisation of their political staff and to personalisation. The downs in their electoral history were often attributed to the lack of popularity of their leaders and to their unusual type of organisation. As a consequence, they strongly increased the powers of leading individuals within the organisation (Wavreille and Pilet, 2016). This led them to rationalise their candidate selection process, and so to reduce the scope of those directly intervening in the decision. However, the evolution of the Greens' candidate selection procedures and practices do not seem to be related to the 2008 political and financial crisis.

The N-VA: centralisation as the after effect of electoral success

The New Flemish Alliance seems a genuine combination of both newness and continuity. The N-VA "rose from the ashes of a dissolved party" (Beyens et al., 2017, 389). It was created in 2001 after the dissolution of the old Volsksunie (VU), which, like most autonomist parties (De Winter, 1998), faced irreconcilable factional divisions (Noppe and Wauters, 2002). The N-VA represented the conservative side of the old party as well as its Flemish-independent faction (De Winter, 2006). The party won only a single candidate in the 2003 federal elections. In 2004, it decided to go for an electoral cartel with the Flemish Christian-democratic party CD&V, which lasted for only two elections but helped the party to grow and made its mediagenic leader better known. The N-VA has become increasingly successful since then, becoming the largest party in Flanders in 2010. It seized almost a quarter of the Chamber of Representatives' seats in 2014 and even entered the Belgian government – despite its ultimate aim, Flemish independence.

What is striking is the strategic mix of ideological and organisational heritage from the former VU and new ingredients. At the local level, the party relied on the VU's local branches and its alliance with the CD&V, but soon managed to develop its own cadre network and attracted many more rank-and-file members than the VU had in its final years (Beyens et al., 2017). In the effort to recruit for the 2012 local elections, and given the predicted success in the polls in 2014, finding motivated, careerist candidates was not an issue at all. An interviewee conceded, "we are in the luxury situation of a party that has grown strongly and which is going to grow again according to the polls, thus we have this luxury, that we would have a large number of MPs." Although the N-VA could be labelled as a successor party (Arter, 2012), we consider it to be a new party given its strong reconstruction of both ideological stances and its organisation, which is the prime focus of this chapter.

Parallel to the large increase in the number of MPs under the N-VA banner, the party also changed its selection procedures. The general principle remained the same, but a closer look reveals some critical modifications regarding the actors in charge of the selection. According to its 2002 statutes, the party selected its candidates in a rather decentralised way, while in the most recent elections in 2014 the main decisions were made at the central level. The selectorates' inclusiveness remained quite constant.

The selection process was in 2002 organised in three main stages. Two different decentralised and exclusive selectorates prepared a draft list (the local electoral college first and the local council second). The third stage consisted of the ratification of the list by the national party council, an assembly of delegates at a decentralised level. If the list was not approved, the (exclusive) party board would make another proposal to be confirmed by the (less exclusive) party council. This process could be characterised as "decentralised with a central control", and rather exclusive at the proposal stage and slightly inclusive at the approval stage.

In the run-up to the 2009 elections, the N-VA used for the first time an assorted procedure with greater intervention of centralised selectorates for the candidates in realistic positions. The party central leadership took charge of the strategic decisions of balancing the profiles within the future parliamentary group and thus decided which positions would be safeguarded. Yet the decision on the candidates' names for these positions was still made by a group of local leaders, but the national selectors could add and modify some names. The selection decision was formally decentralised but, in practice, the central leadership could enlist the desired candidates in the most eligible spots. The national party council then ratified the short list of realistic candidates. The local level selected the other candidates with again confirmation by the party council and a possibility for the party board to alter the list if the council rejected it.

In 2014, the centralisation of the selection procedures was even stronger for these protected candidates. The local level had only a right to check a decision made at the national level but could still decide on the non-realistic positions, as in 2009. The current procedure is thus even more assorted and centralised. As shown in Table 4.1, the BCS figures attest to the greater centralisation at the final decision stage than for the initiative. In 2014, the results testify to an assorted process where candidates for realistic positions point much more than other candidates the national level for their selection (68.4% vs. 41.5%).

Hence, the N-VA selection process underwent a substantial increase of the selectorates' centralisation regarding the most prominent list positions, but not in terms of inclusiveness, which remained constant: national leaders together with some local leaders. Meanwhile the party also experienced an important modification to its process in that the procedure has become assorted when the party was expecting to gain a substantial number of new seats in the Parliament. Centralised selectorates have now almost free hands to decide on the future MPs. Again, we observe that the new party was closer to the ideal of intra-party democracy but that its growth has led it to alter the procedures towards a greater level of control on the outcome for the party leadership.

The workers' party: the top guns and the dogma of democratic centralism

At the most recent elections (2014), for the first time a far-left party entered Parliament. Its electoral popularity has been skyrocketing ever since and now it leads the polls. Although this party may be considered as new in terms of its parliamentary entry, it originates from the old Maoist party Amada (which translates as "all the power to the workers") created in 1970. The Workers' Party of Belgium (PTB in French and PvdA in Dutch –it is the only parliamentary party not organised separately in distinct Flemish and French-speaking organisations) was created in 1979 (Delwit, 2014). The party scored less than 1% until 2010 when its share of the vote rose slightly. This success was attributed to a process of party renewal which encompassed restructuring of the party organisation and a rephrased – less radical – ideology. Besides, it also exploited the popularity of a few of its leaders in the media and managed to attract more members by weakening the membership requirements (Wynants, 2014).

This strategy proved to be successful since the Workers' Party won several dozen councillors at the 2012 local elections. The party formed an alliance with some minor communist parties and succeeded in 2014 in getting two MPs elected at the federal level, and seven MPs elected at the regional level. This entry into the legislative arenas boosted its media coverage and gave the PTB/PvdA an increased legitimacy in the eyes of citizens. Yet the party is said to apply the "Janus tactic": it sends a different message outside than in the intra-party arena. The Marxist-Leninist discourse employed within the party is softened in its communication with voters and by the personalisation strategy for its leaders – with the final aim of the normalisation of the party in the political and media arena (Delwit, 2014; Wynants, 2014).

Despite its relatively new character, its methods of candidate selection do not live up to the standards of inclusive intra-party democracy. The party declares that it follows the principle of "democratic centralism", which implies that decisions taken at an upper level in the party are binding for lower level bodies. The party aims at a collective decision-making process but still leaves the final say to the highest party bodies: the party board, together with the National Daily Management, which comprises the party president, vice-president and secretary general.

Although major decisions are made nationally, the administration of the candidate selection process was decentralised at the provincial level. This party layer consists of three main bodies: the congress gathers delegates from the local level and elects a council which in turn elects a Daily Management. The provincial "Daily Managements", the key selectorates for the 2014 elections, are highly exclusive but take their legitimacy from the step-by-step delegation process according to which the most involved rank-and-file members hold the right to send delegates to the decision-making bodies for candidate selection.

The answers of the PTB/PvdA's candidates to the BCS 2014 confirm that their selectorates were exclusive and rather decentralised (see Tables 4.1 and 4.2): 84.2% of respondents declared that the initiative of their selection happened at the decentralised level. The exclusiveness of the selectorates is reported by 61.4% of the candidates at the initiative stage and by 79.8% for the final decision. Candidate selection in the Workers' Party happens in an exclusive fashion while providing some party members with the right to select the delegates who will in turn determine who will join the decisive party bodies. These "top guns" have all cards in their hands to draw the electoral lists at the decentralised level, while being constantly under the authority of the centralised party bodies. With the national leadership's control of decisions quite strong, we cannot conclude that this newcomer party is implementing the principles of inclusive intra-party democracy.

Recent decades have witnessed the rise of new parties in Belgium. This section has demonstrated that the four new parties in the Belgian political landscape did not, as had been expected, open their selection procedures to a large number of party members. The opposite pattern emerges. The new political actors in the Belgian political arena do not confirm the hypothesis raised in this book, what makes Belgium a rather negative case of change in candidate selection over time. The reasons for the lack of trend towards inclusiveness reflect the will of the party leadership to control the selection. These new parties succeeded in boosting, dramatically or timidly, their electoral success over time. Together with an enlargement of their future parliamentary factions, these parties also faced the need to remain in command of their expanding membership – and this happened at the expense of intra-party democracy.

Selection in traditional parties

This section sketches the evolution of candidate selection procedures in the three traditional party families (the Socialists, the Christian-Democrats and the Liberals) and assesses whether changes were directed towards more inclusiveness. The international trend of party democratisation – between one quarter and one-third of political parties in Western democracies would use primaries for candidate selection (Cross et al., 2016; see also Sandri et al., 2015) does not seem to have reached the Belgian mainstream parties during the last decades, nor as a consequence of the crisis, as they rather reduced the size of their selectorates. Given the mimetism hypothesis (DiMaggio and Powell, 1991), one could indeed not expect traditional parties to open up their selection because even the new parties in the political arena (although most of them are left-wing) did not do so.

The socialist parties traditionally used to organise the so-called "polls" to select their candidates (De Winter, 1980) but this practice declined over the years before its disappearance in the 1980s on the Flemish side and in the 1990s on the francophone one (Put, 2015). Both parties use now delegate congresses to ratify model lists drafted by exclusive committees whose composition varies over time.

Decline in inclusiveness has coincided with centralisation. Until 1992, the Flemish socialist party (now called sp.a) prepared the lists only at the decentralised level but the national level slightly increased its involvement in candidate selection until the current situation where the national party board has to approve all lists before the members' delegates vote (Vandeleene, 2016). A similar pattern is to be found on the other side of the linguistic border at the PS where the national level has been represented since 1999 in the decentralised committees in charge of candidate selection (Put, 2015) and where the party president and his/her entourage hold an informal consultation on all the candidacies (Vandeleene, 2016).

A few changes have appeared over time regarding candidate selection in the Christian-Democratic parties, but again not during the last decade. The Flemish CD&V replaced in the late 1980s its traditional "poll" selection process with a delegates' vote (De Winter, 1988), which took place after the decision was prepared by a committee at the decentralised level and the national party board. Ten years later they reintroduced the members' poll, which would intervene after a decision made by a bureau at the constituency level and the national delegates' assembly. At the 2014 elections, the party applied an assorted process where the non-eligible positions were determined by exclusive selectorates at the decentralised level while the most electable spots were decided by a multiplicity of actors: exclusive committees at the decentralised and centralised levels, an assembly of delegates and a ratification by the party members (Vandeleene, 2016). The degree of centralisation remained quite stable over time while inclusiveness fluctuated, endowing members with a role in the selection or not. The francophone counterpart also reformed its selection procedures some decades ago but these have remained almost unchanged in recent years. While in the late eighties the – now – cdH selected its candidates with exclusive selectorates at both the decentralised and the centralised level, they re-established polls in 1991, as a third step in the process. The procedure looks almost identical nowadays, with a committee at the decentralised level making a proposal to the party board, whose decision is later to be approved by a members' poll. Yet if less than a third of the members participate, the votes are not counted. According to an interviewee, "up to now, we never counted votes from a poll". One may thus conclude that the degrees of centralisation and of inclusiveness remained even over time, but the openness of the process seems IPD window dressing (Vandeleene, 2016; Verleden, 2013).

Finally, contrary to the other traditional party families, the Flemish Open VLD and the francophone MR apply highly dissimilar selection procedures. Both parties used to have fully decentralised processes in the 1980s (De Winter, 2000; Deschouwer, 1993) and changed their rules in the early 1990s. The Flemish liberal party introduced in 1993 a primaries system where party members as well as "registered voters" could approve a list drafted by a decentralised exclusive selectorate (Put, 2015). From 1995 onwards, they kept their decision-making open to members but not to voters anymore, abandoning the open primaries scheme. In 2007, and until now, the Open VLD has organised an assorted process where the head of list is selected prior to the other candidates and can participate in the selection of his/her list counterparts in a committee (Vandeleene, 2016). Never in its recent history did the Open VLD give a formal role to the national party bodies in candidate selection. The MR offers the opposite picture, as the national party headquarters strongly controls the drafting of the lists. This party centralised its selection procedures when it formed an electoral alliance with the FDF in 1993, a regionalist francophone party. The decentralised level could still propose names but this had to be approved by the national committee. In 2003 the party even formed an electoral alliance with three other parties, which resulted in a highly exclusive and centralised process. The party presidents determined the main candidates who were later charged with the selection of their fellow candidates on their constituency list – still to be approved by the four presidents (Put, 2015). The MR ran alone at the last elections of 2014 and maintained a centralised process for the nomination of the heads of list, and the final approval.

Discussion and conclusion

Our argument is that Belgium is a negative case of the impact of the political crisis on candidate selection practices. We demonstrated that no major reform of candidate selection has occurred in this country over the crisis period. We compared two types of parties: the newer parties and the traditional party families. What emerges from our analysis is that changes were more likely to occur among newer parties than among older parties.

As summarised in Table 4.3, it is striking to observe that most new parties applied some changes to their selection procedures over the last decade while no traditional party did so during the same period. Two main conclusions flow from this observation. First, the new parties are more likely to adapt their candidate

Table 4.3 Summary of the evolution of candidate selection procedures over time for the Belgian political parties

	Inclusiveness		Centralisation	
	Since the 1980s	Over the last decade	Since the 1980s	Over the last decade
New parties				
Ecolo	↓	↓	↑	↑
Groen	↓	↓	↑	↑
N-VA	=	=	↑	↑
PTB/PvdA	=	=	=	=
Traditional parties				
sp.a	↓	=	↑	=
PS	↓	=	↑	=
CD&V	↑↓	=	=	=
cdH	=	=	=	=
Open VLD	↑↓	=	=	=
MR	=	=	↑	=

Source: Authors' own elaboration

selection processes than the more established parties. This is obviously due to their growth towards stable professional structures, which implies a rationalisation of the selection process and entailed, in all parties, a (strengthening of the) centralisation, and in the green parties, a shrinkage of the powers endowed to rank-and-file members. Second, some older parties altered candidate selection over time, e.g. the introduction of primaries by the Flemish liberal party or the reduction in size of the socialist selectorates, from members to delegates. Yet these changes took place before the crisis. Over the last decade one cannot notice any significant modification to the selection rules, and certainly not a change that might have been triggered by the crisis context. The study of the newcomers showed that they do not use inclusive selection modes – or that they tend to reduce their selectorates' scope. This probably prevented the traditional parties from enlarging their selection bodies through a copy mechanism.

Several factors can explain the absence of genuine new parties (and hence of innovative forms of selection) triggered by the 2008 financial crisis and subsequent austerity policies. First, one can wonder to what extent "the crisis" was felt as strongly by the Belgian population and parties as by other countries. The banking crisis was largely absorbed through the State nationalising certain banks and covering the debts of others. These operations increased public debt by about 20% percent of GNP, from 86% in 2007 to 107% in 2014, according to Eurostat[3], but the savings and real estate assets of relatively few households were strongly affected in the short term. Second, contrary to the austerity politics of the 2014 federal government, which triggered new social movements (e.g. *Hart boven Hard* and *Tout Autre Chose* – founded in 2014 but not transformed into political parties – yet?), the anti-crisis protests in 2008–2010 were mainly channelled by the main trade unions (see i.a. Rihoux et al., 2009) which had strong connections with the social-democrats and Christian-democrats in the government. Third, the balkanization of the party system, which reached its peak in late 1999 (effective number of parties=9.1) and the exceptionally high electoral sustainability of new political parties (Bolleyer, 2013, 38), meant that almost all "niches" were covered before 2008. Hence, there was simply no space left for new niche parties (Meguid, 2008).

Finally, why did Belgian parties change their selection process at some moments in their history if not because of crisis? Our empirical analysis indicates that there were external and internal causes and that these changes aimed at external and internal objectives. The internal drive for change among new parties was the need for professionalisation, but the reforms were also caused by external factors. We argue that both electoral success and defeats can lead to candidate selection changes. The Greens centralised slightly their processes and dampened inclusiveness as a consequence of an electoral downturn. Conversely, the N-VA expected its number of MPs to grow steadily and consequently adapted the process to control better who enters the parliament. Other contextual explanations could play a role in a process change, such as the occurrence of an early election (Vandeleene et al., 2017) or a redistricting (Put, 2015), but these fall outside this chapter's scope. The parties' objectives when adapting their procedures encompass the search for more voters, by embellishing the party's internal-democratic image towards the electorate, but also internal objectives, e.g. fostering intra-party cohesion and preventing long-lasting intra-party tensions. In any case, we did not find any proof that the financial crisis affected the Belgian party system nor prompted parties to adapt their selection methods. Yet, the substantial rise of the far left PTB/PvdA may have consequences in that respect, and will need to be studied in coming years.

Notes

1 The number of list votes distributed to candidates until they reach the eligibility threshold has been divided by two in 2000, what gave individual candidates more chances to be able to bypass candidates ranked at an upper list position (André et al., 2012).
2 The three surveys were funded by the F.R.S.-FNRS (CDR 1.5314.08F and CDR J.0141.14F) and coordinated by Lieven De Winter, Audrey Vandeleene and Pierre Baudewyns (CESPOL, UCLouvain).
3 see https://tradingeconomics.com/belgium/government-debt-to-gdp

References

André, A., Depauw, S., Shugart, M. S., and Chytilek, R. (2017). Party nomination strategies in flexible-list systems : Do preference votes matter ? *Party Politics*, 23 (5), pp. 589–600. doi:10.1177/1354068815610974

André, A., Wauters, B., and Pilet, J.-B. (2012). It's not only about lists : Explaining preference voting in Belgium. *Journal of Elections, Public Opinion and Parties* 22 (3), pp. 293–313. doi:10.1080/17457289.2012.692374

Arter, D. (2012). Analysing "Successor Parties": The case of the True Finns. *West European Politics* 35 (4), pp. 803–825. doi:10.1080/01402382.2012.682346

Beyens, S., Deschouwer, K., van Haute, E., and Verthé, T. (2017). Born again, or born anew: Assessing the newness of the Belgian political party New-Flemish Alliance (N-VA). *Party Politics* 23 (4), pp. 389–399. doi:10.1177/1354068815601347

Bolleyer, N. (2013). *New parties in old party systems: Persistence and decline in seventeen democracies*. Oxford: Oxford University Press. doi:10.1111/1478-9302.12087_52

Cross, W. P. (2008). Democratic norms and party candidate selection: Taking contextual factors into account. *Party Politics* 14 (5), pp. 596–619. doi:10.1177/1354068808093392

Cross, W. P., et al. (2016). *Promise and challenge of party primary elections: A comparative perspective*. Montreal and Kingston: McGill-Queen's University Press.

De Winter, L. (1980). Twintig jaar polls, of de teloorgang van een vorm van interne partijdemocratie. *Res Publica* 32, pp. 563–585.

De Winter, L. (1988). Belgium: democracy or oligarchy. In Gallagher, M. and Marsh, M. (Eds.), *Candidate selection in comparative perspective*. London: Sage.

De Winter, L. (1998). Conclusion: A comparative analysis of the electoral office and policy success of ethnoregionalist parties. In De Winter, L. and Türsan, H. (Eds.), *Regionalist parties in Western Europe*. London: Routledge, pp. 204–247.

De Winter, L. (2000). Liberal parties in Belgium: From freemasons to free citizens. In De Winter, L. (Ed.), *Liberalism and liberal parties in the European union*. Barcelona: Institut de Ciènces Politiques i Socials, pp. 141–182.

De Winter, L. (2006). In memoriam the Volksunie 1954–2001: Death by overdose of success. In De Winter, L., Gómez-Reino, M. and Lynch, P. (Eds.), *Autonomist parties in Europe:*

Identity politics and the revival of the territorial cleavage. Barcelona: Institut Universitari d'Estudis Europeus, pp. 11–46.

Delwit, P. (2014). *PTB. Nouvelle gauche, vieille recette.* Waterloo: Editions Luc Pire.

Deschouwer, K. (1993). *Organiseren of bewegen? De evolutie van de Belgische partij-structuren sinds 1960.* Brussels: VUB Press.

Dewachter, W. (1967). *De wetgevende verkiezingen als proces van machtsverwerving in het Belgische politieke bestel.* Antwerp: Standaard Wetenschappelijke Uitgeverij.

DiMaggio, P. J., and Powell, W. W. (1991). The Iron Cage Revisited: Institutional Isomorphism and Collective Rationality. In Powell, W. W. and DiMaggio, P. J. (Eds.), *The new institutionalism in organizational analysis.* Chicago: Chicago University Press, pp. 63–82.

Gallagher, M., and Marsh, M. (1988). *Candidate selection in comparative perspective: The secret garden of politics.* London: Sage.

Hazan, R. Y., and Rahat, G. (2010). *Democracy within parties: Candidate selection methods and their political consequences.* Oxford: Oxford University Press.

Hazan, R. Y., and Voerman, G. (2006). Electoral systems and candidate selection. *Acta Politica* 41, pp. 146–162. doi:10.1057/palgrave.ap.5500153

Hooghe, M., and Rihoux, B. (2000). The green breakthrough in the Belgian general election of June 1999. *Environmental Politics* 9 (3), pp. 129–136. doi:10.1080/09644010008414541

Lipset, S. M., and Rokkan, S. (1967). *Party systems and voter alignments: Cross-national perspectives.* New York: Free Press.

Matland, R. E., and Studlar, D. T. (1996). The contagion of women candidates in single-member district and proportional representation electoral systems: Canada and Norway. *The Journal of Politics* 58 (3), pp. 707–733.

Meguid, B. (2008). *Party competition between unequals. Strategies and electoral fortunes in Western Europe.* Cambridge: Cambridge University Press.

Noppe, J., and Wauters, B. (2002). Het uiteenvallen van de Volksunie en het ontstaan van de N-VA en Spirit. Een chronologisch en morfologisch overzicht. *Res Publica* 44, pp. 397–471.

Obler, J. (1974). Intraparty democracy and the selection of parliamentary candidates: The Belgian case. *British Journal of Political Science* 4 (2), pp. 163–185. doi:10.1017/S0007123400009455

Poguntke, T., Scarrow, S. E., Webb, P. D. et al. (2016). Party rules, party resources and the politics of parliamentary democracies: How parties organize in the 21st century. *Party Politics,* 22 (6), pp. 661-678. doi:10.1177/1354068816662493

Put, G.-J. (2015). *All politics is local: The geographical dimension of candidate selection. The case of Belgium (1987–2010).* KULeuven.

Put, G.-J., and Maddens, B. (2011). *De Lijstvormingsprocedures van Vlaamse Politieke Partijen: Onderzoeksnota.* Leuven.

Rihoux, B., Dumont, P., De Winter, L., Deruette, S., and Bol, D. (2009). Belgium. *European Journal of Political Research* 48 (7–8), pp. 903–912. doi:10.1111/j.1475-6765.2009.01852.x

Rihoux, B., and Frankland, E. G. (2008). Conclusion: The metamorphosis of amateur-activist newborns into professional-activist centaurs. In Frankland, E. G., Lucardie, P., and Rihoux, B. (Eds.), *Green parties in transition: The end of grassroots democracy?.* Farnham: Ashgate Publishing, pp. 259–288.

Sandri, G., Seddone, A., and Venturino, F. (2015). *Party primaries in comparative perspective.* Farnham: Ashgate Publishing. doi:10.1017/CBO9781107415324.004

van Haute, E., and Pilet, J.-B. (2007). *Opening and democratizing pillar parties? Internal reforms in Belgian political parties* (Cahiers du CEVIPOL). Brussels.

Vandeleene, A. (2014). Gender quotas and "Women-Friendly" candidate selection: Evidence from Belgium. *Representation* 50 (3), pp. 337–349. doi:10.1080/00344893.2014.951222

Vandeleene, A. (2016). *Does candidate selection matter? A comparative analysis of Belgian political parties' selection procedures and their relation to the candidates' profile.* PhD dissertation. Université catholique de Louvain.

Vandeleene, A., Dodeigne, J., and De Winter, L. (2016). What do selectorates seek? A comparative analysis of Belgian federal and regional candidate selection processes in 2014. *American Behavioral Scientist* 60 (7), pp. 889–908.

Vandeleene, A., Meulewaeter, C., De Winter L., and Baudewyns P. (2017). La relation entre le mode de sélection des candidats et la congruence idéologique entre masses et élites: analyse du cas belge. *Politique et Sociétés* 36 (2), pp. 91–118.

Verleden, F. (2013). De toegang tot de parlementaire elite. Politieke rekrutering en lijstvorming in België in historisch perspectief. Paper presented at *Politicologenetmaal.* Ghent.

Wavreille, M.-C., and Pilet, J.-B. (2016). The Greens in Belgium's federal landscape: Divergent fates. In van Haute, E. (Ed.), *Green parties in Europe.* London: Routledge, pp. 42–58.

Wichowsky, A., and Niebler, S. E. (2010). Narrow victories and hard games: Revisiting the primary divisiveness hypothesis. *American Politics Research* 38 (6), pp. 1052–1071. doi:10.1177/1532673X10369660

Wynants, P. (2014). À la gauche de la gauche: le PTB. *La Revue Nouvelle, Avril-Mai,* pp. 6–8.

5 Leader as a focal point

New political entrepreneurs
and candidate selection in the
Czech republic

Vít Hloušek and Lubomír Kopeček

Introduction[1]

As a consequence of several electoral shocks, the once relatively stable Czech party system (Deegan Krause and Haughton, 2010) has been transformed. In 2010, elections to the Chamber of Deputies, the lower chamber of the Czech parliament, secured parliamentary representation for two new parties: TOP 09 and Public Affairs (VV) (Hanley, 2012). In 2013, there was an even larger electoral shock, when another new party, ANO (meaning 'yes' in Czech), became the second strongest force in parliament. Yet another new party, the populist Dawn of Direct Democracy (or 'Dawn'), likewise crossed the five-percent electoral threshold of the Proportional Representation system, thus winning seats. Other noteworthy changes included the substantial weakening of what were previously the two strongest parties, the Czech Social Democratic Party (ČSSD) and the conservative-liberal Civic Democratic Party (ODS) (see Table 5.1). Viewed retrospectively, a situation had arisen in which voters not only abandoned established parties, but were quite willing to shift their support from new parties to even newer ones. For instance, in the 2013 elections, the bulk of former VV supporters voted for ANO (Median, 2013; Haughton and Deegan Krause, 2015, 70–71).

This chapter focuses on candidate selection in the new, aforementioned political parties. Not all of them were new in terms of their organisational structure. One must distinguish ANO, VV and Dawn from TOP 09, which emerged in 2009 by splitting off from the Christian Democrats (KDU-ČSL), a party with traditions going back almost a century. Ideologically, TOP 09 was a conservative-liberal party. In its organisational structure TOP 09 resembles traditional Czech parties, though unlike them it is unusual in some respects; consider, for instance, the dominance of the parliamentary group over the party as a whole (Kopeček and Svačinová, 2015). For these reasons we leave this party out of our discussion.

The three parties on which our analysis is centred – VV, ANO and Dawn – are entrepreneurial parties (Krouwel, 2006; Krouwel, 2012), in which the political entrepreneur has a key position and uses the party as their own vehicle to enter the political sphere (the description of a set of common party characteristics can be found below). The aim of our chapter is to analyse new patterns of candidate selection introduced by entrepreneurial parties into Czech politics, as well as any

Table 5.1 Votes cast for parliamentary parties in the 2006, 2010 and 2013 elections (% of total/mandates)[2]

Party	2006	2010	2013
ČSSD (social democrats)	32.3 / 74	22.1 / 56	20.5 / 50
ANO (populist, entrepreneurial)	–	–	18.7 / 47
KSČM (communist)	12.8 / 26	11.3 / 26	14.9 / 33
KDU-ČSL (Christian-democratic)	7.2 /13	4.4 / 0	6.8 / 14
ODS (conservative-liberal)	35.4 / 81	20.2 / 53	7.7 / 16
TOP 09 (conservative-liberal)	–	16.7 / 41	12.0 / 26
VV (populist, entrepreneurial, liberal)	–	10.9 / 24	–
Dawn (populist, entrepreneurial)	–	–	6.9 / 14
Other	12.3 / 6	14.4 / 0	12.5 / 0
Total	100.0 / 200	100.0 / 200	100.0 / 200

Source: the Czech Statistical Office.

responses to this behaviour by established parties. The timeframe of our study is 2009–16, during which period there were two elections to the lower chamber of the Czech parliament, which is the country's key electoral arena. Analysing whether parties opt for more or less democratic procedures when selecting candidates for second-order elections is beyond the remit of this chapter.

Context, conceptualisations, hypotheses, and data

Firstly, we must briefly summarise existing trends. The long-established parties, the ČSSD, KDU-ČSL, ODS and the Communist party (KSČM), created their basic mechanisms for cadre selection back in the 1990s. Although they differed from each other in some respects, overall they tended to use exclusive models of candidate selection. For instance, although formally the candidate lists were open to non-partisans, such people rarely appeared on candidate lists in the top places where election is virtually guaranteed.

Key influences in candidate selection are the substantial power of parties' grass-roots organisations – or more precisely of the elites of those organisations – and a circumscribed role for the inner, central party leadership. This is due to the design of the electoral system for the Chamber of Deputies. Since the turn of the millennium, the Czech Republic has been divided into 14 constituencies of varying sizes, the boundaries of which correspond to those of the country's self-governing regions, in which regional party organisations operate. Regional and local elites play an important role in the structure of traditional parties. A consequence of this is that there are 14 separate nomination processes occurring in parallel, primarily at the levels of district and regional organisations (Spáč, 2013, 266–267; Outlý and Prouza, 2013, 101–102). The central leaderships of traditional parties are limited in their ability to influence these processes, even though party statutes do give them certain options in this respect. For example, the central leaderships of ODS,

ČSSD, KSČM, and KDU-ČSL have the right to intervene in the composition of candidate lists after their creation, but in practice they only do this rarely.

In awarding 'safe' places on candidate lists for elections to the Chamber of Deputies, parties show a tendency to give equal representation to the districts making up the region in question. A further characteristic is that candidates are selected by elected bodies (assemblies of delegates) at the regional level, and executive regional bodies, which usually are not formally authorised to select candidates, nevertheless play a substantial role in the process (Spáč, 2013; Outlý and Prouza, 2013). The rank and file have little influence on how candidate lists are compiled or who the candidates are.

The weak influence of the rank and file is correlated with the gradual transformation of traditional party organisation since the 1990s, with professional party elites playing an ever-stronger role. Conversely, the importance of the rank and file diminished over the same period (Kopecký, 2006; Polášek et al., 2012). Party membership today is very low, accounting for less than one per cent of the adult population (Linek and Pecháček, 2005; Van Haute et al., 2015). If this is considered alongside widespread party patronage (Kopecký, 2012), it becomes obvious that traditional parties have been little motivated to make their own practices more democratic.

Voter dissatisfaction with this state of affairs was one of the reasons why the Public Affairs party, which described traditional parties as political dinosaurs, succeeded in the 2010 elections, and why it decided to experiment with party democracy, albeit to a limited extent (Havlík and Hloušek, 2014). Two-thirds of Czechs were dissatisfied with the political situation according to surveys before the 2010 elections. This reflected not only economic problems, but also a series of political scandals and government instability. Surveys indicated the dissatisfaction of three-quarters of Czechs before the 2013 elections. At the same time, the distrust towards traditional political parties culminated in an opening for new parties (CVVM, 2010; CVVM, 2013a and 2013b) which, in terms of organisation, were highly centralised and entrepreneurial.

Our minimal definition of an entrepreneurial party comprises the following characteristics (modified from Hloušek and Kopeček, 2017): (1) The central role of the leader, his personal initiative to launch a new party and his crucial formative influence. (2) The leader uses the party primarily as a vehicle to promote his personal business and political interests. (3) The party seeks an exclusive membership, typically by erecting high barriers for admission. (4) The party is not a 'product' of a promoter/sponsor organisation or social movement, as is the case with mass parties. (5) The party is not connected with parliament, as a cadre party is, and is not founded by MPs seceding from another party. (6) The party is very flexible ideologically and eclectic in its choice of issues, focusing on current views and demands in society.[3]

The basic hypothesis of our analysis does not predict a trend of increasing democracy within parties, but precisely the opposite: the centralisation of candidate selection processes in new political parties. This contradicts the general hypothesis and expectations of the book but stems from the literature on entrepreneurial parties underpinning centralisation and the managerial way in intra-party processes instead of IPD (Hopkin and Paolucci, 1999, 333–334).

Our secondary hypothesis addresses the second research objective of our study: established parties did not respond to the rise of new parties by strengthening their democratic practices, but rather with inertia or even further centralisation of candidate selection.

Public Affairs

Our first case is the Public Affairs party (VV). Its genesis was rather complicated. The party was founded in 2001 as a civic initiative in Prague. It focused on local issues and did not show nationwide ambitions. This changed around the middle of the first decade of the twenty-first century when new members joined the party. In 2009 it expanded beyond the local level for the first time by putting up a candidate for election to the European Parliament, polling 2.4% of the vote. The popular investigative journalist, Radek John, became the new chair and leader of the party, embodying the party's electoral appeal, which combined populism (including the broad use of direct democracy) with the party's central theme: the fight against corruption and 'robber barons and political dinosaurs', i.e. politicians and traditional parties. Despite these promises, after the 2010 elections VV entered into a coalition government with one of the chief 'dinosaurs', the ODS, alongside TOP 09, which initiated the quick political collapse of VV. Its performance in cabinet saw the party initiating or participating in a number of conflicts and scandals, followed by its ultimate disintegration in spring 2012. It did not contest the 2013 elections at all and soon after formally ceased to exist (Havlík and Hloušek, 2014; Havlík, 2015).

According to its 2009 statutes, Public Affairs operated similarly in many respects to established Czech parties. There was a significant difference, though, in that the party recognised the so-called *véčkaři* (the 'Vs') – registered supporters who were not party members. *Véčkaři* were allowed to participate in the election of party leaders, regional party bosses and electoral leaders, as well as in advisory and binding internal party referenda. Originally, these referenda were used to decide virtually all important matters in VV, from personnel to politics to the programme. Soon after the 2010 elections, however, reasonable suspicions were voiced that the party leadership had been rigging the referenda. Furthermore, only a small proportion of the *véčkaři* tended to vote in them: less than 1,000 out of a total of almost 20,000 as of summer 2010 (Hloušek, 2012).

There was another particular characteristic of VV: people wishing to join the party had to spend a period of time as candidates for membership, the conditions of which were strictly defined in detail, and not easy to meet.[4] Thus, in spring 2010, the party had about 1,100 members and about 1,500 membership candidates (Aktuálně, 2010).

The main issue affecting the functioning of VV, however, was the discrepancy between the statutory and actual distribution of power in the party. John, officially the leader of the party, in fact merely represented the party to the media. The real decisions were made by a businessman, Vít Bárta, and his informal shadow body, the so-called Conceptual Council, not mentioned in the statutes and consisting of his close friends and collaborators, many of whom were linked to his private security agency (Kmenta, 2011, 325).

This created a contradiction between an outwardly very democratic and internally very centralist and also rather opaque VV organisation. One of the areas where centralisation was manifest was candidate selection for parliamentary elections. The selection mechanisms for parliamentary and other types of election were not described in the statutes in detail (VV, 2009). According to the statutes, the leaders of the list for parliamentary elections were elected by *véčkaři* in given electoral districts (which correspond with the Czech regions) and the rest of the list was proposed mainly by the regional councils. Even rank and file, and – for local elections – local, party organisations could suggest candidates; but in those as well as other cases the right to actually nominate candidates was reserved for the party's Board (*Grémium*), staffed by members of the party's central executive body, the Council (which was different from the Conceptual Council mentioned above) composed of the chair and vice-chairs of the party as well as unspecified members elected by the Conference of the party, leaders of regional organisations and their deputies, and regional secretaries and chairs of expert commissions. The important role of the Council in compiling candidate lists was confirmed by the provision according to which the Council established a Commission to select candidates for parliamentary elections, and similar Commissions for other types of election. What mattered was not just the fact that these Commissions had only a handful of members; candidate nomination and the make-up of the candidate lists were ultimately subject to approval by the Council. Theoretically, the *Grémium* was the last instance of veto power in regard to the electoral lists but for the reasons presented in the following paragraph, the veto power was not applied.

As the process of transforming VV from a local to a national party was somewhat spontaneous, and prior to the 2010 elections the regional bodies of the party were virtually non-existent, the phase of proposing names of potential candidates was in practice largely performed by local party associations. However, the local organisations only identified suitable candidates, and many of them were not party members. In the next phase, the leaders of the candidate list in each electoral region (constituency) were chosen. Here, democratic principles came into play as leaders of the regions were chosen in primaries in which members and registered *véčkaři* could vote. However, the inclusivity of this process was disrupted by the fact that candidates were preselected by the party's *Grémium* and election was by the first-past-the-post system. In a specific situation where the party's regional structures had not been completely established, the Board often formally confirmed nominations for leadership primaries, these nominations having been informally thrashed out by regional secretaries and the chairs of local party organisations in the given region. The regional leader having been selected, these informal structures then compiled the rest of the candidate list, a process in which the regional leader intervened by suggesting the names of candidates and order of them on the list. Although, before the 2010 elections, the Board rarely intervened in the candidate lists thus obtained, in theory there was no limit placed on the Board's freedom to do so (Spáč, 2013, 237–246).

The Board did intervene in the cases of a few candidates who refused to sign the so-called contract that set out aspects of the relationship between them and the party. The contract also obliged MPs to vote in accordance with decisions made by the VV leadership, and commanded them to express only such opinions in the media that conformed to the official line of the party (Smlouva, 2010). Given that these contracts contravened the constitutional principle of free mandate, they were legally unenforceable; however, they did have a certain disciplinary effect on the party's MPs, at least for a short period following the 2010 elections.

Thus, ostensibly, substantial direct-democracy procedures in the nomination process for the 2010 parliamentary elections were in practice variously diminished and deformed. Further developments strengthened the centralised nature of the party in this and other areas, with the new statutes (VV, 2011) confirming the key role of the Board and bolstering the role of regional party bodies in the selection (but not nomination) of candidates. True, the principle of holding primaries was preserved; but in practice centrally organised preselection was crucial. Despite this, in the history of Czech party politics, VV remains a unique attempt to implement strong intra-party democracy.

ANO

ANO's founding father in 2012 was Andrej Babiš, the owner of Agrofert – a large chemical and agribusiness holding company – and one of the richest people in the country. Babiš defined his new entity as a movement of dissatisfied citizens and, like VV, sharply criticised politicians at the time as corrupt, thieving and incompetent. Unlike VV, he did not put forward a vision of direct democracy; rather he presented the technocratic idea of better governance of the state according to commercial principles, as shown by one of the key ANO slogans, according to which 'the state should be managed as a business' (Havlík, 2015).

Another substantial difference between VV and ANO was that from the outset Babiš was publicly presented as the focal figure of the new political project. The leader's privileged position was enshrined in ANO statutes, allowing him to act independently and unhindered in all matters (ANO, 2013). The establishment of ANO's grass-roots organisation relied on a top-down model managed from Agrofert headquarters, exclusive concept of membership, and was accompanied by the extensive vetting of founding party cadres, involving even human-resources-style checks, and limitations placed on the autonomy of the party's local units. For instance, according to the statutes, the power to confirm regional heads in office lay with the party presidium (ANO, 2013). At the end of 2014 and similarly to VV, ANO had only around 1,800 members; many more – about 6,500 – were candidates for membership (Válková, 2014). A distinctive managerial culture and hierarchy of superordination and subordination was also pressed on the organisation. These are nicely illustrated by the words of one regional leader of ANO: "Mr. Babiš is the boss, he has charisma and knows how to make people dance to his tune. (. . .) There's no way I'd not fulfil a given task, and that's how it should be" (Zeman, 2013; in details Kopeček, 2016).

Professional election consultants and experts played an important role in the ANO campaign for the October 2013 parliamentary elections. In the preparations for the elections, ANO's local organisations were assigned merely service tasks, and this was reflected in the candidate selection process. According to the statutes, the candidate lists were to be put together by regional organisations, specifically by the assemblies of regional organisations – the supreme regional bodies – whose delegates would themselves be elected by assemblies of district organisations. The candidate lists were to be subsequently approved by the Committee of ANO, i.e. the broader party leadership had the power of veto (ANO, 2013). In practice, however, the Committee of ANO was not complete. Similarly, party organisations were not fully developed in many regions, and they were weakened following the intra-party conflict mentioned above. Furthermore, the assembling of candidate lists took place under pressure of time, as the elections were called early. Thus, the job was largely done by regional presidiums, i.e. the executive bodies of regional organisations. A semi-informal circle around Babiš, made up of hired electoral experts and members of the party presidium, had the most important influence. The circle had the final word in allocating the most attractive places at the top of candidate lists, where the probability of election was high (Matušková, 2015). These places were filled by public figures who affiliated themselves with ANO before the election, and were assigned to regions where it was thought they would make the greatest contribution to the party's electoral success. They included, for example, a popular actor, a well-known political commentator, a former university rector and a successful businessman. This situation is redolent of the founding period in the Italian party Forza Italia in the mid-1990s, when the largely informal circle around Silvio Berlusconi played the role of gatekeeper as far as nominations were concerned (Hopkin and Paolucci, 1999).

The degree to which the party centre interfered with the placement of candidates at the top of candidate lists was, nonetheless, limited by the number of celebrities ANO had at its disposal and by the fact that the number of seats allocated per region varied, as well as by lack of time – given that these were early elections. Thus, in reality, the dominance of the ANO leader was not limitless, and the regional organisations retained some influence, even over the top places on the candidate lists (Kopeček, 2016). For example, the candidate list proposed by the regional organisation in Karlovy Vary was simply approved by the Prague centre as suggested, with the party's regional chair as leader. Only a few seats were elected in this region, and according to the election experts working for ANO, the party only had a real chance of winning one. Thus it was simply not worth 'parachuting in' a candidate from outside. In another region, South Moravia, where many more seats were up for election, the regional organisation accepted the three candidates at the top of the list as proposed by the centre, but rejected another candidate (a former university rector) whom the local members considered controversial due to his colourful political past, when he represented different parties.

Babiš accepted this and moved the candidate to another region (Matušková, 2015; Vlčková, 2015).

The party's success in the 2013 elections opened for ANO the possibility of substantial participation in the new coalition government, and this included the position of finance minister for Babiš. ANO subsequently managed to consolidate its party organisation and avoided the serious internal crises that wrecked both VV and Dawn (see below). Further professionalisation and stronger control over the cadres was instrumental in this, as were the establishment of formal rules for candidate selection and amendments to the statutes (ANO, 2015), which gave the party presidium more clout, including the power to nominate candidates for all elected public offices, including elections to the Chamber of Deputies. The formal completion of the unrestricted position of the party leader was a further amendment of the statutes at the beginning of 2017, which supplemented his power to veto candidates on lists (ANO, 2017).

Dawn of Direct Democracy

As with ANO, Dawn of Direct Democracy depended from the outset on a single central figure, Tomio Okamura, a businessman of mixed Japanese, Korean and Czech ancestry, who was involved in the travel industry and enjoyed significant media exposure. In late 2012 Okamura was elected as an independent senator by taking advantage of his image of self-made man and popular tribune who deplored the incompetence of politicians and offered simple solutions – in particular, the direct participation of citizens in political decision-making. Founded in summer 2013, shortly before the early elections called for October, Dawn was able to pick up the threads of VV's participatory rhetoric and anti-corruption and anti-establishment appeals. In these respects Dawn was also similar to ANO. This was augmented by Okamura's mildly xenophobic diatribes against some minorities unpopular with the majority, notably the Roma (Havlík, 2015). However, Dawn's most important assets or source of 'know-how' were probably Okamura himself, his specific charisma and life story, which secured success for the party in the 2013 parliamentary elections.

That this was a one-man show was reflected as well in the way the party statutes were constructed. The leader of Dawn was elected for the comparatively long period of five years. He had 'general responsibility for the party's activities' between the sessions of the party's supreme body (the Congress), and the leader's powers encompassed everything that was not explicitly given to another body (Úsvit, 2013). The statutes were terse, comprising only a few articles, and any changes to them would be difficult to enact; this granted the leader nearly limitless scope for independent decision-making (Kubát, 2015; Kopeček and Svačinová, 2016). Also of essence was the fact that Dawn was impregnably closed to new members; throughout the years of Okamura's leadership, 2013–2015, the party had only nine (sic) members and the leader could veto any new admissions. Okamura not only refused to let any further members in, he also showed no interest in establishing a regional structure for the party, which was not even envisaged by the statutes.

This organisational configuration provided the leader with an even more privileged position than his counterpart in ANO. Sharply contrasting with Okamura's slogans about direct democracy, his firm grasp on the party was crucial for candidate selection ahead of the 2013 parliamentary elections. On this matter the statutes succinctly stipulated that the candidate lists would be compiled and approved by one of the party's bodies, the Committee, consisting of the leader (chair of Dawn), the executive secretary of the party and three further members elected by the Congress (Úsvit, 2013). As with other processes unfolding in Dawn, the candidate lists were largely created by an informal circle of people around the leader – over and above the members of the Committee. As in VV and ANO, the greatest attention was given to choosing leaders of the candidate lists in individual electoral regions and, in the more populous regions, also the candidates in the places immediately below the leader on the lists, as these actually stood a chance of winning a seat. The selection was largely based on the leader's personal contacts. There were criteria, but vaguely applied: regional leaders were expected to broadly chime in with Dawn's goals, especially the notion of direct democracy, and have at least some backing and popularity in the given region, which was important for campaigning (Zilvar, 2017).

Importantly, when choosing people for the leading places on candidate lists, politicians from various other entities were included, in particular from Bárta's VV and several small local parties and civic associations, from whom at least some political experience was expected. Vít Bárta himself became the candidate list leader in one of the regions and generally played the role of *eminence grise* at the founding of Dawn. Testifying to his position is the fact that he was involved in the final debate when the circle around Okamura approved the leaders of the regional candidate lists (Adam, 2017).

Sometimes the selection of candidate list leaders seemed more or less random. In the peripheral and largely rural constituency of Vysočina, the leader chosen at the last movement was a local radio anchor who had conducted an interview with Okamura and 'seemed sympathetic' (Adam, 2017). This arbitrary element was even stronger when candidates were chosen for the other places on the lists: in all regions, candidates were recruited from supporters who put themselves forward, and their order was decided on an *ad hoc* basis with no clear rules by people surrounding Okamura. The regional candidate list leaders wielded some influence here too.

After the elections, the effect of this strategy was that Dawn's parliamentary party was not homogeneous but politically rather colourful. Only three of the 14 MPs elected on the party's ticket were members of Dawn; a further three originated from VV and the rest were largely without party affiliation. Soon after the elections, the lack of connections between the party and its MPs caused a crisis, which was substantially exacerbated by Okamura's unwillingness to allow his own MPs to become party members or to build up permanent organisational party structures, as well as his opaque management of party funds. In the conflict that

occurred in early 2015, not just the majority of the parliamentary party but, ultimately, five of the party's nine members opposed Okamura, who then left and
founded a new party, Freedom and Direct Democracy.

Minimal response by established parties

The electoral success of entrepreneurial parties in the 2010 and 2013 elections
elicited a response from established parties. However, this was largely limited
to their programmes and rhetoric, and they did not attempt to make their own
organisations more democratic. During the period observed, some established
parties did change their statutes – ČSSD in 2009, 2011 and 2015; KDU-ČSL in
late 2002; KSČM in 2012 and 2016; and ODS in 2012 and 2015 – but in ODS and
KDU-ČSL these changes neither introduced new nor strengthened existing democratic practices. If a trend can be observed in established parties in response to the
breakthrough made by new entrepreneurial parties in 2010 and 2013, it is some
strengthening of their leaders' position and weakening of local and regional elites.
However, the beginnings of this organisational adaptation of traditional parties
can be dated to before the rise of entrepreneurial parties, when traditional parties
had responded to the limited weight of central party leadership and the conversely
great importance of regional and local elites. To date, these organisational shake-
ups have met with limited success.

This does not mean that the direct involvement of members in decision-making
would be wholly absent in traditional parties. The statutes of the parties of the left,
ČSSD and KSČM, have provided for the option of holding intra-party referenda
since the 1990s. In practice, such votes are extremely rare in both. There is, then,
a clear difference between the *de iure* and *de facto* status of intra-party democracy
in the two parties. The discrepancy between *de iure* and *de facto* is even more
pronounced in the process of the direct election of the leader by all party members, formally enshrined in ČSSD statutes as an alternative to the election of the
leader by the Congress. Direct election was adopted as an option near the close of
the first decade of the twenty-first century when Jiří Paroubek was the leader of
ČSSD. The reason behind the change was not to make the party more democratic.
A direct election would clearly boost the leader's legitimacy and, conversely, indirectly weaken the influence of regional and local elites (Polášek et al., 2012).
Therefore, the Central Executive Committee, which is dominated by the elites
and which has responsibility for choosing between direct election and election by
Congress, has so far always opted for the latter option. It needs emphasising that
the formal introduction of direct leadership elections occurred prior to the rise of
entrepreneurial parties and in this respect the entrepreneurs' electoral success has
changed nothing.

The change of the ČSSD statutes in 2015, which modified the rules on drawing
up candidate lists, likewise originated from internal party discussions and not in
response to the rise of entrepreneurial parties. The ČSSD statutes (2015) newly
state that 'the final version of the candidate list for elections to the assembly of
municipality, city, region, Senate and Chamber of Deputies shall be decided by a

direct vote of all ČSSD members in the corresponding constituency.' In practice, and compared with the original draft that sought to limit the power of local party elites, this was a significant concession to local and regional party authorities, as the provision for the involvement of local and regional party bodies in the assembling of candidate lists was preserved in the statutes. Under the new system, the rules for putting together candidate lists are to be set by a new intra-party regulation adopted on an *ad hoc* basis for individual elections. Thus, we need to wait for some time before we are able to analyse the real impact of these changes in terms of strengthening internal democracy in party-political practice.

Conclusion

We have analysed intra-party democracy in three new parties: Public Affairs, ANO and Dawn. From the fact that these are all entrepreneurial parties we have derived our basic hypothesis questioning the general assumption that democratic practices in parties would increase in consequence of the rise of new political parties. Our study was based on the premise that the rise of new entrepreneurial parties was accompanied by the centralisation of candidate selection processes. Furthermore, we assumed that established parties do not respond to the rise of new parties by strengthening their own democratic practices. Both of these assumptions contradict the general trend expected in other countries covered by this book.

Of the new entrepreneurial parties, a centralised process of candidate selection involving no democracy is clearly identifiable in ANO and Dawn. These parties were or are managed in a highly centralised manner, and the role of the rank-and-file is effectively eliminated by a combination of the overwhelmingly dominant role of the leader and the organisational make-up of the parties. Dawn has brought this organisational type to the extreme by making membership absolutely exclusive and totally neglecting to build the party on the ground. There is no internal democracy in these parties, not even in the procedure of candidate selection. The explanation of centralised candidate selection and organisation of ANO and Dawn is based on the conceptions of their founding fathers, Andrej Babiš and Tomio Okamura. Babiš and Okamura's conceptions differed in some aspects, which were mainly related to their diverse financial, media, personnel and other resources. However, both political entrepreneurs built the party as their own political vehicle, which allowed them to successfully enter politics. Inclusion of wider grassroots members and supporters to the decision-making party process were alien to them.

In the now defunct VV matters were somewhat different. The party envisaged broad deployment of internal party democracy and the idea was crucial for establishing its profile. However, looking more closely at how, generally, internal referenda were used in practice and, particularly, what role democracy played in the process of compiling candidate lists, we must note that the role of intra-party referenda diminished as time went on and, rather than by rigorous internal democratic procedures, the process of assembling candidate lists for the 2010 elections was marked by an element of spontaneity. True, primaries were used to formally confirm the candidate lists. However, these were preceded by centralised preselection and accompanied by informal mechanisms that limited and deformed intra-party democracy in practice.

Our secondary hypothesis concerning the behaviour of established parties was confirmed for all with the exception of ČSSD. Apart from ČSSD, no established party responded to the rising tide of new parties by introducing new or strengthening existing internal democratic measures. Rather, in established parties the responses to the electoral success of entrepreneurial parties included attempts to centralise decision-making; however, arguably there were other, earlier reasons for that. Even in the ČSSD, where a mechanism for approving candidate lists by all members was introduced, this was not primarily in response to the rise of new parties. This was more probably a compromise outcome of a longer-term internal discussion.

To sum up: the Czech Republic is a country that has not witnessed any strengthening of internal democracy in its political parties since 2010. The newly emergent protest parties are of the entrepreneurial type. By virtue of their structure, they seek centralised organisation and decision-making, and this affects their candidate-selection procedures for parliamentary elections. Established parties also carefully seek to apply a centralist strategy, not just in party organisation and decision-making, but also in the manner in which they conduct electoral campaigns. Figuratively speaking, for most Czech party elites direct democracy and direct elections pose a challenge rather than a welcome change, a threat rather than an opportunity.

For Czech voters and citizens, passive expression of general dissatisfaction with political parties and politicians as a reaction prevails clearly over any demand to foster internal democracy within the parties. Distrust in political parties is so high that it prevents voters even from believing that things can go better with more direct democracy within the parties. The Czechs are apparently opting for exit (from the parties) rather than a voice (within the parties). Together with declining party membership in general and cartel or business-like organisational practices within the parties, conditions for the rise of IPD are not at all favourable.

Notes

1 This text was financially supported by the Czech Science Foundation grant 'The Political Entrepreneurs: The Czech Republic in Comparative Perspective' (code GA17–02226S). The authors would like to thank Peter Spáč for his useful comments on this chapter and Štěpán Kaňa for the translation of the text.
2 ČSSD: Czech Social Democratic Party (*Česká strana sociálně demokratická*); KSČM: Communist Party of Bohemia and Moravia (*Komunistická strana Čech a Moravy*); KDU-ČSL: Christian and Democratic Union – Czechoslovak People's Party (*Křesťanská a demokratická unie – Československá strana lidová*); ODS: Civic Democratic Party (*Občanská demokratická strana*); Public Affairs (*Věci veřejné*); Dawn: Dawn of Direct Democracy (*Úsvit přímé demokracie*).
3 Our definition is based on earlier papers that studied political entrepreneurs in 'old democracies' (e.g. Harmel & Svåsand, 1993; Hopkin & Paolucci, 1999; Lucardie, 2000; Lange & Art, 2011; Bolleyer & Bytzek, 2013; Arter & Kestilä-Kekkonen, 2014).

4 Former Communist party members were barred. Further, candidates had to produce a declaration that they were free from debt, a statement from the state-maintained criminal record repository, a curriculum vitae and a signed copy of the VV ethical code. Further documents could also be requested. Later, external professional personnel agencies were involved in selecting potential members (Stauber, 2015, p. 145). Interestingly, most of these requirements – sometimes in an even more severe form – have been subsequently adopted into the statutes of Andrej Babiš's ANO.

References

Adam. (2017). *Interview with Dawn MP Petr Adam*, 27 January 2017.

Aktuálně. (2010). *Věci veřejné*. Retrieved from www.aktualne.cz/wiki/politika/politicke-strany/veci-verejne/r~i:wiki:631/?redirected=1485255186

ANO. (2013). *Stanovy politického hnutí ANO 2011*. Retrieved from www.anobudelip.cz/file/edee/ke-stazeni/vnitrni-predpisy/ano-stanovy-2013.pdf

ANO. (2015). *Stanovy politického hnutí ANO 2011*. Retrieved from www.anobudelip.cz/file/edee/2015/03/stanovy-ano_cistopis-3.3.2015-2.pdf

ANO. (2017). *Stanovy politického hnutí ANO 2011*. Retrieved from www.anobudelip.cz/file/edee/2017/stanovy-schvalene-iv.-celostatnim-snemem.pdf

Arter, D., and Kestilä-Kekkonen, E. (2014). Measuring the extent of party institutionalisation: The case of a populist entrepreneur party. *West European Politics* 37 (5), pp. 932–956.

Balík, S., and Hloušek, V. (2016). The development and transformation of the Czech party system after 1989. *Acta Politologica* 8 (2), pp. 103–117.

Bolleyer, N., and Bytzek, E. (2013). Origins of party formation and new party success in advanced democracies. *European Journal of Political Research* 52 (6), pp. 773–792.

ČSSD. (2015), *Stanovy České strany sociálně demokratické*. Retrieved from www.cssd.cz/ke-stazeni/stanovy/

CVVM. (2010). *Důvěra ústavním institucím a spokojenost s politickou situací v dubnu 2010*. Retrieved from http://cvvm.soc.cas.cz/media/com_form2content/documents/c1/a3756/f3/101032s_pi100427.pdf

CVVM. (2013a). *Důvěra ústavním institucím září 2013*. Retrieved from http://cvvm.soc.cas.cz/media/com_form2content/documents/c1/a7065/f3/pi130927.pdf

CVVM. (2013b). *Postoje k politickým stranám*. Retrieved from http://cvvm.soc.cas.cz/media/com_form2content/documents/c1/a7100/f3/pv131016.pdf

de Lange, S. L., and Art, D. (2011). Fortuyn versus wilders: An agency-based approach to radical right party building. *West European Politics* 34 (6), pp. 1229–1249.

Deegan Krause, K., and Haughton, T. (2010). A fragile stability. The institutional roots of low party system volatility in the Czech Republic, 1990–2009. *Politologický časopis* 17 (3), pp. 227–241.

Deník Referendum. (2010). *Příznivci Věcí veřejných určili většinu lídrů pro komunální volby*. Retrieved from http://denikreferendum.cz/clanek/5138-priznivci-veci-verejnych-urcili-vetsinu-lidru-pro-komunalni-volby

Hanley, S. (2012). Dynamics of new party formation in the Czech Republic 1996–2010: looking for the origins of a 'political earthquake'. *East European Politics* 28 (2), pp. 119–143.

Harmel, R., and Svåsand, L. (1993). Party leadership and party institutionalisation: Three phases of development. *West European Politics* 16 (2), pp. 66–88.

Haughton, T., and Krause, K. D. (2015). Hurricane season: Systems of instability in Central and East European party politics. *East European Politics and Societies* 29 (1), pp. 61–80.

Havlík, V. (2015). The economic crisis in the shadow of political crisis: The rise of party populism in the Czech Republic. In Kriesi, H. and Pappas, T. S. (Eds.), *European populism in the shadow of the great recession*. Colchester: ECPR Press, pp. 199–216.

Havlík, V., and Hloušek, V. (2014). Dr Jekyll and Mr Hyde: The story of the populist public affairs party in the Czech Republic. *Perspectives on European Politics and Society* 15 (4), pp. 552–570.

Hloušek, V., and Kopeček, L. (2017). Entrepreneurial parties: A basic conceptual framework. *Czech Journal of Political Science* 24 (2), pp. 83–91.

Hloušek, V. (2012). Věci veřejné: politické podnikání strany typu firmy. *Politologický časopis* 19 (4), pp. 322–340.

Hopkin, J., and Paolucci, C. (1999). The business firm party model of party organisation. Cases from Spain and Italy. *European Journal of Political Research* 35 (3), pp. 307–339.

Kmenta, J. (2011). *Všehoschopní - Superguru Bárta*. Praha: JKM.

Kopeček, L. (2016). 'I'm Paying, So I Decide': Czech ANO as an extreme form of a business-firm party. *East European Politics and Societies* 30 (4), pp. 725–749.

Kopeček, L., and Svačinová, P. (2015). Kdo rozhoduje v českých politických stranách? Vzestup nových politických podnikatelů ve srovnávací perspective. *Středoevropské politické studie* 17 (2), pp. 178–211.

Kopeček, L., and Svačinová, P. (2016). Between organizational extremes: Czech parties after a political earthquake. In Sobolewska-Myslik, K., Kosowska-Gąstoł, B. and Borowiec, P. (Eds.), *Organizational structures of political parties in central and Eastern European countries*. Kraków: Jagiellonian University Press, pp. 133–158.

Kopecký, P. (2006), "The Rise of the Power Monopoly: Political Parties in the Czech Republic." In Susan Jungerstam-Mulders (ed.), *Post-Communist EU member states. Parties and party systems*. Burlington: Ashgate, pp. 125–146.

Kopecký, Petr (2012), "Give me 'Trafika': Party Patronage in the Czech Republic." In Kopecký, P., Mair, P. and Spirova, M. (eds.), *Party patronage and party government in European democracies*. Oxford: Oxford University Press, pp. 74–91.

Krouwel, A. (2006). Party models. In Katz, R. and Crotty, W. (eds.), *Handbook of party politics*. London: Sage, pp. 249–269.

Krouwel, A. (2012). *Party transformations in European democracies*. Albany: State University of New York Press.

Kubát, M. (2015), "Przywództwo partyjne w Czechach: pod znakiem gwałtownych przeobrażeń politycznych." In Maciej Hartliński (ed.), *Przywództwo partyjne w państwach postkomunistycznych*, Olsztyn: Uniwersytet Warmińsko-Mazurski, pp. 79–100.

Linek, L., and Pecháček, S. (2005). K důvodům nízkého počtu členů českých politických stran. In Mansfeldová, Z. and Kroupa, A. (eds.), *Participace a zájmové organizace v České republice*. Praha: Slon, pp. 59–80.

Lucardie, P. (2000). Prophets, purifiers and prolocutors. Toward a theory of the emergence of new parties. *Party Politics* 6 (2), pp. 175–185.

Matušková. (2015). *Interview with ANO campaign strategist Anna Matušková*, 19 February 2015.

Median. (2013). *Voliči a voličské motivace*. Retrieved from http://img.ct24.cz/multimedia/documents/52/5187/518640.pdf

Outlý, J., and Prouza, J. (2013). *Navrhování a výběr kandidátů: politické strany v ČR a ve střední Evropě.* Olomouc: Civipolis.

Polášek, M., Novotný, V., and Perottino, M. (2012). *Mezi masovou a kartelovou stranou. Možnosti teorie při výkladu vývoje ČSSD a KSČM v letech 2000–2010.* Praha: Slon.

Smlouva. (2010). *Smlouva o úpravě vzájemných vztahů politické strany a kandidáta politické strany pro volby do Poslanecké sněmovny Parlamentu České republiky konané v roce 2010.* Retrieved from http://data.idnes.cz/soubory/domaci/A100526_KLU_SMLOUVAVV.PDF

Spáč, P. (2013). *České strany a jejich kandidáti. Případ voleb do Poslanecké sněmovny v roce 2010.* Brno: Munipress.

Stauber, J. (2015). Organizační vývoj nových politických stran v České republice pohledem teorie institucionalizace. *Acta Politologica* 7 (2), pp. 133–155.

Úsvit. (2013). *Stanovy politického hnutí Úsvit přímé demokracie Tomia Okamury,* 1 July 2013.

Válková, H. (2014). *Počet členů ANO strmě roste, Okamurův Usvit zamrzl na devíti členech.* Retrieved from http://zpravy.idnes.cz/pocty-clenu-politickych-stran-usvit-dvs-/domaci.aspx?c=A140409_171109_domaci_hv

van Haute, E., Close, C., Paulis, E., and Linek, L. (2015). *MAPP – Party Membership Figures in 32 countries. 1945–2014.* MAPP Project Data Archive. Retrieved from www.projectmapp.eu

Věci veřejné. (2009). *Stanovy Strany Věci veřejné,* 27 June 2009.

Věci veřejné. (2011). *Stanovy Strany Věci veřejné,* 28 May 2011.

Vlčková. (2015). *Interview with former chair of the Brno organisation of ANO Alžběta Vlčkova,* 11 February 2015.

Zeman, B. (2013). Krajský lídr ANO 2011 Procházka, *MF Dnes,* 7 October 2013.

Zilvar (2017). *Interview with Dawn secretary Jan Zilvar,* 24 January 2017.

6 Contagion effects by the AfD?

Candidate selection in Germany

Marion Reiser

Introduction

The Germany party system has long been seen as exceptional amongst European countries for its high stability and continuity (Pogunkte, 2015), and because no Eurosceptic or populist party has gained representation at the national level (Arzheimer, 2015; Schmitt-Beck, 2017). However, in 2013, a new party was formed as a reaction to the European financial crisis: Alternative für Deutschland (AfD; 'Alternative for Germany'). The party criticised the established parties and had a unique position with its critical stance against the Euro rescue package (Berbuir et al., 2015). Despite being created only a few months before the 2013 Federal Elections, the party won 4.7% of the votes and almost reached the 5% threshold to make it into parliament. At the 2014 European elections, the party entered the European parliament with 7% of the votes. Since then, the party has managed to enter all 13 state parliaments which have held elections and has won up to 24% (Saxony-Anhalt) of the vote. In elections held in September 2017 voters granted AfD 94 seats, making it the third largest faction in the Bundestag.

Given its electoral success, AfD has received considerable public and scientific attention, for instance on the ideology and the radicalisation of the party, the type of party, and their voters (e.g. Schmitt-Beck, 2017; Arzheimer, 2015; Bieber et al., 2015). On the contrary, there has been hardly any research into candidate selection. This is striking since the AfD criticises existing parties for their lack of internal democracy and cultivates "a profile based on grassroots democracy" (Levandowsky, 2014, 4). In contrast to this self-perception, however, the party's press coverage regarding internal democracy is rather negative. Based on this, this chapter asks first: how does the AfD as a new party select its candidates for elections in terms of an inclusive participatory process and a representative outcome? Secondly, the chapter analyses whether traditional mainstream parties react to AfD as a new competitor. The isomorphism theory (see the introduction in this volume; Matland and Studlar, 1996) suggests that innovations introduced by parties will set in motion a process of 'contagion' in which rival parties follow in order to compete.[2]

Party system, candidate selection and institutional framework

Germany represents an interesting case to study candidate selection in times of crisis for three reasons. First, the resilient stability of the German party system has long been seen as exceptional amongst European countries and the emergence of AfD challenges this stability.[3] Second, in Germany candidate selection is highly regulated by law in order to guarantee intra-party democracy. Third, the AfD as an anti-establishment, right-wing populist party is criticising the mainstream parties for a lack of internal democracy. Therefore it provides a good case to analyse whether the party is really implementing participative ways of candidate selection and whether the mainstream parties are reacting by changing selection procedures.

The AfD as a new actor in the German party system

The German party system has been characterised by high stability and continuity. In the early 1960s, a two-and-a-half party system – the Social Democratic Party (SPD), the Christian Democratic Union (CDU) with its Bavarian sister party the Christian Social Union (CSU) and the minor party, the Liberal Democratic Party (FDP) – had established itself. The dominance of this party system continued until 1983, when the Green Party entered parliament. Following unification, since the 1990s, the successor party to the SED, the PDS, is represented, with deputies in the Bundestag. In 2007, the PDS merged with the party "Labour and Social Justice – The Electoral Alternative" to form the new united party The Left. Hence, the party system in Germany had developed into a stable five-party system. In contrast to most other European democracies, the party system has been seen as a "role model of stability" (Poguntke, 2015, 242) because of a lack of dramatic changes during the economic crises and a lack of populist parties.

However, shortly before the Federal elections of 2013, Alternative for Germany was founded, claiming to offer a "real alternative" to the mainstream parties and to react to citizens' "feeling of political detachment from the established parties" (AfD, 2016, 6). Initially, the main focus of their programme has been to criticise the measures of the German government during the financial crisis in the EU. In contrast to all other mainstream parties, they were critical of the Euro rescue package and their goal was to dissolve the Eurozone (Schmitt-Beck, 2017). AfD quickly obtained impressive results. In the 2013 parliamentary elections, the party won 4.7%. By the end of 2013, the new party had also attracted more than 17,000 members (Niedermayer, 2016). The party even received 7.1% of the votes in the 2014 European elections, and 12.6% in the 2017 national elections.

As with many other newly founded parties, AfD was already in 2014 torn by internal disputes about its future political orientation, candidates and programmatic decisions (Goerres et al., 2017; Arzheimer, 2015). Two factions fought for influence within the party – an economically-oriented faction which focused on Euroscepticism as the main issue, and a national-conservative faction which increasingly had immigration as its dominant issue (Franzmann, 2016). This second faction gained influence, especially during the refugee crisis in 2015 when immigration was the most salient issue in German politics (Goerres et al., 2017). The conflicts between the two main factions escalated at the party congress in 2015 when Bernd Lucke, founder and Federal spokesman, demanded that the AfD should stick to the Eurosceptic and moderate manifestos while distancing themselves from PEGIDA, a nationalist, far-right protest movement against immigration. Lucke, however, lost the election to be reelected as AfD's spokesman to the national-conservative candidate Frauke Petry (Franzmann, 2016). As a consequence, Lucke and his supporters split from the AfD and founded a new (unsuccessful) party, ALFA. This reflected also a programmatic shift from a Eurosceptic single-issue party to a party which focuses on the issues of immigration. The radicalisation of the party is also reflected in their voters who have right-wing political attitudes concerning immigration, political dissatisfaction, and fears of personal economic decline (Goerres et al., 2017). Hence, since its foundation in 2013, the party has changed both its personnel and its programme in the midst of internal conflicts which remain severe. Nevertheless, the party has been electorally very successful. It has entered all 13 state parliaments which have held elections since then and won up to 24% of the vote and is present in the Bundestag as the third largest party after the SPD and CDU. The short history of the AfD shows that its foundation and success can be explained mainly by two current crises: the European financial crisis and the refugee crisis. The AfD can be seen as a relevant political party and as a new competitor in the German party system.

Candidate selection in Germany

Intra-party candidate nomination in Germany is centrally influenced by the Basic Law, the Party Law and the Electoral Law which stipulate intra-party democracy. The main goal is to ensure that candidate selection within the political parties maintains its democratic standards to prevent Germany from becoming a dictatorship again (Morlok, 2015). The process is decentralised in order to ensure that party leaders cannot accumulate excessive influence. Therefore, electoral laws regulate at which territorial levels candidates are to be selected: According to the German mixed member electoral system which combines a PR and a plurality tier (Manow, 2015) there are two independent forms of candidacies: the district candidacy and the candidacy on the state party list.[4] Constituency candidates must be nominated by either a meeting of the membership of the constituency party or by a meeting of delegates elected by the members of these local party branches. Formally, the Federal or state party executive can put a veto on the nominated candidate (Schüttemeyer and Sturm, 2005). List candidates are selected by party conventions of the state party branch. The selectorate can be either a party primary allowing all party members to nominate their candidates, or delegate conventions. This electoral system is applied for the Federal and most state elections.[5]

Regarding procedures, there are regulations that selections have to be held according to democratic standards: the Electoral Law (§21) rules that every aspirant has to have enough time to present himself and his programme to the convention. The elections have to be held by secret ballot to prevent party leaders from exerting pressure on the delegates. These rules can be enforced by the higher party branches which can veto the decisions of the party conventions at the local or regional level (§21 Electoral Law). Compliance with the formal rules is a pre-condition for the official approval of the candidates and lists (§26 Electoral Law). As such, these rules can even be enforced by regular German courts. They can, for example, make the party repeat an internal election if the formal rules have not been met. Candidates need a minimum age of 18 years and German citizenship and must not be disqualified from voting, e.g. on the grounds of criminal convictions (§12 and §13 Electoral Law). In sum, there is a wide range of regulations regarding intra-party democracy which set a clear framework for the processes of candidate selection.

Democratisation of candidate selection

In recent years, a shared trend towards democratisation in the selection of candidates has been observed (Bille, 2001; Kenig et al., 2015). An increasing number of parties have become more internally democratic by adopting procedures that allow the direct participation of their members to counter the decline of party membership (van Biezen et al., 2012; Scarrow et al., 2000). Since the 1950s, the major German parties used delegate conventions for candidate selection, preferring them in most cases over the more inclusive member conventions (Borchert and Golsch, 2003). For the Federal Elections 2002, Schüttemeyer and Sturm (2005, 541–545) revealed a trend towards more member conventions. However, for the Federal Elections 2009, Reiser (2011, 2018) showed that this trend has not continued since the clear majority of candidates had been nominated by delegate conventions. The question, therefore, is whether the AfD as a new political party reinforces this trend of democratisation in candidate selection. In other countries analysed in this book, it could be observed that these new parties often aim to give voice to those who did not feel represented by mainstream parties. They also criticise existing parties for their lack of internal democracy and promote internal democracy (Cordero and Simón, 2016). This also holds true for the AfD (Lewandowsky et al., 2016) which cultivates a profile based on grassroots democracy (Lewandowsky, 2014) and has an anti-establishment and populist attitude and rhetoric. This could result in more inclusive processes and in the result that their candidates and MPs better reflect the social structure of the citizens. However, there is empirical evidence that during the candidate selection for the Federal Elections 2013 ordinary members – despite formally inclusive selection methods – hardly had any influence. Instead, the process of candidate selection was rather "the project of an elite" and "lacked many basic requirements of real democracy" (Koschmieder, 2015). The question this chapter answers is whether this can be explained by the newness of the party and the heavy intra-party conflicts in its formative phase – or if it is a general feature of the AfD. Additionally, the chapter deals with the contagion effect by analysing whether the traditional mainstream parties changed their selection procedures in the direction of more open and inclusive mechanisms.

Intra-Party Democracy is still a contested concept in terms of meaning and operation (Cross and Katz, 2013). Rahat (2013, 136) argues that intra-party democracy in "candidate selection is perceived in terms of an inclusive participatory process and a representative outcome". Regarding the *process*, the concept is in its core about power distribution within a political party. Most scholars refer to decentralisation and inclusiveness of the selectorate as the two central dimensions. *Centralisation* refers to the question on which territorial level the selection takes place (Hazan and Rahat, 2010). It is argued that the power should be distributed among different party layers and subnational units should have a certain degree of autonomy versus the central level (von dem Berge et al., 2013). The second dimension is *inclusiveness* of the selectorate. Generally, selection processes are evaluated as being more democratic when more persons are involved in the decision (Hazan and Rahat, 2010). Third, the *procedures* of candidate selection processes are important elements which can either be regulated by party statutes or by law (Scarrow, 2005). Freedom of selection refers to secret ballot and the legal possibility of complaint. Fairness includes regularity and a requirement of transparency of the selection process (von dem Berge et al., 2013).

While the focus on the process and thus participation has been the dominant perception within the debate, Rahat (2013, 145) stresses the importance of the *outcome* and thus of representation as another central element. It is argued that parties should be inclusive regarding the eligibility of candidacy and strive for a balanced outcome, e.g. regarding the relevant demographic groups of the population. Research has revealed that parties in which party elites decide upon the nomination of candidates show higher degrees of representation than parties with more inclusive selectorates (Spies and Kaiser, 2014). However, there is also the contrary evidence that more inclusive patterns lead towards a better descriptive representation (e.g. Ashe et al., 2010). In recent years, political parties have increasingly introduced representation correction mechanisms such as quotas in order to guarantee a representative outcome that has not been achieved without rules (Krook, 2009). These rules concern mostly women and minorities but also refer to a wide range of other groups (Krook and O'Brien, 2010; Reiser, 2014).

Data and methods

To analyse candidate selection in the AfD and its effects on the German mainstream parties, a combination of different sources and methods is used: First, there is an analysis of the formal statutes of the AfD and the mainstream parties both at the Federal and regional level. The inclusion of the statutes of the state party branches is relevant because the AfD has been so far mainly successful at the state level. Furthermore, party lists for the Federal elections are also composed by the state party branches (§21 Electoral Law). This makes it possible to examine whether the AfD has formally implemented more democratic means of candidate selection. In order to assess if and how established parties reacted to the emergence of the AfD, the national and state party statutes of the established parties will be examined at two points in time, namely 2013 and 2017.

Second, in order to analyse how selection de facto takes place, the processes of these parties have been scrutinised based on a content analysis of the protocols of the party conventions and associated media coverage. Third, the impact of candidate selection methods on descriptive representation is scrutinised based on the social structure (gender, age and education) of the MPs of the AfD and the five mainstream parties in all parliaments in which the AfD has been represented in May 2017. This includes 13 state parliaments as well as the European Parliament.

Analysis: candidate selection in the AfD and contagion effects

In the following, the central results of the analysis are presented. The first section covers whether the AfD as a new party is implementing more democratic ways of candidate selection. The second section encompasses the examination of the traditional parties by comparing the formal and de facto selection procedures for the Federal elections of 2013 and 2017 in order to assess possible contagion effects in reaction to the emergence of the AfD. The final section scrutinises whether inclusive ways of candidate selection lead towards a political elite that reflects better the social structure of a society in terms of descriptive representation.

Candidate selection in the AfD: more internal democracy?

Does the AfD as a new party implement more democratic ways of candidate selection, based on decentralisation, inclusiveness and procedures? The German Electoral Law sets clear rules regarding *decentralisation*: District candidates are nominated at the local level and state list candidates at the state level. Hence, formally, candidate selection in general and also within the AfD is highly decentralised. While empirical studies for the mainstream parties show that the local and regional party branches also have de facto a high level of autonomy, there are indications that the higher party branches of the AfD influence candidate selection processes at the local and regional level. Koschmieder (2015, 2017) has assessed that Federal party leaders "wielded strong influence on the elections in the different states".

Regarding the *inclusiveness* of the selectorate, the formal regulations in the statutes of the AfD differ between the levels and between the regional branches. At the Federal level, the delegate convention is set as standard for candidate nomination, although the statute allows for the option to have party primaries. However, in the German system, the Federal level is only relevant for the nomination of the party list for the European elections since the state party lists for state and Federal elections are nominated at the state level. At the regional level, the party primary is set as standard in 13 of the 16 regional branches. In four regional branches member conventions are obligatory (Bavaria, Hamburg, Lower Saxony, Saxony-Anhalt), while the other regional branches also have the option – partly depending on the number of members – to have alternatively delegate conventions.[6] Only three state branches – Saarland, Hesse and North Rhine-Westphalia – have set the delegate convention as the standard selectorate.[7] Hence, the AfD has set – within the regulations of the Electoral Law – inclusive selectorates as the standard and thus has allotted their members formally a significant role in candidate selection.

This inclusion of ordinary party members is reflected in the actual nomination processes since the inclusive method of candidate selection has been predominantly adopted in the nomination for the 13 state elections between 2013 and 2017. Except of three cases,[8] these conventions have been party primaries. The same is true for candidate selection for the Federal Elections in 2017. Only in two states delegate conventions took place, while in 14 states the selectorates have been comprised of all members. Hence, in more than 80% of the state party lists' nominations, party members decided upon their candidates. They actively participated in these nominations. On average, 20.2% of the party members of each state participated during the nomination convention. However, the participation of party members differed substantially, between 12.9% in Bavaria and 33.3% in Saarland (see Table 6.1). Hence, the AfD has established formally inclusive candidate selection methods by including party members in the process of candidate selection of state party lists.[9]

The third dimension of democratic candidate selection are the *procedures*. The nomination processes of the AfD have received public attention because of countless scandals and violations against these regulations. Several state party lists of

Table 6.1 Candidate selection of the state party lists of AfD for the federal elections 2017

State	Selectorate	Size of Selectorate	Share of Members participating (%)
Bavaria	Party Primary	450	12.9
Berlin	Party Primary	300	25.0
Brandenburg	Party Primary	241	21.9
Bremen	Party Primary	No information	
Saxony	Delegate Convention	278	15.4
Schleswig-Holstein	Party Primary	120	13.3
Hamburg	Party Primary	124	20.7
Mecklenburg-Western Pomerania	Party Primary	200	33.3
Lower Saxony	Party Primary	407	16.3
North Rhine-Westphalia	Delegate Convention	350	7.6
Thuringia	Party Primary	270	27.0
Hesse	Party Primary	400	18.2
Rhineland-Palatinate	Party Primary	440	24.4
Saarland	Party Primary	133	33.3
Baden-Wurttemberg	Party Primary	600	15.8
Saxony-Anhalt	Party Primary	120	17.1
Overall	**Party Primaries: 87.5%**	**296**	**20.2**

Source: Own dataset based on protocols of the nomination conventions 2013–2017.

the AfD have been declared invalid by the official elections administrator or regular German courts since they have violated legal regulations. For instance, the Saarland Regional Court ruled that the nomination of the state party list for the Federal Elections 2017 has to be repeated since some of the party delegates had not been eligible to nominate the state party list (Saarländischer Rundfunk, 2017). For similar reasons, in 2013, the election of the state party list in Bavaria had to be repeated due to manipulations by regional leaders. Marcus Pretzell (state party leader of the AfD) and his inner circle were accused of using undue methods to orchestrate the selection of candidates for the state election in North-Rhine Westphalia in 2017. The state's elections administrator decided that although there had been irregularities, the process was deemed legal so that the list of candidates was accepted (see for a similar case in Saxony-Anhalt, Bock, 2017). In sum, there have been numerous violations against the state and party rules which are discussed intensively within the party itself and in public.

The candidate selection processes of the AfD have also received public attention since the party excluded the media from several nomination conventions,[10] e.g. the nomination conventions in Baden-Wurttemberg for the state party list for the Federal elections 2017. This has also been controversial within the AfD. Formally, it is not stipulated explicitly by law that party conventions have to be public. However, some professors of party law argue that the exclusion of media is not in concordance with the constitutional role of political parties to participate in the formation of political will (Art. 21 Basic Law) which necessitates publicity (FAZ, 2016). In addition, it has been a usual practice that party conventions are public. Therefore, the exclusion of the media was heavily criticised by other political parties as non-transparent und undemocratic. Also the media argued that this would be a "massive intervention in the freedom of the press" (see Stuttgarter Zeitung, 2016).

In sum, the analysis of intra-party democracy in candidate selection of the AfD reveals mixed results. Selection processes have been formally inclusive since predominantly party members – and not delegates – nominated the state party lists for the regional and Federal elections. In addition, a high share of party members participated in the nomination conventions. Despite the formal inclusive selection methods, there are indications that the national party organisation and the national elites have influenced the candidate selection processes at the subnational level. As regards procedures, candidate selection within the AfD has lacked many basic requirements of intra-party democracy, including violations against formal regulations and intra-party conflicts about fairness, transparency and freedom of candidate selection. This has been explained by the relative newness of the AfD and the lack of experience in these processes of candidate selection (Koschmieder, 2015). This seems to be a reasonable explanation for the elections in 2013 and 2014 since candidate selection took place shortly after the foundation of the party. However, in 2017, the main reason does not seem to be inexperience but rather the intense intra-party conflicts between the different factions of the party. As Gallagher (1988, 3) has emphasised, candidate selection is "a key arena of internal power struggles". The irregularities in the processes of candidate selection can almost exclusively be traced back to the intense intra-party struggles about its programme and personnel (see also Arzheimer, 2015; Koschmieder, 2015). Because of these intense power struggles and their implications, the AfD has been called a "Party of Self-Destruction" (Seils, 2017).

Contagion effects? Candidate selection of the traditional parties

The second aspect tackled in this chapter is whether the traditional parties are implementing more inclusive ways of candidate selection, emulating the practices of new parties. To capture possible changes, the nomination processes of the mainstream parties for the Federal Elections in 2013 and in 2017 are compared.

As discussed, the Electoral Law regulates that candidate selection in Germany is highly *decentralised*. Empirical studies for the mainstream parties show that higher party branches hardly influence the nomination processes at the subnational levels, either by putting a formal veto on the candidate or by other informal means (Schüttemeyer and Sturm, 2005; Reiser, 2011, 2018). Hence, the regional and local party branches dominate the candidate selection processes in Germany while the national party level is also de facto relatively excluded from the procedures.

As regards *inclusiveness*, since the 1950s, the major German parties have used predominantly delegate conventions and rarely party primaries – although a trend to more internal democratisation has been observed (Schüttemeyer and Sturm, 2005). For the Federal Elections 2009, Reiser (2011, 2018) showed that this trend has not continued since 69% of the district candidates of the mainstream parties have been nominated by delegate conventions. This applies also to the selectorates for the nomination of state party lists (see Table 6.2): The analysis of the 64 party statutes clearly shows that delegate conventions are still the standard selectorate for nominating state party lists for Federal Elections. Overall, 91% of the state party lists have been nominated by delegate conventions. The large parties, SPD, CDU and CSU, used delegate conventions in all nominations in 2013 and 2017. The results for the smaller parties (the Greens and the Left) differ between the states. The Greens used party primaries in the three city states, Berlin, Bremen and Hamburg, as well as in Hesse. The Left Party used party primaries only in two states (Bremen and Saarland). The dominance of the delegate convention has clear implications for the participation of the party members: On average, only 4.75% of party members participated in these processes of candidate selection.[11]

The dominance of delegate convention as the standard selectorate of the traditional parties is in clear contrast to the AfD which predominantly uses party primaries (see 6.1). Despite these clear differences, there are no indications of contagion effects with regard to the inclusiveness of candidate selection since the use of these selection methods has been surprisingly stable. No single state branch of the traditional parties has changed the procedure for the nomination of state party lists from 2013 to 2017.

Table 6.2 Candidate selection inclusiveness for state party lists (federal elections 2013 and 2017)

| | Formal Regulation in Statute | | | | | | Selectorates | | | | |
| | Delegate Convention | | Party Primary | | Delegate Convention or Party Primary | | Delegate Convention | | Party Primary | | % of Members in Selectorate |
	2017	2013	2017	2013	2017	2013	2017	2013	2017	2013	2017
SPD		93.8	0	0.0	6.2	6.2	100.0	100.0	0.0	0.0	1.92
CDU/ CSU	93.8	93.8	0.0	0.0	6.2	6.2	100.0	100.0	0.0	0.0	1.56
Greens	75.0	75.0	25.0	25.0	0.0	0.0	75.0	75.0	25.0	25.0	9.12
Left Party	50.0	50.0	0.0	0.0	50.0	50.0	87.5	87.5	12.5	12.5	6.40
Overall	78.1	78.1	6.3	6.3	14.1	14.1	90.6	90.6	9.4	9.4	4.75

Source: Own dataset based on protocols of the nomination conventions 2013 and 2017.

Outcome of candidate selection: more representative?

The third aspect scrutinised is whether inclusive ways of candidate selection lead towards a political elite that reflects better the social structure of society. Therefore, the analysis focuses on regulations regarding candidacy and on descriptive representation in parliaments.

Regarding *candidacy*,[12] the statute of the AfD makes two innovative regulations which reflect the anti-establishment and populist attitude of the AfD. Since they criticise the political class and argue 'against career politicians' (§19 (5) Federal Statute of the AfD), candidates should have at least five years of prior work experience, in which paid work in politics is not counted. As a reaction to lobbyism, aspirants have to commit themselves to not assuming new paid activities during the time of their mandate and the first three years after retirement from the mandate. In addition, they have to commit themselves to reducing their work commitments during the mandate in order to have enough time to be an MP (§19 (1–3) Federal Statute of the AfD). While these regulations might restrict the pool of potential candidates, the AfD regulates that candidacy must not be restricted by any quota (§5 (2) of the Federal Statute). They argue that quotas are a violation against the merit principle and a discrimination against other candidates. In line with the liberal perspective (Bacchi, 2006) they argue for equality of opportunity and against equality of result (AfD, 2016, 56).

Overall, it can be stated that the regulations regarding candidacy are more restrictive than in the other mainstream parties and might have implications for the descriptive representation in parliament. Therefore, the profile of the MPs in terms of gender, age and education will be analysed by comparing it to the profiles of the other parties. With regard to the *gender structure*, MPs of the AfD are predominantly male. Less than 14% of the MPs in the 13 regional parliaments are female, ranging from no female MPs in Bremen and Saarland to 29% in

Table 6.3 Average share and number of female MPs

Party	Regional Parliaments		European Parliament	
	Share	Number	Share	Number
AfD	**13.7**	**24**	**28.6**	**4**
CDU & CSU	21.2	91	20.6	10
SPD	38.9	151	48.1	8
Green Party	50.6	80	54.5	4
Left Party	51.3	78	57.1	14
Liberal Party	21.7	18	33.3	1
Overall	**32.5**	**382**	**39.3**	**41**

Source: Own dataset based on analysis of the websites of parliaments.

Saxony. In the European parliament, the percentage of female MPs corresponds with the share in Saxony. This very low level of female representation of the AfD conforms also to the gender structure of the candidates for the Federal elections in 2013 (Ceyhan, 2016). In comparison with the other parties, these are very low levels of female representation (see also Schroeder et al, 2017).

This result can be explained on the one hand by the rejection of gender quotas in the process of candidate selection of the AfD, since the introduction of gender quotas in Germany increased the number of women in German parliaments (Davidson-Schmich, 2016). This pattern is obvious in this analysis: the SPD, Greens and Left Party, which adopted a 50% party quota, have the highest share of females in the parliaments. The CDU, which employs a 'soft' one-third quota, and the Liberals, who reject gender quotas, have the lowest number of female MPs. This descriptive representation in the AfD reflects the male dominance of their party members since only 16% of the members of the AfD are female (Niedermayer, 2016). In addition, the majority of their voters are male, which is typical for both populist right-wing parties and new parties (Bieber et al., 2015). Hence, the under-representation of women in German parliaments is actually increased by the AfD.

Regarding *age*, the structure of the MPs of the AfD does not differ substantially from that of other parties (see Table 6.4). On average, an MP of the AfD in the 13 state parliaments and in the European parliament is 49.5 years old, which is typical for German MPs. This is mainly explained by the typical career pattern 'Ochsentour' (Herzog, 1975) which implies that politicians need long-term experience in honorary local offices and local party offices as a precondition for a nomination (Reiser, 2018). However, new parties usually have younger MPs without long-term political experience, which is why the result for the AfD is striking.

Regarding *education*, the MPs of the AfD in the state parliaments have a slightly lower level of education: 73% of the MPs in the state parliaments hold a university degree, compared to more than 80% of the other MPs. However, this difference can be mostly explained by significantly lower levels of education in the four outlier state parliaments of Saxony (57%), Rhineland-Palatinate (57%), Mecklenburg-Western Pomerania (56%), and Saxony-Anhalt (60%). In addition,

Table 6.4 Age and education structure (in %)

Party	Average Age		Share of MPs with University Degree	
	State Parliaments	*EP*	*State Parliaments*	*EP*
AfD	**49.3**	**54.1**	72,3	**100.0**
CDU & CSU	49.6	53.5	79.5	91.2
SPD	49.6	53.4	75.4	74.1
Green Party	47.5	49.2	82.6	72.7
Left Party	46,9	55.7	87.9	100.0
Liberal Party	46.6	52.3	76.7	100.0
Overall	**48.9**	**53.1**	**79.6**	90.5

Source: Own dataset based on analysis of the websites of parliaments.

a high level of education can also be observed in the European Parliament, where all MEPs of the AfD have a university degree. Overall, the structure of education corresponds to those of the other parties.

To sum up, the MPs of the AfD are not more representative in descriptive terms. While there are hardly differences between the AfD and the mainstream parties regarding age and education, the share of female MPs of the AfD is significantly lower than that of the other parties.

Conclusion

The foundation and success of the AfD can be explained mainly by two current crises: the European financial crisis and the refugee crisis. The AfD has been characterised as right-wing populist party which criticises the mainstream parties for a lack of internal democracy and speaks out against career politicians. Therefore, the first central question of this chapter has been whether the AfD has introduced more inclusive methods of candidate selection and whether this has led to a better descriptive representation in parliament. The analysis revealed a mixed result. The AfD uses primarily member conventions at the state level to nominate its candidates and thus is significantly more inclusive than the mainstream parties, which predominantly use delegate conventions. However, there are indications that the informal decision-making processes of the AfD are influenced by regional and national party elites and therefore decisions are, de facto, not made by ordinary party members. In addition, media analysis clearly shows that candidate selection of the AfD has been characterised by scandals and violations against democratic procedures such as freedom, fairness and transparency. Several nomination processes even had to be repeated since the state party lists had been declared invalid by the official elections administrator. Next to a lack of experience this seems to be predominantly a result of intense intra-party conflicts within the national and regional party organisations. Also, as regards the outcome of the candidate selection processes, the analysis revealed that MPs of the AfD have even lower levels of descriptive representation than mainstream parties, especially as regards female representation.

The second question of this chapter has been whether the mainstream political parties have reacted to the AfD as a new competitor by introducing new and more inclusive methods of candidate selection. This has been assumed based on contagion theory (Matland and Studlar, 1996) which suggests that political parties will respond to their competitors' actions and follow suit in order not to lose electoral support. The comparison of the selection processes for the Federal elections in 2013 and 2017 showed that there is no evidence that they have reacted in this regard since no single state party branch has modified the procedures. Therefore, the question arises why there is no contagion effect despite the fact that the AfD criticises the mainstream parties for their lack of internal democracy. It is argued that the established parties are not reacting because they do not feel threatened by the AfD with regard to candidate selection and intra-party democracy. Despite its self-image, candidate selection of the AfD is perceived as undemocratic due to the scandals and irregularities. In addition, the AfD factions show low levels of descriptive representation, especially in terms of gender. Furthermore, the AfD has not introduced innovative forms of internal democracy since party primaries and member surveys have been used by the mainstream political parties for a long time. This is in contrast to the Pirate Party which strongly promoted internal democracy and introduced new modes of intra-party democracy but could not establish itself in the German party system (see footnote 2).

Despite this result, there are indications that the mainstream parties have reacted to the AfD regarding their programmatic positions and their rhetoric, mainly in relation to the topic of immigration (Maas, 2016). As a result of the refugee crisis, immigration has become the most salient issue in German politics, and voters express right-wing political attitudes concerning immigration and fears of personal economic decline (Goerres et al., 2017). The AfD has been successful in shaping the public discourse on this issue, and the party is benefitting in current polls while mainstream parties have lost support (e.g. Arzheimer, 2017). The mainstream parties have reacted to the electoral demands and the positions of the AfD programmatically and rhetorically. Examples are the demand of the CSU to introduce an 'Obergrenze' (upper limit) for refugees in their manifesto for the Federal elections (CSU, 2017), or the passing of the Asylpaket II bill by the government parties, which tightened measures to reduce the numbers of refugees (Bundesregierung, 2016). Hence, while there are no indications of contagion effects with regard to candidate selection, programmatic and rhetoric contagion effects can be observed, mainly in relation to the topic of immigration.

Notes

1 Accessibility of all the websites was checked on 21 April 2017.
2 This effect has been confirmed for example for quota contagion in Germany (Kolinsky, 1993; Davidson-Schmich, 2016). However, there is only little systematic evidence under which conditions contagion effects occur (Verge and Kenny, 2013).

3 Next to the AfD, in 2006 the Pirate Party Germany was founded. The party promoted the freedom in the internet and internal democracy. The party seeks to maximize equality between members which is also reflected in the fact that national party leaders have hardly any power and that there are no delegates for intra-party decision processes (Koschmieder, 2015). The Pirates also introduced innovative modes for internal political opinion formation and decision making mediated by the internet such as liquid democracy (Bieber and Leggewie, 2012). The party entered four state parliaments in 2011 and 2012 and was even able to score up to 13% in nationwide polls. However, internal disputes, decreasing media support, and the fact that its core topic was not seen as important by the voters led to a rapid drop in opinion polls (Bieber et al., 2015). After the state election in North Rhine-Westphalia in May 2017 the Pirates are no longer represented in any parliament and thus have (almost) disappeared from the German party system.

4 Candidates may, however, run under both formulas simultaneously, and during the course of time 'dual candidates' have become hegemonic (Reiser, 2014).

5 See for specifics of the state electoral systems www.wahlrecht.de/landtage/. The electoral system for the European parliament is a proportional system with closed lists.

6 The regional branches of Brandenburg, Lower Saxony and Rhineland-Palatine can also opt for a delegate convention; in Berlin, Bremen, Mecklenburg-Western Pomerania, Saxony, Schleswig-Holstein and Thuringia delegate conventions are possible if they exceed a certain number of members; in Baden-Wurttemberg a delegate convention is obligatory if they exceed a certain number of members.

7 In Hesse and Saarland, the regional branches can also opt for a member convention.

8 These have been the nominations for the Saarland (2017) and North Rhine-Westphalia (2017) state elections. In both regional branches the delegate convention is set as the standard selection method. In addition, in the state of Berlin (2016) a delegate convention took place.

9 The party members could also decide whether a single top candidate ('Spitzenkandidat') runs for the Federal elections or a duo of two top candidates. This form of member survey, however, is not an innovation since it has been used also by the mainstream parties occasionally since 1994 (see footnote 10).

10 At other party conventions and meetings – for instance at the meeting of the ENF faction of the European Parliament in Koblenz, including Geert Wilders and Marine Le Pen, – the AfD excluded some media (such as FAZ, Spiegel and the public broadcasting channels) while other media had been accredited by the AfD (WELT, 2017).

11 Additionally, the parties have occasionally used member surveys in order to elect the party's top candidate ('Spitzenkandidat') for the Federal or state elections, e.g. within the CDU: 1994 for the state elections in North-Rhine Westphalia, 2004 and 2016 in Baden-Wurttemberg; within the SPD: 1994 for the General elections, 1995 and 1999 in Berlin and 2001 in Baden-Wurttemberg; within the Green party: 2012 and 2017 for the two top candidates for the Federal Elections.

12 In addition, party membership is a precondition to become candidate (§19 (5) Federal Statute of the AfD). This, however, is a very common feature in most parties both in Germany and worldwide (Hazan and Rahat, 2010).

References

AfD (2016). Programm für Deutschland. Das Grundsatzprogramm der Alternative für Deutschland. Retrieved from https://www.afd.de/grundsatzprogramm/

Arzheimer, K. (2015). The AfD: Finally a successful right-wing populist Eurosceptic party for Germany? *West European Politics* 38 (3), pp. 535–556. doi:10.1080/01402382.2015.1004230

Arzheimer, K. (2017). *Blog posts on the Alternative für Deutschland (AfD)*. Retrieved from www.kai-arzheimer.com/tag/afd/

Ashe, J., Campbell, R., Childs, S., and Evans, E. (2010). 'Stand by your man': Women's political recruitment at the 2010 UK general election. *British Politics* 5 (4), pp. 455–480. doi:10.1057/bp.2010.17

Bacchi, C. (2006). Arguing for and against Quotas: Theoretical Issues. In Dahlerup, D. (Ed.), *Women, quotas and politics*. New York and London: Routledge, pp. 32–51.

Berbuir, N., Lewandowsky, M., and Siri, J. (2015). The AfD and its sympathisers: Finally a right-wing populist movement in Germany? *German Politics* 24 (2), pp. 154–178. doi :10.1080/09644008.2014.982546

Bieber, C., and Leggewie, C. (2012). *Unter Piraten: Erkundungen in einer neuen politischen Arena*. Bielefeld: Transcript Verlag.

Bieber, I., Roßteutscher, S., and Scherer, P. (2015). Anti-party voting in Germany: The Alternative for Germany (AfD) and the pirate party. In de Petris, A. and Poguntke, T. (Eds.), *Anti-party parties in Germany and Italy. Protest movements and parliamentary democracy*. Rome: LUISS University Press, pp. 51–75.

Bille, L. (2001). Democratizing a democratic procedure: Myth or reality? *Party Politics* 7 (3), pp. 363–380. doi:10.1177/1354068801007003006

Bock, M. (2017, July 3). AfD-Zoff. Streit um Liste spitzt sich zu. *Volksstimme*. Retrieved from www.volksstimme.de/sachsen-anhalt/afd-zoff-streit-um-liste-spitzt-sich-zu

Borchert, J., and Golsch, L. (2003). From 'Guilds of Notables' to political class. In Borchert, J. and Zeiss, J. (Eds.), *The political class in advanced democracies*. New York: Oxford University Press, pp. 142–163.

Bundesregierung. (2016). *Asylpaket II in Kraft*. Kürzere Verfahren, weniger Familiennachzug. Retrieved from www.bundesregierung.de/Content/DE/Artikel/2016/02/2016-02-03-asylpaket2.html

Ceyhan, S. (2016). Konservativ oder doch schon rechtspopulistisch? Die politischen Positionen der AfD-Parlamentskandidaten im Parteienvergleich. *Zeitschrift für Politikwissenschaft* 26 (1), pp. 49–76.

Cordero, G., and Simon, P. (2016). Economic crisis and support for democracy in Europe. *West European Politics* 39 (2), pp. 305–325. doi: 10.1080/01402382.2015.1075767

Cross, W. P., and Katz, R. S. (2013). The challenges of intra-party democracy. In Cross, W. P. and Katz, R. S. (Eds.), *The challenges of intra-party democracy*. Oxford: Oxford University Press, pp. 1–10.

CSU. (2017). *Der Bayernplan. Programm der CSU zur Bundestagswahl*. Retrieved from www.csu.de/politik/beschluesse/bayernplan-2017/

Davidson-Schmich, L. K. (2016). *Gender quotas and democratic participation: Recruiting candidates for elective offices in Germany*. Ann Arbor: University of Michigan Press.

FAZ. (2016, November 19). *Ausschluss der Medien rechtens?* Retrieved from www.faz.net/aktuell/politik/inland/afd-parteitag-ausschluss-der-medien-rechtens-14535537.html

Franzmann, S. (2016). Von AfD zu ALFA: Die Entwicklung zur Spaltung. *Mitteilungen des Instituts für Deutsches und Internationales Parteienrecht und Parteienforschung* 22, pp. 23–37.

Gallagher, M. (1988). Introduction. In Gallagher, M. and Marsh, M. (Eds.), *Candidate selection in comparative perspective. The secret garden of politics*. London: Sage, pp. 1–19.

Goerres, A., Spies, D. C., and Kumlin, S. (2017). The electoral supporter base of the alternative for Germany: An analysis of a panel study of German voters in 2015–16. *SSRN Electronic Journal*. Advance online publication. doi:10.2139/ssrn.2942745

Hazan, R. Y., and Rahat, G. (2010). *Democracy within parties: Candidate selection methods and their political consequences*. Oxford: Oxford University Press.

Herzog, D. (1975). *Politische Karrieren: Selektion und Professionalisierung politischer Führungsgruppen*. Opladen: Westdeutscher Verlag.

Kenig, O., Cross, W., Pruysers, S., and Rahat, G. (2015). Party primaries: Towards a definition and typology. *Representation* 51 (2), pp. 147–160. doi:10.1080/00344893.2015. 1061044

Kolinsky, E. (1993). Party change and women's representation in unified Germany. In Lovenduski, J. and Norris, P. (Eds.), *Gender and party politics*. London: Sage, pp. 113–146.

Koschmieder, C. (2015). Internal democracy and candidate selection: The free voters, the alternative for Germany and the pirate party. In de Petris, A. and Poguntke, T. (Eds.), *Anti-party parties in Germany and Italy. Protest movements and parliamentary democracy*. Rome: LUISS University Press.

Koschmieder, C. (2017). Eine demokratischere Alternative? Die Mitgliederparteitage der AfD. In Koschmieder, C. (Eds.), *Parteien, Parteiensysteme und politische Orientierungen*. Wiesbaden: Springer VS, pp. 179–196.

Krook, M. L. (2009). *Quotas for women in politics: Gender and candidate selection reform worldwide*. Oxford: Oxford University Press.

Krook, M. L., and O'Brien, D. Z. (2010). The politics of group representation: Quotas for women and minorities worldwide. *Comparative Politics* 42 (3), pp. 253–272. doi:10.51 29/001041510X12911363509639

Lewandowsky, M. (2014). Alternative für Deutschland (AfD): A New Actor in the German Party System. *International Policy Analysis*. London. Retrieved from http://library.fes. de/pdf-files/id/ipa/10644.pdf

Lewandowsky, M., Giebler, H., and Wagner A. (2016). Rechtspopulismus in Deutschland. Eine empirische Einordnung der Parteien zur Bundestagswahl 2013 unter besonderer Berücksichtigung der AfD. *PVS* 57 (2), pp. 247–275.

Maas, S. (2016, April 18). *Wie etablierte Parteien reagieren. Der Einfluss der AfD auf die Minderheitenpolitik. Deutschlandfunk*. Retrieved from www.deutschland funkkultur.de/wie-etablierte-parteien-reagieren-der-einfluss-der-afd-auf.976. de.html?dram:article_id=351696

Manow, P. (2015). *Mixed rules, mixed strategies: Candidates and parties in Germany's electoral system*. Colchester: ECPR Press.

Matland, R. E., and Studlar, D. T. (1996). The contagion of women candidates in single-member district and proportional representation electoral systems: Canada and Norway. *The Journal of Politics* 58 (3), pp. 707–733. doi:10.2307/2960439

Morlok, M. (2015). The legal framework of party in Germany. In de Petris, A. and Poguntke, T. (Eds.), *Anti-party parties in Germany and Italy. Protest movements and parliamentary democracy*. Rome: LUISS University Press, pp. 113–124.

Niedermayer, O. (2016). *Parteimitglieder in Deutschland. Version 2016* (Arbeitshefte aus dem Otto-Stammer-Zentrum, Nr. 26). Freie Universität Berlin, Berlin.

Niedermayer, O., and Koschmieder, C. (2015). The election campaigns of German anti-party parties. Pirates, free voters and the alternative for Germany. In de Petris, A. and Poguntke, T. (Eds.), *Anti-party parties in Germany and Italy. Protest movements and parliamentary democracy*. Rome: LUISS University Press, pp. 149–162.

Poguntke, T. (2015). The German Party system after the 2013 election: An Island of stability in a European sea of change? In de Petris, A. and Poguntke, T. (Eds.), *Anti-party parties in Germany and Italy. Protest movements and parliamentary democracy*. Rome: LUISS University Press, pp. 235–253.

Rahat, G. (2013). What is democratic candidate selection? In Cross, W. P. and Katz, R. S. (Eds.), *The challenges of intra-party democracy.* Oxford: Oxford University Press, pp. 136–149.

Reiser, M. (2011). Wer entscheidet unter welchen Bedingungen über die Nominierung von Kandidaten? Die innerparteilichen Selektionsprozesse zur Aufstellung in den Wahlkreisen. In Niedermayer, O. (Ed.), *Die Parteien nach der Bundestagswahl 2009.* Wiesbaden: VS Verlag für Sozialwissenschaften, pp. 237–259.

Reiser, M. (2014). The universe of group representation in Germany: Analysing formal and informal party rules and quotas in the process of candidate selection. *International Political Science Review* 35 (1), pp. 56–66. doi:10.1177/0192512113507732

Reiser, M. (2018). *Innerparteilicher Wettbewerb bei der Kandidatenaufstellung: Ausmaß – Organisation – Selektionskriterien.* Wiesbaden: Springer VS.

Saarländischer Rundfunk. (2017, June 1). *AfD-Landesliste ist ungültig.* Retrieved from www.sr.de/sr/home/nachrichten/politik_wirtschaft/afd_saarland_muss_landesliste_neu_aufstellen100.html

Scarrow, S. E. (2005). *Political parties and democracy in theoretical and practical perspectives. Implementing intra-party democracy.* Washington, DC: National Democratic Institute for International Affairs.

Scarrow, S. E., Webb, P., and Farrell, D. M. (2000). From social integration to electoral contestation: The changing distribution of power within political parties. In Dalton, R. J. and Wattenberg, M. P. (Eds.), *Parties without Partisans. Political change in advanced industrial democracies.* Oxford: Oxford University Press, pp. 129–153.

Schmitt-Beck, R. (2017). The 'Alternative für Deutschland' in the Electorate? Between single-issue and right-wing populist party. *German Politics* 26 (1), pp. 124–148. doi:10 .1080/09644008.2016.1184650

Schroeder. W., Weßels, B., Berzel, A., and Neusser, C. (2017). Parlamentarische Praxis der AfD in deutschen Landesparlamenten. WZB Discussion Paper SP V 2017-102.

Schüttemeyer, S. S., and Sturm, R. (2005). Der Kandidat – das (fast) unbekannte Wesen: Befunde und Überlegungen zur Aufstellung der Bewerber zum Deutschen Bundestag. *Zeitschrift für Parlamentsfragen* 36 (3), pp. 539–553.

Seils, C. (2017, April 24). Die Selbstzerstörungspartei. *Cicero.* Retrieved from https://cicero.de/innenpolitik/afd-die-selbstzerstoerungspartei

Spies, D. C., and Kaiser, A. (2014). Does the mode of candidate selection affect the representativeness of parties? *Party Politics* 20 (4), pp. 576–590. doi:10.1177/1354068811436066

Stuttgarter Zeitung. (2016, November 16). *AfD schließt Presse aus – Meuthen gefällt das nicht.* Retrieved from www.stuttgarter-zeitung.de/inhalt.landesparteitag-afd-schliesst-presse-aus-meuthen-gefaellt-das-nicht.d25830cb-da59–41f5-bb29–426d81260dc2.html

van Biezen, I., Mair, P., and Poguntke, T. (2012). Going, going, . . . gone?: The decline of party membership in contemporary Europe. *European Journal of Political Research* 51 (1), pp. 24–56. doi:10.1111/j.1475-6765.2011.01995.x

Verge, T., and Kenny, M. (2013). *Contagion theory revisited: When do political parties compete on women's representation?* EPSA 2013 Annual General Conference Paper 309. https://ssrn.com/abstract=2224780

Von dem Berge, B., Poguntke, T., Obert, P., and Tipei, D. (2013). *Measuring intra-party democracy: A guide for the content analysis of party statutes with examples from Hungary, Slovakia and Romania.* Heidelberg and New York: Springer.

WELT. (2017, January 13). *AfD schließt Medien nach Belieben aus.* Retrieved from www.welt.de/politik/deutschland/article161154671/AfD-schliesst-Medien-nach-Belieben-aus.html

7 New actors, old practices?

Candidate selection and recruitment patterns in Greece

Manina Kakepaki

Introduction

When the 13th Parliamentary Term of the *Hellenic Parliament* ended in April 11th 2012, the Radical Left party of SYRIZA (Coalition of the Radical Left – Συνασπισμός της Ριζοσπαστικής Αριστεράς) had 13 seats, out of 300, and 4.59 percent of the vote. Less than three years later, on the 25th of January 2015, in a party system and a society deeply fragmented and affected by the economic crisis and the bailout agreements between successive Greek governments and the *'Troika'* lenders (IMF, EC and ECB) the 16th Parliamentary Term began. This time SYRIZA gained 36.34 percent of the vote and 149 seats in Parliament and became the main partner in a coalition Government with the emerging anti-memorandum right-wing party, ANEL (Independent Greeks – Ανεξάρτητοι Έλληνες). A few months later, in September 2015, when snap elections were called, SYRIZA and ANEL became once again partners in a coalition government, with minor changes in their electoral and parliamentary representation (Table 7.1).

Ever since the eruption of the economic crisis, the reshaping of the Greek party system and changing voting patterns have been at the centre of academic attention (Voulgaris and Nikolakopoulos, 2014; Teperoglou and Tsatsanis, 2016; Tsirbas, 2016), especially the rise of SYRIZA from a minor party of the left to a governing party (Mudde, 2017; Tsakatika, 2016); the electoral collapse of social-democratic PASOK or the rise of CHRYSI AVGI (Golden Dawn – Χρυσή Αυγή) a neo-Nazi party that after being in electoral oblivion for decades, entered Parliament in 2012, becoming the third largest party at the beginning of the 17th Parliamentary term (Ellinas, 2015).

However there is no study yet about the possible transformations that these changes imply for the patterns of candidate selection and election and the changing socio-demographic composition of MPs. The year 2012 was the starting point not only for a new party system, but also for a new political class. Nearly half of all MPs after the double 2012 elections were newcomers, an unusually high percentage in Greece, where as a rule legislative turnover ranges from 25 to 30 percent (Kakepaki 23:2016).

The aim of this chapter is to offer the first account of how candidate selection mechanisms work and to detect how (and if) these mechanisms have changed

Table 7.1 Distribution of seats in the Greek parliament, 2009–2015 (N except for first time MPs)

Party	13th Term Oct 2009	14th Term May 2012	15th Term June 2012	16th Term Jan 2015	17th Term Sep 2015
Method of Appointment*	Open lists	Open lists	Closed lists	Open lists	Closed lists
SYRIZA	13	52	71	149	145
ND	91	108	129	76	75
Golden Dawn	0	21	18	17	18
PASOK/DIM. SIM.**	160	41	33	13	17
DIM.AR*		19	17		
K.K.E.	21	26	12	15	15
The River				17	11
AN.EL.		33	20	13	10
Union of Centrists	0	0	0	0	9
LAOS	15	0	0	0	0
First time MPs (%)	25	49	12	40	21
Total MPs (N)	**300**	**300**	**300**	**300**	**300**

Source: www.hellenicparliament.gr/

Notes: This is the initial composition of the parliamentary groups. Gray cells indicate that the party did not run in these elections/had not been formed. *Refers to the final stage of the candidate selection process. **In September 2015, Pasok and Dimar appeared in the elections as a coalition under the name Dimokratiki Simparataxi (Democratic Alliance – Δημοκρατική Συμπαράταξη).

in the post 'crisis' period, in order to test two assumptions: first, that new and old political actors are adopting more innovative and participatory modes of candidate selection. Second, to assess whether new (or not so new) methods and practices result in differences in the descriptive representation of parliamentary representatives. In particular the goal is to: a) describe to what extent new political actors emerging after the political crisis are implementing Internal Party Democracy (IDP); b) detect if and how traditionally mainstream parties are responding to trends of internal democratization; and c) study the implications of these changes (or their absence) to descriptive representation in Greece.

Before we proceed, we will provide a brief overview of the electoral system on the issue of 'who selects the candidates'. The Greek system is multi-stage: in the first stage, candidates are selected in long lists, by more inclusive or exclusive electorates. The second stage is the actual voting system through personal preference by all voters. Candidate names are placed in alphabetic order on the ballot paper, and voters select the preferred candidates from their party of choice by marking the symbol of a cross next to the candidate's name.

The Greek Parliament (*Vouli ton Hellinon*) has 300 seats, 250 of them allocated proportionally between all parties that have passed a 3 percent threshold and the remaining 50 given to the party with the highest number of votes.[1] 288 of the 300

MPs are elected in 56 constituencies that vary considerably in size, from eight single-member constituencies to the largest constituency around Athens which elects 44 MPs (Athens B'). The remaining 12 MPs are elected from closed lists in one nationwide constituency, the 'State' Constituency (*Epikrateias*) which is usually reserved for senior party figures or individuals of wider appeal with a symbolic value.

The open list system was introduced in its present form in the 1926 general elections and was abandoned only once in 1985 in favour of a closed list. It is interlinked with the origins of the Greek party system, characterized by strong personal and clientelistic traits, where candidates resembled 'independent political entrepreneurs' (Cotta and Verzichelli, 2007, 428) that mobilized voters through personal networks and operated as political patrons. Through time, organized parties stepped in as intermediaries, (Lyrintzis, 1984; Pappas and Asimakopoulou, 2012). However, the process has never been really contested. Closed lists are used only when snap elections are called within eighteen months of previous general elections. An unwritten code of ethics applies. The ordering of the candidates in the closed lists must follow the ranking order of the previous elections under an open list system, so as to respect the will of the voters. Only in unrealistic positions are changes made, usually with the consent of the candidate. The justification for the use of closed lists when the period of eighteen months has not elapsed relates to the heavy cost of the campaign, since candidates are expected to run personal campaigns in order to attract personal votes and be elected.

Theoretical background

The global economic crisis had deep political implications and posed serious challenges to representation. On the one hand, new social movements to emerge after 2008 demanded more direct ways of political participation whilst on the other hand new actors that became politically relevant promoted internal party democracy as their inherent characteristic. If democratization of party life is the remedy to the declining levels of trust and participation witnessed all over Europe (Cross and Katz, 2013), we must clearly define which aspects of democratization are deemed most relevant. We adopt the typology suggested by Hazan and Rahat (2010) in order to measure intra-party democracy in the candidate-selection process, by focusing on the dimensions of a) who selects, b) at what level and c) how representative is the outcome of selection. On the issue of 'who selects' the candidates, the process can be more or less inclusive. A totally exclusive process is one when a single person (usually the party leader) selects all candidates, whilst, at the other extreme, the process is totally inclusive when all voters choose their candidates. In between positions include selectorates by party members, party delegates or party elites. Following that, we adopt the view that "[d]emocratization of the candidate-selection process is expressed as a widening of participation in the process; that is, when the selectorate following a reform of the candidate-selection method is more inclusive than previously" (Hazan and Rahat, 2010, 54). The centralization/decentralization pole refers to the level where selection takes place. A procedure is more centralized if a national party agency or the party leader makes the selection and more decentralized if local or regional selectorates select candidates. Finally, on the issue of representation, we are interested not only in the representation as presence but also in the representation of ideas.

Hypothesis, data and methods

In order to describe the candidate-selection methods used by the main political actors after 2012, we focus on SYRIZA and Nea Demokratia (ND) the parties that have formed the two leading poles in 'a still fluid party system' (Tsirbas, 2015). Although several new political actors emerged after the political crisis in Greece, SYRIZA had the most significant electoral gains. Most 'new' parties emerging after 2012 had a rather short-term success as evident from their declining electoral appeal (ANEL), weakening parliamentary cohesion (To Potami),[2] electoral vanishing (DIMAR) or lack of consolidation (Enosi Kentroon). Only Chrysi Avgi remains a case of a 'new' actor with an electoral appeal that still holds; however, the party's candidate-selection methods are totally leader-oriented with a very strict hierarchical structure and militia-like branches. It is the only party without any published document regarding its party organization structure or a party Statute available online, therefore totally lacking in transparency as an index of IPD (Rahat and Shapira, 2017).

The 'old' actors of the Greek party system that have suffered minor or major electoral loses are ND, PASOK and KKE. We focus on ND as the only mainstream party of the old bipartyism that despite its electoral losses is still the main challenger for office and has a substantial numerical representation in Parliament. PASOK had until January 2015 the lowest turnover of the three, proving elite circulation theories which claim that when a party suffers from a major electoral loss, most experienced MPs are and the ones less likely to lose their seats (Kakepaki, 2015, 178–179). As for KKE, its candidate selection methods and overall party strategy remain largely constant and unaffected by the reshaping of the Greek party system (Eleftheriou, 2014).

Therefore the SYRIZA and ND relevance is twofold: on the one hand their size, with a combined share of vote in the September 2015 elections of 63.3 percent and share of seats in the 17th Parliamentary Term of 76 percent, makes them the dominant political actors. On the other hand, it makes it easier to distinguish more clearly between two different cases and therefore tests the main goals of this chapter. ND represents a traditional party and SYRIZA a party that has recently became a mainstream party. By focusing on the two we can check if new parties are more open in selecting their candidates than traditional parties and the "contagion" effect from new to traditional parties.

Therefore, after having established our case for putting emphasis on SYRIZA and ND we proceed to the main hypotheses that we aim to test:

Hypothesis 1: Syriza as a 'new' political actor is implementing more inclusive ways of candidate selection by adopting elements of Internal Party Democracy (IPD).

Hypothesis 2: ND is a traditional party implementing more inclusive ways of candidate selection as a response to the trend for IPD.
Hypothesis 3: New ways of candidate selection result in a more diverse profile of the new MPs.

In order to check our hypotheses we will use data from multiple sources, employing a multi-method analysis. Since candidate-selection methods are largely based on 'unwritten' rules from party elites that are less easy to detect and analyze, our approach went beyond a typical analysis of party documents, although party statutes were collected in order to detect the degree of centralization, exclusiveness and representation allocated to candidate selection. Semi-structured interviews were used with select MPs elected in the September 2015 Parliament and party cadres from SYRIZA and ND, in an attempt to further elaborate on the candidate selection methods adopted by these two parties after 2012 (for the selection process, see Appendix). Our findings are topped with data on the socio-demographic profile of MPs collected under the research project So.Da.Map.[3]

For the time period covered in this chapter, closed party lists were used in June 2012 elections (following the May 2012 elections and candidates' ranking order) and in September 2015 elections (following the January 2015 elections and candidates' ranking order). As a result, the June 2012 and September 2015 candidate lists – and elected MPs – largely reflect the selection process adopted in the elections preceding them, since very limited changes were introduced in the lists. We focus on the candidate-selection process employed by SYRIZA and ND before the May 2012 and January 2015 elections with the exception of September 2015 for SYRIZA. In that case, the party split and the formation of LAE (Popular Unity – Λαϊκή Ενότητα) from 25 former SYRIZA MPs meant that some previously successful candidates were no longer in the SYRIZA ballot, resulting in empty slots and a 'reshuffling' of the ballot's ranking order.

Results

The case of SYRIZA: top-down approach fit for minor actors?

Technically SYRIZA is not a 'new' party *per se*, for it has appeared in national elections since 1993, under different forms and names. However almost all (94 percent) of its current MPs first entered Parliament after 2012, making this a case of an 'old' party with a brand new political class (Table 7.2). Under the name SYRIZA it contested national elections for the first time in 2004. Being a minor party of the Radical Left until 2012, its parliamentary representation ranged from 10 seats for its predecessor SYNASPISMOS in 1996, to 14 seats, the highest number achieved prior to its electoral rise in 2012, in 2007.

Article 13§3 of SYRIZA's statute in effect until 2012 describes the candidate-selection method employed by the party: "The selection of candidatures is decided by the Prefectural Committees or through primaries at the Prefectural level [. . .]. The Central Political Committee holds the right to amend these choices with an

Table 7.2 Composition of the 17th Parliamentary Term (September 2015) by party and first election of MPs

	Total MPs (N)	MPs elected before 2012 (%)	MPs elected after 2012 (%)
SYRIZA	145	6.2	93.8
ND	75	52.0	48.0
Golden Dawn	18	0.0	100.0
Democratic Alliance (PASOK/DIMAR)	17	64.7	35.3
KKE	15	46.7	53.3
The River	11	18.2	81.8
ANEL	10	40.0	60.0
Union of Centrists	9	0.0	100.0
ALL	300	24.0	76.0

Source: Data from the project So.Da.Map (own calculations)

elevated majority of 60 percent, after deliberation with the Prefectural Committees" (SYRIZA, 2005, 13).

In detail the process was the following: local members' groups proposed a list of candidates to the Prefectural Committee (Nomarchiaki Epitropi) of their electoral district. Prefectural Committees (PC) are party organs at the intermediate level, one in each electoral district (with the exception of the large electoral districts in Athens, where more PC operate). Prefectural Committees then deliberated and decided on the final list which was sent to the central party organ, the Central Committee (Kentriki Epitropi) for approval by vote. All accounts agree on the deliberative nature of the process and the call for consensus throughout all stages of candidate selection. Very rarely (if ever) were the PC's proposals contested by the central organs. The use of primaries was a provision on paper that was never actually activated whilst the vote approval by the Central Committee had also a procedural character.

On the issue of representation, besides the legal obligation for gender quotas in candidates' lists,[4] representation of ideas was taken most into account, since SYRIZA, as opposed to ND, has been a party with different ideological streams and tendencies officially recognized and represented in the party's organs.[5] Territorial representation was not considered of upmost importance. Sometimes in smaller constituencies local party cadres welcomed assistance from central party elites, with the inclusion in party lists of more prominent party members from the central party organs: "many constituencies accepted or even asked for a party cadre from central office [. . .] let's give to the contest a more 'political' meaning. This was often their demand: 'give us a hand". (Interview 7).

Incumbency was not really an issue until 2012. SYRIZA elected a handful of MPs mostly in the urban centres. Therefore, although the party presented candidates and contested elections in all 56 electoral districts, up to May 2012 past results and electoral projections made the candidates in the majority of the constituencies where SYRIZA had never gained seats 'unrealistic' or 'symbolic'. "Our viewpoint, until 2012 was for the party to plead for candidates. We would say 'please come', not everyone was willing to participate. That enabled the party to coordinate centrally things, so instead of pressing X member, let's press Y. Because Y is young and she is a woman. And I have such a planning that I'd rather select her. Their role is symbolic anyway. And that made it easier for X to agree to step down. Nothing was at stake". (Interview 7)

Therefore, the process before SYRIZA became a mainstream actor was closer to the inclusive and decentralized pole. The electoral success of SYRIZA in May 2012 raised the issue of whether the process ought to become more centralized and exclusive. The May elections produced a hung Parliament, and new elections were called for June under a closed party list system. That list, if it was to follow the ranking order of the May 2012 results, was set to produce the biggest until then number of SYRIZA MPs.

> "In June 2012 we had the same ballot [. . .] knowing that the 52 [MPs] elected in May, even in the worst case scenario would rise to 70–75 [. . .] there was an idea to make use of our right [to change the ranking order in order to introduce other candidates and secure their election]. But we have a democratic culture [. . .] ok this may be within our authority, but this is too much a political burden to lift in such a case"
>
> (Interview 7).

As a result, the June 2012 Parliamentary group of SYRIZA was a product of the previous candidate-selection process, meaning that realistic positions were acquired under a system mostly designed and used for unrealistic and symbolic positions. In January 2015, when it was clear that SYRIZA was about to become the government, the process became more centrally organized, though on paper, with a new Statute in effect (Syriza, 2013, 43) it remained almost identical. The only change was the creation of a special body (Special Electoral Committee) under the aegis of the Central Committee "whose composition reflected the power balance and tendencies of SYRIZA at the time" (Interview 7). This committee instructed all Prefectural Committees to follow the procedure described above, with the exception that this time they were asked to provide a long list of candidates exceeding the available slots in the ballot, thus allowing for political manoeuvring. The SEC decided on the short list and sent it back to the PC for approval.

Since offers to participate in the ballot were abundant, the role of the SEC was rather to monitor what was already in full supply. Incumbency became a central criterion (all elected MPs from 2012 were included in the ballots) whilst a 'good' personal record of preferential votes defined candidates as electable and in most cases ensured their place in the ballot. SYRIZA had also decided on a policy of cooperation with other political forces opposing the memorandum, so that was to be reflected in the ballots

In September 2015, the political events of the preceding months (Referendum in July 2015, third Memorandum of Understanding voted by the Greek Parliament, party split in SYRIZA from MPs opposing the MoU) leave SYRIZA with a deep ideological and political trauma. Candidate selection follows the January 2015 process, with one major difference: because of the snap elections, closed party lists are used. That makes candidate selection easier to coordinate centrally and therefore the process becomes even more exclusive and centralized. The Special Electoral Committee's target is to produce lists that will secure a more cohesive parliamentary group, less prone to differentiate from the central party line. As a rule the list follows the ranking order of the previous (January) elections, so incumbents that did not leave the party are re-elected. The seats previously occupied by MPs that left SYRIZA are filled either with extra-parliamentary Ministers of the January government (10 out of the 42 new MPs) or with those down the list trusted to be loyal to the party.

"Things happened until September 2015 [. . .] it's not that we, ingrained with a democratic culture became suddenly undemocratic [. . .]. We were overthrown, some blackmailed us 'I am not going to vote' [the MoU]. They ruined the picture and in this war we need soldiers, people willing to give the battle. So we are allowed to put X in the corner"

(Interview 7).

These three partially different selection processes have an effect in the descriptive representation of newcomers (Table 7.3). SYRIZA MPs elected for the first time in September 2015 are much less representative in terms of gender, with 11.6 percent being female as opposed to 25.6 percent in January 2015 and 43.1 percent in the dual 2012 elections. They have more ties with their constituency of election (76.5 percent in 2015J and 73.0 percent in 2015S are 'native sons and daughters' compared to 66.1 percent in 2012). Their mean age at the time of

Table 7.3 Socio-demographic profile of SYRIZA's new MPs

	May / June 2012 (N =65)	*January 2015 (N = 82)*	*September 2015 (N = 42)*
Female (%)	43.1	25.6	11.6
Local Government Post (%)	33.8	37.8	26.2
Born in Constituency of Election (%)	66.1	76.5	73.0
Mean Age (years)	52	50	57
Lawyers (%)	3.1	8.5	16.3
University education (%)	78.5	78.0	85.7
New technocrats (Economists, University professors) (%)	13.8	10.1	23.8
Farmers/unskilled workers (%)	7.2	0.0	2.3

Source: Data from the project So.Da.Map (own calculations).

election is 57 years in 2015S, compared to 50 in 2015J and 52 in 2012 thus making them an older cohort. In 2015S 16.3 percent are lawyers, which is the most traditional political profession in Greece compared to only 3.1 percent in 2012. New technocratic professions (university professors and economists) are predominant in September 2015 (23.8 percent), with a much more modest appearance in the previous cohorts, whilst 85 percent have a university degree, compared to 78 percent of the previous cohorts. The data reveal that gradually SYRIZA MPs become more representative of the parliamentary elite: male, with more traditional political professions, ties with the community and more middle class. When candidate selection was designed for symbolic seats (as was the case in 2012), representation was more diverse in gender and sectorial terms but less so in territorial terms. When candidate selection targeted realistic seats in January 2015, representation correction mechanisms came forward and promoted candidates with a more traditional profile. This trend is even more pronounced in September 2015: closed lists combined with the need to secure a more cohesive parliamentary group promoted older males with governing skills and a clear technocratic profile.

From the preceding analysis, our Hypothesis 1, that Syriza as a 'new' political actor is implementing more inclusive ways of candidate selection by adopting elements of Internal Party Democracy (IPD) is mostly verified. However since the party's candidate-selection mechanisms are not 'new' but follow the party's tradition, these elements do not imply the use of new technologies. Before 2015 the selection process was closer to the decentralized and inclusive pole, with a small degree of competition between candidates, since personal campaigning was outside the culture and values of the party's candidates and most seats were unrealistic. Regional party elites (the Prefectural Committees) were in charge of the candidate selection method, with the national party elites (Central Committee) having a rather supervisory and typical role in the process. Also it was rather inclusive since ordinary party members belonging to the local members' group were given a say in the process by proposing candidate names that were discussed at the regional level. After 2015, the process becomes more centralized and exclusive, though it still retains some of its previous characteristics. Territorial representation becomes more important once chances of constituents having one of their own MPs in Parliament are realistic. Intra-party competition between candidates appears (though on paper prohibited by the party's code of ethics) and is experienced by old party cadres as an uncomfortable side-effect of the party's electoral appeal. Our Hypothesis 3 that SYRIZA's more inclusive and democratic methods will result in a more socially diverse and representative of society mix of candidates is again mostly verified. The 2012 cohort is more socially diverse and representative of society especially in terms of gender, age and occupation. In September 2015 the Hazan and Rahat (2010) argument, that a party's attempt to ensure party-centred representation can bias representation as presence is confirmed.

The case of Nea Demokratia: A ballot designed to maximize success

Nea Demokratia (ND) is the only party of the Third Hellenic Republic with a continuous parliamentary presence under the same name. The right-wing conservative party founded by Konstantinos Karamanlis in 1974 has always served either as the party in Office or as the party in Opposition. ND is a party that runs elections in order to win, although undoubtedly electoral projections made that wish more or less realistic at time. Its ballots were always designed on the premise of vote maximization, rendering the majority of seats either realistic (candidates with high probability to become MPs) or pragmatic (candidates with low probability that strive for a good personal voting number as a future investment or with the aim of securing a place in the state apparatus). For the time period discussed in this chapter, ND experienced first a rise in its share of seats in parliament, from 91 in 2009 to 129 after the June 2012 elections, followed by a decline to 76 seats after the January 2015 elections. ND, at the beginning of the crisis, as opposed to SYRIZA, had an already established parliamentary group, with incumbents having to face fierce intra-party competition in order not to lose their seats. Incumbency is therefore one of the key features in candidate selection.

> "The leading figures of each constituency, that's what counts. Even for who else is going to participate [in the ballot] [. . .] now think about it: in the last few years, we had election after election; governmental changes; in a constituency that ND previously had 3 seats it has now one. So you can understand the battle for who's gonna be that 'one'"
>
> (interview 2)

ND's statute in effect until 2016, stated a dual procedure in article 19 (ND, 2013, 29–31): on the one hand local party branches made their suggestions to the party's Executive Committee; on the other hand individual aspirants could make an application to the central party branch. These two pools of candidates were added to a long list; in that list serving MPs were included ex officio. The party leader made the final selection and decided on the party list. By all accounts, this procedure remained more on paper. In reality the party leader and a close circle of trusted party executives were in charge of the process. Therefore, this was a rather centralized and exclusive procedure which, because of its central character, secured aspects of representation that were of importance to the party.

All interviewees agreed that territorial and local dimensions were of importance since a vote maximization strategy meant that specific regional or local subgroups within an electoral district ought to be represented: "The locals must find someone in the ballot they can identify with, common heritage matters as a form of expression of certain social groups. If you have a constituency with a large population of Pontians, or Vlachs,[6] you must present to these people someone who shares their customs and characteristics" (interview 6).

Another dimension taken into account for selection in the ballot in smaller constituencies were ties with the community either through experience in Local Government or through an occupation that enables personal communication with the voters (lawyers, doctors) and may result in personal favours: "[In order to get re-elected] it doesn't matter how many good things you did for your constituency; but how many people you helped, personally" (Interview 5).

The ballot paper is tailored differently in order to fit the needs of the voters in different size constituencies. In large constituencies, what is stated to be of prime importance is media access and good use of it by prospective candidates. As a general rule, and as opposed to SYRIZA in the past, ND does not have a pool of local party members that view participation in the ballot as part of their partisan duty. The prospect (or not) of electoral success is of key importance for offers. "Availability was always linked to forecasts related to the party's share of the vote. When it appears that we are going to lose, there is not much interest" (interview 6).

This lack of interest can be explained by the low turnover rate whenever the party loses seats in Parliament. ND is a party with very low levels of parliamentary elite circulation (Table 7.4). Incumbents are the ones most likely to get reelected whilst this inertia is reversed only whenever the party increases significantly its share of seats, and whenever there is a change in leadership.

This 'new leader' effect, although hard to access empirically seems to be a key factor in the candidate-selection processes. In ND the election of its leader, after the stepping down of its founder Konstantinos Karamanlis in 1980 due to him becoming President of the Republic, has always been an open, competitive process; since the focus of this chapter is on candidate selection and not on leadership elections, we will not analyze this dimension, but instead come to the tentative conclusion that for ND changes in candidate representation are not so much related to the 'contagion' effect of the most inclusive and decentralized approaches adopted by SYRIZA, but come as a reaction to intra-party demands to 'refresh' the party image in conjunction with a leadership change. Most accounts on the organization structure of ND agree on the leader-oriented

Table 7.4 Turnover in ND, 1996–2015

Election Year	Share of Seats	Parliamentary Turnover (in %)	Difference in share of seats from previous Parliament (in %)	Runs elections under new leader
1996	108	23	−3	Yes (Miltiades Evert)
2000	125	33	16	Yes (Kostas Karamanlis)
2004	165	32	32	No
2007	152	19	−4	No
2009	91	13	−40	No
2012 May	108	34	19	Yes (Antonis Samaras)
2012 June *	129	12	19	No
2015 Jan	76	16	−41	No
2015 Sep*	75	2	1	Yes (Vangelis Meimarakis)

Source: Data from the project So.Da.Map (own calculations). Percentages are rounded.

Notes: * Elections with closed lists.

structure of the party (Alexakis, 2001) and the absence of intra-party demo-cratic procedures.

> "There is a leader-oriented dimension in the process, in line with the party's character. Because of the party's structure the role of the leader is elevated, regardless of whether other processes intervened [. . .] For as long as parties remain incapable of organizing democratically, the democratic legitimacy of their leader will extend as an outlet"
>
> (Interview 5).

For the period analyzed, we focus on elected MPs in the 2012 and January 2015 elections. This cohort entered Parliament under a new leader (Antonis Samaras). In September 2015, although the party ran the elections under another leader (Vangelis Meimarakis) the obligation to keep the ranking order of the previous ballot resulted in an almost identical parliamentary group to January 2015, with its share of seats also nearly the same.

> "[In September 2015] some changes were made voluntarily. Those that did not get any preference vote [in January 2015] in the large constituencies, in Athens B' for instance, the last ten candidates. They had only 100 personal votes, they knew that they did not stand a chance to get elected, so for a variety of reasons, even for the expenses [a non reimbursable deposit each candidate has to pay] they withdrew and were replaced with ten others".
>
> (Interview 2)

After a second electoral defeat in September 2015, intra-party elections for the selection of a new leader were held in January 2016. Newly elected Kyri-akos Mitsotakis, son of former Prime Minister Konstantinos Mitsotakis, set out to make changes to the candidate selection process. An amended Party Statute was voted in the 10th Party Conference in April 2016. Article 30 devotes only a few words to the process: "The President of the party compiles the ballots for National and European elections. For the selection of candidates he applies an evaluation system; creates a Candidates' Register and may ask the opinion of party members" (ND, 2016, p. 21). This process introduced what is seen by many in ND as a huge innovative measure: the opening of an online reg-istration system in which all interested individuals can upload their applica-tion without any intermediaries.[7] Those applying are called for an interview at the central party office by experienced party members, MPs and Human Resources experts. Then, a long list is comprised, including those that were selected through the interview process, serving MPs and other individuals. The final shortlist will be the product of deliberation between a closed party com-mittee and the leader. Since this process has not yet produced an electoral list and has not been tested in elections we cannot tell whether it will bring about changes in actual representation. Officially though the candidate-selection process becomes more exclusive and centralized with the cutting off of any in the middle selection stages:

> for the first time we give every citizen the opportunity to express their interest without intermediaries. In the past, they would come to the party's headquarters, search someone close to the president, go to the party's local branch in their district. With this registry you do not need anyone in between.
>
> (Interview 2)

Finally, in order to test Hypothesis 3, we present some basic socio-demographic variables of ND MPs elected in the 2012 and January 2015 elections (Table 7.5). We split them into two categories, those entering Parliament for the first time after 2012 ("the Crisis cohort") and all others. This distinction between a 'pre' and a 'post' crisis political class can only be applied in ND, since SYRIZA MPs are in numerical terms almost exclusively a 'post' crisis political class.

The "crisis" cohort shows clear signs of a less traditional parliamentary profile: 19.7 percent are women, compared to 11.9 percent of the older cohorts, have stronger ties with the constituency and come less from the traditional legal professions (19.4 percent compared to 31.2 percent of the previous cohort). Finally, they have less family networks (defined as another family member elected MP in previous Parliaments), although this is a dimension that still matters for the conservative party.

In sum, Hypotheses 2 and 3 are partly verified. ND remains a mainstream actor that up until 2015 did not change its candidate-selection practices, with IPD being at a low level. The process is quite centralized and exclusive, but younger cohorts appear to be more diverse in socio-demographic terms. These attributes may have less to do with different candidate-selection mechanisms (since these have not changed in the period under consideration) and more with other aspects of electioneering and an overall trend of more diversity in MPs as part of a modernization process (Cotta and Best, 2007). A tentative explanation that needs further research is that the widespread anger of the voters after the eruption of the crisis was partly experienced in ND as 'voting the rascals out' by giving a personal preference vote to new candidates, whilst still voting for the party. As one MP said, "we are the shock absorbers of the political system. We reap all success but also get blamed for every failure" (Interview 5).

Table 7.5 Socio-demographic profile of ND's MPs, 2012 and 2015 (in %)

	The "Crisis" Cohort (N=66)	All others (N=94)
Female	19.7	11.9
Local Government Post	56.1	40.4
Born in Constituency of Election	88.9	56.7
Lawyers	19.4	31.2
Family Networks	13.3	18.8

Source: Data from the project So.Da.Map (own calculations).

Conclusions

This chapter examined the ways 'new' political actors that emerged in the Greek party system after the 2012 earthquake elections select their candidates, and the extent to which their methods have affected more established parties. We argued that the reshaping of the Greek party system was not so much followed by the emergence of new actors, but rather by the strengthening of old ones (SYRIZA, Golden Dawn) which gained a new audience. Our analysis of SYRIZA's candidate-selection methods revealed that IPD was in the 'DNA' of the (old) party and did not come as a reaction to pressures generated by the political crisis and subsequent calls for more democracy. On the contrary, the crisis and the fact that SYRIZA became a new mainstream party, ready to govern, resulted in a more centrally coordinated process without the use of any innovative measures that could press traditional parties to mimic them. This is evident on the descriptive characteristics of SYRIZA MPs: after 2015 they resemble more those of an archetypical candidate: male, middle-aged, from politics-related professions and with ties to the community.

ND, as a traditional mainstream party did not have to respond to an IPD trend, since SYRIZA mechanisms were not perceived as innovative or successful, and therefore worthy of replicating. In that sense, we find no contagion effect between the two parties. ND's mechanisms remained closer to the centralized and exclusive pole, whilst electoral defeat and leadership change seem to be the basic drivers for change. An innovative measure was introduced under the current leadership (an online candidate's registration system) that so far has not produced an outcome and therefore cannot be adequately evaluated. In sum, SYRIZA and ND have candidate-selection methods that differed substantially at the beginning of the period under investigation, and then slightly converged once SYRIZA acquired more realistic chances to govern and the role of central party elites became crucial. On the other hand, the personalized character of the electoral system, through open lists and preference voting, means that the final outcome (the elected representatives) cannot be totally controlled with representation correction mechanisms since incumbency and territorial representation prevail at the expense of gender and sectorial representation.

Acknowledgements

Since all interviews were conducted on the condition of anonymity I wish to thank collectively all MPs and party cadres who were interviewed.

Notes

1 For a detailed description of the Greek electoral system, see www.ipu.org/parline-e/reports/2125_B.htm.
2 At the time of writing, six from the eleven MPs initially elected with the party *To Potami* in September 2015 were no longer in its parliamentary group. Two of them moved to other parties (one in ND and another in DIMOKRATIKI SYMPARATAXI) and the

remaining four became independent MPs. See: www.hellenicparliament.gr/Vouleftes/ Ana-Koinovouleftiki-Omada/. In November 2017, the leader of To Potami run as a candidate for the leadership of a new coalition that also included Dimokratiki Symparataxi. The new coalition, named Movement of Change (Κίνημα Αλλαγής) aims to group together all forces of the centre-left, thus indicating a tendency for the party to abandon its autonomous course.

3 Source of funding: General Secretariat of Research and Technology. Data for all MPs elected until January 2015 national elections are available at www.socioscope.gr/ deputies

4 Article 34 of Presidential Decree 26/2012 states that at least one-third of political parties' candidate lists, both for national and constituency lists must be filled with candidates of each sex. However, because candidates are selected from open lists, with no reserved seats, gender representation is Parliament is not guaranteed.

5 For the selection of the Central Committee, candidates representing various ideological streams run in different ballots, such as in the first SYRIZA conference in 2013 (see: https://leftgr.files.wordpress.com/2013/07/1cebf-cf83cf85cebdceadceb4cf81ceb9cebf-cf83cf85cf81ceb9ceb6ceb1_ceb5cebacebc-2.pdf)

6 Pontian Greeks (people descending from Pontos) and Vlachoi are ethnic groups to be found mostly in central and northern Greece.

7 The platform is in operation here: https://ananeosi.nd.gr/main/. The web address includes the word "ananeosi" that literally means renewal but the term is used also to describe legislative turnover.

References

Alexakis, E. (2001). *Η Ελληνική Δεξιά: Δομή και ιδεολογία της Νέας Δημοκρατίας 1974– 1993* [The Greek Right: Structure and ideology of New Democracy 1974–1993]. Athens: Sakkoulas.

Cotta, M., and Best, H. (Eds.). (2007). *Democratic representation in Europe. Diversity, change and convergence*. Oxford: Oxford University Press.

Cotta, M., and Verzichelli, L. (2007). Paths of institutional development and elite transformation. In Cotta, M. and Best, H. (Eds.), *Democratic representation in Europe. Diversity, change and convergence*. Oxford: Oxford University Press, pp. 417–173.

Cross, W. P., and Katz, R. S. (2013). *The challenges of intra-party democracy*. Oxford: Oxford University Press.

Eleftheriou, K. (2014). Ρωγμές στον Μονόλιθο. Το ΚΚΕ στις εκλογές του 2012 [Cracks in the monolith. KKE in the 2012 elections]. In Voulgaris, Y. and Nikolakopoulos, I. (Eds.), *2012 The double earthquake elections*. Athens: Themelio, pp. 151–184.

Ellinas, A. (2015). Neo-Nazism in an established democracy: The persistence of Golden Dawn in Greece. *South European Society and Politics* 20 (1). http://dx.doi.org/10.1080/ 13608746.2014.981379

Hazan, R. Y., and Rahat, G. (2010). *Democracy within parties: Candidate selection methods and their political consequences*. Oxford: Oxford University Press.

Kakepaki, M. (2015). Is there politics without professional politicians? [Υπάρχει πολιτική χωρίς επαγγελματίες πολιτικούς;]. In Demertzis, N. and Georgarakis, N. (Eds.),*The political portrait of Greece*. Athens: EKKE-Gutenberg, pp. 168–187.

Kakepaki, M. (Ed.). (2016). *Political representation in contemporary Greece: Characteristics and profile of Greek MPs 1996–2015* [Η πολιτική αντιπροσώπευση στη σύγχρονη Ελλάδα. Χαρακτηριστικά και φυσιογνωμία των μελών του Ελληνικού Κοινοβουλίου, 1996–2015]. Athens: EKKE – Papazissis.

Lyrintzis, C. (1984). Political parties in Post-Junta Greece: A case of 'Bureaucratic Clientelism'? *West European Politics* 7 (2), pp. 99–118.

Mudde, C. (2017). *SYRIZA. The failure of the populist promise*. London: Palgrave Macmillan.

Nea Demokratia. (2013). *Καταστατικό* [Statute] Retrieved from http://politike.al/wp-content/uploads/2016/03/Statuti-i-Nea-Demokracia-ne-Greqi.pdf

Nea Demokratia. (2016). *Καταστατικό* [Statute] Retrieved from https://nd.gr/katastatiko

Pappas, T., and Assimakopoulou, Z. (2012). Party patronage in Greece: Political entrepreneurship in a party patronage democracy. In Kopecký, P., Mair, P. and Spirova, M. (Eds.), *Party patronage and party government in European democracies*. Oxford: Oxford University Press. doi:10.1093/acprof:oso/9780199599370.003.0008

Putman, R. D. (1976). *The comparative study of political elites*. Englewood Cliffs, NJ: Prentice-Hall.

Rahat, G., and Shapira, A. (2017). An intra-party democracy index: Theory, design and a demonstration. *Parliamentary Affairs* 70, pp. 84–110.

SYNASPISMOS. (2005) *Καταστατικό* [Statute] Retrieved from www.syn.gr/downloads/syn_katastatiko.pdf

SYRIZA. (2013). *Καταστατικό* [Statute] Retrieved from www.syriza.gr/page/katastatiko.html#.WUzzC-vyiUk

Teperoglou, E., and Tsatsanis, E. (2016). Realignment under stress: The July 2015 referendum and the September parliamentary election in Greece. South *European Society and Politics* 21 (4). doi:10.1080/13608746.2016.1208906

Tsakatika, M. (2016). SYRIZA's Electoral rise in Greece: Protest, trust and the art of political manipulation. *South European Society and Politics* 21 (4). doi:10.1080/13608746.2016.1239671

Tsirbas, Y. (2016). The January 2015 parliamentary election in Greece: Government change, partial punishment and hesitant stabilisation. *South European Society and Politics* 21 (4). doi:10.1080/13608746.2015.1088428

Voulgaris, Y., and Nikolakopoulos, I. (Eds.). (2014) *2012 Ο Διπλός Εκλογικός Σεισμός* [*2012 The Double Earthquake Elections*]. Athens: Themelio.

Appendix
Interviews

In order to engage with MPs and party officials a targeted approach was adopted. After an initial literature review and off-the-record discussions with party members and key informants, select party officials and MPs (former or current), with knowledge of and/or active roles in the candidate selection process were approached. Due to time restrictions, thirteen people were initially selected, six from SYRIZA and seven from ND. From SYRIZA five accepted and one did not respond, whilst from ND three accepted and five either declined or did not respond. In all cases, the aim of the interview was clearly stated, as well as the anonymity of the interview. From the three interviewees from ND two did not consent to a recording of the interview, therefore notes were kept. In all other cases, interviews were recorded, with the duration of the interviews ranging from 28 to 56 minutes. In one case, two SYRIZA party officials were interviewed together (interviews No 7 and 8). For the case of SYRIZA, the main reasons for refusal seemed to be lack of time due to various government-related obligations; for ND refusal was mostly related to hesitation to talk about a subject that they felt should not be discussed outside the party.

1 Interview with SYRIZA cadre (6.2.2017)
2 Interview with ND cadre (8.2.2017)
3 Interview with SYRIZA MP (16.2.2017)
4 Interview with SYRIZA MP (1.3.2017)
5 Interview with ND MP (1.3.2017)
6 Interview with ND cadre (7.3.2017)
7 Interview with SYRIZA cadre (9.3.2017)
8 Interview with SYRIZA cadre (9.3.2017)

8   Representation in crisis

The Icelandic case

Gunnar Helgi Kristinsson and
Eva H. Önnudóttir

Introduction

Dramatic system failure such as the global credit crunch that hit a great number of economies in 2008 is likely to be followed by loss of confidence in conventional methods of representation. Iceland was among the countries which were hit especially hard by the global credit crunch in 2008, triggering protests and political turmoil unprecedented in the history of modern democracy in Iceland (Önnudóttir et al., 2017; Önnudóttir, 2016). Political trust fell dramatically in 2008 and has recovered only to a limited extent, and far from reaching pre-2008 levels (Indriðason et al., 2017). The main pillars of the Icelandic party system include four established parties, the Left-Green Movement (LGM) (left-wing), the Social Democratic Alliance (SDA) (centre-left), the Progressive Party (PP) (centre-right) and the Independence Party (IP) (right-wing). In the last three elections (2009, 2013 and 2016), four new parties have entered parliament. The Civic Movement (CM – centre) received 7% of votes in 2009, but the party dissolved before the 2013 election. In 2013, two new parties were elected into parliament; Bright Future (BF – centre) with 8% of the vote and the Pirate Party (Pr – centre-left) with 5%. Both were re-elected in 2016, Bright Future with 7% and the Pirates with 15%. These three all had roots in the protest movement, and all of them are placed close to the centre on the left-right divide. In 2016, Reform (R), a new centre-right party, won the biggest share an insurgent party has received since 1987 with 11% of the vote. Reform does not have roots in the protest movement and advocates mainstream methods of political representation.

Voter confidence that their political interests are being taken care of, even as they devote their time to other matters, lies at the essence of representation (Pitkin, 1967). Loss of confidence can lead to a search for new solutions, but convincing alternatives to conventional methods of representation may not be easy to find. In general, the political forces which have emerged in response to the crisis have reacted by introducing reforms that have to do with increasing the opportunities for citizens to participate in political decisions and introducing greater intra-party democracy within political parties (Close et al., 2017). The number of new parties in Iceland gaining representation indicates that the Icelandic party system is in flux. Moreover, the economic crisis placed demands for democratic reforms on the agenda (Bernburg, 2016). However, party primaries have been used extensively to select candidates in Iceland since the early 1970s and therefore are hardly likely to be the main focus of the discussion about democratic reforms. Instead, a discussion about adopting some sort of preferential voting took place and demands were made for more direct democracy. Since the crisis, both the established parties and the new parties have used a mix of candidate selection methods. Thus, we can compare the impact of primaries on representation between the established and the new parties which have emerged since the crisis.

Furthermore, we test Hazan's and Rahat's (2010) claim that party primaries undermine party organizations by reducing participation, representativeness and responsiveness, and by weakening intra-party competitiveness in the post-crisis era in Iceland. Their main argument is that the primary agents of political representation in contemporary democracies, the political parties, need to be able to control their representatives to act coherently and in a responsible manner, and to open up the choice of party candidates to a broad group of voters may undermine the parties as representative institutions. However, there are numerous other ways a party can control their representatives, such as the impact of the party leadership on representative's career paths and whether they hold an office for the party or not (Kristinsson, 2011).

The political context in Iceland since 2008

The 2009 election was an early election held in the wake of the global credit crunch of 2008 that was followed by an economic and political crisis in Iceland (Önnudóttir et al., 2017). The government coalition of the Independence Party and the Social Democratic Alliance fell at the end of January amidst massive protests in the streets of Reykjavík, and an early election took place in April 2009. The combined losses of the Independence Party, widely blamed for the crash, and the Social Democratic Alliance in the 2009 election amounted to ten percentage points, but the Social Democrats improved their share of the votes. The left-wing government (SDA and LGM) won the election and the first purely left-wing majority in Icelandic political history took over. After a difficult four-year term, however, the 2009 left-wing coalition suffered a crushing defeat in the 2013 election. The combined vote of the two coalition parties fell from 52% four years earlier to 24%, amounting to the greatest electoral loss (of 28 percentage points) ever suffered by an Icelandic government (Indriðason et al., 2017). The two parties had risen to power on the shoulders of the protests in 2008–09, promising to introduce a Nordic welfare state model and equitable sharing of the burdens imposed by the financial crash of 2008. Iceland's success in dealing with the crisis won acclaim by international experts from Paul Krugman (2012) to Joseph Stiglitz (Bloomberg Markets magazine, 2011) and international organizations such as the IMF (2011) and OECD (2012).

In October 2016, the right-wing coalition of the Progressive Party and Independence Party (which replaced the left-wing government in 2013) suffered a fate similar to its predecessor, although on a more modest scale. Amidst blooming economic recovery, the combined vote shares of the two coalition partners fell from 52% in 2013 to 41% in 2016. The chain of events which started with the financial meltdown in October 2008 has primarily become a crisis of confidence in the political system and its main actors. The combined vote shares of the four traditional actors (LGM, SDA, PP and IP) of the Icelandic party system fell from 90% in 2009 to 75% in 2013 and 62% in 2016.

Trust in parliament dropped from 42% in February 2008 to 13% in February 2009, and in 2017, it was 22%.[1] Bernburg's (2016) analysis of the political protests in 2008–09 describes how the financial crash led to quotidian disruption in Iceland, meaning that the public's taken for granted assumptions and expectations about their way of life were threatened by big and sudden events. He also describes how the protest evolved into a platform for a call for democratic reforms, challenging the authorities at the time; and the crisis was framed as one of credibility for the political system. Önnudóttir et al. (2017) argue that the 2009 election in Iceland was a critical election in the sense that sharp alternations of pre-existing voting patterns occurred, and they maintain that there are signs of realignment, with voters shifting their alliances from one party to another in the subsequent election in 2013. The credibility crisis of the established party system, increased volatility between elections, and a disruption in Icelanders' expectations about how the society works have provided fertile ground for new parties.

It can be argued that lower levels of trust have led to support for participatory innovations and more direct forms of democracy. Such demands were prominent in the debate on constitutional reform which was initiated by the establishment of the Constitutional Council in 2011. Party primaries, however, were never presented as a serious alternative. This may be attributed to the fact that the Icelandic experience indicates that party primaries are easily compatible with conventional party representation. The idea of overthrowing the power of party elites using party primaries therefore never carried much weight.

Representation and trust in government

We may design any number of tools to monitor representatives, but even the most conscientious application of the agency tools suggested by principal-agent theory will leave room for shirking (Davies et al., 1997; Miller, 2000). The case may, of course, be made that we might not want excessive trust in government, e.g. because the government is not trustworthy (Hardin, 1999). However, a government that does not enjoy the trust of its citizens is likely to be neither popular nor efficient. The chief task of constitutional design must be to make representation tenable and government trustworthy. Historically, as Hardin points out, the agencies making judgements on the trustworthiness of politicians were the political parties; however, party monopoly of the representative function typical of much of the 20th century has itself become a contested issue. Demands are increasingly being made for more direct forms of participation, including the right to choose individual representatives whether that be through party primaries or a more open ballot structure (such as a personalized or a preferential vote). Thus, we have seen not only increasing interest in personal representation (Colomer, 2011; Karvonen, 2009) but also in party primaries (Sandri et al., 2015) and other devices for personalizing politics.

The logic behind the claim that declining trust in government leads to demands for personal representation is fairly simple. If representation through conventional channels such as parties and representative government is considered weak, the principals, in this case voters, will have to become more active in taking care of their own interests. This leads to calls for more direct forms of democracy and more personal representation (Hetherington, 2005). The precise forms that demands for democratic innovations take may, however, vary. After all, the full menu for such innovations is quite extensive (Smith, 2009; Geissel and Newton, 2012). Historical contingencies may influence the way such innovations are presented as potential cures for the malaise of representation. If we accept that demands for greater personalization of politics reflect distrust of the political parties, the question is how the parties respond most efficiently. In this respect, it is important to keep in mind that parties choose electoral systems and are likely to fit them to their needs (Colomer, 2005; see also Ware, 2002).

In an influential contribution, Hazan and Rahat (2010) maintain that democratizing the nomination procedure may not be advantageous to the wider democratic system. Inclusive and decentralized nominations are likely to deinstitutionalize the party organizations, with negative consequences for participation, representativeness, intra-party competition and responsiveness. Data on party nominations in Iceland, where inclusive primaries have been practiced since the beginning of the 1970s, may be used to test some of Hazan's and Rahat's hypotheses. This has been done by Indridason and Kristinsson (2015) for the period 1971 to 2009, who found little support for the de-institutionalization thesis. We intend to look at the post-crash situation, covering the elections of 2009, 2013 and 2016. For this purpose, we use data from the Icelandic National Election Study (ICENES) including both candidates and voters, to reflect on the predictions we derive from Hazan's and Rahat's approach. Thus, we should expect those of the Icelandic parties practising nominations through primaries to suffer detrimental effects on participation in their membership organizations, produce less representative candidates, have smaller intra-party competition with greater incumbency effects and smaller responsiveness (through impaired ability to act in unison). This pattern should apply to both the established parties and new parties.

The development of party primaries in Iceland

While it is difficult to pinpoint specific features of the political system that may have contributed to the crash, different actors saw it as vindication of an incongruous conglomerate of criticisms and reform ideas. The "truth commission" (Special Investigative Commission, 2010) established to investigate the issue wrote an extensive report detailing the process that led to the crash but steered clear of a systematic interpretation concerning system failures. A separate commission established by the ministries interpreted the results as a call for a stronger public service while the third one – established by Althingi, the national parliament – maintained that parliament needed to be strengthened (Forsætisráðuneytið, 2010; Alþingi, 2010). The president emphasized the importance of the presidency in reviving trust in the political system while some of the political parties supported the demand for a constitutional assembly to revise the constitution. Among the demands for democratic innovations which the crash put on the agenda, were a greater measure of direct democracy and greater involvement of voters in selecting individual representatives at the election level.

Because all of the Icelandic parties had experimented to a greater or lesser extent with primaries since the beginning of the 1970s, the debate was more about introducing a personalized vote at the election level, e.g. preferential vote, and not about greater intra-party democracy regarding primaries. While the parties varied in the extent to which they embraced the primaries – the most enthusiastic being the Independence Party and the Social Democrats – they all experimented with such methods at some point (Indriðason and Kristinsson, 2015). The original impetus to the introduction of primaries in the 1970s had been growing scepticism about party control in different spheres of society and criticism of the power of closed party elites (Kristjánsson, 1994).

The primaries were never undisputed, and on the left, e.g. in the Left Green Movement or its predecessor, the party was still seen as an instrument of social change that could be undermined by the primaries. Such criticism seemed borne out by successive crises in the parties most willing to practice primary elections in the 1980s where they may have played a role in internal strife and splits. Two innovations at that time are likely to have balanced out such tendencies. In the first place, the introduction of a new electoral formula in the primaries reduced the incentives of individual politicians to cultivate a personal following. In the early primaries, the method of voting was that of limited voting where voters could cast a limited number of votes among chosen candidates without ranking them. This proved a highly unstable system and was replaced by rank-ordered plurality, which is a plurality formula and, strictly speaking, gives the electoral majority control over all seats (Indriðason and Kristinsson, 2015). Secondly, the parliamentary parties weakened the incentive to cultivate a personal following through more assertive party leadership in the parliament and the strategic distribution of positions such as the posts of ministers and committee chairs to enhance cohesion (Kristinsson, 2011). Parliamentarians who could not be relied on to act as team players were not likely to be nominated by the party leaders for positions of influence. This was another powerful incentive to comply with the party line rather than to win personal popularity points.

Against this background, nominations through party primaries were hardly likely to appeal, especially to sceptics of established methods of representation after the crisis. Adherents of preferential voting advocated the introduction of the single transferable vote instead that would have transferred the rank ordering of party lists from the nomination stage to the actual parliamentary election. The vote would still be a party vote as would the distribution of seats between lists based on proportionality, but voters would decide who, among the party candidates, would be selected. The introduction of such a rule in parliamentary elections was believed to enhance individual accountability among members of parliament to voters and weaken the control of party leaderships in parliament.

The first government bill on the introduction of preferential voting along these lines had already happened in July 2009 (Forsætisráðuneytið, 2009). The idea resurfaced at various times during the following years, including the work of the Constitutional Council, which was set up in 2011 to revise the constitution. The basic idea of preferential elections enjoyed considerable support among voters. In the consultative referendum on the output of the Constitutional Council in October 2012, 69% of voters declared support for the idea that 'preferential voting in parliamentary elections will be allowed to a greater extent than is presently the case' (Statistics Iceland, 2013).

Why preferential voting did not, in the end, replace the primaries remains open to interpretation. In the first place, there was no consensus among the political parties on the issue. The Independence Party was in many ways sceptical, preferring to maintain control over its own nomination processes. Scepticism was also considerable in the other parties, especially the Progressive Party and to some extent the Left-Green Movement. Enacting such a radical reform – with so little known about the likely effects – was considered risky among the political establishment. The link between preferential voting and other measures on the constitutional agenda did not help the issue either. The draft constitution written by the Constitutional Council met with considerable criticism from academics and legal experts and, in the end, failed to win approval in its current form. Finally, while the voters expressed broad approval of the basic concept of preferential voting, they are unlikely to have understood the issues involved very well or given the matter high priority.

Candidate selection after the crisis

Parties that have used primaries in recent elections use them to select the top candidates on their lists within each of the six constituencies in Iceland. Rules vary concerning the number of seats for which results in the primaries are binding, but usually, they influence primarily the first 5 to 10 out of 16 to 26 places on the list (the precise number varies depending on district magnitude).

Table 8.1 presents an overview of how candidates report that they were nominated within each party since 2009. The established parties have continued to use primaries to select their candidates in all three elections since 2009 except for the Progressive Party, which uses extended constituency party conferences to put lists together. The Independence Party and the Social Democratic Alliance tend to use more inclusive types of primaries although in recent elections the fully open primary is in retreat. The Left-Green Movement tends to use closed primaries confined to party members. The four new parties that have gained representation since 2009 have used a mix of selection methods. In 2009, Civic Movement selected its candidates in open meetings where an agreement was reached about the list positions of its candidates. Since the meetings were not confined to party

Table 8.1 How candidates were nominated on the party list, 2009, 2013 and 2016

	2009	*2013*	*2016*
Left-Green Movement			
Open primary	18.6	1.2	3.8
Partially-open or closed primary	30.5	26.7	15.0
Other, e.g. party delegate conference, selection committee or party leadership	50.8	72.1	81.3
Social Democratic Alliance			
Open primary	21.5	3.4	5.5
Partially-open or closed primary	13.9	50.6	17.8
Other, e.g. party delegate conference, selection committee or party leadership	64.6	46.1	76.7
Civic Movement**			
Open primary	100.0		
Partially-open or closed primary	.0		
Other, e.g. party delegate conference, selection committee or party leadership	.0		
Pirate Party			
Open primary		63.2	21.1
Partially-open or closed primary		17.6	70.4
Other, e.g. party delegate conference, selection committee or party leadership		19.1	8.5
Bright Future			
Open primary		.0	.0
Partially-open or closed primary		.0	5.7
Other, e.g. party delegate conference, selection committee or party leadership		100.0	94.3
Progressive Party			
Open primary	9.7	.0	.0
Partially-open or closed primary	22.2	11.9	10.3
Other, e.g. party delegate conference, selection committee or party leadership	68.1	88.1	89.7
Reform			
Open primary			2.7
Partially-open or closed primary			0.0
Other, e.g. party delegate conference, selection committee or party leadership			97.3
Independence Party			
Open primary	23.9	11.5	8.3
Partially-open or closed primary	26.9	28.7	28.3
Party delegate conference/selection committee	43.3	39.1	38.3

Source: *The Icelandic National Election Study, post-election candidate survey. In 2009 candidates were asked 'Who made the decision about your nomination?' and response categories were: In an open primary, in a closed primary, at a party delegate conference, by party leaders and other. In 2013 and 2016 candidates were asked 'Who was most influential in deciding on your candidacy nomination?" and response categories were: Open primary election, supporters of my party (primary election), party members in my constituency, party leadership in my constituency and national party leadership. **The responses from candidates of the Civic Movement were all recoded as selected in an open primary. The Civic Movement used the same method to select of their candidates or in open meetings with members/supporters of the party where all participants reached an agreement about the party lists.

members, they had the essential characteristics of open primaries. In 2013, the Pirate Party selected its candidates in open primaries where all voters could participate; but in 2016, the party shifted to closed primaries where participants had to be party members. The shift from open primaries to closed ones seems to reflect the development of a tighter organizational structure in 2016 compared to 2013. The two other new parties, Bright Future in 2013 and 2016, and Reform in 2016 used decentralized candidate selection committees to select candidates. In general, the smaller use of party primaries before the 2016 early election as compared to earlier elections (cf. Table 8.1) is likely to reflect the special circumstances in which the elections took place and lack of time for organizing proper primary elections.

Participation

One of Hazan's and Rahat's (2010) claims is that party primaries undermine participation in political parties. According to this, primaries emphasize quantity over quality, and although parties may be successful in attracting instant party members, they are likely to be both inactive and short-lasting. The increase in the number of party members following primaries is primarily instrumental and may drop off afterwards 'showing that membership had become merely the way by which one could vote in the primaries, and no longer a permanent link between the voter and the party' (Rahat and Hazan, 2001, 315). With Iceland's long experience of party primaries, such trends should have become highly apparent in the Icelandic political parties.

Examining party membership after the crisis and using data from the post-election voter survey of ICENES, one can see that party membership has not been on the decline despite the widespread use of primaries (Table 8.2). The parties using primaries have not seen their share of party members decline or those using the party delegate method increase. In 2009, 50% of those who were party members said that they were members of the Independence Party, and in 2016, this number had risen to 55%. Not surprisingly, fewer respondents report that they are members of one of the new parties. However, there is an interesting contrast between the Bright Future and the Pirate Party. The proportion of party members in the Bright Future, which did not use primaries to select its candidates, was extremely low both in 2013 and in 2016, whereas the proportion increased in the Pirate Party, which used party primaries to select its candidates for both elections. Thus, the Pirate Party's use of primaries could explain the increase in the number of their members as well as the absence of primaries and the extremely low proportions who say that they were members of the Bright Future, both in 2009 and in 2013.

The general trend of either a stable or an increase in party membership, regardless of whether parties use primaries to select candidates, is not in line with what we should expect if primaries were mainly detrimental to participation in political parties, as Hazan and Rahat claim. It might be argued, however, that the need for candidates to attract personal supporters could make membership less meaningful to many of those who are officially members. In this case, they should be less involved in party activities than in parties that do not use primaries. In ICENES 2013, party members were asked three follow-up questions about how actively they were involved in their party: whether they paid membership fees, whether they had attended at least two party meetings per year, and whether they held party office of some kind (Table 8.3). Payment of membership fees is more common in the Progressive Party than the others, with 85% of the members paying fees. Second in membership fees payment are the Left-Green Movement (74%) followed by about half of the members of the Social Democrats and the Independence Party with no fees paid by members of the Bright Future and the Pirate Party. About other forms of activity (going to meetings and holding a party office), the pattern is quite different. The Progressive Party shows the least activity among the established parties while the Left-Green Movement (which is much smaller than the others) is the most active one. On the whole, the patterns lend no support to the thesis that primaries undermine participation in political parties.

Intra-party competition

Hazan and Rahat (2010) suggest that party primaries lead to increasing incumbency advantage, meaning that incumbents stand a greater chance of securing a place high enough on the party list to secure their election. Incumbents generally do have an advantage over competing candidates (Hirano and Snyder, 2009) regardless of whether they are nominated by their party's leadership, in a primary or by a different method. The argument, however, is that they enjoy a greater advantage when primaries are used compared to other methods.

Our data offer only limited possibilities to evaluate whether party primaries heighten the advantage of incumbents. Due to the low number of elected candidates in our data, we combine the candidate data from 2009, 2013 and 2016 and analyse to see if there is a difference, depending on whether they are selected in a primary (open or closed) or by other means, whether they are elected or not, focusing on unsuccessful candidates that are placed next to or below the elected on the party list. In Table 8.4 we present the results, both for all parties together and for new and established parties separately.

As the number of current and former incumbents is too low to draw inferences about the impact of incumbency among the new parties, and given that most of their Members of Parliament (MPs) are new parliamentarians, we cannot draw any inferences about incumbency advantage among those parties. However, the pattern for the established parties is in line with the trend for all parties. Among those selected in primaries, the proportion of elected new parliamentarians is higher, whereas among those who are elected, incumbents are more often chosen by different means, e.g. a selection committee, and to a lesser extent, in primaries. Accordingly, primaries do not seem to favour incumbent MPs in Iceland. The explanations for these differences could, however, be high turnover rates and increasing volatility of voters who have supported different parties from one election to the other since the 2009 election. Furthermore, the only two parties that do not use party primaries in any of the constituencies to select candidates are

Table 8.2 Voters – self-reported party membership

	Left-Green Movement	Social Democratic Alliance	Civic Movement	Pirate Party	Bright Future	Progressive Party	Reform	Independence Party	Other parties/ refuses to say what party	N*
2009	7.3	19.3	.9			14.6		51.2	6.7	342
2013	3.4	19.1		.3	.5	13.5		55.4	7.7	377
2016	7.5	13.7		4.6	.4	13.7	2.5	56.8	.8	241

*Number of respondents who are party members

Source: Icelandic National Election Study, post-election voter survey. Respondents were asked 'Are you a member of a political party?' and if yes: 'What political party/ies are you a member of?

Table 8.3 Voters – activity of party members

	Left Green Movement	Social Democratic Alliance	Pirate Party	Bright Future	Progressive Party	Independence Party
Pays membership fees %	73.7	45.9	–	–	84.8	53.7
n	19	85	4	4	61	226
Goes to at least two meetings per year	57.9	34.9	–	–	27.9	28.3
n	19	86	4	4	61	226
Holds a party office	42.1	15.1	–	–	11.5	13.3
n	19	86	4	4	61	226

*Source: Icelandic National Election Study, post-election voter survey. Respondents which were party members were asked three yes or no question: 'Do you pay membership fees?', 'Do you go to a least two meetings per year held by (PARTY)?' and 'Do you hold some party office for (PARTY)?'.

Table 8.4 Incumbency advantage, 2009, 2013 and 2016

			Selected by party leadership/ party delegate conference / other	Selected in a primary, open or closed
	New MP	Elected	60.0	80.8
		Placed after the elected	.0	3.8
		Placed lower on the party list	40.0	15.4
		n	20	26
All parties	Incumbent MP	Elected	19.2	47.8
		Placed after the elected	15.4	21.7
		Placed lower on the party list	65.4	30.4
		n	26	46
	New MP	Elected	71.4	100.0
		Placed after the elected	.0	.0
		Placed lower on the party list	28.6	.0
		n	7	3
New parties	Incumbent MP	Elected	.0	50.0
		Placed after the elected	.0	.0
		Placed lower on the party list	1.0	50.0
		n	1	2
	New MP	Elected	53.8	78.3
		Placed after the elected	.0	4.3
		Placed lower on the party list	46.2	17.4
		n	13	23
Established parties	Incumbent MP	Elected	20.0	50.0
		Placed after the elected	16.0	20.5
		Placed lower on the party list	64.0	29.5
		n	25	44

*Source: Icelandic National Election Study, post-election candidate survey.

the two new parties, Bright Future and Reform. Thus, it is impossible to distinguish between incumbency effects (most of their candidates are newcomers) and the impact of candidate selection on the electoral success of those parties' candidates. In this respect, our findings regarding intra-party competition remain inconclusive.

Representativeness

Among the claims made concerning the effects of primaries is that they undermine the representativeness of parties (Hazan and Rahat, 2010). Instead of party institutions working deliberately to produce representative lists, this line of argument suggests that a one-stage candidate selection method, such as party primaries, is unlikely to contribute to such an outcome.

Respondents in the surveys were asked to place themselves ('In politics, people sometimes talk about the 'left' and the 'right'. Where would you place your own views on a scale from 0 to 10, where 0 means the most left and 10 means the most right?') and candidates were asked a follow up question about where they would place their party on a left right scale. The table 8.5 shows mean difference between self-placement of party voters and candidates' placement of their party on a scale from 0 to 10

Using congruence on the left-right scale between parties (as placed by their candidates) and their voters (self-placement) as a proxy for how representative the parties are, we see that congruence seems to be driven by how far parties are from the centre rather than the selection methods (Table 8.5). The Left-Green Movement, which is furthest to the left, and the Independence Party, which is furthest to the right, are those least representative when using congruence as a proxy with their voters, except for the Independence Party in 2009. The parties at the centre have more policy congruence with their voters, regardless of whether they use primaries to select their candidates, e.g. the Pirate Party, or a selection committee, e.g. the Bright Future. While this does not rule out the possibility that primaries influence how representative parties are of their voters, it seems unlikely to be a major one.

Responsiveness

Finally, we analyze whether candidate selection methods affect responsiveness using ideological agreement within parties. Ideological agreement within parties is considered relevant for their ability to act in unison, and hence, responsively. In Iceland's party-centred system, ideological agreement within parties plays an important part in responsiveness given that parties' actions are based on and supported by ideological agreement within the parties. That is because, in party-centred systems, cohesive parties are the ones that can act in unison and thus be responsive, while individual politicians have limited options to be responsive without the support of their party.

The analysis here is focused on intra-party disagreement (which we use as a proxy for responsiveness) and how far or close candidates place themselves to their party on the left-right scale. Intra-party disagreement within parties is greater in the Pirate Party and the Independence Party in all three years, and in the Social Democratic Alliance in 2009 (Table 8.6). In all three parties, primaries have been the main tool to select candidates. Among those parties where intra-party disagreement is less, there is no clear difference depending on what selection method they use to select their candidates. For example, intra-party disagreement is on a similar level in the Social Democratic Alliance in 2013 and 2016 as it is within Reform in 2016. Keeping in mind that the parties use primaries mainly to select their top candidates, it might be that intra-party disagreement, as a proxy for responsiveness within parties, depends on how each candidate was selected on the list. Candidates selected in a primary might be in less agreement with his/her party compared to candidates within the same party selected by other means, e.g. a selection committee.

Table 8.5 Representativeness: policy congruence between party voters and parties

	Left Green Movement	Social Democratic Alliance	Civic Movement	Pirate Party	Bright Future	Progressive Party	Reform	Independence Party
2009	1.38	.74	.42			.54		.25
2013	1.47	.49		.04	.02	.34		1.01
2016	1.48	.40		.35	.55	.47	.24	.79

Table 8.6 Responsiveness: intra-party disagreement between candidates and their parties – each party

	Left-Green Movement	Social Democratic Alliance	Civic Movement	Pirate Party	Bright Future	Progressive Party	Reform	Independence Party
2009	.91	1.27	.71			.88		1.09
2013	.70	.79		1.16	.67	.58		1.01
2016	.88	.97		1.03	.70	.75	.87	1.03

*Source: The Icelandic National Election Study, post-election candidate survey. Candidates were asked to place themselves ('In politics, people sometimes talk about the 'left' and the 'right'. Where would you place your own views on a scale from 0 to 10, where 0 means the most left and 10 means the most right?') and their party ('using the same scale, where would you place your party?') on a left-right scale. The table shows mean difference between self-placement of candidates and party voters on a scale from 0 to 10. Intra-party disagreement is the absolute distance between candidates' self-placement and where they place their party on an 11 point left (0)-right (10) scale.

In contrasting intra-party agreements between candidates that are selected in a primary and those selected by other methods, there is a tendency for candidates who are selected in a primary to place themselves further away from their party on the left-right scale (Table 8.7). This difference could be explained by factors other than the candidate selection method such as party age, how far the party is placed towards the ends of the left-right spectrum, and party socialization. One could expect that there is less responsiveness regarding more intra-party disagreement on the left-right dimension within new parties, both because they have not yet stabilized themselves and because their ideological profile might be driven by other factors than the traditional left-right scale. The parties' placement on the left-right scale or how far they are towards the ends of it is also of importance if candidates tend to place themselves closer to the centre than they place their party. The longer a candidate has been an incumbent for a party, the more likely it is that he/she agrees with his/her party. This agreement could be due to party socialization and because candidates that agree with a party are more likely to have been successful in securing a seat high enough on the party lists to be elected as MPs.

To examine the interplay between the impact of candidate selection and age of parties (old parties contrasted with new), in intra-party disagreement (proxy for responsiveness), as well as the impact of the distance of the party from the ideological centre (controlling for possible greater disagreement within parties towards the extremes due to candidates placing themselves closer to the centre then their party), and incumbency, we ran a linear regression model. We distinguish between the impact of the age of parties and candidate selection method on intra-party disagreement by interacting candidate selection method with whether the party is an established or a new party.

The model (Table 8.8) results in some significant outcomes, but explained variance (R^2: 0.07) is very low. Positive coefficients indicate more disagreement, and we see that those who are selected in primaries and belong to parties which are towards the ends on the left-right scale are in a lesser agreement with their party. Other main effects are negligible.

Interestingly, the impact of primaries on intra-party disagreement depends on whether the party is old or new. In Figure 8.1, we plot this interaction effect. It shows that candidate selection method has no impact on responsiveness regarding

Table 8.7 Responsiveness: intra-party disagreement between candidates and their parties, and candidate selection method

	2009	2013	2016
Primary/open or closed	1.00	.93	.91
Party leadership/party delegate conference/other	.95	.75	.87

Source: *The Icelandic National Election Study, post-election candidate survey. Distance between candidates' self-placement and their placement of their party on an 11 point left (0)-right (10) scale. Zero indicates lowest distance (high congruence) and 10 highest distance (low congruence).

Table 8.8 Linear regression on intra-party disagreement (responsiveness)

	B
	(st.err)
Constant	1.29
	(26.358)
Selected in a primary	.48***
	(.130)
Old party	.03
	(.101)
Selected in a primary*old party	−.32*
	(.159)
Incumbency, reference=never been elected:	
New MP	−.15
	(.186)
Been elected for one term	−.30
	(.205)
Been elected for two terms or more	−.24
	(.181)
Placement on party list (seat)	.01
	(.006)
Distance of party on left-right from the mean within each election	.30***
	(.049)
Election year	−.0004
	(.013)
R2	.07
N	866

*Response variable: Intra-party disagreement, distance between candidates and their party on left-right. Significance levels: *p<0.05; **p<0.01; ***p<0.001. Source: The Icelandic National Election Study, post-election candidate survey

intra-party disagreement among the old parties, but it is of importance for the new parties. Within the new parties, candidates that are selected in primaries are in more disagreement with their party compared to candidates who are selected by other methods. This indicates that the primaries have no long-term effects on responsiveness within parties but that in new parties, the method of selection by committee may produce slightly greater responsiveness than the use of primaries.

Our findings on the impact of party primaries and their consequences for how political parties work and how representative they are have led to mixed conclusions. For this study, we tested Hazan's and Rahat's (2010) claims that they have detrimental effects on party membership, how representative candidates are, how they undermine the chances of new candidates, and how they affect intra-party disagreement. The only claim receiving (weak) support is that intra-party disagreement is higher within new parties since 2009 when candidates are selected by primaries as opposed to other selection methods. Whether this is due to the parties' age or political turmoil which was offset by the economic crash in Iceland in 2008 is hard to tell.

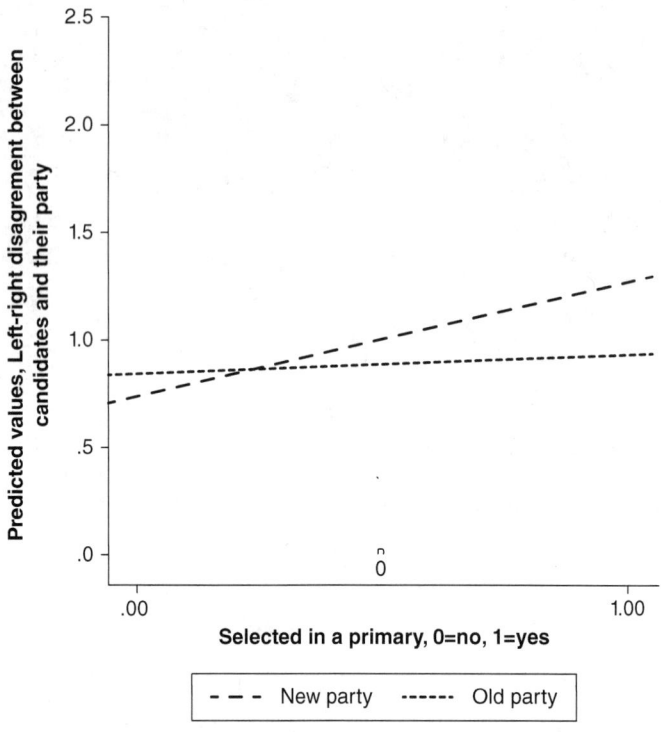

Figure 8.1 Responsiveness: intra-party disagreement in new and old parties – marginal effect of primaries

Conclusion /discussion

There seems no doubt that the economic crash of 2008 produced a crisis of confidence in the Icelandic political system with considerably lower levels of trust in politicians than before the crash. This generated considerable interest in democratic innovations among sections of the population, including more direct forms of democracy and personalized representation. Paradoxically, the established political parties in Iceland were already practicing decentralized and inclusive nominations. This meant that demands for representative reforms were unlikely to aim at opening up the nomination processes – the primaries were already in place.

Since 2009, the four established parties in Iceland have lost their former status with generally a combined vote of about 90% down to 62% in 2016, and four new parties have entered the parliament – thus the Icelandic party system is in flux. Three of the new parties, the Civic Movement (which has ceased to exist), the Bright Future, and the Pirate Party, mobilized anti-establishment sentiments and a demand for more involvement of citizens in policy-making. The fourth new party, Reform, has also attracted voters who have less faith in the political system, but it is different to the other new parties in the sense that it has many features in common with the established parties.

Both the established parties and the new parties have used a mix of candidate selection methods since the crisis. We show that primaries – as practiced by the Icelandic political parties – need not undermine participation, representation, intra-party competitiveness or responsiveness. In fact, they seem for the most part compatible with conventional conceptions of representation. Therefore, the reform movement after the crash has looked for solutions elsewhere, such as direct democracy or highly personalized forms of representation, which might have posed a far more serious threat to party representation than the primaries. The established elites, however, were far more sceptical of these ideas than the reform movement or their voters. It remains to be seen whether the reform movement will manage to push through more citizen involvement or whether the system in place will continue unchanged, including the widespread use of primaries.

Note

1 Source: https://datamarket.com/data/set/1wb6/traust-til-stofnana-skv-thjodarpulsi-capacent #!ds=1wb6!1xyh=1&display=line

References

Alþingi. (2010). *Þingmannanefnd um skýrslu rannsóknarnefndar Alþingis*. Retrieved from www.althingi.is/thingstorf/thingmalalistar-eftir-thingum/ferill/?ltg=138andmnr=705

Bernburg, J. G. (2016). *Economic crisis and mass protest: The Pots and Pans revolution in Iceland*. Oxon: Routledge.

Bloomberg Markets magazine. (2011). *Iceland shows Ireland did 'Wrong Things' saving banks*. Retrieved from www.bloomberg.com/news/articles/2011-02-01/iceland-proves-ireland-did-wrong-things-saving-banks-instead-of-taxpayer

Close, C., Kelbel, C., and van Haute, E. (2017). What citizens want in terms of intra-party democracy: Popular attitudes towards alternative candidate selection procedures. *Political Studies* 65 (3), pp. 646–664. doi:10.1177/0032321716679424

Colomer, J. M. (2005). It's parties that choose electoral systems (or Duverger's laws upside Down), *Political Studies* 32, pp. 1–21. http://doi.org/10.1111/j.1467-9248.2005.00514.x

Colomer, J. M. (Ed.). (2011). *Personal representation: The neglected dimension of electoral systems*. Colchester: ECPR Press.

Davies, J., Schoorman, D., and Donaldson, L. (1997). Toward a stewardship theory of management. *Academy of management. The Academy of Management Review* 22 (1), pp. 20–47. http://doi.org/ 10.5465/AMR.1997.9707180258

Forsætisráðuneytið. (2009). *Dómsmálaráðherra leggur fram frumvörp um persónukosningar til Alþingis og sveitarstjórna*. Retrieved from www.forsaetisraduneyti.is/frettir/nr/3806

Forsætisráðuneytið. (2010). *Viðbrögð stjórnsýslunnar við skýrslu rannsóknarnefndar Alþingis*. Retrieved from www.forsaetisraduneyti.is/media/Skyrslur/Skyrsla-starfshops-6-mai2010.pdf

Geissel, B., and Newton, K. (2012). *Evaluating democratic innovations: Curing the democratic malaise?* London: Routledge.

Hardin, R. (1999). Do we want trust in government? In Warren, M. (Ed.), *Democracy and trust*. Cambridge: Cambridge University Press, pp. 22–41.

Hazan, R., and Rahat, G. (2010). *Democracy within parties. Candidate selection methods and their political consequences*. Oxford: Oxford University Press.

Hetherington, M. (2005). *Why trust matters*. Princeton: Princeton University Press.

Hirano, S., and Snyder, J. M. Jr. (2009). Using multimember districts elections to estimate the sources of incumbency advantage. *American Journal of Political Science* 53 (2), pp. 292–306. http://doi.org/10.1111/j.1540-5907.2009.00371.x

IMF. (2011). *Iceland's recovery: Can the lessons be applied elsewhere?* Retrieved from www.imf.org/external/pubs/ft/survey/so/2011/SurveyartF.htm

Indriðason, I., and Kristinsson, G. H. (2015). Primary consequences. The effects of candidate selection through party primaries in Iceland. *Party Politics* 21(4), pp. 565–576. http://doi.org/0.1177/1354068813487117

Indriðason, I. H., Önnudóttir, E. H., Þórisdóttir, H., and Harðarson, Ó. Þ. (2017). Re-electing the culprits of the crisis? Elections in the aftermath of a recession. *Scandinavian Political Studies* 40 (1), pp. 28–60. http://doi.org/10.1111/1467-9477.12081

Karvonen, L. (2009). *The personalisation of politics*. Colchester: ECPR Press.

Kristinsson, G. H. 2011. Party cohesion in the Icelandic Althingi. *Stjórnmál og stjórnsýsla – Icelandic Review of Politics and Administration* 7 (2), pp. 227–248.

Kristjánsson, S. (1994). *Frá flokksræði til persónustjórnmála. Fjórflokkarnir 1959–1991*. Reykjavík: Félagsvísindastofnun Háskóla Íslands.

Krugman, P. (2012). *The Times Does Iceland*. Retrieved from https://krugman.blogs.nytimes.com/2012/07/08/the-times-does-iceland/

Miller, G. (2000). Above politics: Credible commitment and efficiency in the design of public agencies. *Journal of Public Administration Research and Theory* 10 (2), pp. 289–327.

OECD. (2012). *Restoring public finances, 2012 update*. Paris: Author.

Önnudóttir, E. H. (2016). The "Pots and Pans" protest and requirements for responsiveness of the authorities. *Icelandic Review of Politics and Administration* 12 (2), pp. 195–214. https//doi.org/10.13177/irpa.a.2016.12.2.1

Önnudóttir, E. H., Schmitt, H., and Harðarson, Ó. Þ. (2017). Critical election in the wake of economic and political crisis: Realignment of Icelandic party voters? *Scandinavian Political Studies* 40 (2), pp. 157–181. doi:10.1111/1467-9477.12085

Pitkin, H. (1967). *The concept of representation*. Berkley: University of California Press.

Rahat, G., and Hazan, R. (2001). Candidate selection methods: An analytical framework. *Party Politics* 7 (3), pp. 297–322.

Sandri, G. Seddone, A., and Venturino, F. (Eds.). (2015). *Party primaries in a comparative perspective*. Farnham: Ashgate.

Smith, G. (2009). *Democratic innovations*. Cambridge: Cambridge University Press.

Special Investigative Commission. (2010). *Report of the Special Investigation Commission*. Retrieved from www.rna.is/eldri-nefndir/addragandi-og-orsakir-falls-islensku-bankanna-2008/skyrsla-nefndarinnar/english/

Statistics Iceland. (2013). *Results for referenda by 20 October 2012*. Retrieved from http://px.hagstofa.is/pxen/pxweb/en/Ibuar/Ibuar__kosningar__thjodaratkv/KOS04108.px

Ware, A. (2002). *The American direct primary. Party institutionalization and transformation in the North*. Cambridge: Cambridge University Press.

9 Candidate selection in Ireland

New parties and candidate diversity

Theresa Reidy

Introduction[1]

Irish political parties began to enhance the internal decision-making roles of their members from the 1990s. One member, one vote (OMOV) was introduced for candidate selections at all elections; members were given voting rights at party leader elections and some parties (i.e., Labour Party, Green Party, Fianna Fáil) empowered members to vote on key decisions such as entering government. The Green Party and Fine Gael were early adopters of greater internal party democracy while Fianna Fáil was the last of the mainstream parties to embrace these reforms at its 2012 annual party congress known as an Ard Fheis in Ireland (Cross and Blais, 2012b; Galligan, 2003; Reidy, 2011; 2016). However, all of the older parties retain power centrally to set the selection parameters, an important qualifying point and one which is especially relevant in the Irish case because of its multi-member system of PR and more recently the introduction of legislative candidate gender quotas (Reidy, 2016). Many new parties emerged in the febrile years of the economic crisis from 2008 and this chapter seeks to document and evaluate the candidate recruitment strategies of these parties. The analysis will demonstrate that while all aspired to extensive internal party democracy, few were able to achieve this at their early elections and many of the new parties used recruitment techniques which were more exclusive than the old parties in the system. However, the emergence of new parties did change the profile of candidates contesting elections and their continued involvement in party politics is likely to have important consequences in terms of descriptive representation.

Ireland was one of the first countries to require financial assistance from international organisations when the economic crisis hit. The package of financial measures agreed in 2010 with the European Commission, European Central Bank and International Monetary Fund came to be known as the 'troika bailout'. Many commentators identified weak governance as a contributory factor to the economic crash leading to intense scrutiny of the political system during the 2011 election. Politicians had tended to emerge from small elite groups and Ireland had one of the most gender imbalanced parliaments in the EU in 2011, contributing to public demands for gender quotas (introduced in 2012) and more diversity in politics (Farrell, 2016). Collectively, the crisis and the bailout were to have a profound impact on electoral politics in Ireland. The long dominant ruling party, Fianna Fáil, was routed from office and replaced with a new coalition in 2011 in what was then the third most volatile election in Western Europe since 1945 (Mair, 2011). Several new parties and non-party candidates contested the election on platforms of political and economic reform. However, most were unprepared for the election and struggled to have an impact. The 2011 election was especially volatile but as Peter Mair has argued it resulted in a reordering of the party system and the replacement in government of one of the old parties in the system with two other old parties. There was no new political movement which capitalised on the uncertainty.

Voter dissatisfaction was again widespread in 2016 but on this occasion the picture changed quite a bit. Some of the new groups that had survived from 2011 mounted more organised and ambitious campaigns while further new parties and groups emerged over the course of the 2011–16 parliamentary term. The 2016 election, also among the ten most volatile elections since 1945, resulted in considerable fragmentation of the political landscape, with some of the new parties and groups gaining representation in parliament. Ireland's two and a half party system has been fracturing since the 1980s and the party system has become reasonably porous. New parties emerged in the 1980s partly in response to the prolonged recession during that decade and undoubtedly the economic crisis from 2008 was also a contributory factor in the more recent wave of new party formation. However, the impact of the crisis should not be overstated. It accelerated a process of party system fragmentation which had been in train for some time, as can be seen from Table 9.1. The combined vote share of the three largest parties (Fine Fáil, Fine Gael and Labour) has been oscillating at recent elections and small parties, micro parties and non-party candidates have gained a growing foothold in electoral politics.

There are three notable points about the political fragmentation during the crisis elections. First, new political parties were formed and contested elections during the period. Most of the new parties were on the left of the spectrum and they generally offered left-wing critiques of the neo-liberal economic model in operation in Ireland. All the new parties on the left were united in their opposition to

Table 9.1 First preference votes at general elections in Ireland 2002–2016

	2002	*2007*	*2011*	*2016*
Fianna Fáil	41.5	41.6	17.4	24.3
Fine Gael	22.5	27.3	36.1	25.5
Labour	10.8	10.1	19.4	6.6
Sinn Fein	6.5	6.9	9.9	13.8
SP-PBP Alliances	–	1.1	2.7	3.9
Greens	3.8	4.7	1.8	2.7
Others	14.9	8.3	12.5	23

Source: Department of Housing, Planning and Local Government

the fiscal retrenchment measures introduced by successive governments. While support for the new parties on the left has grown over the 2011 and 2016 elections, they remain a considerable distance from government. Second, there is no substantive party of the far right and issues such as immigration have gained little traction in public debate (O'Malley, 2008; Reidy and Suiter, 2017). Third, Ireland has a large number of non-party candidates, known as independents. There is a long history of these candidates gaining seats in parliament and they have previously provided support for minority governments. Non-party candidates will often do well when there is a sharp drop in support for one of the larger political parties as was the case in 2011 (Fianna Fáil) and 2016 (Fine Gael and Labour). But their increased support in 2016 has also been linked to growing political disaffection and an anti-politics mood (Reidy and Suiter, 2017).

Proportional Representation by the Single Transferable Vote (PR-STV) is the electoral system used at elections in Ireland. At present, the country is divided into 40 constituencies which return 158 MPs and between three and five per constituency. The electoral system is an important structuring variable which shapes how parties select their candidates (Marsh, 2007). Firstly, PR-STV is used by parties as the voting system for internal party decisions. Second, as more than one MP is elected in each constituency, large parties will usually select from two to five candidates per constituency depending on a number of factors, such as their support in that area, incumbency, geography and gender. Third, as there are often candidates from the same party competing against each other within a constituency, personality, political record and constituency service can be as important as party label in the election but also in the party selection.

The threshold for getting on the ballot in Ireland is relatively low and this in part contributes to the large number of non-party candidates. There are three routes onto the ballot; a candidate can collect the signatures of thirty registered electors; they can lodge a deposit of €500 with the returning officer or they can present a certificate of political party affiliation. The number of candidates contesting general elections peaked at 566 in 2011 but fell only marginally to 551 in 2016 (Reidy, 2016).

This chapter is focused on the internal democracy procedures of the new political parties and groups which emerged during the economic crisis and competed at general elections in 2011 and 2016, specifically their candidate selection rules. In the Irish case, the analysis includes parties of the far left, centre left, centre right and some of the non-party candidates that were to coalesce into groups, especially at the 2016 election. The chapter will document the recruitment strategies adopted by the parties following Rahat and Hazan (2001). The chapter will then go on to discuss the changing profile of candidates at Irish elections, paying particular attention to the impact that the introduction of legislation on candidate gender quotas was to have in 2016. The new parties and groups have brought more than ideological diversity to politics in Ireland; their candidates come from more varied occupational backgrounds and have quite different political experience to those that compete from the traditional parties in the system. Section two provides some contextual information on the parties in the study and sets out the criteria for case selection. The specific recruitment approaches of the groups are documented in section three and some comparison to the old parties in the system is provided. The evidence presented is drawn from a series of interviews with party staff (Socialist Party, People Before Profit, Independents4Change), party leaders (Social Democrats, Renua, Independent Alliance) and from the party constitutions and charters where they were available (Social Democrats, Renua). Section four presents a comparative profile of candidates at the 2011 and 2016 elections. Section five has some concluding remarks and discusses preliminary implications of the changes being wrought in the Irish political system through the addition of more ideological and candidate diversity among its political parties.

Parties and groups competing at elections since the economic crisis

Ireland has a diverse party political landscape and in 2017 there were twenty political parties listed on the official register of parties. Nearly all of the parties contest every election but only a small number have candidates elected to public office. The 'old' or 'traditional' party system includes Fianna Fáil, Fine Gael, the Labour Party, Sinn Féin and the Green Party. All of these parties have competed at elections since at least the 1980s and as a result lie outside the analytical scope of this work. The core focus of this chapter is on the political parties and groups which have emerged since the economic crisis started in Europe in 2008. In the Irish case, some caution is required in relation to the categorisation of the groups and parties as 'new'. Quite a number of the parties included in this study have roots in earlier political movements, and reorganisations within parliament have delivered further new political vehicles but all of those considered here have either officially registered, or organisationally operated, as new political parties or groups during the time frame of interest. Finally, only parties or groups that have had members elected to parliament (Dáil Éireann)[2] are included, thus some of the smallest political parties are excluded. Five parties are included and some contextual information is set out in this section.

The first cluster of parties considered are located on the far left of the ideological spectrum. Beginning with the Socialist Party and People Before Profit, these two parties were to coalesce under the umbrella, United Left Alliance (ULA), in 2011. The coalition dissolved during the 2011–16 parliamentary term and a new movement on the left, the Anti-Austerity Alliance (AAA), formed outside parliament. This movement emerged primarily as a grass roots protest group opposed to the introduction of water charges, and other fiscal retrenchment measures, and it was closely associated with many members of the Socialist Party whose candidates were to contest the 2016 election under the Anti-Austerity Alliance banner. Opposition to fiscal retrenchment measures was the key factor driving support for AAA candidates in 2016 (Farrell, Marsh and Reidy, 2018). A close relationship was also retained with People Before Profit at the 2016 election. In 2017, the Anti-Austerity Alliance was to re-brand as Solidarity and it retained its relationship with People Before Profit. The current name for the overall group is Solidarity-People Before Profit.

Several parties formed in parliament through realignments of political affiliations. The Social Democrats was founded by three non-party MPs in 2015 and positioned itself on the centre-left as its name would suggest. The three founding MPs were particularly critical of the government's fiscal retrenchment policies and sought to capitalise on the strong anti-government sentiment in the lead up to the 2016 election. Renua Ireland formed as a splinter group from the centre-right Fine Gael. A small number of Fine Gael MPs and Senators (members of the upper house) were expelled from the party in 2013 over an abortion vote and some of the renegade group were to go on to form a new party in 2015. Their formation was not connected with the economic crisis. Positioned on the centre-right, their first election was in 2016.

Non-party candidates are prevalent at elections in Ireland, much more so than in any other European country (Weeks, 2009). There is no screening process or political recruitment phase that they must pass through. As a result, this type of candidate is usually outside the scope of candidate selection research. However, in 2016, the formation of the umbrella group, the Independent Alliance, means that this group of candidates deserve some attention. Non-party candidates are quite diverse, both in terms of their ideological orientations and their pathway to the ballot (see Galligan, 2003; Reidy, 2011; 2016 for further discussion). 2016 marked an important departure for non-party candidates in that some were to choose both formal and informal routes of co-operation. Opinion polls prior to the 2016 election suggested that non-party candidates were likely to be very successful. However, they faced a challenge in that it would be difficult to have an impact on government formation unless they had at least a loose organisational structure. But most non-party candidates were unwilling to forego their political autonomy. Many of the non-party candidates sought to capitalise on the strong anti-system and anti-party sentiment among the electorate. Party discipline is very high in Ireland (De Pauw and Martin, 2009) and during the 2011–2016 parliamentary term, the use of the party whip to ensure government bills were passed was especially controversial, often because the laws enacted involved tax increases, new taxes, expenditure cuts and reductions in services. Many MPs, both within parties and non-party MPs, complained that the use of the party whip was excessive and that this undermined democracy.

Nevertheless, the Independent Alliance emerged as an umbrella political grouping for a number of non-party candidates. Though it did not register as a political party, the group adopted many of the procedures associated with a political party, including candidate-selection procedures. A second group that is also discussed in this chapter is Indepedents4Change. This group operated in the opposite direction. While it registered as a political party, the group did not develop centralised procedures in relation to candidate selection but several candidates contested the election under the brand. In addition to these specific groupings, there were also a number of alliances which became more formalised after the election partly as a result of the government formation negotiations, e.g. rural independents. These groups did not organise in advance of the 2011 or 2016 elections and show no signs of formalising their co-operation and hence are excluded from this analysis.

Having identified the new parties and groups which competed at the 2011 and 2016 general elections, in section three an overview and evaluation of their recruitment strategies is provided. The strategies are grounded in the political recruitment literature and some discussion is also provided in relation to how many of the new parties embraced approaches that have become more common-place among the traditional parties in the system in recent years.

New parties and groups and their recruitment strategies

This chapter seeks to understand how new parties behave when they emerge in a political system that is already characterised by reasonable levels of internal party democracy. Following Rahat and Hazan (2001) parties are evaluated in terms of how inclusive-exclusive and centralised-decentralised their selection procedures are.

'Older' parties

All of the older parties in the Irish system (Fianna Fáil, Fine Gael, the Labour Party, Sinn Féin and the Green Party) have embraced internal democratisation reforms and can be located on the inclusive end of the spectrum (Rahat and Hazan, 2001). The parties use OMOV for selection decisions and candidate selection takes place at the level of the electoral district (constituency for general elections and local electoral area for local elections). The movement toward greater internal party democracy began in 1989 when the Green Party introduced postal voting for party members to select candidates (Galligan, 2003). The Green Party emerged from grass root environmental groups which had a strong record of participatory approaches to decision making and that it was a first mover in this area was not surprising. Fine Gael was to follow suit in the late 1990s after a recommendation from an internal party commission looking at its rules but within a decade, there was a clear contagion effect with all of the older parties moving toward greater democratisation of their internal party decision-making (Galligan, 2003; Reidy, 2011; 2016). Party members are also empowered in the selection of party leaders, albeit with considerable variation in the weighting of the membership votes and the conditions under which members are involved. The Labour Party and the Green Party operate the most expansive selectorates for party leadership elections (Cross and Blais, 2012b). Fianna Fáil was the last of the old parties to move to giving all registered members a vote in candidate selection processes at Dáil, European Parliament and local elections. Consistent with the expectations from the research literature, it took this decision after its catastrophic performance at the 2011 election (Cross and Blais, 2012a.

It would be wrong to suggest that the old parties in the Irish system provide a form of internal political nirvana. All of the older parties experience internal tensions to varying degrees in relation to the recruitment of candidates and the choice of party leaders (see Galligan, 2003; Reidy, 2016). The main axis of contention derives from the ongoing retention of power in all of the parties by a party leadership or executive branch to define the selection choices presented to the selectorate. As Scarrow et al. (2002) observe, there is an inclination among party elites to retain power at the centre and to resist democratisation reforms. This reflection is particularly pertinent in the Irish case due to the complexities presented by the electoral system. Ireland has multi-member constituencies and many parties can expect to win more than one seat within a constituency (Gallagher and Marsh, 1988). As discussed earlier, this preferential voting system means that parties will often run more candidates than the number of seats that they expect to win. Geography, age of candidates, proximity to other candidates, and gender most importantly in 2016, influence the overarching requirements which the central party sets out for local constituency organisations when they are being asked to make their selections. The introduction of the gender quota legislation for the 2016 election tilted the balance of power further towards party elites but this tension between participation and representativeness is a well-established one (Rahat, 2009) and not easy to resolve.

The primary concern of this chapter is to evaluate the internal procedures of parties and groups established since the economic crisis. Specifically we are interested in the question of how far the new parties and groups embraced the idea of more open participation and consequent internal party democracy. In the next part of this section, the candidate-selection procedures of the new groups and parties that contested elections in 2011 and 2016 are considered. To aid this analysis, table 9.2 provides a summary of the candidate-selection rules for each of the parties in the system.

Table 9.2 Summary information on parties

New Party/Group	Candidate Selection Method in 2011 and 2016	'Older' Party	Candidate Selection Method in 2011 and 2016
United Left Alliance (2011)		Fianna Fail	OMOV at district level
Anti-Austerity Alliance – People Before Profit (2016)	OMOV at district level		
Social Democrats	Interview by national party group	Fine Gael	OMOV at district level
Renua Ireland	Interview by national party group	Green Party	OMOV at district level
Independent Alliance	Interview by national party group	Labour Party	OMOV at district level
Independents4Change	Not applicable	Sinn Féin	OMOV at district level

Source: Party constitutions and author interviews with party leaders and staff

Internal procedures in new political parties and groups

Far left parties have played only a minor part in electoral politics in Ireland since independence in 1921. While parties of the far left have long competed at elections, it was not until the late 1990s that these parties began to win seats in parliament, and opinion polls in advance of the 2011 election showed that their support levels were increasing. The two main parties in this space are the Socialist Party and People Before Profit, both of whom had existed for some time and had roots in party politics for some decades. However, they are included in this analysis as they formed a new alliance before the 2011 general election, although organisationally the parties remained separate and this also pertained for candidate recruitment. The same is true of the parties in 2016 when they contested the election under the banner Anti-Austerity Alliance-People Before Profit. In 2011, they jointly put forward 20 candidates and this number jumped to 31 in 2016. Both parties have separate rules and procedures governing candidate selection but there are many common features.

For both parties, the selectorate for candidates at general elections includes all members of the party and decisions are taken at constituency level. The threshold for participation in party decision-making is modest and in the case of People Before Profit, members are only required to have joined six weeks prior to the selection convention to be entitled to vote. In both parties, members are notified about conventions in writing, and also often by phone (information provided in interviews with officials from both parties in April 2016 and May 2017). Both parties are quite small and tend to only run one candidate in each constituency. Decisions on where candidates will run are taken formally by the national executive committee in both parties. In 2016, there were five constituencies where there were candidates from both People Before Profit and Anti-Austerity Alliance; in three instances this was the direct result of the parties having autonomous organisational structures but it was for strategic electoral reasons in the other two (Reidy, 2016). The Socialist Party explained in interviews that there is a good deal of flexibility in relation to overall decisions on candidate numbers and constituency organisations can come forward and suggest running a candidate but all candidates must be ratified by the national executive committee which is elected directly by members.

What is clear from the rules in this left-wing coalition of parties is that the internal structures display reasonable levels of democracy and there is also flexibility in how they carry out their activities. Support for the parties on the far left has increased in recent years and first in 2011 the United Left Alliance, and then in 2016 Anti-Austerity Alliance-People Before Profit, capitalised on this, increasing the number of candidates they fielded and the number of public representatives they had elected. However, there are still only a small number of occasions when there are formal contests for party positions or candidate roles. Smaller parties tend to have less centralised approaches to candidate selection (Lundell, 2004). A full review of party rules is planned by Solidarity in late 2017 and there is a sense among party elites that as the organisation grows, some greater codification of rules will have to occur. Following the selection structures advanced by Rahat and Hazan (2001) leads to a classification of the group's procedures as being on the inclusive end and moderately decentralised.

Hereafter, the parties that are discussed were formed during the period 2011–16, indeed most during 2015. This is an important point in that Katz and Mair (1994) discussed the three faces of party organisation, referring to the party in public office, the party on the ground and the party central office. But for the remaining parties and groups in this section, it is only meaningful to think about the party in public office. Most of the parties were formed within the Dáil and had a number of incumbent MPs and senators, but none of these parties were at an advanced stage of organisation when the election was called in 2016. They did not have functional membership bases, party staff or elites in the manner that Katz and Mair describe. Hence, the parties are one dimensional and this is an important context for understanding the limited organisational arrangements that are described.

One of the main practical reasons for the limited organisational base of the new parties was lack of funding. Party finance rules have been tightened considerably over three decades in Ireland after a series of corruption scandals (Byrne, 2012). There are strict limits on donations to candidates and parties and there are also expenditure limits for candidates at elections. These changes are important because one by-product of them is that it is more difficult to raise money to establish a new party. The party founders cannot use their own money nor can they rely on donations from generous benefactors. However, once parties reach a two per cent electoral threshold or have candidates elected to office, they are eligible for generous state funding.

The Social Democrats formed just months before the 2016 election and consequently put preliminary procedures in place to manage candidate selection. The party was founded by three MPs within parliament and jointly they formed the co-ordinating committee of the party. As the party formed in parliament, they did not have a formal membership in place and candidate selection for the 2016 election was organised through a series of interviews with the party leaders. An open call for candidates was issued through the media and the party ran 14 candidates following the interview process with the three founding MPs. Policy compatibility and electability were the key selection priorities highlighted by party leaders (in interviews with the author in May 2016) but the cost of contesting elections was a background limiting factor which was also mentioned as explaining the low candidate numbers. During interviews in Autumn 2016 with party staff and leaders, ensuring that internal party procedures would be more democratic in the future was identified as a key priority and quite a bit of progress in this direction has been achieved. The party has agreed a new constitution, held its first national conference at which it elected its officer board through a vote of the membership. Candidate selection conventions for future elections will use OMOV within constituency branches (Social Democrats Constitution, 2016).

Turning to the other side of the ideological spectrum, Renua Ireland was formed in March 2015, giving it a little more time to organise. Like the Social Democrats, it also formed in parliament and had a number of incumbent MPs.

The party had a preliminary constitution which set out an interview process for candidate selection (Renua Constitution, 2015). Each candidate that came forward was interviewed by three members of the national board of the party. The national board included all the elected founding members of the party (MPs and Senators) and the chairman of the party. In interviews with former party MPs and the current party leader, policy compatibility was identified as the most important criterion in choosing candidates. The party organises its beliefs around six core policy areas which include enhancing local democracy, being pro-life (opposed to the use of abortion in all circumstances) and espousing pro-business policies. The party estimated that it interviewed between three and six candidates per constituency but there is some doubt about this figure as the party had to extend its nomination deadlines on a number of occasions and did not meet its own stated target of running a candidate in each constituency (Reidy, 2016). All of Renua's incumbents lost their seats, no new candidates were elected and the party leader at the 2016 general election resigned. Leadership of the party passed to a member of local government. The party did pass the two percent threshold required to receive funding under the electoral acts but it has struggled to gain any traction in public debates. Its internal party procedures remain at an embryonic stage and it is not certain if the party will contest a further election.

Procedures for the party Independents4Change are difficult to classify. The party was officially registered in 2014 and five candidates contested the election in 2016 under the party affiliation. Four of these were incumbent MPs and a fifth candidate was a constituency colleague at local government of one of the MPs. The party did not have formal candidate selection rules in 2016 and personal relationships formed among the incumbent MPs were the basis for their decision to come together in a 'quasi' party. While there is ideological congruence among the members of the party, they continue to operate as an independent collection of non-party MPs.

Moving to non-party candidates, most of these self nominate to get onto the ballot. The only notable group which operated a recruitment process was the Independent Alliance. Again, this group formed in parliament with five MPs and two Senators coming together to establish an umbrella alliance with ten founding principles. The Alliance did not have a formal constitution but it did operate selection procedures for candidates seeking to contest under the alliance brand. In common with many of the parties which formed within parliament, the alliance opted for an interview strategy for its recruitment process. The interview panels consisted of the founding members and electability was the key criterion for this group. Just two of their 21 candidates had not previously contested an election and one of these was a prominent journalist with a national newspaper. The Independent Alliance joined the minority government which formed after the 2016 election and the umbrella coalition remains intact. However, there are no plans to develop the group into a political party and thus it is unlikely that more inclusive candidate selection strategies will develop as the group will not have a card-carrying membership.

There is one striking pattern to be found in the candidate-selection practices of the new parties. The ULA (AAA-PBP at the 2016 election) is the only party with a grass-roots membership and a party network across the country. Among the new parties, it alone operated an inclusive and moderately decentralised approach to candidate selection. All of the other parties/groups were formed out of new coalitions among non-party MPs or were splinter groups from larger parties. Their origins lay in elite parliamentary politics not grass-roots mobilisation and their candidate-selection strategies to a great extent flowed from this. These parties/ groups employed exclusive electorates within highly centralised decision-making approaches.

Renua lost all its seats at the election, Independents4Change show no signs of formalising their arrangements and the Independent Alliance is clear that it is an umbrella structure and will not be evolving into a political party. The Social Democrats have perhaps the most clearly thought-out plan for developing their internal structures but it remains to be determined what their electoral destiny will be. Their three incumbent MPs were returned in 2016 but one MP has already left to join another party.

On the evidence presented here, it is clear that the new parties and alliances which formed do not display high levels of internal party democracy in parliament. The processes are national and exclusive. In interviews with the author, many spoke of a desire to develop greater internal party democracy but there is little concrete evidence to suggest this is happening in Independents4Change, the Independent Alliance or Renua. Party swapping is not especially prevalent in politics in Ireland and the 2011–16 Dáil term stands out as having delivered considerable internal movement among the incumbents. Irish politics has long been used to incumbents MPs and would-be candidates leaving parties to contest as non-party candidates. That Dáil term was notable for movements also taking place in the opposite direction and quite a few incumbents were involved in party formation. However, it is an open question as to whether many of these new parties will survive another election.

The far left alliance deviates from this picture in that it has clear, democratic internal procedures but this point must be tempered by the fact that both iterations of the alliance were formed around two older parties, both of which continue to exist and which have not ceded much internal organisational power to the umbrella coalitions that they have cooperated within either at the 2011 or the 2016 elections.

In many ways, the Irish case presents an example where the older parties had already embraced some internal democratisation in the late twentieth century (Bille, 2001) and the spill-over effect within the system operates in the opposite direction to that posited in many of the other chapters in his volume. In some of the interviews with representatives from the newer parties and alliances, it was clear that they were acutely conscious that internal party democracy was important and they did not want to be rated unfavourably against other parties which already had good practices in place. Therefore, we might conclude that further democratisation is to be expected albeit with the caveat that some of the groups, but not the individuals, discussed here may have a short shelf life.

Changing candidate profiles in Ireland

The new parties and groups which contested the elections in 2011 and 2016 may have a mixed record on internal party democracy but undoubtedly they did diversify politics in Ireland. The data presented in tables 9.3–9.5 point to the diverse

Table 9.3 Gender profile of candidates in new parties and groups

Party	Number of Candidates	Female	%
ULA (2011)	20	5	25
AAA-PBP	31	13	41.9
Renua	26	8	30.8
Social Democrats	14	6	42.9
Independents4Change	5	2	40
Independent Alliance	21	5	23.8

Source: Data derived and adapted from *How Ireland Voted 2011* and *2016*

Table 9.4 Occupational background of candidates in new parties and groups (in %)

Occupation	AAA- PBP	R	SD	Ind4Ch	Ind All	ULA
Farmer	0	8	0	0	0	0
Commerce	0	31	29	20	33	5
Higher professional	3	31	7	–	10	–
Lower professional	26	15	43	40	24	10
Non-manual employee	23	8	14	20	19	5
Manual employee	13	0	0	20	5	20
Other	35	8	7	–	10	50
Unknown	–	–	–	–	–	10

Source: Data derived and adapted from *How Ireland Voted 2011* and *2016*

Table 9.5 Political experience of candidates in new parties and groups (in %)

Party	Member of Parliament	Local Government	Previous Experience	New Candidate	Total
ULA (2011)	5	30	25	40	100
AAA-PBP	10	26	26	38	100
Renua	15	12	8	65	100
Social Democrats	28	14	29	29	100
Independents4Change	80	20	–	–	100
Independent Alliance	19	62	9.5	9.5	100

Source: Data derived and adapted from *How Ireland Voted 2011* and *2016*

Note: Member of Parliament includes the Upper and Lower Houses in Ireland and the European Parliament gender profile, occupational background and political experience of candidates in new political parties and groups.

Gender

The gender profile of candidates at general elections altered radically at the 2016 election following the introduction of candidate gender legislation in 2012. In 2011 just 15.2% of the candidates contesting the election were women. In advance of the election, there had been a significant debate about political reform, and the need for greater diversity in political life was a prominent part of that campaign (Reidy and Buckley, 2017). The new government acted early in its term and gender quota legislation was introduced which required that parties have at least 30 percent of their candidates from both genders. Parties which failed to meet this threshold would incur a 50 percent penalty in their funding under the electoral acts. As Buckley, Galligan and McGing (2016) argue, the severe financial penalties included in the legislation were a significant factor in the 100 percent compliance by all of the political parties with the legislation at the 2016 election.

In 2016, the Social Democrats and the AAA-PBP were the two parties with the highest overall proportion of women on their ticket (see table 9.3). In 2011, AAA-PBP, which was then contesting as the ULA, was also towards the top of the table in terms of its gender profile. In general, left leaning parties have had a stronger gender balance, in Ireland and internationally, and this is reflected in the numbers in table 9.3 for both 2011 and 2016 (Studlar and McAllister, 1991; Thames and Williams, 2013). Interestingly, the Independent Alliance also put effort into increasing its overall gender balance and this was mentioned in interviews with the author, even though the quota did not apply in their case as they were not registered as a political party. On balance, we can conclude that new entrants tend to have a stronger gender profile but it is difficult to separate out the specific dynamic forces in this case owing to the change in the legislative environment.

Descriptive representation extends beyond gender and Table 9.4 provides an occupational background of the parties and groups covered in this study. The occupational categories are drawn from the *How Ireland Voted* book series. Data presented in the *How Ireland Voted* book series (Reidy, 2011; Reidy, 2016) shows that commerce and professional backgrounds predominate among candidates at elections across all of the parties and this is especially true for some of the older parties. Farming, although in decline as an occupational background, continues to be important in particular for Fianna Fail and Fine Gael. In contrast, we can see from Table 9.4 that the non-manual employee, manual employee and the other categories are quite significant for the new parties and groups and that fewer of their candidates are drawn from business or, in particular, the higher professional category. Renua is something of an outlier. The highest proportion of its candidates are drawn from business and the higher professions. The party was essentially a splinter group from Fine Gael so the fact that its occupation profile mirrors that party is not entirely surprising. Many of the other parties lie on the left of the spectrum and the occupational diversity evident is consistent with expectations about those parties.

Finally, it is also possible to present data on the political experience of candidates in the new groups and parties. Table 9.5 provides an overview of the political backgrounds of the candidates. Unsurprisingly, we find a large proportion of the candidates who contested the elections were new candidates. The figure is highest at 65 percent for Renua in 2016. On balance, the new system entrants run more candidates with no political experience than the older parties in the system (see Reidy, 2016). The Independent Alliance has the lowest proportion and, as discussed earlier, this is in part a function of their focus on electability when choosing candidates.

Reflecting a common international experience of local government as a pipeline into national politics (Fox and Lawless, 2004; Mariani, 2008), we can also see that many of the candidates were drawn from local government and this is especially the case for the Independent Alliance. Independents 4 Change stand out among all the parties in that 80 percent of their candidates were already members of parliament and just one further councillor was added to the ticket. The figures reinforce the point that this party was formed as a parliamentary cadre.

Conclusion

Only a small number of new parties and groups managed to organise effectively for the 2011 election but by 2016 the picture had altered considerably and quite a few groups were to have candidates on the ballot paper in constituencies across the country using new political party affiliations. However, even in 2016, the parties and groups were in their infancy in organisational terms and the analysis presented here shows that only the Anti-Austerity Alliance-People Before Profit coalition had inclusive candidate-selection procedures in place. But as discussed in section three, to a great extent the organisational structures of this party predate the crisis. While the other parties and groups are all clearly cognisant of the reasons why internal democratic procedures are meritorious and the Social Democrats are already moving in this direction, it is clear that building a party structure is an onerous and time-consuming task and it takes more than one election cycle to achieve. The new parties formed in the later years of the parliamentary term struggled to develop party structures. Most had no membership base in place. Onerous party finance rules meant that many of the parties were unable to source funds to pay for even a rudimentary administrative support system before their first elections. The burden of party organisation therefore fell heavily on the incumbent public representatives who may have been able to divert some parliamentary resources to party building but even here, there would have been limitations on what was allowed, especially during the election campaign. The long-established parties in the system adopted elements of internal party democracy from the 1990s and in the Irish case a pull factor towards internal democratisation came from within the system rather than being driven by new entrants.

The new parties and groups did improve diversity in politics in Ireland. The gender pattern would have improved in any case because of the quota legislation but the new parties were among the strongest performers in relation to gender.

Furthermore, their candidates were drawn from a wider occupational background than has traditionally been the case with the older parties. They also brought new people into the political system and a significant proportion of their candidates had not previously contested elections in Ireland.

Notes

1 The author is particularly grateful to the many candidates, public representatives and party and alliance staff that have been so generous of their time and knowledge in interviews on internal party structures over many years. The information gathered through these interviews provide the basis for much of the analysis in this chapter. A full list of interviewees and interview dates is available from the author.
2 The official name for the lower house of parliament in Ireland is Dáil Éireann, commonly, the Dáil.

References

Bille, L. (2001). Democratizing a democratic procedure: Myth or reality? Candidate selection in Western European parties, 1960–1990. *Party Politics* 7 (3), pp. 363–380.

Buckley, F., Galligan, Y., and McGing, C. (2016). Women and the election: Assessing the impact of gender quotas. In *How Ireland voted 2016*. New York: Springer International Publishing, pp. 185–205.

Byrne, E. (2012). *Political corruption in Ireland 1922–2010: A crooked harp*. Manchester: Manchester University Press.

Cross, W., and Blais, A. (2012a). Who selects the party leader? *Party Politics* 18 (2), pp. 127–150.

Cross, W. P., and Blais, A. (2012b). *Politics at the centre: The selection and removal of party leaders in the Anglo parliamentary democracies*. Oxford: Oxford University Press.

Depauw, S., and Martin, S. (2009). Legislative party discipline and cohesion in comparative perspective. *Intra-Party Politics and Coalition Governments*, pp. 103–120.

Farrell, D. (2016). Political reform in a time of crisis. In *Austerity and recovery in Ireland: Europe's poster child and the great recession*. Oxford: Oxford University Press, pp. 160–176.

Farrell, D.M., Marsh, M. and Reidy, T. (2018). *The post-crisis Irish voter*. Manchester: Manchester University Press.

Fox, R. L., and Lawless, J. L. (2004). Entering the arena? Gender and the decision to run for office. *American Journal of Political Science* 48 (2), pp. 264–280.

Gallagher, M. and Marsh, M. (1988). *The secret garden of politics: Candidate selection in comparative perspective*. London: Sage, p. 103.

Galligan, Y. (2003). Candidate selection: More democratic or more centrally controlled? In *How Ireland voted 2002*. London: Palgrave Macmillan, pp. 37–56.

Hazan, R. Y., and Rahat, G. (2010). *Democracy within parties: Candidate selection methods and their political consequences*. Oxford: Oxford University Press.

Katz, R. S., and Mair, P. (1994). The evolution of party organizations in Europe: the three faces of party organization. *American Review of Politics* 14, pp. 593–617.

Lundell, K. (2004). Determinants of candidate selection: The degree of centralization in comparative perspective. *Party Politics* 10(1), pp. 25–47.

Mair, P. (2011). The election in context. In *How Ireland voted 2011*. London: Palgrave Macmillan, pp. 283–297.

Mariani, M. (2008). A gendered pipeline? The advancement of state legislators to congress in five states. *Politics and Gender* 4(2), pp. 285–308.

Marsh, M. (2007). Candidates or parties? Objects of electoral choice in Ireland. *Party Politics* 13 (4), pp. 500–527.

O'Malley, E. (2008). Why is there no radical right party in Ireland? *West European Politics* 31 (5), pp. 960–977.

Rahat, G. (2009). Which candidate selection method is the most democratic? 1. *Government and Opposition* 44 (1), pp. 68–90.

Rahat, G., and Hazan, R. Y. (2001). Candidate selection methods an analytical framework. *Party Politics* 7 (3), pp. 297–322.

Reidy, T. (2011). Candidate selection. In *How Ireland voted 2011*. London: Palgrave Macmillan, pp. 47–67.

Reidy, T. (2016). Candidate selection and the illusion of grass-roots democracy. In *How Ireland voted 2016*. New York: Springer International Publishing, pp. 47–73.

Reidy, T., and Buckley, F. (2017). Democratic revolution; Evaluating the political and administrative landscape after the great recession reforms. *Administration* 65 (2).

Reidy, T., and Suiter, J. (2017). Who is the populist Irish voter. *Statistical and Social Inquiry Survey of Ireland.*

Scarrow, S. E., Webb, P., and Farrell, D. M. (2002). From social integration to electoral contestation. In Dalton, R. J. and Wattenberg, M. P. (Eds.), *Parties without partisans: Political change in advanced industrial democracies*. Oxford: Oxford University Press, pp. 343–361.

Studlar, D. T., and McAllister, I. (1991). Political recruitment to the Australian legislature: Toward an explanation of women's electoral disadvantages. *Western Political Quarterly* 44 (2), pp. 467–485.

Thames, F. C., and Williams, M. S. (2013). *Contagious representation: Women's political representation in democracies around the world*. New York: NYU Press.

Weeks, L. (2009). We don't like (to) party. A typology of Independents in Irish political life, 1922–2007. *Irish Political Studies* 24 (1), pp. 1–27.

10 The hurricane in the Italian parliament

M5S and its MPs, selection procedures, profiles and legislative behaviour

Antonella Seddone and Stefano Rombi

Introduction

This chapter presents an analysis of the impact of inclusive methods for selecting candidates by addressing the case of the Italian Parliament elected in 2013, focusing in particular on the *Movimento 5 Stelle* (M5S). Italy and the M5S provide an enlightening case study for investigating emerging patterns in party organisation combined with the use of inclusive procedures for party decision-making, allowing an understanding of how they could impact on parliamentary dynamics.

Several reasons justify this choice of case study. Firstly, in the last ten years, Italy has experienced a spread of primary elections (especially open ones) that have been organised at both local and national levels (mainly by left-wing parties) for selecting candidates and party leaders (Pasquino and Valbruzzi, 2016). The *Partito Democratico* (PD), in particular, in its statute recognises open primary elections as the main selection method for choosing nominations. Moreover, it also uses primaries to appoint its party leader. As often happens in political systems where primary elections are introduced by parties but are not ruled by public law, the PD's experience stimulated a form of contagion effect (Hazan and Rahat, 2010; Sandri et al., 2015a). As a result, some right-wing parties overcame their scepticism towards such inclusive procedures, as in the case of the *Lega Nord* (LN), and other coalitions of parties at local level promoted inclusive procedures for selecting their candidates or party leader. The spread of primary elections among parties traditionally centred on the figure of the party leader, who usually determines nominations (and could rarely be challenged by alternative candidates for the party leadership), has to be interpreted as an indicator of the routinisation of such inclusive selections within the Italian political system (De Luca et al., 2013).

Secondly, the Italian political system offers a privileged viewpoint for understanding the consequences of the economic crisis for the political system. The early resignation of Silvio Berlusconi in November 2011 created an opening for a technocratic government led by Mario Monti, supported by a large coalition including both left-wing and right-wing political parties (McDonnell and Valbruzzi, 2014). External pressure from the EU, requiring institutional reforms and austerity policies, and the prompt response by Monti's government produced an unusual political context. The traditional parties were basically left out of the political agenda but, at the same time, they were forced to support a political line often far from their ideological stances. This entailed a redefinition of parliamentary dynamics: moving from the traditional adversarial model to – in practice – a more consensual model (Marangoni and Verzichelli, 2015). The technocratic government was thus interpreted as the abdication of an incapable political elite, which had simply surrendered to pressures from EU institutions and supported austerity policies that strengthened citizens' disaffection with politics, thus offering fertile ground for new political parties and actors criticising the political elite for its inefficacy.

This leads to the third factor, which in our view makes Italy a crucial case study: the *Movimento 5 Stelle*. Compared with other parties that emerged in Europe just after the economic crisis, the M5S obtained greater success, becoming a pivotal actor within the Italian political system. De facto, the unexpected result obtained by M5S in the 2013 general election disarticulated the bipolarism characterising political competition during the so-called Second Republic. Furthermore, it introduced new patterns in political parties' organisation, hitherto unconventional in Italian politics. The peculiar organisational features of the party make M5S a compelling case study. It entered the Italian political system as a protest movement: criticising political parties and explicitly refusing the label of 'political party', claiming to be different from the other political actors, described as being unable to address the needs and demands raised by citizens. The new party embraced a series of original features. First of all, its organisation relies largely on the use of the internet as the main arena of discussion for party members and supporters. Secondly, the party promotes the inclusiveness of its party members in party decision-making. It is worth pointing out that this claim often appears more as rhetoric rather than as a substantial and effective modality of the management of party internal life. In addition to a set of internal votes aimed at defining the political line, the party resorted to closed primary elections organised on the web to select candidates to be included into the closed lists for the 2013 Italian general election. The use of such an inclusive method was aimed at overcoming the limits imposed by the electoral law in force: a proportional system with closed lists not allowing preferential votes (Pasquino, 2007). With closed primary elections, the party sought to involve its members in the process of composing the electoral lists to be presented for the subsequent general election.

Our aim is to assess whether inclusive methods for selecting MPs had an impact on the socio-political profile of selected candidates. Literature on this theme suggests that larger selectorates struggle to facilitate processes of renewal. With reference to candidate selections, Hazan and Rahat (2010) – as well as Wauters (2012), regarding party leader inclusive selections – argue that, for example, there is no evidence that primary elections have the capacity to increase the number of women candidates. The same could be argued concerning age. The literature still lacks strong empirical confirmation on the potential patterns of renewal induced by inclusive selection methods. In this regard, Sandri et al. (2015b) found only weak evidence from primaries aimed at selecting party leaders. Therefore, this chapter will clarify (RQ1) *whether and to what extent primary elections may have facilitated the renewal of political elites in parliament*, by comparing the M5S parliamentary group (PG) with the other PGs in parliament.

Secondly, we focus on the impact of inclusive selection methods on party cohesion in parliament. The literature on this issue (Cordero and Coller, 2014; Hazan and Rahat, 2010) suggests that when MPs obtain their nominations from larger selectorates, they tend to adopt more rebellious behaviour in parliament. Any processes by which nominations are defined entails a close and strong relationship between selectorates and nominees. As a consequence, whereas the party (party elites or party executive offices) plays a crucial and central role in setting up nominations, MPs, once elected, will be more prone to follow the party line with their parliamentary behaviour supporting the party. By contrast, in cases of larger selectorates (party members or electorate), MPs would be less tied to their own party. Therefore, their parliamentary behaviour might be more rebellious towards the party line, on the one hand, and more responsive to their larger selectorates, on the other hand. That having been said, in this chapter we focus on two further research questions: (RQ2) *to what extent do inclusive selection methods facilitate rebellious behaviour by MPs; namely can inclusiveness affect party cohesion in parliament?* In addition, assuming that MPs are responsive to their selectorates, we aim to clarify (RQ3) *whether and to what extent the level of inclusiveness in candidate selection methods impacts on MPs' responsiveness, i.e. understanding whether, when selected by larger bodies, MPs tend to be more focused on responding to claims and demands coming from their own constituencies.*

The next section offers an overview of the case study, by highlighting specificities and peculiarities of rules adopted by M5S for its legislative primaries in 2013. We take into account the requirements for running as a candidate and the rules on selectorate inclusiveness. Then, the following section, addressing RQ1, presents the results of the M5S legislative primaries in terms of sociological representation, by analysing MPs' socio-political profiles: (i) the main characteristics of selected candidates, and (ii) their differences compared with the other MPs elected in the 2013 general election. RQ2 and RQ3 are addressed in the subsequent sections, which present the methodological approach adopted and the main results of inferential analyses aimed at assessing the extent to which the support obtained in primary elections may have affected MPs' parliamentary behaviour in terms of party rebellion and responsiveness. The last section summarises the main findings.

Italy and the 5 Star Movement, an overview of the case study

The 2013 general election represented a turning point for the Italian political system as well as for the story of M5S, which, having competed in local and regional elections, was making the grade at national level (Turner, 2013; Lanzone and Rombi, 2014; Tronconi, 2015). This election was called after the resignation of Mario Monti, who was leading a 'technocratic government' that was supposed to help Italy overcome the economic crisis and meet the financial obligations established in the European Treaties. As mentioned before, it was precisely during Monti's government that, as a consequence of its austerity policies, there formed in Italy a strong and deep detachment from politics (Di Virgilio et al., 2015; D'Alimonte, 2013). M5S was able to intercept this sense of dissatisfaction by gaining credit as the sole political actor able to cope with a mediocre and corrupt political elite unable to respond to citizens' demands (Bobba and Seddone, 2015). Despite its activism in previous years, the Meet-up organisations – linked to the movement, tasked with organising and mobilising activists at local level – became less relevant during the 2013 election campaign. Notably, the party experienced a sort of centralisation, as the extensive online activity by its leader, Beppe Grillo, demonstrates. He also committed himself to a series of rallies in the largest Italian cities. A combination of both online and offline events characterised the M5S campaign strategy while the mainstream media were shunned. The unexpected outcome of the electoral race, unforeseen by polls, came after a brief election campaign, characterised by a high level of negativity and a critical climate of opinion (Ceron and d'Adda, 2016). The high level of electoral volatility was mainly due to the large electoral support obtained by the M5S, as more than one quarter of Italian electors voted for the new party.[1]

The so-called *Parlamentarie* – a neologism coined by M5S and then commonly adopted in Italy to refer to legislative primaries for selecting candidates for parliament – could be included in the aforementioned online events organised by M5S during the election campaign. M5S decided to promote primary elections to select its candidates for parliament in order to respond to the growing public hostility towards the proportional electoral system that did not offer citizens the opportunity of preferential voting.[2] To be fair, primary elections cannot be considered as M5S's specific 'product'. On the contrary, the *Partito Democratico* is commonly recognised as having 'ownership' of the use of such inclusive methods for selecting candidates at local and national levels (Sandri and Seddone, 2015). The M5S simply adapted the 'model' of the open primary election already implemented in Italy in compliance with its specific organisational features. It organised an online closed primary election, which was held on 3 and 6 December 2012.[3] In order to avoid any risk of instant membership, M5S introduced a requirement for participation in candidate selection: registration as a party member at least three months before the primary date (September 2012) and identity verification by uploading the ID card onto the online platform within Grillo's website.

With regard to the candidacy requirements, a series of criteria were established. Candidates had to prove they had a clean criminal record, were not enrolled in other political parties, and were resident in the electoral district in which they were offered as a candidate. As a sign of distance from other political parties, candidates were requested not to have served for more than one electoral mandate in the past. Moreover, there was a crucial requirement to meet: the right to run for nomination was afforded only to those who had already been candidates but were not elected during the local and regional elections in which the 5 Star Civic Lists or M5S had already participated between 2008 and 2012. According to Gualmini

(2013), this choice has to be interpreted as a means of ensuring greater control by the head of the movement over the candidates. Lack of experience as elected officials potentially creates greater dependency and thus loyalty to the political line. A total number of 1,486 candidates ran for the 945 seats available.

In terms of the electoral rules, up to three preferential votes were allowed. The allocation of the candidates' names within the closed list was supposed to be organised according to the number of votes obtained in the legislative primaries, and thus – for each electoral district – the following logic was applied: the higher the number of votes, the higher the position in the closed list.

According to the official figures, due to the strict regulations previously cited, 31,612 selectors were entitled to participate, namely 12.3% of the total M5S members (n=255,339). However, only 20,252 (64.1%) finally participated. The valid votes totalled 57,252, meaning that very few chose not to cast all three preferential votes allowed.

From *parlamentarie* to parliament

This section deals with the impact of inclusive selection methods on the dimension of representation (RQ1). In particular, it provides a descriptive analysis of the socio-political profile of Italian MPs, taking into account incumbency, age and gender.

When considering the composition of the Italian Parliament elected in the 2013 general election, it must be taken into account that, in addition to M5S, three other parties adopted primary elections to select their nominees: the *Partito Democratico*, the *Sinistra Ecologia e Libertà* (SEL), and the *Sudtiroler Volkspartei* (SVP). In particular, whereas SVP selected its candidates through a closed process, allowing only party members to participate, PD and SEL organised open primary elections. It has to be noted that the inclusiveness level was not the only difference compared to the M5S legislative primaries. Indeed, both the PD and the SEL introduced mechanisms aimed at ensuring gender balance within their electoral lists. In particular, the Democratic Party allowed its selectors to cast up to two preferences, provided that they were addressed to candidates of different genders. In the case of ballots presenting a double preference for candidates of the same gender, the vote was considered null. A similar procedure was used by SEL, which supplied two different lists of candidates (one for males and one for females) for each chamber, consenting selectors to express one preference per list. In addition, it should be noted that while M5S allowed its members to decide on the nominations for all the positions in the list, PD and SEL maintained control over nominees to be placed at the head of the list.

The results in terms of gender balance as well as of renewal in parliament are quite remarkable (Table 10.1). The magnitude of the political change that resulted from the 2013 Italian general election at parliamentary level could be effectively summarised by the amount of re-elected MPs: 35.9%, meaning that a large renewal occurred in terms of parliamentary composition (De Lucia, 2013). This high rate of general renewal comes from a range of different factors. The entrance

Table 10.1 Parliament 2013: Outgoing, elected, re-elected, and newly elected by party

	Electoral result (%)*	N Outgoing (1)	N Elected (2)	N Re-elected (3)	N New MPs (4)	Renewal rate	Confirmed Rate
PD	25.4	290	407	145	262	64.4	35.6
SEL	3.2	0	44	0	44	100.0	0.0
Other C-L	0.9	26	16	7	9	56.3	43.8
PdL Area	25.1	382	206	149	57	27.7	72.3
LN	4.1	81	36	23	13	36.1	63.9
M5S	25.6	0	163	0	163	100.0	0.0
Monti Coalition	10.6	102	67	14	53	79.1	20.9
Others	5.1	64	6	1	5	83.3	16.7
Total	100	945	945	339	606	64.1	35.9

Data for Lower Chamber (data do not include Valle D'Aosta and foreign districts).
Source: Adaptation from De Lucia (2013)

into parliament of M5S could be considered one of the main causes, because none of its MPs was an incumbent or had previously served in parliament. Similarly, the whole SEL parliamentary group is composed only of newly elected MPs, since the party had not obtained any seats in the previous legislature. Furthermore, within the PD a number of 'historical' MPs decided to renounce their nominations, and this – combined with the result of the open legislative primary election promoted for selecting candidates to be included in closed lists – triggered a renewal dynamic (64.4% of the Democratic MPs are newcomers). PD and SEL also included a specific requirement for candidacy in their open primary election: candidates were allowed to compete for the nomination only if they had served in parliament for fewer than two mandates.[4]

This remarkable change is also evident in the data on gender balance, since the rate of elected women increased from 20.2% to 30.8%. The only parties resisting this general trend were the *Lega Nord* (LN) and the *Popolo della Libertà* (PDL), showing the lowest renewal rates – respectively 36.1% and 27.7% of newly elected MPs.

Exactly how candidate selection methods and their inclusiveness may affect the dimension of representation remains controversial in the literature. With regard to gender balance, Wauters (2012), working on the Belgian leadership selections, argues that inclusive selection methods may be more beneficial for women than exclusive methods. By contrast, studies on Taiwan and Iceland (Fell, 2006; Kristjansson, 1998) underline that inclusive selection methods would be a barrier for the representation of women. Moreover, Hazan and Rahat (2010) argue that whereas Israel in the 1950s had the highest levels of women's representation in the world, after the introduction of more inclusive candidate-selection methods the country registered declining representation for women. The case of M5S seems more similar to the Belgian one. Despite the quota of women running in the online primaries being quite marginal (13% out of 1486 candidates), they

Table 10.2 A comparison between M5S's elected MPs and other Italian elected MPs

	M5S	*Other Italian MPs*
Gender		
Women	38%	29%
Age (avg)	37	50
Education		
Middle school	1.2%	1%
High School	31.9%	26.2%
University	66.9%	72.8%
N	*163*	*772*

Source: Candidate and Leader Selection.

registered higher support in terms of votes if compared to the male candidates (on average, 86 votes were obtained by women, compared to 39 votes for men). When considering the education profile, other peculiar features emerge among *Parlamentarie* candidates. Indeed, if compared to average Italian citizens (Istat, 2016), they boast far higher educational levels: 47.4% have a university degree, while 46.2% have a high school diploma. Interestingly, the number of votes obtained in closed primaries seems to reward this high level of education: graduates obtained on average 58 votes, namely 19 more than the average for non-graduates.

Figures detailed in Table 10.2 show that, compared to all the Italian MPs elected to parliament,[5] M5S's elected representatives reflected the innovative features presented above. First of all, within a general pattern of increasing gender balance (at least by Italian standards), M5S provides a higher presence of women within its parliamentary group – 38%, which is 9 percentage points more than the other PGs. In addition, they are much younger, with an average age equal to 37 years old, against the other Italian MPs who average 50 years old. Finally, as concerns educational level, the high education profile for M5S MPs (66.9%) is confirmed, just as for *Parlamentarie* candidates. Actually, it should be underlined that this indicator registers a higher percentage for the other Italian MPs. According to the data presented so far, *Parlamentarie* – even within the strict rules stated by Grillo – provided a competitive arena for a set of quite young and well-educated candidates.

Party unity and party responsiveness

Although the literature argues that the method of candidate selection can affect the parliamentary behaviour of the nominees (Hazan and Rahat, 2010), the case of M5S elected MPs deserves some clarifications. Firstly, at least theoretically, M5S's hyper-closed primaries (Rombi and Seddone, 2017) impacted less on MPs' behaviour than open primaries involving a large selectorate. By adopting open primaries as a method of candidate selection, the relationship between the nominee and the constituency of selection becomes very similar to the relationship between the elected MP and his/her electoral constituency. This is absent in the case of online closed primaries, as in the case of M5S. Given that the Italian electoral system does not allow for preferential voting, the inclusiveness of the method of candidate selection may be intended as a mechanism to lead Italian MPs to take into account requests that do not come directly from their own party.

Secondly, unlike the selection mechanism adopted by PD and SEL,[6] all the M5S parliamentarians elected in 2013 have been selected through the same procedure. This prevents an assessment of the impact of the selection method within Grillo's party parliamentary group. However, although the selection method does not change among the M5S MPs, it is possible to take into consideration the electoral support received during the online primaries as a factor that could contribute to explaining their parliamentary behaviour.

The concept of parliamentary behaviour could be examined by looking at two dimensions: party unity and responsiveness. Party unity is defined as 'the observable degree to which members of a group act in unison' (Sieberer, 2006, 151). We can talk about party cohesion when MPs share values and preferences: it is the consequence of a bottom-up process. By contrast, party discipline is the result of a top-down process where the major role is played by the party leadership imposing its will.

As has been said, party unity can be achieved 'because the members agree with each other or because they are being made to act in accord with each other despite their personal preferences (or, perhaps, a combination of the two)' (Bowler et al., 1999, 5). Moreover, it is worth noting that 'discipline is needed when cohesion is low and is not needed in its more coercive forms when cohesion is high' (Bowler et al., 1999, 5).

The second dimension of parliamentary behaviour that we take into account is MPs' responsiveness. It concerns the relationship between citizens and their delegates. More specifically, it relates to the ability of representatives to take into account demands coming from the citizens they represent, and to translate them into policies (Powell, 2004). The literature on this issue is extensive, but sometimes controversial. On the one hand, responsiveness is at the basis of representative democracies (Dahl, 1971), but on the other hand Riker (1982) has argued that responsiveness is conceptually impossible. Diamond and Morlino (2005) have suggested that responsiveness should be considered as one dimension, among others, of the quality of democracy.

In this chapter we rely on Eulau and Karps' (1977) concept of responsiveness, referring to the congruence of a district's positions on policy issues and its delegate's policy orientation. This means that policy-responsive representatives are attentive and effective in promoting policy proposals well-accepted by their electoral district. For our purposes, we also consider a further component: allocation responsiveness; that is 'the representative's efforts to obtain benefits for his/her constituency through pork-barrel exchanges in the appropriations process or through administrative interventions' (Eulau and Karps, 1977, 241). It has to be underlined that in this chapter we are not interested in identifying the specific matter of policy issues handled by MPs; rather, we want to identify their engagement in demands raised by their own constituency, regardless of their specific content.

As anticipated, all M5S MPs are subject to the same incentives, in terms of both election and selection methods. On the one hand, they have been elected through a closed lists system: no preferential voting was admitted. On the other hand, they have been selected by a system of online closed primaries where, in every Italian region, M5S members were entitled to choose among dozens of candidates. We focus precisely on the support obtained by the nominees with the aim of assessing whether and to what extent the process of candidate selection may have affected party unity and the policy responsiveness of M5S MPs. In particular, we hypothesise that:

H1: the higher the support received by the nominee, the higher the propensity for parliamentary rebellion.

H2: the higher the support received by the nominee, the higher the level of responsiveness.

We expect that nominees with a larger (s)electoral base do not feel compelled to adopt party-centred behaviour, since they have more incentives than nominees with scarce (s)electoral support for cultivating a personal vote to achieve reselection (Shomer, 2009). We suggest that when MPs can rely on larger support, this affords them leverage in their relationship with the central office and the party elite. The primary vote is in this case the expression of personal support for the candidate, namely a personal trust that in the absence of a preferential vote – as was the case in the 2013 general election – represents the main incentive for the MP elected to address supporters' demands. The number of votes – rather than the percentage – obtained in primary elections are an effective measure of the external support of MPs.[7] The larger the support, the higher the opportunity to be free from party control and thus the greater likelihood to act responsively and – if required in order to fulfil selectors' demands – also to rebel.

As pointed out by Hazan and Rahat (2010) in relation to the Israeli case, candidates selected through inclusive procedures are inclined to increase their activity within parliament (such as signing a high number of bills) in an attempt to cultivate a personal, candidate-centred responsiveness. In the case of M5S MPs, we expect that this propensity will be higher for nominees with a larger electoral base.

We test our hypotheses through two inferential models designed to assess whether and to what extent the level of selectors' support explains the parliamentary behaviour of M5S MPs in terms of party unity and policy responsiveness. The dataset encompasses all M5S MPs elected in 2013, including those who changed parliamentary group in the months after the election, i.e. 163 MPs, 36 of whom switched from M5S to other parties. All data are collected from 15 March 2013 to 19 April 2015.

In Model 1 (Table 10.3), the dependent variable is represented by the index of parliamentary rebellion, calculated as the percentage of rebel votes – namely the number of votes cast by M5S MPs in dissent from the party line. This variable is employed as a proxy of party unity. In Model 2, the dependent variable is, instead,

Table 10.3 Multivariate linear regression: Parliamentary rebellion

Dependent variable: % of parliamentary voting in contrast with the parliamentary group (Model 1)		
Independent variables		
Number of votes	−0.130 (0.000)*	−0.089 (0.000)
Control variables		
Age		0.509 (0.004)***
Gender		−0.005 (0.067)
Education		−0.009 (0.062)
Social Capital		−0.007 (0.001)
Party's office		−0.069 (0.026)
Switchers		−0.034 (0.079)
Model information		
Observations	163	162
Adjusted R^2	0.01	0.24

Source: own elaboration.

Note: Entries are standardised beta coefficients; standard errors in parentheses. ***$p \leq 0.01$; *$p \leq 0.1$. In the second column, there are 162 observations because the social capital variable has one missing value.

the index of policy responsiveness, namely the ratio between the MP's parliamentary activity devoted to the constituency where they were selected and their whole parliamentary activity. In both cases, the parliamentary activity is understood as: bills proposed and questions (by speech or by written documents), reports, opinions (by speech or by written documents), and resolutions both in parliament and in commissions.

As anticipated, the independent variable, in both models, is the number of votes received by each nominee at the online primaries. It is a continuous variable, ranging from the 602 votes obtained by Paola Carinelli to the 22 votes of Alessio Tacconi. Furthermore, the analyses include a set of control variables:

a) three sociographic variables: age, gender and education for each M5S MP;
b) the index of social capital for each Italian region (Bordandini and Cartocci, 2014), aimed at controlling for the social environment of the (s)electoral constituency;
c) the role played by M5S within the party organisation. This variable has five different values according to the role played by the MPs within the M5S organisation: no role (0); member (1); assistant organiser (2); co-organiser (3); organiser (4). One can assume a positive relationship between the centrality of the role played within the organisation and party-centred parliamentary behaviour both in terms of party unity and policy responsiveness;
d) a dichotomous variable, which makes a distinction between those MPs elected within the M5S lists and who switched to other parliamentary groups (1) and all others (0). It can be supposed that the switchers, during their stay within M5S, were more likely than others to indulge in rebellious behaviour and constituency-oriented parliamentary acts.

As shown by Table 10.3, the greater the (s)electoral support received by M5S MPs in legislative closed primaries, the less they vote differently to their group line (β = -0,130; p $\leq$ 0.1). Although the coefficient is very low to achieve grounded conclusions, we must point out that the result is in contrast with our first hypothesis (H1). When including control variables, the explanatory power of the independent variable totally disappears. The control variable 'age' is the only one that is statistically significant.[8] It is positively correlated with the index of parliamentary rebellion (β = 0.509; p $\leq$ 0.01): the higher the age of the MP, the higher is his/her propensity for rebellion. These results suggest that the youngest MPs were more inclined to follow the party elite's recommendations, coming from Beppe Grillo. Contrary to the more experienced M5S MPs, the youngest began their political socialisation within M5S's organisation. It is very likely that this contributed to increase their level of loyalty with respect to the indications stemming from the party elite.

According to the findings presented in Table 10.4, as concerns the relationship between the level of policy responsiveness and electoral performance at the closed online primaries, our second hypothesis (H2) is not confirmed. The coefficient β of the independent variable 'number of votes' is close to zero and not statistically significant, with an irrelevant variation as a result of the inclusion of the control variables. While the β coefficient is not robust, the only statistically significant variable is 'education' (β = -0.163; p $\leq$ 0.05): the lower the level of MPs' education, the higher their level of responsiveness toward their (s)electoral constituency. To sum up, according to our analyses, the magnitude of electoral support obtained during the legislative primaries has no impact on the parliamentary behaviour of M5S MPs. This result could be interpreted in the light of the peculiar features of the party. In particular, it seems that the online nature of

Table 10.4 Multivariate linear regression: policy responsiveness

Dependent variable: % of parliamentary act related to the MP's electoral constituency (Model 2)

Independent variables		
Number of votes	0.008 (0.002)	0.023 (0.003)
Control variables		
Age		−0.073 (0.024)
Gender		−0.014 (0.405)
Education		−0.163 (0.376)**
Social Capital		0.027 (0.009)
Party's office		−0.050 (0.159)
Switchers		0.042 (0.479)
Model information		
Observations	163	162
Adjusted R^2	−0.01	−0.01

Source: own elaboration.

Note: Entries are standardised beta coefficients; standard errors in parentheses. **p $\leq$ 0.05. In the second column, there are 162 observations because the social capital variable has one missing value.

the M5S legislative primaries is detrimental to their ability to influence the parliamentary behaviour of the nominees. In fact, online primaries involve a very limited number of selectors, so that a few tens of votes are enough to get a nomination. Most likely, MPs have no incentive to base their parliamentary work on the requests of such a low number of voters.

In any case, these results have to be interpreted in the light of very low (or negative) adjusted R^2. This value indicates that the variance of the residuals is higher than the variance of the dependent variable, meaning that – despite previous literature findings – the level of support obtained in primary elections has no significance in explaining the changes in MPs' rebel votes. In particular, party rebellion seems to be affected by other factors, and we suggest that in this case contextual factors should be considered. The uncertainty of the electoral law for the following general election may have affected the MPs' parliamentary strategies. The proposal for a new PR electoral system – providing a combination of blocked head of the lists and preferential votes – could have led MPs to adopt more loyal behaviour in order to be able to achieve a safe place at the top of the list, demonstrating loyalty and cohesion with the party line. With regard to responsiveness, we clearly see that our independent variable does not help in explaining the changes in responsive parliamentary behaviour, but once other socio-political variables are included in the model the adjusted R^2 increases to 0.24, suggesting that in this regard personal profile counts for more.

Conclusions

The case of Italy is particularly helpful to understanding how a political system may react to the entry of new political parties. In this chapter, we focused in particular on the *Movimento 5 Stelle*. This party represents a true novelty for its organisational structure – based mainly on the web – and for its intra-party dynamics, where party members are entitled to have a say in party decision-making. This, it has to be pointed out, is true at least in theory, but in practice the party leadership influences intra-party democracy remarkably. The party had the ability to capitalise on the negative climate of opinion during the 2013 Italian general election (Bobba et al., 2013), obtaining almost a quarter of the votes in its first national electoral competition. The *Movimento 5 Stelle*, furthermore, tried to take advantage of the diffusion of primary elections in Italy – introduced more than ten years ago by the centre-left mainstream parties – to offer its party members the possibility to have a say in the selection of candidates to be included in the blocked list for the general election. This represents an absolute novelty for the Italian political system, since primaries have so far been used for selecting candidates for monocratic electoral offices. Interestingly, this choice led the other parties to use open primaries – meaning even more inclusive procedures – for choosing nominations.

This chapter focused on the effects of the *Parlamentarie* in terms of representation, party rebellion and policy responsiveness. In particular, we aimed to assess how and to what extent these closed primaries may have affected the representation in the Italian Parliament in terms of generational renewal and gender balance. Our purpose was also to test whether the level of support (in terms of the number of votes) obtained in primary elections could have an impact on MPs' parliamentary behaviour.

The analysis showed that in the selection process, women – although largely under-represented – have attained more electoral support than men; the same applies to graduates, which were a relative majority and obtained more votes than others. Limiting the analysis to the elected members in parliament, the M5S MPs are younger and have a better gender balance than the rest of the parliament. From the point of view of sociological representation, M5S's selection of candidates had some innovative effects on the parliamentary class, but with regard to the parliamentary behaviour of the MPs, the results are different. As the inferential analyses clearly showed, the selection method and, especially, the (s)electoral performance of the online primary's candidates had no effect on their degree of rebellion against the party or on their level of policy responsiveness. These findings, basically, contradict our hypotheses and previous literature results. Nevertheless, they could be interpreted in the light of the Italian political scenario where the uncertainty about the electoral law could have redefined MPs' incentives in their parliamentary behaviour. Furthermore, it has to be considered that the rules set by *Movimento 5 Stelle* for candidacy were quite restrictive. According to Hazan and Rahat (2010, 112), restrictive candidacy requirements are indicative of the 'attempt by the party to control the supply side of potential candidates'. This would relate to the need to strengthen party cohesion. Fulfilling the (exclusive) eligibility criteria would induce candidates to be more prone to follow the party line once elected. With hindsight, this could also be valid for M5S, since the candidacy for *Parlamentarie* was allowed only to those candidates who had failed local elections. In the absence of a structured (and prepared) political elite, Grillo resorted to those who already had (even if small) a network of supporters at local level. Even if not elected, they at least had experience on the election campaign, and that was sufficient for the kind of primary election organised.

To conclude, in terms of political outputs, the selection method adopted by M5S seems not entirely able to replace the absence of preferential voting, which – along with the single-member district – seems to be the only institutional tool that could give rise to a parliamentary class that is more constituency-centred than party-centred.

Notes

1 M5S obtained 25.6% of the votes for the Lower Chamber. It has to be pointed out that, when also considering the votes cast by Italians resident in foreign countries, the votes obtained by the *Partito Democratico* were slightly higher: 25.5% against the 25.1% gained by M5S. Furthermore, the PD is the primary party in the Senate.

2 Law No. 240/2005 was declared to be not in compliance with principles stated in the Italian Constitutional Chart by the *Corte Costituzionale* in 2014 (verdict 1/2014).

3 *Parlamentarie* were organised just after the second round of the centre-left open primary election to select the head of the coalition, held the 2nd December 2012.

4 It should be underlined that the party granted a few exceptions, allowing incumbent MPs serving in parliament for more than two legislatures to run in open primaries, or in other cases they were assigned to top-list positions.
5 See Table 1A in the annex, where a detailed overview of these figures is provided for each parliamentary group.
6 Both PD and SEL organised legislative primaries for selecting their candidates to be included in closed lists, but they opted for preserving the top list for a set of nominees directly selected by the party élites.
7 We tested both measurements, and the analyses produced the same results. Furthermore, relying on a calculation of votes in percentages would have, in the end, cancelled out the real difference between candidates' support in primary elections. Thus, in order to avoid any bias, we simply opted for using the absolute number of votes gained by candidates in primary elections.
8 The average age of M5S MPs is 37 years old: from a minimum of 25 to a maximum of 62.

References

Bobba, G., Legnante, G., Roncarolo, F., and Seddone, A. (2013) 'Candidates in a negative light. The 2013 Italian election campaign in the media. *Rivista italiana di Scienza Politica* 43 (3), pp. 353–380.
Bobba, G., and Seddone, A. (2015). Issues without owners, candidates without ownership. An analysis of 2013 Italian general election campaign. *Quaderni di Scienza Politica* 22 (1), pp. 37–60.
Bordandini, P., and Cartocci, R. (2014). [Quante Italie?] Il ritorno al tradizionale cleavage tra Nord e Sud del Paese. *Cambio* 4 (8), p. 47.
Bowler, S., Farrell, D., and Katz, R. S. (1999). Party cohesion, party discipline, and parliaments. In Bowler, S., Farrell, D. and Katz, R. S. (Eds.), *Party discipline and parliamentary government*. Columbus, OH: Ohio State University Press, pp. 3–22.
Ceron, A., and d'Adda, G. (2016). E-campaigning on Twitter: The effectiveness of distributive promises and negative campaign in the 2013 Italian election. *New Media & Society* 18 (9), pp. 1935–1955.
Cordero, G., and Coller, X. (2014). Cohesion and candidate selection in parliamentary groups, *Parliamentary Affairs* 68 (3), pp. 592–615.
Dahl, R. (1971). *Polyarchy*. New Haven: Yale University Press.
D'Alimonte, R. (2013). The Italian elections of February 2013: The end of the Second Republic? *Contemporary Italian Politics* 5 (2), pp. 113–129.
De Luca, M., Porcellato, N., Rombi, S., and Seddone, A. (2013). *Gli iscritti della Lega Nord e le primarie. Report basato su indagine CAWI*. Candidate and Leader Selection. Retrieved from www.cals.it/wp-content/uploads/2015/11/LN_reportWS2014_.pdf
De Lucia, F. (2013). Il Parlamento 2013: Nuovo e al femminile. In De Sio, L., Cataldi, M. and De Lucia, F. (Eds.), *Le elezioni Politiche 2013*. Roma: CISE – Centro Italiano Studi Elettorali, pp. 136–140.
Di Virgilio, A., Giannetti, D., Pedrazzani, A., and Pinto, L. (2015). Party competition in the 2013 Italian elections: Evidence from an expert survey. *Government and Opposition* 50, pp. 65–89. doi:10.1017/gov.2014.15
Diamond, L. J., and Morlino, L. (Eds.), (2005). *Assessing the quality of democracy*. Baltimore: Johns Hopkins University Press.
Eulau, H., and Karps, P. D. (1977). The puzzle of representation: Specifying components of responsiveness. *Legislative Studies Quarterly* 2 (3), pp. 233–254.

Fell, D. (2006). Democratisation of candidate selection in Taiwanese political parties. *Journal of Electoral Studies* 13 (2), pp. 167–198.

Gualmini, E. (2013). Da movimento a partito. In Corbetta, P. and Gualmini, E. (Eds.), *Il partito di Grillo*. Bologna: Il Mulino, pp. 7–28.

Hazan, R. Y., and Rahat, G. (2010). *Democracy within parties: Candidate selection methods and their political consequences*. Oxford: Oxford University Press.

Istat. (2016). *Rapporto Annuale 2016. La situazione del paese*. Roma: Istituto Nazionale di Statistica.

Kristjánsson, S. (1998). Electoral politics and governance: Transformation of the party system in Iceland, 1970–1996. In Pennings, P. and Lane J-E. (Eds.), *Comparing party system change*. London: Routledge, pp. 167–182.

Lanzone, M. E., and Rombi, S. (2014). Who did participate in the online primary elections of the five star movement (M5S) in Italy? Causes, features and effects of the selection process. *Partecipazione e conflitto* 7 (1), pp. 170–191.

Marangoni, F., and Verzichelli, L. (2015). From a technocratic solution to a fragile grand coalition: The impact of the economic crisis on parliamentary government in Italy. *The Journal of Legislative Studies* 21 (1), pp. 35–53.

McDonnell, D., and Valbruzzi, M. (2014). Defining and classifying technocrat-led and technocratic governments. *European Journal of Political Research* 53 (4), pp. 654–671.

Pasquino, G. (2007). Tricks and treats: The 2005 Italian electoral law and its consequences. *South European Society & Politics* 12 (1), pp. 79–93.

Pasquino, G., and Valbruzzi, M. (2016). Primary elections between fortuna and virtù. *Contemporary Italian Politics* 8 (1), pp. 3–11.

Powell, G. B. (2004). The chain of responsiveness. *Journal of Democracy* 15 (4), pp. 91–105.

Riker, W. H. (1982). *Liberalism against populism*. San Francisco: W. H. Freeman.

Rombi, S., and Seddone, A. (2017). Rebel rebel. Do primary elections affect legislators' behaviour? Insights from Italy. *Parliamentary Affairs*. doi: doi:10.1093/pa/gsw036.

Sandri, G., and Seddone, A. (Eds.). (2015). *The primary game. Primary elections and the Italian Democratic Party*. Novi Ligure: Epoké Edizioni.

Sandri, G., Seddone, A., and Venturino, F. (Eds.). (2015a). *Party primaries in comparative perspective*. Farnham: Ashgate Publishing.

Sandri, G., Seddone, A., and Venturino, F. (2015b). Understanding leadership profile renewal. In Cross, W. and Pilet, J-B. (Eds.), *The politics of party leadership: A cross-national perspective*. Oxford: Oxford University Press. doi:10.1093/acprof: oso/9780198748984.003.0006

Shomer, Y. (2009). Candidate selection procedures, seniority, and vote-seeking behavior. *Comparative Political Studies* 42 (7), pp. 945–970.

Sieberer, U. (2006). Party unity in parliamentary democracies: A comparative analysis. *The Journal of Legislative Studies* 12 (2), pp. 150–178.

Tronconi, F. (ed.). (2015). *Beppe Grillo's five star movement: Organisation, communication and ideology*. Farnham: Ashgate Publishing.

Turner, E. (2013). The Grillini in Italy: New horizons for internet-based mobilization and participation. *Social Movement Studies* 12 (2), pp. 214–220.

Wauters, B. (2012). *Democratization versus representation? Women party leaders and party primaries in Belgium*. In ECPR Joint Sessions of Workshops. Ghent University, Department of Political Science.

Annex

Table 10.5 Socio-graphic characteristics of the Italian main parliamentary groups' MPs (in %)

	Partito Democratico	Sinistra Ecologia Libertà	Movimento 5 Stelle	SVP	Forza Italia	Unione di Centro	Lega Nord	Scelta Civica	Centro Democratico	Fratelli d'Italia	Others	All MPs
Female rate	38.6	27.3	38.0	14.3	18.5	14.3	15.2	14.3		12.5	18.2	30.5
Age (mean)	49	46	37	47	54	60	47	53	59	48	47	48
Middle school	0.5	2.3	1.2	–	1.5	–	6.1	–	–	–	–	1.1
High school	26.4	34.1	31.9	28.6	23.6	–	39.4	18.4	27.3	37.5	18.2	27
University degree	73.1	63.6	66.9	71.4	74.9	100	54.5	81.6	72.7	62.5	81.8	72
N	417	44	163	7	195	7	33	49	11	8	11	945

Source: Candidate and Leader Selection.

Table 10.6 Descriptive statistics of the control variables

	N	Min	Max	Mean	St. Deviation
Age	163	25	62	37.0	7.897
Gender	163	0	1	0.62	0.487
Education	163	2	4	3.66	0.502
Organisational role	163	0	4	1.31	1.264
MPs Switchers	163	0	1	0.22	0.426
Social Capital	162	58.9	144.4	97.53	22.594

Source: Candidate and Leader Selection.

11 New political parties in Latin America

A new way of selection and new elite profiles?

Mélany Barragán and Asbel Bohigues

Introduction

Candidate selection is vital to political parties: those who are eventually elected to office will be successful candidates previously chosen by the parties, and they will determine much of how the party appears and what it does (Hazan and Rahat, 2006, 2010). For that reason, backing a winning candidacy is a meaningful source of power for every political party, especially taking into account that holding political office is the principal aim of any party or politician (Kirchheimer, 1990, 344).

The use of internal elections as a method of candidate nomination has risen intensely in recent decades (Sandri et al., 2015). On the one hand, the appearance of new parties has informed the population about problems of democratic accountability, transparency and internal democracy. In that sense, new parties may reveal to citizens demands that were not previously known. On the other hand, against a background of sharp decline in party legitimacy, internal elections have emerged as a method of party reform in several countries (Torcal, 2015).

However, the introduction of methods of promoting internal democracy and the holding of primary elections do not necessary alter the profiles of elites. Recent studies have evidenced that the direct election of candidates does not modify the characteristics of the candidates nominated (Hazan and Rahat, 2010; Wauters and Pilet, 2015). The main reason for this is the persistence of strong party control over primaries: candidates who are less connected to the party are less likely to win, and also less likely to remain a candidate throughout the primary.

In spite of the emergence of new parties and the importance of candidate-selection procedures, there is a scarcity of pertinent studies focused on Latin America. Although some authors have written about specific parties, or have compared a small group of parties, there are no systematized works comparing a large number of political parties. A few factors may explain this circumstance: first, the difficulties in obtaining information about the organizational development of parties and internal party democracy; second, tensions between formal procedures and informal rules; and, finally, incessant changes in terms of candidate-selection processes (Freidenberg, 2003).

In order to contribute to the scholarly literature on candidate selection, this chapter describes political recruitment, candidate selection, and models of party democracy in Latin America. From a comparative approach, this work combines two dimensions: the new/traditional party dichotomy and the mechanisms of internal democracy. All these are linked to their impact on elite profiles.

Specifically, this chapter proceeds as follows: first, an overview of Latin American parties and elites; second, a review of candidate-selection procedures in the region; and, finally, an analysis of the impact on elite profiles. To that end, four paradigmatic parties will be examined: Movement for Socialism (Bolivia), PAIS Alliance (Ecuador), United Socialist Party of Venezuela, and Citizens' Action Party (Costa Rica).

Latin American politics: an overview of its parties and elites

One of the main characteristics of Latin American parties and party systems is their diversity: their development does not take any particular form.[1] In fact, over the last two decades, all Latin American countries have reformed their instruments of party law and organization (Molenaar, 2012). However, in spite of the existence of many works that attempt to describe and systematize all these reforms, the scholarly literature which links these processes with the transformations and crises of party systems remains scarce.

Nevertheless, among the main reasons for all these legal and organizational changes is that, from Mexico to Argentina, many of the traditional parties have entered into crisis. Between 1958 and 1993, Venezuela's two major parties, AD and COPEI, together drew an average of 78% of the vote in national elections.[2] But by 1998, a mere 3% of Venezuelans cast their ballots for these parties. Something very similar happened in Bolivia: in 1980, three parties – ADN, MNR, MIR – dominated politics. Together they received an average 67% of the vote. In 2002, ADN attracted only 3% of the vote, and neither ADN nor the MIR fielded a presidential candidate in the 2005 election (Lupu, 2016).

Disenchanted by corruption, poverty and inequality, voters have been drawn to new movements which promise redistribution of wealth and punishment of the traditional parties (Murillo et al., 2010). New parties, seeking to enter into the system, try to offer to the electorate new models of party democracy. Often, new organizations introduce into their discourses recipes against exclusion and disaffection, proposing mechanisms of internal democracy such as primaries. But, for the most part, these new parties hope to assume the capacity to break up the established political order: they emerge as an alternative in terms of discourse, organizational models, and elites.

Between 1978 and 2007, one-quarter of the region's established parties broke down, deeply fragmenting the party systems. New parties have emerged as instant electoral vehicles for prominent personalities, and fragmentation has made it easier for political outsiders to win elections (Lupu, 2016). In fact, with the exception of Bolivia, Panama and Venezuela, the number of parties competing in elections has increased (Alcántara and Tagina, 2016).

However, this doesn't mean that the parties on offer have been stable during this period: since the transitions to democracy, many parties have born and disappeared (Torcal, 2015). Those parties that were too rigid to evolve, and those that relied most heavily on patronage have sometimes found it particularly difficult to mobilize support without access to state resources (Burges, 1999; Levitsky and Way, 1998; Morgan, 2011).

Nevertheless, Latin American party systems have been fluid as a result of political mobilization in combination with social policy innovation (Mainwaring and Scully, 1995). Thus, the emergence of new political and economic trends has produced new political alignments and, therefore, changes to the party system's composition. Furthermore, other factors must be taken into account, such as the emergence of new leaders and alliances, programmatic shifts and party splits.

When Hugo Chávez came to power in 1999, a new political cycle started in Latin American politics (Alcántara, 2016). After decades of neoliberalism and right-wing Governments, there was a turn to the left (Levitsky and Roberts, 2013) that had an impact on party systems. New parties emerged and, although it is difficult to characterize all of them, one of their main attributes is their connection with social movements or demands for political change (Lupu, 2016).

In order to distinguish between traditional and new parties, it is first necessary to briefly describe the evolution of Latin American party systems. In spite of the permanence of some historical parties – for example, the APRA in Peru or UCR in Argentina – following the transitions to democracy new parties were incorporated in the party systems – FSLN in Nicaragua, FMLN in El Salvador, *inter alia* – and have remained ever since. On the opposite side, some traditional parties have disappeared – DCG in Guatemala, MPD in Ecuador, PS in Bolivia – and others had a relatively short life – CR in Peru, in Guatemala, CMR in Venezuela, or MFE in Ecuador, among others. In some cases, these parties were mere electoral platforms without the expectation of continuity; in others, electoral failure caused their extinction.

In any case, parties that emerged before and after transitions usually shared similar structures and models of democracy. Since the mid-1990s, parties have relied on vertical structures, where a few leaders at the central level concentrate power and control the party's direction (Wills-Otero, 2016). While in some cases stronger party roots have sought to produce stable links between the represented and their representatives, and have helped parties to survive in times of crisis, in other cases, highly personalized parties have concentrated power into just one or few leaders. In both cases the parties ensure continuity of the model – with some distinctions in the case of populism – and limit the role of the citizenry in politics.

Meanwhile, some entirely new parties have emerged in Latin American politics in recent years: PAIS in Ecuador, MORENA in Mexico, or LIBRE in Honduras are just a few examples. The majority of these new parties may be considered a symptom of transformation, having considerable voter support and being conceived as a real alternative to the old parties (Torcal, 2015). They bring new proposals and models of democracy, marking a difference in the manner of engaging in politics.

In spite of the arrival of new parties, certain continuities have remained in terms of elite profiles (Table 11.1). There remains a predominance of men in middle-age

Table 11.1 Elite profiles in traditional and new parties

	Traditional Parties				New Parties				Total			
	Women (%)	Age	Education (%)	Main Profession (%)	Women (%)	Age	Education (%)	Main Profession (%)	Women (%)	Age	Education (%)	Main Professions (%)
Argentina	26.8	52.3 (0.8)	22.4 High School 55.4 Bachelor 22.2 Postgrad.	24.6 Lawyer 10.3 Professor 7.0 Businessman	37.8	47.3 (1.3)	3.8 High School 60.7 Bachelor 35.5 Postgrad.	26.7 Lawyer 19.6 Businessman 14.1 Economist	30.8	52.2 (1.02)	26.4 High School 52.3 Bachelor 21.3Postgrad.	22.4 Lawyer 11.9 Professor 5.9 Businessman
Bolivia	16.5	44.8 (9.4)	19.7 High School 50.8 Bachelor 29.5 Postgrad.	12.6 Lawyer 10.3 Businessman 9.1 Farmer	–	–	–	–	16.5	44.8 (1.2)	19.7 High School 50.8 Bachelor 29.5 Postgrad.	12.6 Lawyer 10.3 Businessman 9.1 Farmer
Chile	11.0	48.1 (10.1)	4.9 High School 60.3 Bachelor 34.8 Postgrad.	19.3 Lawyer 10.5 Businessman 10.1 Professor	–	–	–	–	11.0	48.1 (1.3)	4.9 High School 60.3 Bachelor 34.8 Postgrad.	19.3 Lawyer 10.5 Businessman 10.1 Professor
Colombia	10,1	45.6 (1,0)	1.9 High School 38.6 Bachelor 59.5 Postgrad.	19.1 Lawyer 9.1 Bureaucrat 7.8 Engineer	37.3	43.4 (1.3)	0.0 High School 46.5 Bachelor 53.5 Postgrad.	20.0 Businessman 10.1 Lawyer 7.1 Trader	12.9	45.2 (1.0)	1.7 High School 39.9 Bachelor 58.4 Postgrad.	15.8 Lawyer 11.4 Bureaucrat 8.0 Businessman
Costa Rica	36.7	47.2 (1.0)	5.5 High School 52.3 Bachelor 42.2 Postgrad.	15.0 Businessman 14.1 Professor 13.7 Lawyer	35.1	49.7 (1.2)	10.2 High School 59.3 Bachelor 30.5 Postgrad.	11.9 Professor 7.2 Lawyer 6.0 Businessman	30.3	48.6 (1.1)	8.8 High School 54.6 Bachelor 36.7 Postgrad.	17.0 Professor 13.6 Lawyer 13.6 Businessman
Dominican Republic	14.0	47.6 (0.9)	8.0 High School 63.2 Bachelor 28.8 Postgrad.	15.6 Lawyer 14.9 Trader 10.1 Businessman	25.0	47.3 (1.0)	6.2 High School 67.2 Bachelor 26.6 Postgrad.	16.0 Lawyer 15.0 Trader 9.0 Businessman	15.1	47.6 (0.9)	7.1 High School 64.9 Bachelor 27.9 Postgrad.	17.5 Lawyer 14.2 Trader 8.1 Businessman
Ecuador	13..9	46.4 (1.1)	9.3 High School 55.3 Bachelor 35.4 Postgrad.	24.3 Lawyer 14.6 Businessman 5.8 Professor	31.5	45.4 (1.3)	1.2 High School 61.3 Bachelor 37.5 Postgrad.	25.0 Lawyer 18.2 Professor 9.1 Journalist	22.9	45.9 (1.3)	7.3 High School 58.4 Bachelor 34.2 Postgrad.	24.6 Lawyer 12.7 Professor 8.1 Businessman
El Salvador	15.6	47.2 (1.2)	14.2 High School 69.0 Bachelor 16.8 Postgrad.	13.9 Businessman 8.2 Farmer 7.6 Bureaucrat	–	–	–	–	15.6	47.2 (1.2)	14.2 High School 69.0 Bachelor 16.8 Postgrad.	13.9 Businessman 8.2 Farmer 7.6 Bureaucrat
Guatemala	6.8	49.3 (1.0)	11.9 High School 68.9 Bachelor 19.2 Postgrad.	16.8 Businessman 13.6 Trader 11.9 Lawyer	12.9	46.2 (1.3)	9.8 High School 52.9 Bachelor 37.3 Postgrad.	25.0 Businessman 10.5 Lawyer 5.2 Trader	10.0	47.2 (1.1)	10.2 High School 64.0 Bachelor 25.8Postgrad.	18.3 Businessman 10.7 Trader 10.0 Lawyer
Honduras	10.8	52.3 (1.1)	25.3 High School 60.1 Bachelor 14.6 Postgrad.	17.2 Businessman 10.9 Lawyer 6.7 Farmer	33.1	42.0 (1.4)	20.1 High School 61.8 Bachelor 18.1 Postgrad.	15.2 Businessman 10.5 Lawyer 7.3 Farmer	17.9	48.1 (1.2)	23.8 High School 61.5 Bachelor 14.7 Postgrad.	16.7 Businessman 11.5 Lawyer 6.4 Farmer

Country	%	Age (SD)	Education	Top professions	%	Age (SD)	Education	Top professions	%	Age (SD)	Education	Top professions
Mexico	24.7	44.0 (1.1)	2.4 High School; 61.2 Bachelor; 36.4 Postgrad.	18.4 Bureaucrat; 12.0 Professor; 9.0 Lawyer	28.6	46.3 (1.2)	0.0 High School; 85.7 Bachelor; 14.2 Postgrad.	10.1 Bureaucrat; 9.0 Professor; 6.0 Businessman	24.8	45.1 (1.2)	3.8 High School; 64.1 Bachelor; 32.0 Postgrad.	17.0 Bureaucrat; 10.0 Professor; 8.6 Businessman
Nicaragua	10.0	50.9 (1.1)	7.7 High School; 64.5 Bachelor; 27.8 Postgrad.	12.0 Lawyer; 9.5 Businessman; 8.0 Farmer	11.8	46.9 (1.3)	0.0 High School; 41.2 Bachelor; 58.8 Postgrad.	17.6 Lawyer; 11.6 Manager; 11.6 Doctor	23.4	48.1 (1.2)	6.6 High School; 48.4 Bachelor; 44.9 Postgrad.	13.0 Businessman; 12.5 Lawyer; 7.1 Manager
Panama	12.3	48.9 (1.1)	10.3 High School; 59.3 Bachelor; 30.2 Postgrad.	18.9 Businessman; 13.8 Doctor; 8.7 Professor	—	—	—	—	12.3	48.9 (1.1)	10.3 High School; 59.3 Bachelor; 30.5 Postgrad.	18.9 Businessman; 13.8 Doctor; 8.7 Professor
Paraguay	6.9	43.3 (0.9)	11.5 High School; 55.0 Bachelor; 33.5 Postgrad.	20.6 Businessman; 19.5 Trader; 14.2 Lawyer	21.1	55.0 (1.0)	0.0 High School; 100.0 Bachelor; 0.0 Postgrad.	9.5 Lawyer; 9.5 Businessman; 9.5 Trader	9.3	45.3 (1.0)	18.6 High School; 70.2 Bachelor; 20.2 Postgrad.	19.6 Lawyer; 13.7 Businessman; 12.5 Trader
Peru	20.1	51.8 (1.2)	7.7 High School; 41.2 Bachelor; 51.1 Postgrad.	18.8 Professor; 15.5 Lawyer; 13.5 Doctor	30.2	49.1 (0.9)	5.2 High School; 51.3 Bachelor; 43.5 Postgrad.	25.0 Businessman; 14.2 Lawyer; 10.1 Bureaucrat	20.8	49.4 (1.2)	3.7 High School; 50.6 Bachelor; 45.7 Postgrad.	18.5 Businessman; 16.1 Professor; 14.7 Lawyer
Uruguay	6.8	—	21.6 High School; 59.5 Bachelor; 18.9 Postgrad.	13.3 Professor; 10.0 Lawyer; 6.7 Doctor	16.1		0.0 High School; 65.0 Bachelor; 35.0 Postgrad.	29.0 Lawyer; 12.3 Doctor; 9.3 Bureaucrat	11.7	49.3 (1.2)	20.4 High School; 60.3 Bachelor; 19.4 Postgrad.	15.0 Lawyer; 9.3 Professor; 7.9 Doctor
Venezuela		49.3 (1.2)				47.2 (1.0)			9.2	48.0 (1.2)	7.4 High School; 52.6 Bachelor; 40.1 Postgrad.	16.8 Lawyer; 15.0 Professor; 9.3 Journalist

Source: Project of Parliamentary Elites in Latin America. University of Salamanca (1994–2017).

Note:
(1) Standard deviation in brackets for the age variable.
(2) Data not available for the case of Brazil.
(3) There are no new parties in Chile, El Salvador or Panama. In terms of age, the percentage varied between 45.2 in Colombia and 52.2 in Argentina. In some countries like Argentina, Guatemala, Honduras and Nicaragua, the average age within new parties has decreased. This may be explained by the promise of a rupture with the old ruling elites and a clear rejection of "partitocracy" (Guillman, 2010). However, the figure in the Dominican Republic has been stable and in Paraguay it has been increased by almost ten years, indicating the absence of a generational replacement. Finally, the presence of politicians with university degrees is a constant in all countries, and having experienced university training is a common feature among candidates (Putnam, 1977; Rosón, 2006; Best and Cotta, 2007). However, although university-trained legislators are quite frequent in modern democracies, in Latin America there is a much diversity in terms of education. The country whose elites carry the highest educational credentials is Colombia, while the countries where more people have not attended university are Argentina, Honduras and Uruguay.

with high educational credentials. Nevertheless, one of the main characteristics of new parties is the inclusion of new actors, especially those considered traditionally "vulnerable" (Guchin Mieres, 2012). And, among these groups, women play an important role: the number of women in politics has risen with the emergence of new parties.

Argentina and Costa Rica are the countries with the highest percentage of women in politics, partly due to regulations. Argentina was the first Latin American country where a gender quota law was passed[3] and Costa Rica is a case (together with Ecuador) where quotas further apply to the internal structures of political parties.[4] On the other hand, countries like Guatemala or Dominican Republic show the lowest level of women in politics. In the former, the country lacks a Quota Law, while in the Dominican Republic, the law only provides for a 33% quota of female representation.[5]

Candidate selection in Latin American politics: changes and continuities

Parties can select their candidates in many different ways. In some cases, a legal framework establishes that political parties should democratically elect their candidates but does not specify applicable legal provisions. Sometimes, laws allow parties to choose whether or not they want to hold primaries. In other cases, legislation lays down the procedure by which candidates should be selected.

The aim of this section is to develop a framework to describe candidate selection models in Latin America, in order to identify similarities and differences in the nomination procedures among countries. The model does not attempt to provide a complete explanation of institutional adoption, but to clarify the role of nomination of candidates to run in elections. Political parties throughout Latin America rely increasingly on primary elections to select candidates, and these are touted as moves toward openness and internal party democracy (Carey and Polga-Hecimovich, 2006). Nowadays, parties are regulated by constitutional frameworks or internal regulations that specify requirements for selecting leadership positions within the party. This includes selecting candidates to run for public office as well as selecting candidates for executive positions within the party.

While in most countries in the region candidates were traditionally selected by the party elite, the institutionalization of party systems during the third wave of democratization brought the candidate selection process to the forefront of political debate. As a consequence, citizens now expect primary elections to promote intra-party democracy and to reduce party control over the selection of candidates preferred by the establishment (Sacristan, 2007).

However, the adoption of primary elections reveals differences among countries. In that sense, one of the first aspects to address has to do with the mandatory nature of the mechanism: while some political systems impose primaries on political parties, others regulate its implementation but give parties the option to not hold primaries. These include both open and closed primaries, establishing different degrees of intra-party competition. In general, primaries have been introduced in the last two decades, although there were some earlier experiences in countries such as Costa Rica or Honduras (Table 11.2).

The introduction of primaries is a consequence of various factors: on the one hand, elites have assumed that mechanisms of internal democracy are useful to connect with new voters; on the other hand, there are pressures from international cooperation to deepen the processes of democratization. Additionally, there is a belief that primaries can contribute to achieving electoral success (Freidenberg, 2014).

In that sense, the arrival of the new century evidenced the crisis of legitimacy of many traditional parties, which had been conceived as oligarchic and non-transparent organizations. Traditional elites maintained firm power, limiting the participation of the base and exercising absolute control over candidacies. In response to that circumstance, public opinion began to demand new instruments of participation, transparency, cooperation and tolerance (Freidenberg, 2007).

However, primaries have also emerged from internal party divisions. For example, in 1985 Honduras introduced compulsory mechanisms of internal democracy to solve problems between party factions or groups. Later, PT in Brazil adopted this model to fight against internal divisions and to achieve cooperation and consensus among groups. Notably, the holding of primaries may allow changes in the conditions of intra-party competition (Bruhn, 2014). For example, in 2005, the anti-apparatus candidates of Mexico's PAN pressured elites into establishing more competitive mechanisms for candidate selection. Finally, the experiences of other countries provided examples and conditioned the probability of adopting these instruments, producing a contagion effect (Sandri et al., 2015).

Two large groups of countries may be distinguished: one composed of countries where primaries are compulsory, and another with non-compulsory elections. When elections are not compulsory, there are two possible settings: the existence of regulation if parties agree to hold internal elections, or the absence of the same. Finally, there is a marginal group of countries without a specific regulation (Table 11.3).

Costa Rica is the country with the longest tradition of compulsory internal elections (since 1949), although it relaxed its system in 2010. Uruguay introduced compulsory primaries in 1996, replacing the double simultaneous vote in place since 1922. One year later, in 1997, Panama regulated the holding of primaries for presidential elections, and in 2002 it extended that process to the selection of all party candidates. These countries were pioneers in the introduction of primaries, but the main reforms developed after 2000.

In the last decade, different Latin American countries introduced reforms regarding candidate-selection processes. Several countries adopted provisions for internal democracy; some for the first time in their history. In 2003 Peru prescribed in its law of political parties several procedures for the internal democratic election of all party candidates and all those in charge of internal party functions. One year later, the Dominican Republic introduced national primaries for the selection of party candidates overseen by the Electoral Council, and Honduras added the regulation of primaries to its electoral code.

Table 11.2 Electoral laws

Country	Source of Law	With reference to the Party Statues	Primary Elections (by Law)	Primary elections (In practice)	State-supervised/organized
Argentina (1985–2001)	Law	No	No	Yes	No
Argentina (2001–2006)	Law	No	Yes	Yes	Only if parties so request
Argentina (2009)	Law	Yes	Yes	Yes	Yes
Bolivia (1999)	Law	Yes	Yes	Yes	Yes
Bolivia (2001)	No	–	–	No	–
Brazil	No	–	–	No	
Colombia (1994)	Law	Yes	No	Yes	Yes (National Electoral Council)
Costa Rica (1949)	Constitution	Yes	Yes	Yes	No
Costa Rica (2010)	Electoral Code	Yes	Unspecified	Yes	Yes (Electoral Court)
Chile (1996)	Law	No	No	Partially	Electoral Organism
Chile (2012)	Law	No	No	Yes	
Ecuador (1978–2009)	No	–	–	No	
Ecuador (2009)	Law	Yes	Yes	Yes	Yes (National Electoral Council)
El Salvador (1985–2013)	No	–	–	No	
El Salvador (2013)	Constitution and Law	Yes	Unspecified	Yes	No
Guatemala	Law	Yes	No	No	No
Honduras (1985)	Law	Yes	Yes	Yes	Yes (Electoral Court)
Honduras (2004)	Law	Yes	Yes	Yes	Yes (Electoral Court)
Mexico (2014)	Law	Yes	Unspecified	Yes	–
Nicaragua	No	–	–	No	
Panama (1997)	Law	Yes	Yes	Yes	No

Panama (2002)	No	–	No	–
Panama (2006)	Law	Yes	Yes	No
Paraguay	Law	Yes	Yes	No
Peru (2003)	Law	Yes	Yes	Yes
Dominican Republic (1994–2004)	No	No	No	–
Dominican Republic (2004)	No	–	Yes	No
Uruguay (1998)	Law	Yes	Yes	Yes (National Electoral Council)
Venezuela	Constitution and Law	Yes	Yes	Yes (National Electoral Council)

Source: adapted from Freidenberg and Dosek (2016).

Table 11.3 Legislation and candidate selection in Latin America: primary elections

Non-compulsory		Compulsory	Non-specific regulation
No regulation	*Regulation (if parties agree to hold primary elections)*		
Bolivia, Brazil, Guatemala, Nicaragua	Chile, Colombia	Argentina, Costa Rica, Dominican Republic, Ecuador, Honduras, Panama, Paraguay, Peru, Uruguay and Venezuela	El Salvador, Mexico

Source: Authors' own elaboration.

In 2008, Ecuador stipulated in its Constitution that political organizations need to function in a democratic matter, and that they must appoint their candidates through internally democratic processes. Argentina followed the same path in 2009, after a failed attempt at reform in 2002, with a special particularity: here primaries are not only compulsory for parties, but also for voters. Finally, in Venezuela, the electoral branch of Government is awarded the power to organize the internal elections of the political associations mentioned in the Constitution (Art. 293).

At the other end of the spectrum are countries with non-compulsory primaries. On the one hand, Bolivia, Brazil, Guatemala and Nicaragua have no regulation. Within this group, Bolivia is an interesting example, because its Constitution stipulates that indigenous organizations' candidates may be elected in line with the democratic norms customary within their communities (Molenaar, 2012). On the other hand, Chilean and Colombian electoral laws present regulations if parties agree to hold primary elections. In both cases, parties may choose between primaries regulated by law, or closed elections regulated by their own statutes (Table 11.4.).

Finally, Mexico and El Salvador do not have a specific regulation, and some leeway is hence given to the parties themselves. Even though many efforts have been made at regulating internal democracy, there are no specific norms for organizing candidate selection. The consequence is a low and late score for implementation of that mechanism. In El Salvador, ARENA held primary elections for the first time in 2014, and FMLN in 2016. In Mexico, PAN shows the highest levels of internal democracy, as compared to PRI and PRD (Freidenberg and Dosek, 2016).

Together with the legal regulations, information from personal and anonymous interviews may provide a clearer perspective wherever informal rules and perceptions serve to complete the analysis of internal democracy; such a strategy has already been successfully used to analyze Spanish parliamentary elites (Coller,

Table 11.4 Primary election by political parties (non-compulsory and non-specific regulation)

Country	Political Party	Primary Elections	Since (Year)
Bolivia	MAS, UN, PDC	NO	
Brazil	PT, PMDB, PSDB, PDB, PR, PP	NO	–
Guatemala	LIDER, UNE, FCN, PP, GANA	NO	–
Nicaragua	FSLN, PLI	NO	–
	PLC	YES	1996
Chile	UDI, PCCh	NO	–
	RN, PDC, PPD, PRSD, PS, Alianza (coalition)	YES	2013
	Concertación (coalition)	YES	1993
Colombia	Partido de la U, Centro Democrático, PLC, PDA, PCR	NO	–
	PCC	YES	1998
El Salvador	ARENA, GANA,PCN	NO	–
	FMLN	YES	2016
Mexico	PRI, PAN, PRD	YES	1999
	MORENA	YES	2015

Source: Project of Electoral Reforms in Latin America. University of Salamanca.

Note: The last column applies only to political parties which hold primary elections.

Jaime and Mota, 2018). Exploring the perceptions of elites is important because it allows understanding of how party members interpret successive electoral reforms as well as the implementation of new mechanisms of internal democracy. Moreover, this allows study of whether there is a direct connection between effective regulation and the attitudes of the political elite.

Figure 11.1 shows that, except in some cases – mainly Dominican Republic and El Salvador – the trend is toward fewer parliamentarians who believe that decisions are taken at the top of the party hierarchy. Or, in other words, the majority of parliamentary elites agree that their parties allow for plurality and participation of the party bases. The predominance of this assumption in the region responds to the same logic: electoral reforms have been accompanied by a discourse of democratization by elites, and politicians conceive the participation of their bases as a strategy for innovation and transparency. In this way, there is good reason to expect that transparency in internal party decisions should be an electoral asset: cynicism toward political parties is widespread through the region and parties are among the least trusted institutions (Carey and Polga-Hecimovich, 2006).

These percentages indicate a new reality in terms of organizational dynamics: an empowerment of party members has occurred, and every day there are more instruments of inclusion (Rahat and Hazan, 2001). The majority of countries are displaying higher levels of intra-party democracy, member participation and openness of internal decision mechanisms. This also connects with the political transformations commenced at the beginning of the 21st century: the arrival of

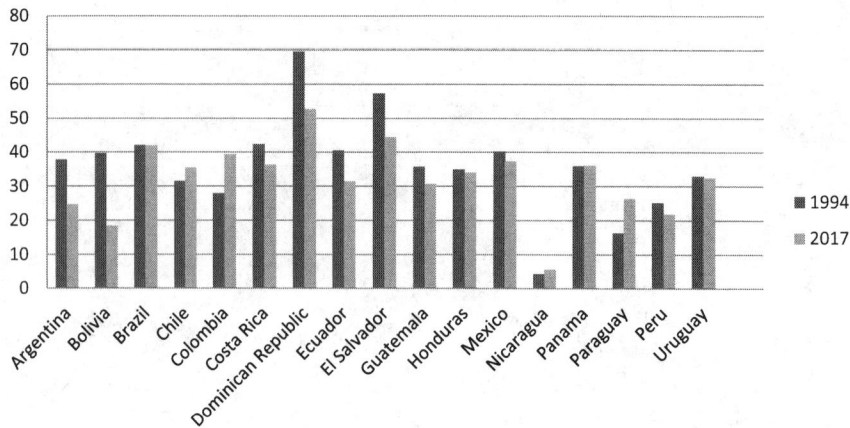

Figure 11.1 Percentage of deputies who claim, "In my political party, decisions are taken at the top"

Source: Project of Parliamentary Elites in Latin America. University of Salamanca (1994–2017).

Note: Response categories included in the figure: "agree" and "strongly agree".

new political forces, the greater inclusion of society in politics, and the demands for change have all contributed to altering internal party dynamics and increasing the participation of the bases.

According to this perception of internal democracy, the greater part of parliamentarians state that their party's leaders are not too powerful (Figure 11.2). Only the Dominican Republic and Panama deviate from this general trend. And this is especially relevant because, traditionally, Latin American politics have been characterized by strong personalism, with powerful leaders. However, according to the perceptions of elites, party leaders do not enjoy the same influence and control as before, and this may be because, in times of change or crisis, a more horizontal internal party structure may be more electorally successful (Wills-Otero, 2016). As was mentioned above, recent political changes have increased the role of participation and, inasmuch as leaders are less powerful and more people can participate in the decision-making processes, more options are becoming available and representation may be improved.

Finally, when elites are questioned about candidate selection, the larger part agree that candidates are democratically elected (Figure 11.3). In this respect, electoral reforms have put the candidate-selection process at the centre of debate and have raised the perception of internal democracy in comparative terms with respect to the past. Moreover, the emergence of new parties and the crisis of representation have imposed a discourse of internal democracy. The final purpose is to alienate parties from oligarchic models and to transform them into fresh organizations with a higher degree of freedom, transparency and pluralism. And, in this

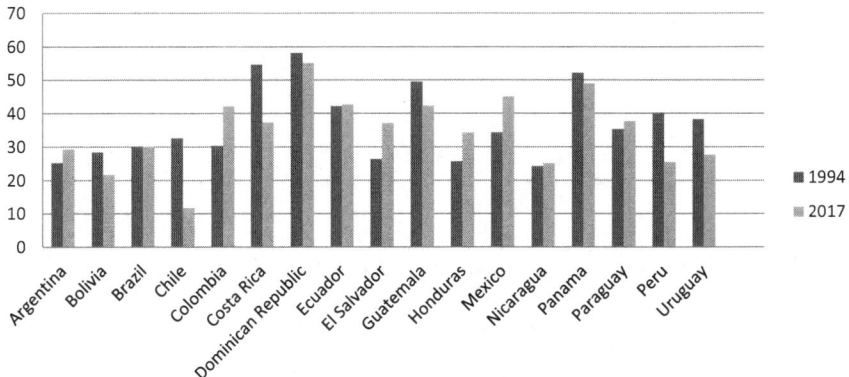

Figure 11.2 Percentage of deputies who claim, "The party leader is too powerful"

Source: Project of Parliamentary Elites in Latin America. University of Salamanca (1994–2017).

Note: Response categories included in the figure: "agree" and "strongly agree".

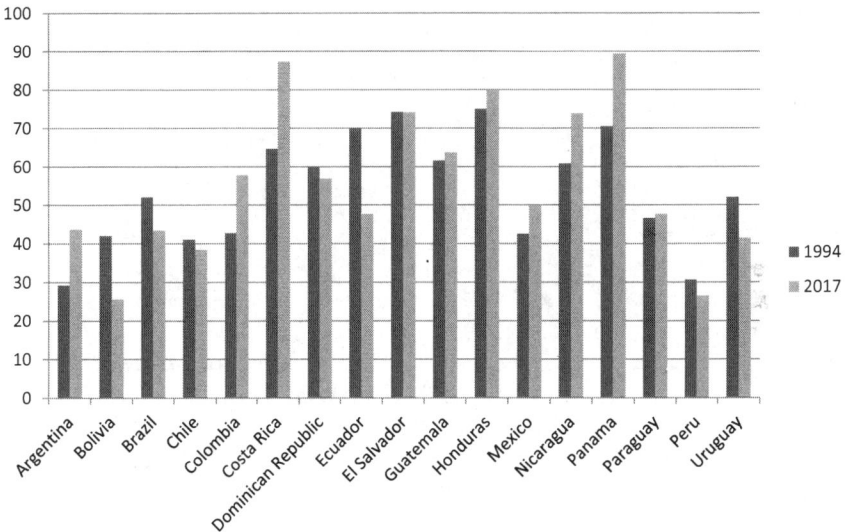

Figure 11.3 Percentage of deputies who claim, "Candidates are democratically elected."

Source: Project of Parliamentary Elites in Latin America. University of Salamanca (1994–2017).

Note: Response categories included in the figure: "agree" and "strongly agree".

respect, the emergence of new social demands and the increase of political dis-affection have caused the arrival of fresh parties. Anti-establishment discourses have flourished in the last decade and, challenged by disaffected electorates, these new organizations propose new ways of pursuing politics. Nevertheless, this is not always translated into the adoption of democratic procedures for candidate selection.

Times of change? the experience of PAC, MAS, PAIS and MRV-PSUV

The beginning of the 21st century witnessed an unprecedented wave of electoral victories by leftist presidential candidates in Latin America (Levitsky and Roberts, 2013; Cameron and Hershberg, 2010). While the rest of the world reeled from the economic fallout of the 2008 financial crisis, South America was going strong, and leftist and centre-left leaders took office. The first evidence of that change occurred in 1998, when Hugo Chávez was elected president of Venezuela. After that, other leftist candidates arrived in the presidency: Luiz Inácio Lula da Silva in Brazil (2002), Néstor Kirchner in Argentina (2003), Tabaré Vázquez in Uruguay (2004), and Evo Morales in Bolivia (2005) being examples. These electoral victories opened a new political cycle that impacted on the political life of the region, but also had an effect on the role played by parties and leaders (Lupu, 2016). For that reason, it is relevant to consider some of the iconic parties that have emerged in the last decade and to determine whether they exhibit considerable differences in terms of internal democracy and elite profiles.

As mentioned above, political changes were accompanied by the emergence of new parties that had never before held office. Among these are the four highlighted cases: PAC (Costa Rica), MAS (Bolivia), PAIS (Ecuador) and MRV-PSUV (Venezuela) (Table 11.5). These parties have been chosen for analysis because they represent a novel way of restoring political faith after a period of crisis (Lupu, 2016). The significant increase in political mobilizations and the change in electoral cycles have facilitated their rise. But, at the same time, the political environment where they developed presented a considerable challenge.

On the one hand, these parties had to represent disgruntled voters and build an anti-system discourse. On the other hand, they needed to become embedded in the institutional system. In order to achieve that, one of their first missions was to find and empower political cadres to embrace positions in different levels of government (Van Cott, 2007). In addition, these new elites had to be demarcated from the traditional parties and integrate (at least in terms of discourse) new groups, ideological currents, and movements which had as their common objective the regeneration of the political system (Levitsky *et al.*, 2016). For all that, the selected bodies represent an example of the appearance of new parties that had to face new demands, articulate original discourses, and establish alternative ways of organization.

More specifically, these four parties have specific features that make it possible to analyze them separately. In the first place, as shown in the table, they may be

Table 11.5 Parties' evolution

	PAC	MAS	PAIS	MRV-PSUV
Country	Costa Rica	Bolivia	Ecuador	Venezuela
Foundation	2000	1995	2006	2008 (MVR, 1997)
Ideology 1–10	4,1	2,7	3,4	1,6
	(0,9)	(1,2)	(2,1)	(0,9)
In Government	2014–2018	2005–2009	2007–2013	1998–2001
		2009–2014	2013–2017	2001–2007
		2014–2020		2007–2013
				2013–2019
Presidents	Luis Guillermo	Evo Morales	Rafael Correa	Hugo Chávez
	Solís	2005–2020	2007–2017	1998–2013
	2014–2018		Lenín Moreno	Nicolás Maduro
			2017–2021	2013–2019
Primaries	Yes	No	Yes	Yes

Source: Authors' own elaboration.

Note: For ideology, the source is the Project of Parliamentary Elites in Latin America. University of Salamanca (1994–2017). Standard deviation in brackets.

involved in the left-turning wave and represent, in some way, a new model of democracy. Further, beyond their programmatic axes, their members are usually self-identified as occupying left-wing positions when asked to placed themselves on a scale where "1" is "left wing" and "10" is "right wing". With the exception of PAC, closer to the centre, these parties show clear positioning on the left wing. This is especially relevant given that in Bolivia, Ecuador and Venezuela, old party systems collapsed at the beginning of the 21st century. Such circumstances may well have had an impact on their ideological positions and, therefore, it may be significant to analyze the impact on their party organization and the profiles of their elites.

Following the collapse, the programmatic alignment of establishment parties along a left-right axis failed to take hold. Taking advantage of this situation, new movements began competing for, winning, and exercising power. By agglomerating tens of organizations, political actors and social bases, they built new political realities incorporating new demands and policies. And, above all, they defended an anti-establishment discourse that transcends the traditional divisions between left and right (Lupu, 2016).

Secondly, the four parties here analyzed have all been successful in electoral competition: MVR/PSUV won the presidency in 1998, MAS in 2005, PAIS in 2009, and PAC in 2014. As shown in Table 11.5., with the exception of Costa Rica, all these parties have held office for two or more consecutive mandates and still remain in power – a clear sign of consolidation of forces in their respective party systems. Moreover, PAIS and MVR/PSUV have already survived a change of leadership: Nicolás Maduro arrived in office after the death of Hugo Chávez, and Lenín Moreno relieved Rafael Correa. No other new parties, including those that could be considered as Left-Turn, have had such electoral success in their respective party systems. Regarding the rest of the left-turn parties, most already existed before 2000 and had a strengthened trajectory in the political system (Levitsky and Roberts, 2013).[6]

Another important feature to highlight is the role played by society in the creation and configuration of these parties: the origin of the PAC party is a platform based on encouraging citizen participation and involvement in politics (Frajman, 2014); MAS was founded as a political instrument that initially grouped together peasant, trade union and indigenous movements (Anria, 2013; Barrientos Garrido, 2016); PAIS also appeared following the axes of political revolution and Latin American integration (Freidenberg, 2012): finally, MVR-PSUV resulted from the fusion of political and social forces that supported Hugo Chávez, head of the Bolivarian Revolution.

However, not all these parties have taken the same position regarding candidate-selection processes. While PAC and PSUV did not introduce any modifications to regulation, PAIS modified the law and established the obligation to hold primary elections. Finally, MAS is the only case where candidates are not selected in competitive processes. The main reason for this is the party's low level of institutionalization: MAS emerged as a movement and never introduced mechanisms of control in order to select its candidates. For a long time, there was no control over those who joined in the movement, and the MAS strategy comprised a general openness in the admissions of new members. One further consideration is the existence of strong local organizations within the movement with the capacity to select candidates in assembly (Harten, 2007).

On average, candidates are nominated by the grass-roots organizations present in electoral districts which represent the social bases of the movement. Due to the strong weight of local communities, these organizations,[7] are in charge of conducting screening, preselection and candidate-nomination processes according to the norms and procedures they themselves deem adequate (Anria, 2016). Usually, they decide in a consensual manner, trying to incorporate candidates who represent the local interests of the movement. Then they communicate their decision to the National Political Commission.

Thus, only PAIS includes in its program the adoption of primaries. PAC and PSUV do not have to, because their regulations contain the relevant mechanism, and MAS maintains non-competitive candidate-selection processes. In general, new parties do not necessarily promote their internal democratization, but rather reflect the partisan culture of their countries.

Finally, in terms of profiles, there are not many differences in comparison with the traditional parties (Table 11.6 and annex). Probably the main difference is the greater presence of women and younger people, in part because these parties try to attract social groups traditionally not included in professional politics. Even as these parties try to offer new models of democracy, they also try to fight against decreasing party identification by providing new political cadres (Childs and Webb, 2011).

Additionally, in terms of education, their members show higher levels of instruction, the number of deputies with postgraduate studies being higher. However,

Table 11.6 Profiles of elites

	PAC	MAS	PAIS	MRV-PSUV
Women (%)	50.0	47.6	37.1	11.8
Age	51.3 (1.2)	45.9 (1.2)	44.3 (1.3)	42.0 (1.2)
Education	0.0 High School	53.2 High School	5.0 High School	11.8 High School
	33.3 Bachelor	33.9 Bachelor	63. 7 Bachelor	47.1 Bachelor
	66.7 Postgrad.	12.9 Postgrad.	31.3 Postgrad.	41.2 Postgrad.
Profession	25.0 Teacher	11.7 Trader	21.4 Lawyer	11.8 Professor
	16.7 Professor	11.7 Trade Unionist	12.2 Professor	11.8 Engineer
	8.9 Doctor	10.0 Bureaucrat	8.2 Businessman	11.8 Trader

Source: Project of Parliamentary Elites in Latin America. University of Salamanca (1994–2017).

Note: Standard deviation in brackets.

Bolivia is the exception with 53.2% of legislators with only high school levels of education. Finally, there is more heterogeneity in terms of profession. The differences in terms of education and occupation may be linked with the inclusion of new groups but also with the existence of more professionalized politicians. The sociodemographic and political changes that have occurred in recent decades have allowed the entry into politics of a better-trained elite (Vergara, 2013).

Still, over and above these small differences, it is difficult to speak generally of a new breed of elites. Even after the inclusion of new mechanisms of candidate selection and internal democracy, old patterns remain, and politics seem still to be reserved for specific groups.

Conclusions

This chapter has attempted to provide a general overview of candidate-selection processes in Latin America, focusing attention on the differences between old and new parties in terms of regulation, but also the profiles of elites. Through a comparative exercise, new and old parties have been identified, along with their elites, in order to provide a photograph of the region. Electoral reforms have been systematized, explaining the causes and consequences of the adoption of instruments for internal democracy, and focusing on primary elections. Finally, four new parties have been examined, giving attention to their candidate-selection processes and the profiles of their elites.

In the last decade, Latin American has seen a number of changes in terms of candidate selections. Political disaffection has caused the emergence of new parties and the region has been tending generally toward more inclusive procedures as a solution to the growing distrust in political parties. In absence of state regulations, pressures to include the bases in decision-making processes have had a direct impact on intra-party democracy. Anti-establishment discourses, the turn toward the left and the emergence of new leaders have modified Latin America's party systems as well as its candidate-selection procedures.

Against a background of sharp decline in party legitimacy and frequent party infighting, internal elections emerged as a solution for party reforms in several countries of the region. In this regard, primaries are expected to deliver different goals: promoting intra-party democracy, solving conflicts between party factions, and strengthening party links with society. Nevertheless, some differences among countries and political parties persist.

Although primary elections have gained importance over time, some important features must be underlined. First, primaries are, in about half of Latin American countries, a largely party-specific phenomenon. The non-existence of specific regulation suggests that party characteristics may play a relevant role in the adoption of primaries. In that sense, the adoption of primaries is a party decision more than a national policy.

Finally, the chapter provides data on the social profile of MPs to explore if new parties and/or new selection methods have brought parliaments more social diversity. In that sense, even when the introduction of primary elections and intra-party democracy allow the entry into politics of traditionally marginalized groups such as women or young people and promote more social diversity, there remains a predominance of old patterns: men of middle-age with high education levels.

Notes

1 See annex, Table 11.7.
2 See annex, Table 11.8.
3 Law 24.012 (1991).
4 Law 8.765 (2009).
5 Art. 68 Electoral Code (2000).
6 Some examples are the *Frente Amplio* (Broad Front, or FA) in Uruguay, which was created in 1971; the Brazilian PT in 1980; the Chilean left-wing parties that have ruled since the arrival of democracy; and the FSLN and FMLN, which had existed in Nicaragua and El Salvador for decades.
7 Some examples are Peasant Federations or Trade Unions.

References

Alcántara, M. (2016). Los ciclos políticos en América Latina (1978–2015). *Sistema* 242–243, pp. 5–22.
Alcántara, M., and Tagina, M. L. (2016). *Elecciones y cambio de élites en América Latina, 2014 y 2015*. Ediciones Universidad de Salamanca.
Anria, S. (2013). Social movements, party organization, and populism: Insights from the Bolivian MAS. *Latin American Politics and Society* 55 (3), pp. 19–46.
Arnson, C., and Perales, J. R. (2007). *The 'New Left' and democratic governance in Latin America*. Washington, DC: Woodrow Wilson International Center for Scholars, Latin American Program.
Azcargorta, J., and Hernández, I. (2007). PSUV: ¿partido hegemónico o partido único? *Temas de Coyuntura* 56, pp. 7–23.
Barrientos Garrido, M. R. (2016). El MAS-IPSP, una maquinaria electoral. In Alcántara, M. and Tagina, M.L (Eds.). *Elecciones y cambio de élites en América Latina, 2014 y 2015*. Salamanca: University of Salamanca Press, pp. 123–148.

Best, M. and Cotta, M. (Eds.) (2007). *Democratic representation in Europe: diversity, change and convergence*. Oxford: Oxford University Press.

Bruhn, K. (2014). Choosing how to choose. *Estudios Mexicanos* 30 (1), pp. 212–240.

Cameron, M., and Hersberg, E. (Eds.). (2010). *Latin America's left turns. Politics, policies, and trajectories of change*. Boulder: Lynne Rienner.

Carey, J.M. and Polga-Hecimovich (Eds.). (2006). Primary elections and candidate strength in Latin America. *The Journal of Politics* 68 (3), pp. 530–543.

Childs, S., and Webb, P. (2011). *Sex, gender and the conservative party: From iron lady to kitten heels*. London: Palgrave Macmillan.

Coller, X., Jaime, A. M., and Mota, F. (2018). *Political power in Spain: The multiple divides between MPs and citizens*. London: Palgrave Macmillan.

Cotta, M., and Best, H. (2007). *Democratic representation in Europe: diversity, change, and convergence*. Oxford: Oxford University Press.

Frajman, E. (2014). The general election in Costa Rica, February/April 2014. *Electoral Studies*, 35 (1), pp. 61–66.

Freidenberg, F. (2003). *Selección de candidatos y democracia interna en los partidos de América Latina*. Salamanca: University of Salamanca.

Freidenberg, F. (2007). *La tentación populista: una vía al poder en América Latina*. Madrid: Síntesis.

Freidenberg, F. (2012). Ecuador 2011: Revolución Ciudadana, estabilidad presidencial y personalismo político. *Revista De Ciencia Política* 32 (1), pp. 129–150.

Freidenberg, F. (2014). Semilla de la Discordia. *Voz y voto*, 1.

Freidenberg, F., and Dosek, T. (2016). Las reformas electorales en América Latina (1978–2015). *Reformas políticas* 25.

Guchin Mieres, M. K. (2012). *El Estado ecuatoriano y las mujeres: ¿nuevos sujetos de la revolución ciudadana?* Ecuador: FLACSO Ecuador.

Guillman, A. (2010). Juventud, Democracia y participación ciudadana en Ecuador. *Revista Latinoamericana de Ciencias Sociales*, 8 (1), pp. 329–345.

Harten, S. (2007). ¿Hacia un partido "tradicional"? Un análisis del cambio organizativo interno en el Movimiento Al Socialismo (MAS) en Bolivia. *Nuevo Mundo Mundos Nuevos. Nouveaux mondes mondes nouveaux-Novo Mundo Mundos Novos-New world New worlds*, 7.

Hazan, G., and Rahat, R. Y. (2001). Candidate selection methods an analytical framework. *Party Politics*, 7 (3), pp. 297–322.

Hazan, R. Y., and Rahat, G. (2006). Candidate selection: methods and consequences. *Handbook of Party Politics* 4, pp. 1545–1591.

Hazan, R. Y., and Rahat, G. (2010). *Democracy within parties: Candidate selection methods and their political consequences*. Oxford: Oxford University Press.

Kirchheimer, O. (1990). The catch-all party. In Mair, P. (coord). *The West European Party System*. Oxford: Oxford University Press, pp. 50–60.

Kitschelt, H., Hawkins, K. A., Luna, J. P., Rosas, G., and Zechmeister, E. J. (2010). *Latin American party systems*. New York: Cambridge University Press.

Levitsky, S., Loxton, J., Van Dyck, B., and Domínguez, J. I. (Eds.). (2016). *Challenges of party-building in Latin America*. Cambridge: Cambridge University Press.

Levitsky, S., and Roberts, K. M. (Eds.). (2013). *The resurgence of the Latin American left*. Baltimore: JHU Press.

Levitsky, S. and Way, L.A. (1998). Between a shock and a hard place: The dynamics of labor-backed adjustment in Poland and Argentina. *Comparative Politics*, pp. 171–192.

Lupu, N. (2016). *Party brands in crisis: Partisanship, brand dilution, and the breakdown of political parties in Latin America*. Cambridge: Cambridge University Press.

Mainwaring, S., and Scully, T. (Eds.). (1995). *Building democratic institutions: Party systems in Latin America*. Stanford: Stanford University Press, pp. 1–36.

Molenaar, F. F. (2012). *Latin American regulation of political parties: Continuing trends and breaks with the past Working Paper Series on the Legal Regulation of Political Parties*, 17.

Morgan, J. (2011). Bankrupt representation and party system collapse. University Park: Penn State University Press.

Murillo, M. V., Oliveros, V., and Vaishnav, M. (2010). Electoral revolution or democratic alternation? *Latin American Research Review* 45 (3), pp. 87–114.

Paramio, L. (2006). Giro a la izquierda y regreso del populismo. *Nueva Sociedad* 205, pp. 62–74.

Putnam, R. D. (1977). Elite transformation in advanced industrial societies: An empirical assessment of the theory of technocracy. *Comparative Political Studies* 10 (3), pp. 383–412.

Rosón, M. D. M. M. (2006). La carrera parlamentaria: ¿La calidad importa? In Alcántara, M. (ed.) *Políticos y política en América Latina*. Fundación Carolina, pp. 175–211.

Sacristán Romero, F. (2007). Influencia de las elecciones primarias abiertas en el seno de los partidos políticos latinoamericanos. *Revista De Estudios Políticos* 136, pp. 179–212.

Sandri, G., Seddone, A., and Venturino, A. P. F. (Eds.). (2015). *Party primaries in comparative perspective*. Burlington: Ashgate Publishing, Ltd.

Siavelis, P., and Morgenstern, S. (2008). *Pathways to power: Political recruitment and candidate selection in Latin America*. University Park: Pennsylvania State University Press.

Tanaka, M. (2015). Agencia y estructura, y el colapso de los sistemas de partidos en los países andinos. In Torcal, M. (Eds.) *Sistemas de partidos en América Latina. Causas y consecuencias de su equilibrio inestable*. Barcelona and Buenos Aires: Anthropos.

Torcal, M. (2015). *Sistemas de partidos en América Latina. Causas y consecuencias de su equilibrio inestable*. Barcelona and Buenos Aires: Anthropos.

Van Cott, D. L. (2007). *From movements to parties in Latin America: The evolution of ethnic politics*. Cambridge: Cambridge University Press.

Vergara, L. G. (2013). Elites, political elites and social change in modern societies. *Revista de Sociología* 28, pp. 31–49.

Wauters, B., and Pilet, J. B. (2015). Electing women as party leaders: Does the selectorate matter? In Cross, M. and Pilet, J. B. (Eds.) *The politics of party leadership: a cross-national perspective*. Oxford: Oxford University Press, pp. 73–89.

Wills-Otero, L. (2016). The electoral performance of Latin American traditional parties, 1978–2006: Does the internal structure matter? *Party Politics* 22 (6), pp. 758–772.

Wolf, J. (2013). Towards post-liberal democracy in Latin America? A conceptual framework applied to Bolivia. *Journal of Latin American Studies* 45, pp. 31–59.

Annex

Table 11.7 New and old parties in Latin America

	Traditional Parties	*New Parties (2000–2017)*
Argentina	UCR (1891), PS (1896), PDP (1914), PC (1914), PJ(1946), PDC (1954), UP (1955), PCP(1958), MID (1963), PF (1973), UCD (1982), PSA (1982), PH (1984), MST (1992), PFG (1993), PAIS (1995)	CC (2002), PV (2003), PRO (2005), MLS (2006), IS (2006), GEN (2007), UCyB (2008), PSOL (2008)
Bolivia	MNR (1942), PDC (1954), ADN (1979), UCS (1989), MAS (1995)	FUN (2003), CP (2013), MDS (2015)
Brazil	PLB (1945), PSB (1947), PCdoB (1962), PDL (1979), PT (1980), PMDB (1980), PSC (1985), PV (1986), PSDB (1988), PS (1995)	PR (2006), PPS (2006), PSD (2011)
Chile	PC (1912), PS (1933), PDC (1957), PH (1984), PPD (1987), RB (1987),UDI (1988), PRS (1994)	PRI (2006), PV (2006), PI (2009), PP (2010), IC (2012), MIRAS (2012), EP (2012), RD (2012), PL (2013), *Ciudadanos* (2013), *Amplitud* (2014), MAS (2014), FRP (2015), PC (2015), ANDH (2015), UP (2015), *Todos* (2015), URD (2015)
Colombia	PL (1848), PC (1849), PCR (1998)	MIRA (2000), PDA (2005), PSUN (2005), POC (2009), AV (2009),CD (2013)
Costa Rica	LN (1951), PUSC (1983), ML (1994), RC (1995)	PAC (2000), FA (2004), ASE (2004), RN (2005)
Dominican Republic	PRD (1939), PRSC (1963), PLD (1973)	PRM (2014)
Ecuador	PSE (1926), PSC (1951), ID (1978), PACHAKUTIK (1995),	SP (2002), PAIS (2006), CDN (2012), AVANZA (2012), CREO (2012), SUMA (2012), MUP (2014), UE (2014), FE (2015), MAEA (2016)

(*Continued*)

Table 11.7 (Continued)

	Traditional Parties	*New Parties (2000–2017)*
El Salvador	PDC (1960), PCN (1961), FMLN (1980), ARN (1981), CD (1998)	–
Guatemala	PAN (1989), MR (1995)	GAN (2002), UNE (2002), PU (2002), UCN (2006), EG (2007), VV (2007), FCN (2008), WINAQ (2011), PRI (2013), ANN (2015)
Honduras	PL (1891), PN (1902), PDC (1968), PINU (1970)	LIBRE (2011), PAC (2011)
Mexico	PRI (1910), PAN (1939), PV (1985), PRD (1988), PT (1990)	NA (2005), MC (2010), MORENA (2014), ES (2014)
Nicaragua	PCN (1851), PLI (1944), FSLN (1961), PLC (1968), PRN (1993), MRS (1995)	ALN (2006)
Panama	PPA (1931), PP (1956), PRD (1979), MOLIRENA (1982), CD (1998)	–
Paraguay	PC (1887), PLRA (1887), PCOM (1928), PRF (1951), PH (1984),PT (1989), PEN (1991)	PSS (2000), PPQ (2001), UNCE (2002), FA (2002), PDP (2007), PCPS (2009)
Peru	APRA (1924), AP (1956), PPC (1966), PPS (1989), UP (1994), PDSP (1997), SN (1999)	AP (2001), PH (2001), TP (2003), PNP (2005), RN (2005), SU (2008), FP (2010), FAJVyL (2012), TyL (2012), *Vamos Perú* (2013), PK (2016)
Uruguay	PN (1836), PC (1836), FA (1971), PT (1984)	PI (2002), UP (2013), PERI (2013), UC (2013)
Venezuela	PC (1931), AD (1941), URD (1945), COPEI (1946), MEP (1967), LCR (1971), *Tupamaro* (1979), ORA (1987), ICN (1995), *Patria para Todos* (1997)	PJ(2000), PODEMOS (2002), UPV (2004), UNT (2006), PSUV (2008), PD (2008), *Socialismo y Libertad* (2008), UVP(2009)

Source: Authors' own elaboration

Table 11.8 List of parties

Country	Acronym	Name in Spanish	Name in English
Argentina	UCR	Unión Cívica Radical	Radical Civic Union
Bolivia	AD	Acción Democrática	Democratic Action
Bolivia	ADN	Acción Democrática Nacionalista	Nationalist and Democratic Action
Bolivia	COPEI	Comité de Organización Política Electoral Independiente	Independent Political Organizing Committee
Bolivia	MAS	Movimiento al Socialismo	Movement for Socialism
Bolivia	MIR	Movimiento de Izquierda Revolucionario	Revolutionary Left Movement
Bolivia	MNR	Movimiento Nacionalista Revolucionario	Revolutionary Nationalist Movement
Bolivia	PDC	Partido Demócrata Cristiano	Christian Democratic Party
Bolivia	PS	Partido Socialista	Socialist Party
Brazil	PMDB	Partido do Movimento Democrático Brasileiro	Brazilian Democratic Movement Party
Brazil	PP	Partido Progresista	Progressive Party
Brazil	PR	Partido da República	Party of the Republic
Brazil	PSDB	Partido da Social Democracia Brasileira	Brazilian Social Democracy Party
Brazil	PT	Partido dos Trabalhadores	Workers' Party
Bolivia	UN	Frente de Unidad Nacional	National Unity Front
Chile	CCH	Partido Comunista	Communist Party
Chile	PDC	Partido Demócrata Cristiano	Christian Democratic Party
Chile	PPD	Partido por la Democracia	Party for Democracy
Chile	PRSD	Partido Radical Socialdemócrata	Social Democrat Radical Party
Chile	PS	Partido Socialista	Socialist Party
Chile	RN	Renovación Nacional	National Renewal
Chile	UDI	Unión Demócrata Independiente	Independent Democratic Union
Colombia	CD	Centro Democrático	Democratic Center
Colombia	PCC	Partido Conservador Colombiano	Colombian Conservative Party
Colombia	PCR	Cambio Radical	Radical Change
Colombia	PDA	Polo Democrático Alternativo	Alternative Democratic Pole
Colombia	PLC	Partido Liberal Colombiano	Colombian Liberal Party
Colombia	PdeU	Partido Social de la Unidad Nacional	Social Party of National Unity
Costa Rica	PAC	Partido de Acción Ciudadana	Citizens' Action Party
Ecuador	MFR	Movimiento Fuerza Ecuador	Movement Forward Ecuador
Ecuador	MPD	Movimiento Popular Democrático	Democratic Peoples' Movement

(*Continued*)

Table 11.8 (Continued)

Country	Acronym	Name in Spanish	Name in English
Ecuador	PAIS	Alianza PAIS	Alliance Party
El Salvador	ARENA	Alianza Republicana Nacionalista	Nationalist Republican Alliance
El Salvador	FMLN	Frente Maribundo Martí para la Liberación Nacional	Farabundo Martí National Liberation Front
El Salvador	GANA	Gran Alianza por la Unidad Nacional	Grand Alliance for National Unity
El Salvador	PCN	Partido de Conciliación Nacional	Party of National Conciliation
Guatemala	ADN	Acción de Desarrollo Nacional	National Development Action Party
Guatemala	DCG	Democracia Cristiana Guatemalteca	Guatemalan Christian Democracy
Guatemala	FCN	Frente de Convergencia Nacional	National Convergence Front
Guatemala	GANA	Gran Alianza Nacional	Grand National Alliance
Guatemala	LIDER	Libertad Democrática Renovada	Renewed Democratic Liberty
Guatemala	PP	Partido Patriota	Patriotic Party
Guatemala	UNE	Unidad Nacional de la Esperanza	National Unity of Hope
Honduras	LIBRE	Libertad y Refundación	Liberty and Refoundation
Mexico	MORENA	Movimiento Regeneración Nacional	National Regeneration Movement
Mexico	PAN	Partido Acción Nacional	National Action Party
Mexico	PRD	Partido de la Revolución Democrática	Party of the Democratic Revolution
Mexico	PRI	Partido Revolucionario Institucional	Institutional Revolutionary Party
Nicaragua	FSLN	Frente Sandinista de Liberación Nacional	Sandinista National Liberation Front
Nicaragua	PLC	Partido Liberal Constitucionalista	Constitutionalista Liberal Party
Nicaragua	PLI	Partido Liberal Independiente	Independent Liberal Party
Peru	APRA	Partido Aprista	American Popular Revolutionary Alliance
Peru	CR	Cambio Radical	Radical Party
Venezuela	CMR	Clase Media Revolucionaria	Revolutionary Middle Class
Venezuela	PSUV	Partido Socialista Unido de Venezuela	United Socialist Party of Venezuela

Source: Authors' own elaboration.

12 Party-protective institutions and candidate selection for Mexico's Chamber of Deputies

Joy Langston

Introduction

The difficult economic situation of the post-2008 world affected politics by promoting new voices which lashed out at established political elites in different nations, such as the Tea Party and Occupy Wall Street in the United States, or the Movimiento 15M in Spain. Growing anger against traditional politics and political parties allowed for new types of participation and political action, including mass protests, sit-ins, and marches. The drive to affect politics often rouses otherwise underserved populations to participate politically; but success in the longer term requires that new actors participate in the political arena more formally, including running for office on an existing party's ballot or forming a new electoral organization. In some nations, economic crisis and political stalemate have driven political parties to decentralize and open selection processes so they are able to integrate these new voices (see the Introduction to this volume). In other cases, however, economic downturns, crises in public security, or political stagnation do little to obligate parties to open their control over ballot access to societal actors. Party leaders are able to manipulate institutional rules to isolate their organizations from pressures to admit new actors or more citizen participation (Coppedge 1993). Under these circumstances, party leaders often open or close access to their valuable party label due to internal rather than external pressures.

Where party leaders are strong – that is, where they control ballot access, party finance, and even electoral commissions – they may be able to manipulate political institutions to isolate party organizations from outsider demands for political change, even after profound political or economic crises. For example, in Mexico's 2009 mid-term legislative elections, social and media elites were angered over the inability of the political class to offer solutions to a host of problems, including rising violence caused by organized crime and the lack of economic growth, and called for a general "strike" in the form of a null vote campaign against the parties' candidates in the elections. In 2012, social networks led by students (#Soy 123) shook up the presidential campaign when a small student protest grew to a movement against unfair campaign practices and the return to power of the former hegemonic party, the Institutional Revolutionary Party (or PRI).

Yet, these attempts to open the parties' internal decision making processes, including candidate selection, failed. In fact, as Mexican citizens' views of parties and Congress have become more negative over time (Moreno and O'Neil, 2014), the parties have grown less open to citizen participation in the candidate-selection process. Since the mid-2000s, Mexico's three major parties, with the partial exception of the centre-right National Action Party (PAN), have centralized candidate-selection procedures either to the national headquarters or to the governors' mansions, or some combination of the two. Even the PAN, which for decades had decentralized candidate selection (with party conventions with elected delegates at the constituency level) has become less – rather than more – open to membership participation in deciding which politician will win access to the party's ballot.[1] Federalism in democratic Mexico, as in Argentina, has allowed powerful governors to win control over the resources that matter to ambitious politicians, including candidate selection (De Luca et al., 2002; Langston 2010). As a result, the national party headquarters of the nation's largest parties share some of their power with directly-elected state executives.

To demonstrate the general point of declining openness in candidate selection in Mexico, the author has collected data on the forms of selection at the plurality district level of the three major parties: the former hegemonic Party of the Institutional Revolution (PRI); the centre-left Party of the Democratic Revolution (PRD); and the PAN (that governed the nation between 2000 and 2012) for the 2009, 2012, and 2015 election cycles to the Chamber of Deputies, the lower house of congress. These parties were chosen because they were the largest in Mexico between 1989 and 2015. The data includes how the candidate was selected – be it in a democratic primary or convention of delegates, or by the national party headquarters (or some other non-democratic or closed nomination procedure).[2]

Literature on candidate-selection procedures

As alluded to in Gallagher and Marsh's 1988 book title, *The Secret Garden of Politics*, candidate selection often involves informal practices and negotiations. Because these informal practices determine winners and losers, there can be great variation among parties within the same nation. Or, as in the case of Mexico, almost every selection procedure is legal in the party statutes, so party leaders are formally empowered to select among many methods that range from open primaries to semi-open conventions, to candidate impositions.

Formal and informal party leaders, such as governors, may wish to impose candidates for several reasons – the pressures of electoral competition; internal party divisions; or the relations between co-partisan governors and their president. Party leaders face a dilemma: they want to place their favoured allies into the legislature but at the same time they do not want to divide the party or lose the election. However, these party leaders often find it imperative to convince voters that they are open to citizen participation and, more generally, greater party democracy as part of a wider democratization movement (Fields and Siavelis 2011; van Biezen, 2001). And in fact, in several newer democracies such as Argentina (De Luca et al., 2002; Jones, 1997, 2002), Mexico (Bruhn, 1997; Wuhs, 2008) and Taiwan (Wu, 2001), party leaders and factions made attempts at more inclusive nominations. However, many of these efforts failed because powerful forces within the parties did not believe more open selection processes would serve their interests, and they were able to stymie greater participation by party activists or voters.

Political institutions, especially federalism and the electoral system, have powerful effects on selection processes, although these effects are often mitigated by other institutions (Gallagher and Marsh, 1989; Lundell, 2004; Shomer, 2013). The nation's ballot structure is principal among the institutions that can isolate parties from citizens' preferences and render candidate- selection methods more closed. In closed-list proportional representation (PR) systems, voters in legislative races cannot change the rank of the names of the candidates on the lists. In this case, electors react foremost to party labels for guidance. In single-member-district (SMD) and open-list PR systems, on the other hand, the legislative hopeful must make contact with voters and use personal reputation to help win the race (Carey and Shugart, 1995). Here, the personal image of the politician weighs more in voters' choices, so selection processes should be more decentralized to capture more popular, local candidates. Mexico has a mixed-majoritarian electoral system with 60 percent of the 500 seat Chamber of Deputies filled through plurality races and 40 percent through closed list PR.

However, the plurality seats in Mexico do not provide a tight connection between voter and representative that can lead to more open, decentralized nominations (Fiorina, 1981; Carey and Shugart, 1995). Single term limits were instituted in Mexico in the 1930s and were only partially revoked in the 2013 electoral reforms. Thus, parties are not forced to choose the most popular candidates in open nominations (although local candidates are the norm even in closed impositions) because voters cannot return the same representative to office in the next election. The second electoral tier does not have a second ballot, such that PR candidates need not campaign, and the national party headquarters control these lists as well.

Mexico also has high entry barriers to new parties. It takes several years to establish a new electoral option and the barriers to win seats in the Chamber are quite high (the party must win at least three percent of the national vote).[3] Independent candidacies were prohibited until the 2015 elections, and still, it is difficult for a candidate without a party label to appear on the ballot and win public campaign funds. Even when a candidate runs under a party's label, public sources of campaign finance are controlled by party headquarters and doled out to district candidates with few guidelines. Other restrictions have cropped up on legislative candidates' ability to communicate directly with voters, such as prohibitions on taking out radio and television advertising.

Mexican party leaders are able to manipulate institutional rules because they control their caucuses in Congress, which make and remake electoral rules to protect their interests. Party leaders ignore their members' calls to open selection processes because they control the formation of new parties (through their ability to influence the National Electoral Institute, formerly IFE and now INE) and campaign finance. Even when public protests lead to greater opportunities to participate, such as the electoral reform in 2012 that allowed independent candidacies and consecutive re-election, Mexico's parties manipulated these rules to reduce citizens' participation and thus prevent a closer connection between voter and representative. Another important reason why political parties can manipulate electoral rules is their control over the hiring and firing of councillors to the state and federal electoral commissions, and judges to the electoral tribunals.

Federal governments also have a strong effect on party organization and candidate selection; parties in federalist systems, for example, often engage in organisation building at the level of the state or province because the state political arenas hold resources, government jobs, and candidacies for state and local elected posts (Riker, 1964). Governors can act as gatekeepers to an array of political posts: those in the state bureaucracy, state party, and of course, elected positions. In many federal regimes around the world, governors are quite powerful. They can take on sovereign debt; control their state assemblies to avoid accountability; influence the judicial system; and allow certain economic groups greater access to government largesse than others. The political leader assures allies' loyalty through control over which party politician wins a spot on the ballot, and ambitious career politicians respond most favourably to those who determine their future political careers. A strong state executive should not support open nomination methods because closed procedures allow control of valuable, scarce resources, with which the leader can benefit or punish ambitious state politicians from the party, and enhance their loyalty. All things being equal, federalism should decentralize but not necessarily democratize candidate selection.

In addition, the governors in Mexico are powerful political actors because they control resources that are crucial in developing longer-term political careers. They are able to support their co-partisan candidates in their campaign activities, recruit their allies to important government posts, and at times deliver government largesse. All of these resources are fundamental to building successful political careers. As a result, they wield influence over candidate selection (Jones et al., 2002; Luca et al., 2002; Montero, 2004; Samuels, 2003). In fact, directly elected state executives in the developing world may be more powerful than their counterparts in Europe and the United States because of weak accountability institutions. As a result, governors often have the wherewithal to support their co-partisan candidates' campaigns by lending materials and manpower for canvassing and rallies. Furthermore, state executives often have influence over the electoral boards in their states. Because of the campaign support, even strong national parties might be willing to allow their co-partisan state executives to control ballot access.

Electoral competition is another important consideration for candidate-selection methods. Van Biezen and Hopkin (2006) write that one should expect that where the party has had very bad results in the past, it would allow open nominating procedures, to attract more popular candidates who are not necessarily members of the party and interest voters in participating in and then voting for the party.[4] However, one could argue the opposite: greater electoral competition at the district level implies that many party politicians are interested in winning the nomination because of a higher probability they will win the seat. A party may find it difficult to impose a candidate in this situation because candidates who lose might leave the party and run under a different label (Bermúdez and Cordero, 2016). To reduce this possibility, parties may be willing to implement either primaries or democratic conventions.

Given these considerations, we offer the following hypotheses:

Hyp. 1: New political parties are not more likely to implement open candidate-selection methods under institutions that isolate party operations from voters. Furthermore, established parties should not open their nomination procedures even as the number of years that democracy has survived grows.

Hyp. 2: The higher the level of competition in a district, the more likely one will see an open candidate-selection process.

Hyp. 3: When a party holds a state government, the probability of more open candidate selection in the districts in that state falls.

Mexico's economic and political problems after 2008

The global financial crisis of 2008 and 2009 was particularly hard on Mexico as the dramatic economic slowdown in its largest trading partner – the United States – caused a sharp drop in imports of Mexican products. Fear among international investors meant Mexican companies found it harder to win foreign direct investment. These factors led to a sudden currency devaluation as the Mexican peso fell against the U.S. dollar. As a result, the nation's Gross Domestic Product (GDP) fell by a dramatic 6.6 percent in 2009 (Sidaoui, Ramos-Francia and Cuadra, 2014). Two years later, oil reserves and production in Mexico began to drop, causing more hardship in the nation's finances due to its dependence on oil revenues (up to 40 percent of government revenue comes from petroleum exports) to finance spending and run the government (Villarreal, 2010). At the same time as the economy faltered, the war on drug cartels heated up, with 2009 and 2010 ranking as two of the most violent years in recent times.

As a result of these and other problems – including the party's inability to respond to the needs and demands of its voters – several prominent critics of the government called for a "*voto nulo*," or null vote campaign in the 2009 mid-term legislative elections. As a critic of the *voto nulo* campaign wrote, "The cynicism of the majority of our political class is well known, as is the inefficiency of our institutions that were theoretically created to attend to the needs of the population."[5] An academic supporting the null vote pointed out that many citizens were growing indignant of politicians, in part because of the enormous amount of money spent on parties and elections that could have been spent on social programmes and because of the growing sense of political cynicism.[6] As a result, the campaign grew rapidly on Facebook and Twitter. Felipe Calderón criticised the null vote proponents, reminding them that if they found their political class wanting, they could join a party or form a new one to participate more fully in politics. Still, the president later called for an electoral reform;[7] but as we will see below, Mexico's parties still did not open candidate selection to greater citizen participation. While the 2012 electoral reform legalised independent candidates and consecutive re-election, party leaders have manipulated these new rules as well, assuring their continued monopoly over access to elected offices.[8]

Specifics on candidate selection in Mexico, 2009, 2012 and 2015

Mexico's candidate-selection procedures are covered both by federal laws and party statutes. However, because of the institutions that protect parties and their leaders against the demands and pressure of voters, the parties have used the electoral reforms (especially the 2008 reform) to allow parties to impose their favoured candidates through the guise of open procedures.[9] As a result, candidate selection is rarely affected by the demands for fair and open procedures. The level of centralisation and openness of candidate selection in Mexico seems to change with every election due to factors internal to the parties. If the party has a strong presidential candidate who demands open nominations, they will allow greater participation; if the party has a strong candidate who implicitly desires closed nominations, party leaders will impose candidates. And if the party in question is suffering an internal crisis, one faction may push closed procedures to protect its quota of candidacies. In the pages below, the author presents both the specific rules of each party as well as a short synopsis of its candidate-selection methods for the 2009, 2012, and 2015 electoral cycles.

The centre-left Party of National Action (PAN) is a long-lived party that acted as the loyal opposition to the PRI's overwhelming electoral and political hegemony (Mizrahi, 2003). The party grew up as a decentralised organisation: it developed in several cities and depended on its "families" to keep it alive outside of Mexico City. The PAN's traditional rules for selecting candidates were open to party militants and decentralised to the level of the election, such that candidates to the federal congress were chosen in district conventions made up of interested militants (Mizrahi, 2003; Wuhs, 2008). When the label grew more competitive during the 1990s, the party experienced growing pains as new types of ambitious politicians began to compete for candidacies against the ideological "true believers." A dilemma existed for the party: to choose popular candidates who had some ideological proximity to the party's ideals.

As a result of growing internal pressures, the PAN's statutes began to reflect attempts by the party leadership to resolve these issues.[10] The most important problem was to establish who is permitted to vote in the internal nomination processes. The PAN established decades before that it would be difficult to become a member of the party, because its members could vote in internal decisions, most importantly, the candidacies. The statutes clarify which members exercise full rights (active members) versus those with lesser rights (adherents). The decision to allow adherents to vote depends on each election and is made by the National Election Commission of the PAN. To reduce cheating in their nomination processes, the party's national headquarters reserves its right to cancel any pre-candidate's registration. If any problems lead to cancelling a candidacy, the national office can impose its choice of candidate. The PAN began to close candidate-selection processes to its membership gradually from the late 1990s onward: the party was concerned with the ideological backgrounds of its newer candidates as well as their willingness to toe the party line (Wuhs, 2008). Once the party took the presidency, it became far more normal for its national headquarters to reserve legislative candidacies – even among the 300 plurality districts – for its favourites, rather than politicians who were willing to compete in a contested nomination.

However, where the party label is weak or unpopular, (for example, where the party won less than ten percent of the vote in the last elections) the PAN's statutes formally allow for either an open primary of all registered voters or a direct designation candidate by the national office. These same rules hold if the overall turnout in the district was less than 40 percent, the result of a public opinion poll shows that the party's candidates hold less than 20 percent of voters' preferences, or if only one prospective candidate is inscribed in the nomination process (Art. 43), or at the simple request of the state party office. As a result, a lack of party popularity in a district can lead to opposing outcomes: an open nomination or a simple top-down imposition.

Success in the 2000 and 2006 presidential elections, as well as in many states, had brought new conflict to the PAN as it became a party that could defeat the PRI (Mizhari, 2003). Even though the PAN was once considered a decentralised and internally democratic party, by 2009, after almost ten years in power, this began to erode. In 2009, the national party leader decided that at least 30 to 40 percent of the 300 plurality districts would be directly determined by the CEN.[11] A few days later, that figure rose to 65 percent. From press reports in 2009, it appeared that the PAN's decision to make an inordinately high number of top-down impositions stemmed from weakness, not strength: that is, the party's leadership was concerned the party would lose seats in the Chamber, and so to avoid internal party conflict, they chose to impose these candidates instead.[12]

A second reason the PAN uses impositions instead of its once-favoured delegate conventions at the district level is conflicts caused by the primaries.[13] Open candidate selections tend to cause problems when more than one strong group competes for the nomination, which sometimes drive party leaders to impose candidates. In 2009, the president stymied attempts by the PAN governors to control nominations to the Chamber.

Next, we turn to the PRI. When Mexico's authoritarian system began to break down in the late 1980s and into the 1990s, the balance between the powerful federal government and the states began to shift. In the late 1990s, during the last hegemonic PRI administration, governors of all parties won a fiscal reform which allocated state governments rule-based outlays of federal matching funds and shared tax revenues. State executives (who were all from the PRI until 1989) had always been responsible for supporting their co-partisan candidates in winning huge margins of victory over their weak opponents. And, as competition grew, the PRI's governors used their ability to support the candidates' campaigns through spending and materials to win more power over ballot access.

By 2009, the PRI had not held the presidency for almost 10 years and its governors were extremely strong bases of power within the party (Hernández Rodríguez, 2008; Langston, 2017). Candidate selection for Chamber hopefuls depended on governors in those states where the PRI governed[14] and more on the CEN leadership where they did not. For this cycle its leaders and governors made the decision to choose the vast majority (237 of the 300) of their candidates in delegate conventions with only one alternative on the ballot.[15] As a result, even though the former leader of the PRI, Roberto Madrazo, had promised party primaries to decide local and federal candidacies, it soon became apparent that without the support of his party's governors, the party would lose votes, and the internal democratisation process was scrapped. Because of the gender quota rule then in effect, where the party used democratic selection methods, it did not have to respect the gender quota, and thanks to the 2008 electoral reforms, the parties could now decide which among their different methods were "democratic."

The argument the PRI used to legitimate candidate impositions centred on party unity: if only one candidate competed for the candidacy and the other hopefuls agreed to this, then the candidate-selection process was considered a success.[16] Another was that impositions made it easier for the party to win back competitive districts that had been lost to other parties in previous elections.[17] At least in some states, public opinion polls were carried out to determine the most popular options for each district, although it is not clear this occurred in every state. At the point in which these pre-candidates were announced, the other politicians in the districts had already been informed they had not been chosen and had agreed not to publicly complain, or even turn in their paperwork.

In 2012, the PRI was in a far stronger electoral position than it had been in 2009 and open nominations fell off sharply (see Table 12.1). The party's presidential candidate, Enrique Peña Nieto, was expected to win the election easily and lift the party's vote totals in most of the races, including those for the Chamber, held concurrently. Once Peña Nieto had won the presidency, almost no plurality district candidates were chosen in competitive contests in 2015.

The centre-left PRD was created in part by former members of the PRI who were displaced by the hegemonic top-down candidate selection process. As a result, the party always emphasised the importance of internal democracy, especially in leadership and candidate selection (Bruhn, 1997). The most recent version of the PRD's statutes state clearly that the centre-left party's candidates will be chosen through the universal, free, and secret vote of the citizens, unless 60 percent of the attendees of the Political Council at the level in which the election is held determine otherwise. Even if the Political Council decides that other methods should be employed, it must still use 50 percent free and secret balloting for at least half of the candidacies. Yet, the party leadership has stated several times since the mid-2000s that organising primaries in the 300 plurality districts is too expensive and conflictual.

As is customary in the PRD, the candidate-selection processes in 2009 and 2012 were filled with infighting among its powerful factions. First, the PRD in both election cycles had to deliver a set number of SMD candidacies to its

Table 12.1 Closed nomination procedures for three electoral cycles, PAN, PRD, and PRI (in %)

	2009	*2012*	*2015*	*Number*
PAN	68.8	44	62.5	594
PRD	82	46	100	573
PRI	80	97	100	600
Total				1767
Average Closed	**76.9**	**62.3**	**87.5**	

Source: Author's data.

alliance partners (53 out of 300 in 2009 and 145 in 2012).[18] Further, factional leaders within the party fought to impose their candidates – especially in districts that are either competitive or bastion – to enlarge their group's influence within the party. With the fracturing of the left in 2012, the PRD not only had to contend with its factions, but with other left-wing parties who joined the coalition, as well as with a popular presidential candidate, Andrés Manuel López Obrador, at the helm.[19]

The PRD's leadership hit upon a combination of public opinion polling to select the most popular candidates (except in the Federal District which is the PRD's largest bastion) to avoid some of the traditional internal battles, accusations of cheating, and other intrigues that had plagued their primaries. The positive aspects of polling are that they can choose the most popular candidate and second, if they are credible, they demonstrate to losers their lack of popularity among voters, reducing incentives to leave the party (Langston, 2003). The problems with employing opinion polls to choose candidates is that first, the losers often argue that they lost because the poll data was manipulated;[20] and second, the party cannot make political deals among factions to keep all on board. Interestingly, where the PRD had a good chance to win districts in the 2012 cycle, its leader was adamant that polls *not* be employed.

After López Obrador left the PRD and formed MORENA (National Movement for Moral Rejuvenation) as a rival to the PRD, the remaining PRD factional leaders have been unwilling to commit to open nomination procedures. In 2015, central party headquarters of the PRD had the final decision on all candidacies, not just a final veto, as had been the case before. Under the rules used by the PRD, the state branches came up with lists of names for each district in their states and sent them to the national nominating convention, which then voted on a list imposed by the national leaders. As far as is possible to glean from newspaper accounts and the party's own documents, no candidates were chosen via primaries or conventions. Opinion poll results were used in only a few cases.

Table 12.1 helps show that all of the major parties in Mexico decide a majority of their 300 plurality districts without much input from their activists or members. Instead, they impose both their SMD and their PR candidates. Worse yet, this trend has continued since the 2009 economic crisis and the later political problems. The newest party in Mexico, one that won the three points necessary to gain a seat in the Chamber in 2015, is the Social Encounter Party (PES). Its candidate-selection method for federal Chamber candidates in plurality districts was also by imposition: or as they wrote, a "decision made by the National Party Committee."[21] As a result, new parties in Mexico did not promote democratisation in candidate-selection procedures because they were not open to citizen participations themselves.

Data and methods

This section will test the various hypotheses laid out above using a database constructed by the author out of the candidate-selection procedures of the nation's three main parties (the centre-right PAN, the centre-left PRD, and the centrist PRI) for the 2009, 2012 and 2015 legislative contests. The database is based on a sample of 200 districts for each party for each electoral cycle. The regression models *do not* include the PRI and the PRD in the 2015 races because there was almost no variation in selection – party leaders made almost every one of these decisions, at times with the input of lower level party branches, and at others, without their information or opinions.

The dependent variable, "democratic nomination," is binary with a zero signifying a closed procedure and a one, a democratic nomination. Democratic nominations include primaries and conventions with more than one candidate on the ballot. The two most important explanatory variables are first, whether the district for the candidacy in question was made in a district of the governor's party or not; for example, the candidacy of the first district of the state of Sinaloa is included in the PRI's sample, so the variable would include a one for the year 2009 and a zero for 2012 and 2015 because the governor changed from a member of the PRI to a member of the PAN in 2010. District competitiveness was measured as a three-point ordinal scaled variable, 1 for losing districts and 2 for competitive districts and 3 for bastion districts.

To determine whether a selection process was open or closed was at times difficult; parties sometimes reported one type of method to the IFE and at times carried out a different procedure in practice. This required a check of newspaper accounts to understand how the parties chose their candidates in each district in each state. For the 2015 electoral cycle, the national office of the PRD simply made the final decision on all candidates. The PRI's impositions are made both by its governors and national party office, but it is impossible to know exactly which of the two political actors made each decision.

Several socio-demographic controls were included in the models; the INE provides a measure of the percentage of rural precincts in each district, and so as the proportion rises, a higher number of voters live in rural precincts, so that a positive sign on this variable represents a more rural district. Using data from the National Institute of Statistics and Geography (INEGI) that provides socio-demographic information for each federal electoral district (carried out in 2010), the author was able to identify the number of residents per district with access to Social Security benefits (IMSS). As Bruhn and Wuhs note (2016), members of the national parties chose candidates for 200 PR seats in all three parties, although there is some input from the state branches in the PAN, and in the case of the PRI, some of the PR ranked lists were informally negotiated with the governors. Election years exclude the 2009 elections as a comparison. The population is taken from INEGI data.

Three election cycles are included in the PAN Model (2), but the number of cases equals 590 instead of 600 because some information on nominations could not be found. In competitive districts, the PAN is more likely to nominate via an open or democratic method, such as delegate conventions. Co-partisan governors appear not to have any effect on the willingness of the PAN to employ open or closed nominations. The two socio-demographic variables reach the same conclusion: the PAN tends to use more democratic methods in urban areas with higher incomes (as measured by the percentage of residents with social security benefits). When the PAN was about to lose power in 2012, its leaders appeared more willing to open candidate selection as shown by the positive and significant 2012 variable (2009 is the excluded year variable).

As can be seen in Figure 12.1 above, the PAN demonstrates that the probability of a democratic nomination rises when it runs in competitive districts, as there

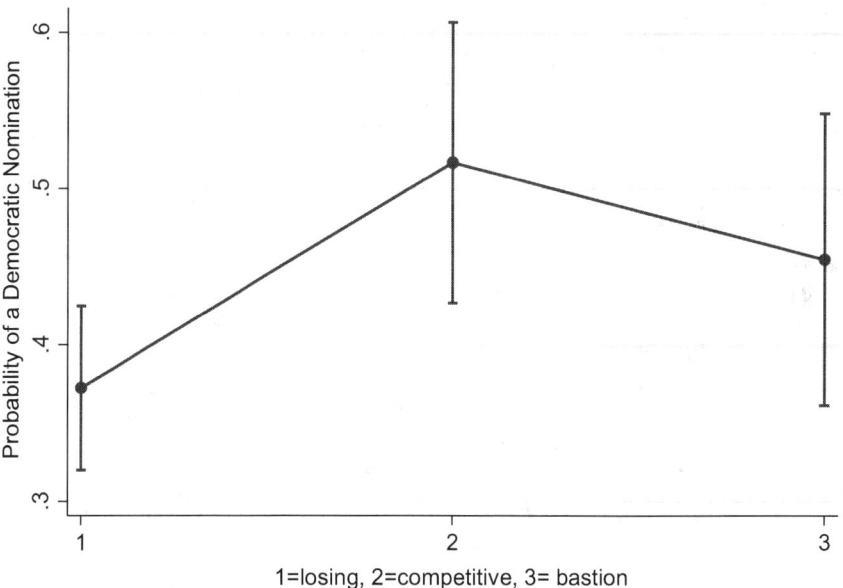

Figure 12.1 Predicted probabilities of district competitiveness for the PAN, 2009, 2012, and 2015

Source: The regression models in Table 12.2.

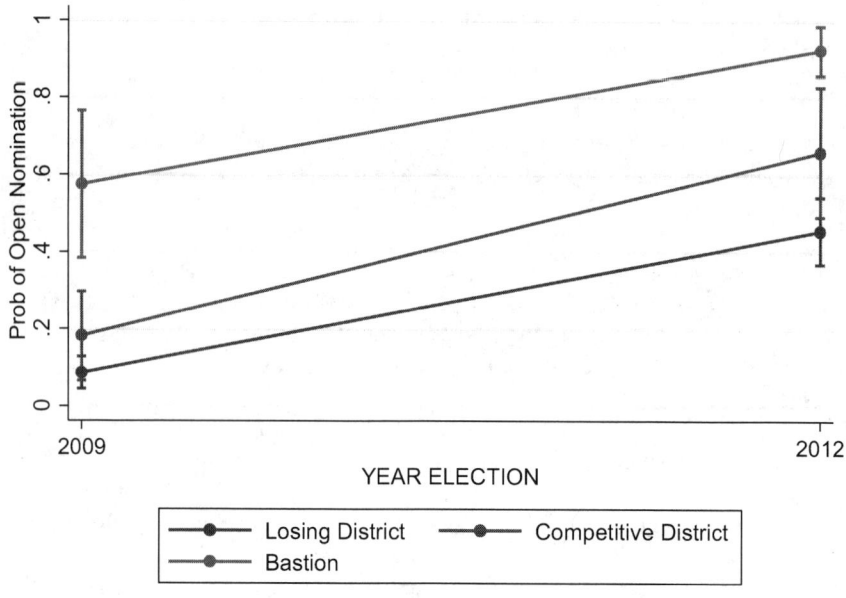

Figure 12.2 PRD predicted margins for election year and district competitiveness, 2009
     and 2012

Source: The regression models in Table 12.2.

is no overlap between the intervals in the losing and competitive districts in the predicted margins graph.

For the PRD (again, because of a lack of variation, 2015 is excluded), the number of cases is 373 instead of 400 because of missing data. The model's findings parallel those of the PAN in terms of the effects of competition on strategies over candidate selection: in both competitive and bastion districts, the PRD is more likely to use a democratic nomination than in losing districts. It appears that the pressures of intra-party competition where the party has a chance to win the district race overcome other considerations. Even when taking into consideration other variables, the PRD was far more likely to use open nominations in 2012 than in 2009, most likely because of the insistence of its presidential candidate, López Obrador.

From the PRI model (4) in Table 12.2 above, one can see the strong importance of its co-partisan governors, at least in 2009 and 2012, when there was some variation. Furthermore, district-level competition is also highly significant, although the signs are in the opposite direction from those of the PAN and the PRD. Figure 12.3 above illustrates the predicted margins of the co-partisan governors and district competition.

If a district lies in a state with a co-partisan governor, the PRI is less likely to use democratic nominations, regardless of whether the district is more or less

Table 12.2 Logistic models of democratic nominations, Mexico

		Model 1	Model 2	Model 3	Model 4
		All Parties	PAN	PRD	PRI
		2009 &2012	All years	2009&2012	2009&2012
Co-Partisan Governor		−.244	0.14	0.682*	−1.68***
		[.16]	[.24]	[.39]	[.36]
District Type	Losing (excluded)				
	Competitive	0.09	.64***	.85**	−1.48***
		[.184]	[.23]	[.408]	[.48]
	Bastion	.577***	0.37	2.7***	−.89**
		[.172]	[.26]	[.46]	[.46]
Election Year	2009 (excluded)				
	2012	0.19	1.07***	2.38***	−4.01***
		[.127]	[.217]	[.322]	[.48]
	2015		0.31		
			[.22]		
Party	PAN (excluded)				
	PRD	−.355**			
		[.154]			
	PRI	−.812***			
		[.163]			
Formal Sector Employment		−1.15	3.1***	−.42	−5.5***
		[.779]	[1.1]	[1.8]	[1.87]
Rural District		−.67***	−.64*	−.47	0.363
		[.24]	[.347]	[.527]	[.7]
Logged State Population		0.338***	.37**	.866***	0.24
		[.103]	[.13]	[.235]	[.268]
Constant		−4.7**	−8.6***	−15.5***	1.28
		[1.92]	[2.6]	[4.37]	[4.8]
Number of Observations		1367	590	373	400
Pseudo R2		0.052	0.076	0.307	0.426

Source: Author's Data

competitive. Finally, the paper considers the PRI's selection methods, and finds very different outcomes from those of the PAN and the PRD: specifically, competition has the opposite effect on the PRI as it does on the PAN and the PRD. For the PRI, as competition rises, there is a significantly lower probability of a democratic nomination

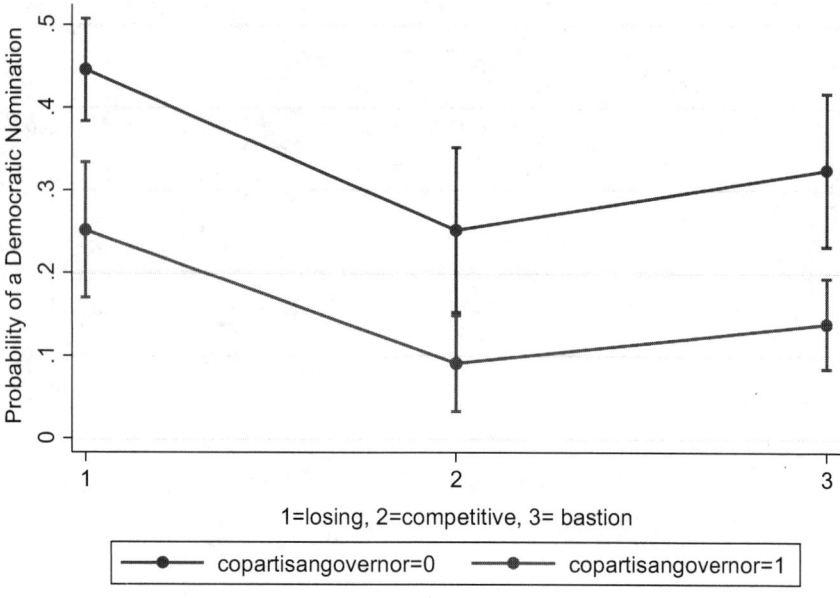

Figure 12.3 Predictive margins for the PRI: Co-partisan governor and type of district, 2009 and 2012

Source: Regression model, Table 12.2.

Conclusions

The Mexican case demonstrates that when party leaders can control and manipulate institutions they can isolate their parties from demands for greater participation from their activists and regular citizens as well. Party leaders are able to do so because they control their caucuses in Congress, where electoral rules are made and reformed, and because they influence the hiring and firing of the councillors and judges on the electoral commissions and tribunals. As a result, since the transition to democracy in 2000, the three main parties were able to gradually close down participation, either by voters or by party activities, in their nominations, rather than open them to more democratic participation.

However, even in the face of party-protective institutions, the parties show differences in how electoral competition affects their propensity to open or closed nominations. In the face of electoral competition, the PRI shuts down internal competition over candidacies, while the PAN and the PRD democratise, at least in the 2009 and 2012 cycles. The weakest party, the PRD, has a long history of conflictual nominations, and so when it split in 2015, it simply shut down any pretence of openness and allowed its remaining factions to determine candidates, albeit with lower level opinions. Only the PAN, with its long history of open, democratic, and decentralised nomination procedures, has been able to partially avoid the tendency to restrict internal party democracy. But even for the historically open and decentralised party, its 12 years in office drove its leaders to centralise selection, as party leaders attempted to control who won ballot access, both to strengthen their position within the party and to maintain some ideological consistency.

Notes

1   See Mizrahi, 2003 and Wuhs, 2008 for more on the PAN's earlier forms of candidate selection.
2   Unfortunately, in the case of the PRI, it was impossible to distinguish between gubernatorial and national party control over selection.
3   See the Ley General de Partidos Políticos. Accessed, May 1, 2017. www.diputados. gob.mx/LeyesBiblio/pdf/LGPP_130815.pdf.
4   This is made explicit in the party statutes of two main parties (the former opposition parties), the center-left PRD and the center-right PAN. In the case of the PAN, if the party's past electoral performance did not reach 20 percent of the vote, then an open primary of all registered voters (rather than a closed party primary) is allowed to enhance participation. Further, if the voter turnout is less than 40 percent in the last election, then open primaries are allowed.
5   Rodriguez Araujo, O. ¿Para qué sirve el voto nulo? *La Jornada*, June 4, 2009, p. 31.
6   Crespo, J. (2009), "Razones para no votar", *Excélsior*, 16 de febrero.
7   Zuckerman, L. "Juegos de poder," *Excélsior*, May 19, 2015.
8   Zepeda, A. "Candidatos independientes: 7 estados piden 3% de firmas de padrón," *Excélsior*, September 10, 2015. The article lists the attempts by local deputies in state assemblies to make independent candidacies in state elections almost impossible, such as requiring a higher percentage of supporters, copies of voter identifications, restricting losing pre-candidates from participating as independents, among others.
9   In the 1996 electoral code, the parties were obligated to use democratic procedures for a certain number of candidacies, and the IFE determined which types of selection were considered democratic. This opened the way to many challenges against their parties from candidates against the selection methods. In 2008, the party leaders used the reform to close this loophole and the party law now states that if a party claims the procedure is open, then the candidate must prove it is not.
10 PAN statutes, www.pan.org.mx/documentos-basicos/, www.pan.org.mx/wp-content/ uploads/2013/04/Estatutos-XVI-Asamblea-Nacional.pdf (2012).
11 Anonymous, "Nominará CEN-PAN un Tercio de Candidatos a San Lázaro." *El Financiero*, January 12, 2009.
12 Hernández, E. "Alistan 'dedazo' en blanquiazul." *Reforma*, January 12, 2009. In this report, the PAN stated that the impositions were a way to confront the problems of internal battles over candidacies and to improve the electoral results for the PAN in at least 15 states.
13 Saldierna, G. "El CEN panista designará a los candidatos donde hubo anomalías, *La Jornada,* March 10, 2012, p. 12.
14 Guerrero C. & Ramírez, I. "Acusa PRI injerencia en SLP." *Reforma*, January 15, 2009. In early January of 2009, the PRI's Commission of Internal Procedures approved the method of candidate selection for federal deputies: delegate conventions. In the next line below, the authors reported that the PRI's 18 governors had already turned their lists of "unity" candidates into the CEN for each of their respective states!
15 Anonymous, "PRI prepara convención para elegir a sus candidatos." *El Universal*, February 1, 2009. The state PRI branches examined the candidates' papers, before sending them to the National CPI, which then determined which registered pre-candidates

would make it to the convention. Also, Anonymous, "Chiapas: registran Pre Candidatos del PRI para Diputados Federales," accessed June 30, 2016, http://villaflorestimes. blogspot.mx/2009_01_01_archive.html.

16 Anonymous, "Rechazan 23 solicitudes de precandidatos en el PRI." *El Universal,* January 30, 2009.

17 Anonymous, "Registra PRI a precandidatos a diputados en Tabasco." *El Universal,* January 26, 2009.

18 Anonymous, "Define el PRD Candidatos en Colima, Querétaro y Sonora." *El Financiero,* March 20, 2009. See Alma E. Muñoz, "Analiza PRD elegir con sondeos a sus candidatos para julio próximo," *La Jornada,* 2 de febrero de 2012, p. 12.

19 Muñoz, A. "Tenso ambiente en el PRD por la distribución de candidaturas," *La Jornada,* 10 de febrero de 2012, p. 13. Even though the Progressive Movement's presidential candidate requested that polls be used in every district, the leader of the PRD rejected this idea because the party had to *"incorporate all the components of the essential plurality"* (emphasis mine) of the PRD in its selection process.

20 Muñoz, A. "Jaloneos por encuestas en el PRD." *La Jornada,* February 13, 2012, p. 8. For example, in the 2012 cycle, one of the leading factions claimed it had won 45 of the 86 districts where polls were used to identify the most popular candidate.

21 http://encuentro.social/pdf/proceso_electoral/federal/2014-2015/Convocatoria%20 Proceso%20Federal.pdf. Interested pre-candidates had to bring their forms in person to Mexico City.

References

Bermúdez, S., and Cordero, G. (2017). Who is recruiting our crew? Contextual determinants of MPs selection. *Acta Politica* 52 (3), 265–285.

Bruhn, K. (1997). *Taking on Goliath: The emergence of a new left party and the struggle for democracy in Mexico.* University Park: Pennsylvania State University Press.

Bruhn, K., and Wuhs, S. (2016). Competition, decentralization, and candidate selection in Mexico. *American Behavioral Scientist,* 60 (7), pp. 819–836.

Carey, J., and Shugart, M. (1995). Incentives to cultivate a personal vote: A rank ordering of electoral formulas. *Electoral Studies* 14, pp. 417–439.

Coppedge, M. (1993). Parties and society in Mexico and Venezuela: Why competition matters. *Comparative Politics* 25, pp. 253–274.

Field, B., and Siavelis, P. (2011). The genesis of candidate selection procedures in democratizing countries: A framework applied to Europe and Latin America. *Democratization* 18 (3), pp. 797–822.

Fiorina, M. (1981). *Retrospective voting in American national elections.* New Haven, CT: Yale University Press.

Gallagher, M., and Marsh, M. (Eds.). (1988). *Candidate selection in comparative perspective: The secret garden of politics.* London: Sage.

Harmel, R. (1981). Environment and party decentralization: A cross-national analysis. *Comparative Political Studies* 14, pp. 75–99.

Hernández Rodríguez. (2008). *El centro dividido. La nueva autonomía de los gobernadores.* Mexico City: El Colegio de México.

Jones, M., Saiegh, S., Spiller, P., and Tommasi, M. (2002). Amateur legislators – professional politicians: The consequences of party centered electoral rules in a federal system. *American Journal of Political Science* 46 (3), pp. 656–669.

Langston, J. (2017). Democratization and authoritarian party survival. Mexico's PRI. Oxford: Oxford University Press.

Langston, J. (2003). Rising from the Ashes? Reorganizing the PRI's State Party after Electoral Defeat. *Comparative Political Studies* 36, pp. 293–318.

Luca, M., Jones, M., and Tula, M. (2004). Back rooms or ballot boxes? Candidate nomination in Argentina. *Comparative Political Studies* 35 (4), pp. 413–436.

Lundell, K. (2004). Determinants of candidate selection: The degree of centralization in comparative perspective. *Party Politics* 10–1, pp. 25–47.

Mizrahi, Y. (2003). *From Martyrdom to power*. South Bend: University of Notre Dame Press.

Montero, A. (2007). The limits of decentralisation: Legislative careers and territorial representation in Spain. *West European Politics* 30 (3), pp. 573–594.

Moreno, A., and O'Neil, S. (2014). El malestar democrático en México. In Meixueiro, G. and Moreno, A. (Eds.), *El comportamiento electoral mexicano en las elecciones de 2012*. Mexico City: Centro de Estudios Sociales y de Opinión Pública and Cámara de Diputados, pp. 318–325.

Partido Encuentro Social. Rules for candidate selection. (2015). Retrieved from http://encuentro.social/pdf/proceso_electoral/federal/2014-2015/Convocatoria%20Proceso%20Federal.pdf

Riker, W. (1964). *Federalism: Origin, operation, significance*. Boston: Little, Brown.

Samuels, D. (2003). *Ambition, federalism, and legislative politics in Brazil*. New York and Cambridge: Cambridge University.

Shomer, Y. (2014). What affects candidate selection processes? A cross-national examination. *Party Politics* 20 (4), pp. 533–546.

Sidaoui, J., Ramos-Francia, M., and Cuadra, G. (2014). The global financial crisis and policy response in Mexico. BIS Papers No 54, pp. 279–298. Retrieved from www.bis.org/publ/bppdf/bispap54q.pdf

van Biezen, I. (2000). On the internal balance of party power: Party organizations in new democracies. *Party Politics* 6, pp. 395–417.

van Biezen, I., and Hopkin, J. (2006). Party organization in multi-level contexts: Theory and some comparative evidence. In Hough, D. and Jeffrey, C. (Eds.), *Devolution and electoral politics*. Manchester: Manchester University Press, pp. 14–36.

Villarreal, A. (2010). *The Mexican economy after the global financial crisis specialist in international trade and finance*. Washington, DC: Congressional Research Service. Retrieved from https://fas.org/sgp/crs/row/R41402.pdf

Wuhs, S. (2008). *Savage democracy: Institutional change and party development in Mexico*. University Park: Pennsylvania State University Press.

13 The limits of party change

Candidate selection in Portugal in the age of crisis

Marco Lisi

Introduction

The process of candidate selection has faced new challenges with the emergence of the Eurocrisis. On the one hand, domestic pressures on parties have increased, through the emergence of new competitors, an increase in anti-party feelings and new forms of mobilization (Kriesi, 2014; Della Porta et al., 2017). On the other, a growing tension between responsibility and responsiveness has emerged during the crisis (Mair, 2013), and this has particularly affected political representation, the role of legislators and their performance. Several authors have argued that some countries are experiencing a process of de-consolidation (or de-institutionalization) with a qualitative deterioration of democratic principles and institutions (Streeck, 2014; Foa and Mounk, 2017). This is particularly true for Southern Europe, where the Eurocrisis has boosted growing support for reforms vis-à-vis the political system and for the replacement of the 'old' political elite, which has ultimately led to major changes in both electoral alignments and political actors, outside and inside the parliamentary sphere (Freire and Lisi, 2016; Morlino and Raniolo, 2017).

To what extent have the economic crisis and subsequent austerity measures affected the way parties select their candidates? What is the impact of the economic crisis on the representation capacity of political parties? In particular, has the social and ideological representativeness of party organizations changed over the recent period? We investigate these questions and test our hypotheses focusing on the Portuguese case. Portugal is a suitable case to examine the impact of the economic crisis on candidate selection due to the deep economic and political turmoil that has affected the country since 2010. Drawing on data collected before and after the economic crisis, this chapter aims to shed more light on the relationship between hard economic conditions and the process of candidate selection.

Portugal is also an interesting case study for its institutional and political characteristics. First, Portugal has a proportional representation system with 22 multi-member constituencies and closed lists. The conversion of votes into mandates is done through the Hondt highest average formula. As previous studies have noted (Riera, 2011; Shomer, 2012), this feature is crucial in influencing the process of candidate selection. On the other hand, voters do not have a choice in selecting their preferred representative, and candidates' names do not appear in the ballot list. This means that the election of MPs depends more on the place attributed by the party selectorate in the list than on the electorate's votes. Another important characteristic is that there is a wide variation in district magnitude. While Lisbon and Oporto are very large districts (47 and 39 seats, respectively), there are two groups with a low and medium-district magnitude. As a consequence, small parties (polling below 5%) can only aspire to win seats in the two largest districts.

The second important feature is the resilience of the Portuguese party system. Despite the huge political and economic crisis, the main characteristics of party competition have remained unchanged, with alternation in government between mainstream parties, low levels of volatility and party system fragmentation and the failure of new parties to break existing patterns of competition (Freire, 2016). This is an anomaly in the Southern European context, where new challenger parties have successfully reshaped the configuration of the party system and have raised (or deepen) new political cleavages (Verney and Bosco, 2014; Bosco and Verney, 2016).

Nonetheless, the economic and political turmoil that affected Portuguese politics since 2011 has indeed fostered the emergence of new parties, mainly on the left of the political spectrum. The first was the PDR (Republican Democratic Party, *Partido Democrático Republicano*), a personal party led by Marinho e Pinto, a former magistrate who was elected as a MEP in the 2014 elections. The party adopted a populist rhetoric and one of the main issues it tried to politicize was the lack of representativeness of the political establishment. Although the PDR can be positioned in the middle of the political spectrum, it displays on several issues – e.g. European integration – ambiguous programmatic positions and an unclear strategy of alliances. The second was LIVRE (Free), a left-libertarian party also founded in 2014 when it obtained 2.4% of the votes in the European elections (Lisi and Fernandes, 2015). The main innovation of this new party was the adoption of open primaries. It is worth noting that this method, although attracting growing attention and gaining relevance in the European landscape (Sandri et al., 2015a), is still very rare. The primaries conducted by LIVRE defined not only who would be a candidate but also the order of candidates within the closed lists. The process is open to non-members, while the criteria for eligibility are very permissive as they require signing LIVRE's statement of principles and obtaining at least 12 endorsements among those registered in the internal census (Cancela et al., 2016). Overall, this was a major innovation in Portuguese party politics and political recruitment, which aimed to renew the political system and to foster political participation.

The chapter is structured as follows. The next section discusses the connection between economic crises and candidate-selection processes and derives some hypotheses to be tested. Section three presents data and methods, while the subsequent section examines in detail candidate selection in Portugal before and after the crisis. Section five analyzes how the crisis has influenced candidate selection in terms of outcomes, taking a longitudinal look at legislators' profile and internal ideological homogeneity. In the final section, we summarize the main results and discuss their implications for the process of candidate selection.

Table 13.1 Main political parties in Portugal

Party name	Vote (%), 2015 legislative elections	Institutional position	Party family
BE	10.2	External support	Left-libertarian
CDS-PP	*	Opposition	Conservative
PCP	8.3**	External support	Communist
PS	32.3	Government	Socialist
PSD	38.6	Opposition	Liberal

* In the 2015 elections the PSD and CDS-PP formed the coalition PàF (*Portugal à Frente*).
** Since 1987 the PCP run with the Green Party (PEV, *Partido Os Verdes*) in the electoral coalition CDU (*Coligação Democrática* Unitária, Unitary Democratic Coalition).

Candidate selection in the age of crisis

It has been argued that reforms of candidate-selection methods are likely to take place when there are potential or actual changes at different levels: for the political system, for inter-party competition and, finally, for the intra-party distribution of power (Barnea and Rahat, 2007, p. 377–378). Arguably the most important arena is the latter one, because parties enjoy relative autonomy in deciding whether to adopt democratizing reforms or not, regardless of the political environment. Yet it is true that opposition status is a key factor triggering party change and facilitating the adoption of democratizing reforms, as happens, for instance, in the case of party leadership selection (Chiru et al., 2015). However, studies have failed to address the link between changes in the political environment and democratizing reforms.

Economic crises are exogenous shocks that create deep changes in both the electoral arena and the mobilization of civil society outside the electoral moment (Kriesi, 2012). In particular, the 'Great Recession' is expected to influence indirectly the process of candidate selection in two ways. On the one hand, the Euro-crisis has unveiled the incapacity (or unwillingness) of political elites to deal with social demands, thus aggravating the legitimacy crisis of democratic regimes and popular discontent (van Biezen and Piccio, 2013, 28; Torcal, 2014). On the other hand, the crisis has already had important effects on the European party system, such as the erosion of mainstream parties, the emergence of new forms of collective mobilization, high levels of volatility and changing patterns of government (Verney and Bosco, 2014).

However, if we look at party change, the links between the crisis and organizational reforms are less clear. Party organizational changes are often seen as general trends that travel across countries and party systems and that are mainly the results of (common) external shocks – e.g. changes to the institutional environment, introduction of public funding or technological developments. One important arena of party change is the reform of leadership and candidate-selection methods. Regarding the first dimension, empirical research has highlighted the growing adoption of one member one vote (OMOV) to choose the party leader (Krouwel, 2012; Pilet and Cross, 2014). As for candidate-selection methods, a number of studies found that these procedures have changed considerably in Europe, namely through the adoption of more inclusive criteria of recruitment (Bille, 2001; Kittilson and Scarrow, 2003; Krouwel, 2012; Sandri et al., 2015a). These reforms represent important innovations in party organizations and they have stimulated the debate about intra-party democracy and the emergence of new arenas of political participation (Cross and Katz, 2013). It has been argued that this change might significantly affect party politics, namely in terms of members' attitudes, patterns of participation, intra-party competition, the profile of MPs, as well as the degree of responsiveness (Hazan and Rahat, 2010; Sandri et al., 2015a).

Another approach to party change emphasizes the importance of informal mechanisms and discretionary decisions for the adoption of intra-party reforms (Panebianco, 1988). This paradigm is important because it argues that party change may originate from strategic choices taken by party elites, while other idiosyncratic factors that are hardly generalizable may also be responsible for the implementation of intra-party democracy. Considering political recruitment, changing patterns of informal rules may be consequential for the representativeness of MPs, for example by selecting younger candidates, especially when the process is centralized in national party elites. This means that even in the presence of party inertia at the organizational level, patterns of political recruitment may still experience important changes. An external shock – such as the crisis in the Eurozone – may have an indirect effect by leading the party selectorate to change informal mechanisms for candidate selection.

Since the onset of the economic crisis, Portugal has presented favourable conditions for party change, namely with the (potentially) explosive combination of an economic and political crisis. Regarding the first dimension, the country experienced a situation of bankruptcy during the second socialist government led by José Sócrates (2009–2011), leading the main parties – Socialist Party (*Partido Socialista*, PS), Social Democratic Party (*Partido Social Democrata*, PSD) and Social Democratic Centre-Popular Party (*Centro Democrático Social-Partido Popular*, CDS-PP) to sign the Memorandum of Understanding (MoU) with the so-called Troika (European Central Bank-International Monetary Fund-European Commission) in May 2011. As a consequence, a comprehensive package of austerity measures was implemented, which caused significant deterioration in economic indicators. GDP fell abruptly between 2010 and 2013, unemployment skyrocketed from 8.5% in 2008 to 16.2% in 2013, and both the public deficit and the public debt reached record levels.

Yet the crisis that hit Portugal did not merely affect the economy. On the contrary, the country has experienced a deep and long-standing disenchantment on the part of voters towards the democratic regime. Despite the overall support for democratic values, several indicators associated to specific support, such as satisfaction with democracy, trust in government, trust in parliament or trust in political parties, had been traditionally low in Portugal compared to other West European countries, but plunged even lower in the aftermath of the economic crisis (Freire et al., 2015; Freire, 2016). Using data from two national surveys before and after the emergence of the economic crisis (2008 and 2012), several studies have found that support for political parties declined significantly in 2012 (Teixeira et al., 2016), whereas partisan identities also achieved historical lows (Lisi, 2015).

Overall, there is clear evidence that the economic and political context Portugal experienced after 2010 provided fertile grounds for party renewal or change. Citizens' discontent led to the adoption of new and intense forms of mobilization (Fernandes, 2017) and the emergence of new parties, such as the populist PDR and the left-libertarian LIVRE. Given the growing electoral dealignment and increasing electoral pressures, it is plausible to expect that in times of crisis parties will increasingly adopt democratizing reforms for selecting parliamentary candidates.

> H1: During the economic crisis, parties are prone to open their process of candidate selection.

As mentioned above, during the recent economic crisis in Portugal negative attitudes towards political representation and anti-party sentiments have shown a positive trend. This has led not only to the emergence of new forms of citizen mobilization, but also to the rise of new political actors (social movements and challenger parties, see Freire, 2016). These new forces have tried to mobilize dissatisfied voters by introducing a new cleavage, namely the anti-establishment divide. Their concern regarding the need to strengthen the representativeness of political parties and, at the same time, the fading of traditional cleavages (see Morlino and Raniolo, 2017, 113–115) may lead new actors to emphasize descriptive representation. In other words, the crisis might pressure political parties to select representatives that share the social identity of the groups most affected by the crisis and with a less partisan background. Hence, we hypothesize the following:

> H2a: During the crisis, the main political parties are expected to enhance their representation capacity, in particular by recruiting more MPs belonging to particular societal groups – i.e. young and women – and affiliated to civil society organizations.
> H2b: During the crisis, the main political parties are expected to recruit a higher proportion of MPs with no previous partisan or political experience.

However, we know that social representation is not always linked to opinion representation (Widfeldt, 1995). A declining (or increasing) capacity of social representation does not necessarily imply a change in the ideological position of representatives. Empirical research has found that the crisis has challenged the identity of mainstream parties. On the one hand, austerity politics has forced left-wing actors to redefine their strategies and programmatic stances (see March and Keith, 2016). On the other, the issue of European integration has become highly divisive within moderate parties. Both issues are key for understanding the success of challenger parties in the euro zone (Hobolt and Tilley, 2016). Therefore, one important outcome of the Eurocrisis may be related to the decrease in internal ideological homogeneity, i.e. MPs belonging to the same party are more likely to display different attitudes or political preferences. One party is ideologically homogeneous when their members share the same opinions and beliefs. This dimension is germane not only to legislative output, but also to intra-party functioning, in particular to candidate selection. According to the literature (Bille, 2001; Rahat and Hazan, 2001; Hazan, 2013), parties with more inclusive and decentralized methods of candidate selection are more prone to display lower levels of internal ideological homogeneity.

As several authors have noted (Montábes and Ortega, 1999; Lisi, 2015), the process of candidate selection in Portugal is an important source of intra-party conflict. In particular, this dimension mirrors the internal distribution of power and bargaining between the leader and intra-party factions. During the crisis, external pressures – namely electoral volatility and policy constraints – are expected to foster centrifugal tendencies within the parties. Indeed, a recent contribution has shown that the crisis has led to lesser correspondence among government parties in core policy issues (Belchior et al., 2016). Given that in Portugal we did not observe any important change in the way MPs are recruited, if we observe a change in the degree of internal ideological homogeneity, this might be due to the impact of the Eurocrisis. As a consequence, our final hypothesis is as follows:

> H3: The economic crisis has been pushing deputies towards more heterogeneous positions, thus decreasing the degree of internal ideological homogeneity.

Data and methods

The data used here are based on three distinct sources. The first is related to MPs' biographies as reported in the Parliament website. A data set was created for the 230 MPs elected in national elections between 2009 and 2015, covering all parties represented in the Portuguese Parliament (BE, CDS-PP, PCP, PEV, PS and PSD).[1] The data set includes the main socio-demographic variables (gender, age, education, profession), as well as membership in civic association or interest organizations (trade unions, business groups and professional organizations). We also include the variable 'party leadership', which measures whether an MP is (or has been) a member of executive or representative party bodies at the national or local level. Finally, the analysis includes the variable 'institutional experience', which gauges whether legislators have held previous positions in government (national or regional levels) or as members of the European Parliament (MEP).

The second type of sources draws from face-to-face interviews with MPs from all parties represented in the Parliament. The interviews were conducted after the 2015 legislative elections (between September 2016 and February 2017) and covered a wide range of topics, such as MPs' activities, their links with voters and the process of candidate selection. We were able to conduct 8 interviews, with an average length of 35 minutes.[2]

Finally, the third source is based on three surveys of Portuguese MPs conducted between 2008 and 2017 within three distinct projects on political representation (see Freire and Viegas, 2009; Freire ct al., 2013; Freire et al., 2017). The survey was applied to the parties with parliamentary representation using face-to-face interviews, with a response rate of between 53.5% and 70%.[3]

The process of candidate selection in Portugal: between continuity and change

Constitutional rules for the presentation of candidates do not establish restrictive requisites[4] and party organizations in Portugal are key gatekeepers in the selection of parliamentarians and in holding them accountable. This control is strengthened by the Parliament's rules that grant numerous privileges and powers to party directorates and parliamentary groups (PG). For instance, the distribution of resources (e.g. question time), the setting of the parliamentary agenda and the election of decision-making bodies is managed at the PG-level. In addition, procedural rules and institutional constraints contribute to strengthening the level of cohesion of Portuguese parties. As a number of authors have noted (van Biezen, 2003; Teixeira, 2009), this phenomenon originated from the democratic transition, where the main priority was to strengthen and consolidate party organizations, in particular the party in central office.

In order to examine the process of political recruitment – both formally and informally – we will use the criteria elaborated by Rahat and Hazan (Rahat and Hazan, 2001; Hazan and Rahat, 2006; 2010) for the analysis of the candidate-selection process, namely the degree of centralization and the level of selection. With regard to the first dimension – centralization vs decentralization – Portuguese parties display relatively high levels of centralization (Freire, 2001; Teixeira, 2009; Freire and Teixeira, 2011). In general, the party in central office is responsible for the choice of prospective MPs, while party leaders often have the final say on the party list to be submitted to voters (Table 13.2). Although the Constitution establishes that MPs' mandates are based on national representation rather than on territorial criteria, parties are the main *de facto* gatekeepers for achieving political representation. In a recent comparative work, Krouwel (2012, 252) considers Portugal in the group of countries (along with Greece, Italy, and the Netherlands) characterized by a process of 'candidate selection substantially in the hands of the elite'.

Nonetheless, there are some relevant differences between parties (Table 13.2). The PCP presents a higher concentration of powers within national party bodies, as the Central Committee has the responsibility to prepare candidate lists, which are then ratified by regional organizations. Despite the high degree of centralization, the principles of 'democratic centralism' establish a bottom-up process with the intervention of local and regional structures, which assume direct responsibilities for candidate selection. In practice, however, it is the secretariat – the executive body of the Central Committee – that prepares a draft list, which easily achieves a consensus within party branches. Therefore, the inclusive and

Table 13.2 Candidate-selection process in the main Portuguese parties

Degree of decentralization	Degree of inclusiveness		
	Low	Medium	High
Low	CDS-PP; (PDR)		
Medium	PSD	PS	
High	BE; PCP		(LIVRE)

Source: party statutes.

Note: Parties in parentheses are not currently present in the Parliament.

deliberative process is more a formal mechanism to legitimize the final choice than a power the select the names of potential candidates (Freire and Teixeira, 2011). Finally, the PCP clearly differs from other parties for the collective character of the decision-making process, with no explicit intervention of the party leader.

The PS's statutes indicate that the choice of MPs depends on regional party bodies (federations), although the National Political Commission has the final say on the composition of candidate lists. In 2003 the PS statutes introduced a quota of 30% of the seats to be chosen by the main national party body. Indeed, this rule has been traditionally used by the party leader to strengthen his discretionary powers and autonomy. Moreover, it is worth mentioning the importance of informal practices within the PS. In this regard the campaign coordinator – usually a member of the main executive party body – negotiates with regional party bodies the composition of party lists months before the election day in order to neutralize potential conflicts and to achieve a consensual solution.

The CDS-PP also adopts a centralized process based on the selection of MPs through the decision of the National Council. The process is more centralized than for the two major parties (PS and PSD) because the party has a weak organizational structure and party branches often fail to find and propose candidates for every district. Moreover, the party leader also has the informal right to define the head of the list, while the National Council can veto the candidates selected by decentralized party bodies. According to our interviews, political experience is a crucial factor in influencing the choice of candidates, as well as the competence and the area of expertise of prospective legislators. Territorial representation is also an important criterion that guides party elites in candidate selection.

The PSD's statutes present a higher decentralization, at least formally, through the intervention of regional and local party bodies. From this viewpoint, these bodies can propose their own names, although they have to be approved by the National Political Commission. In practice, however, the power of decentralized structures depends to a great extent on the strength of the party leader. When the party leader enjoys considerable authority, it is easier to control the process and to veto political figures designated by local or regional structures.[5] In the PSD two more aspects need to be taken into account. On the one hand, party leaders often play a decisive and authoritative role in the elaboration of party lists, especially with regard to the allocation of national figures. Strategic considerations are crucial in order to decide the head of the party lists, a practice that is known as the 'parachuting' of candidates on to the lists. On the other, the negotiation that takes place between national and regional party structures is asymmetric because the most powerful districts are also more successful in designating their own candidates compared to the less important local bodies, which remain subordinated to the decisions taken at the national level. Both features also apply to a great extent to the CDS-PP, especially through the informal quota of the party leader in the elaboration of the final list, although in this case the power of local structures is more limited.

Finally, the process of candidate selection for BE's candidates is more decentralized and participatory. The national Convention establishes the rules for the choice of candidates, while local party structures have the authority to propose the names of prospective MPs, even if the final list is ratified by the national party bodies (Freire and Teixeira, 2011, 40–41). From this viewpoint, the party makes an effort to maintain a permanent link between local organizations and the national party bodies, without any direct intervention of the party leadership. The goal is to foster the mobilization of grassroots members and to favour a deliberative process in order to select the 'best' candidates. Our interviews with BE MPs suggest that social representation is one of the most important principles adopted by the party in the choice of prospective candidates. It is also important to stress that the BE has usually adopted the principle of rotation for elected deputies, therefore it is in this party that political or partisan experience is less relevant.

As for the degree of inclusiveness of the selectorate, with the exception of LIVRE (see below), none of the Portuguese parties attribute the right to select prospective MPs to members or sympathizers. One important aspect of the process of candidate selection for Portuguese parties is the gap between formal rules and the *de facto* practice followed by the main actors involved in the elaboration of party lists, namely with regard to the power attributed to national party bodies (Freire and Teixeira, 2011, 46). Moreover, party statutes are deliberately vague with regard to the process of candidate selection, increasing the importance of informal rules. Finally, it is worth emphasizing that national party bodies often establish informal criteria for the selection of prospective MPs according to strategic considerations – i.e. in terms of age, gender, profession, etc. – especially when decentralized structures have the power to propose the name of the candidates.

Unlike the selection of party leaders (Lisi, 2015), candidate selection has remained highly centralized in national party bodies and highly oligarchical, with crucial decision-making powers in the hands of national party elites. This findings provides evidence against our first hypothesis. However, in the aftermath of the crisis two 'experiments' took place. The first is related to the adoption of open primaries by LIVRE, the second is the introduction of primaries within the PS.

The main innovation in terms of candidate-selection methods was implemented by the newly created party LIVRE by introducing open party primaries. It is worth noting that the main rationale for the adoption of more inclusive methods of candidate selection was based on the imprint of the party's genetic model, which was centred on a strong emphasis on participation and more horizontal ties among members, emphasizing the use of instruments of direct democracy for adopting key decisions (alliance strategy, leadership, policy orientations, etc.). This contrasts with the main rationale behind the introduction of primary elections, which depends on a party's reaction to a (internal or external) crisis (Sandri et al., 2015b, 190). Eligibility for the primaries only required signing L/TdA's[6] statement of principles and obtaining at least twelve endorsements among the proponents registered in the internal electoral census (LIVRE/TdA, 2015). A recent study has shown that endorsements were crucial in determining the candidates selected through primaries (Cancela et al., 2016). This means that open methods of candidate selection had only limited consequences for the profile of prospective representatives; ultimately LIVRE's candidates were those displaying more political (and partisan) experience, more visibility in mass media and those who are formally members of the main party bodies.

The second important innovation in candidate selection in Portugal took place within the PS. The debate on the introduction of democratizing reforms emerged in the aftermath of the 2011 general elections and the subsequent withdrawal of the socialist Prime Minister (and PS leader) José Sócrates. Competition for the party leadership raised the issue of democratizing candidate selection, as advocated by one of the competitors. Francisco Assis defended the need to introduce open primaries for selecting prime ministerial and mayoral candidates. This was mainly a strategic move aimed at increasing support by deepening party democratization. Yet this issue was a divisive one, as revealed during the 2013 congress. After an intense debate, the new socialist leader (António José Seguro) decided to accept open primaries for local offices, in the attempt to neutralize internal opposition. In addition, the new statutes approved in 2012 also established the possibility of adopting primaries for candidates to MPs.

The proposal to adopt open primaries was unexpectedly taken up again by the secretary general after the poor performance at the 2014 European elections. António Costa, the mayor of Lisbon, decided to challenge the incumbent leader by demanding a new election for party leadership. Instead of organizing a closed primary (the method normally used to select the party leader), Seguro decided to open the competition but only for prime ministerial candidates. This was considered a strategic move, a 'rush forward' against the challenger's greater popularity and the growing difficulties in controlling the party apparatus. In the end Costa won a landslide victory and Seguro was forced to resign.

Costa decided to institutionalize party primaries by including this method of candidate selection in the new party statutes approved in 2015. The problem is that the party organization has not defined yet the rules that should manage the selection of candidates through primaries (art. 59°-6). In fact, one of the most divisive issues between Costa and the challenger that ran in the leadership contest in June 2016 was the call for primaries for local and national public offices. After the congress a working group was created within the PS in order to analyze the possibility of conducting party primaries before the 2017 local elections. However, the party secretariat has delayed the decision *sine die* and has been critical towards primaries because of the problems of 'instant membership' that these may bring and the excessive control of local bosses on grassroots mobilization.[7]

Both primaries represent an important shift in traditional practices adopted for the selection of politicians, introducing innovative methods of candidate selection. These experiences constitute a radical change vis-à-vis previous patterns of recruitment in Portugal, in terms of both inclusiveness and decentralization. By introducing party primaries, new dynamics and potentially relevant effects for the Portuguese political system, with unpredictable outcomes in the foreseeable future.

Candidate-selection methods and the crisis: representativeness and ideological homogeneity

This section is dedicated to the analysis of the relationship between candidate-selection methods and the representation capacity of Portuguese parties before and after the crisis. The empirical analysis proceeds in two steps. First, we map the evolution of descriptive representation during the crisis. Second, we look at deputies' careers in order to elucidate whether the crisis has had an impact on MPs' political profile. We are particularly interested in examining how the representation capacity of distinct parties, adopting different criteria for political recruitment, has changed over time, i.e. whether the crisis has led to a higher (or lower) representation capacity of parties. Regardless of the stability of candidate-selection methods, MPs' profile may have changed due to informal criteria used in the process. It is likely that party leadership has been more sensitive to represent a great variety of social groups in order to improve their public image and to positively impact their electoral performance.

The literature on the evolution of party organizations suggests a general decline of parties' representative capacity. Parties have faced growing difficulties recruiting members and mobilizing young voters, with an increasing bias over time (Whiteley, 2009). This trend also applies to Portuguese parties, whose members usually are male, middle-aged, belonging to liberal professions and with high socio-economic status (Lisi, 2015, 73–78; Lisi and Cancela, 2017). Previous studies have found that Portuguese MPs have traditionally displayed an 'elitist' profile. i.e. they have above-average levels of education, with high socioeconomic status and mostly with a partisan career (Freire, 2001). In addition, the proportion of young MPs (below 35 years old) has declined over time and representatives present low levels of civic engagement compared to other Western democracies. Recent studies have found that this pattern has been relatively stable until 2011 (Lisi, 2013; Fonseca de Almeida, 2015).

We start our empirical analysis by considering MPs' socio-demographic profile. Generally speaking, Portuguese parties do not display any significant change in MPs' characteristics (Table 13.3). The only exceptions are the PCP and CDS-PP. On the one hand, both parties show an increase in the proportion of women (from approximately 20% to more than 40%).[8] On the other hand, we can observe a decrease in the proportion of young MPs (18–35 years old).

Table 13.3 Change of MPs' profile after the crisis: summary

	BE	PCP	PS	PSD	CDS-PP
Gender	No change	More women	No change	No change	More women
Age (18–35)	No change	–	No change	No change	–
Education	No change	More educated	No change	No change	No change
Civic engagement	+	+	+	+	+
Interest groups	No change	No change	No change	No change	No change
Political capital	+	+	+	+	+
Political experience	+	+	+	+	+

Source: see appendix.

Note: (–) means that there has been a decline in the specific variable; (+) means that there has been an increase.

Yet it seems that the proportion of representatives belonging to a civic organization has increased in all parliamentary parties. The most evident cases are parties at the extreme of the ideological spectrum. For communist MPs, for example,
associational membership has grown from 13.3% (2009) to 35.3% (2015), while
for the CDS-PP the proportion has increased from 14.3% to 33.3%.

Another important change is related to the variable 'political capital', measured
as the proportion of legislators having a previous post within the party (at the
national, regional or local level). Over the period 2009–2015, the proportion of
MPs holding a party office has increased over time. In addition, political experience seems also to have become more important for the choice of MPs. The BE is
the party with a lower percentage of representatives with no previous experience
in representative offices at local, national or supranational level (approximately
one third). On the contrary, PCP and PSD's deputies present the higher level of
professionalization, with a substantial increase over time.

The fact that partisan and political experience matters for political recruitment
is in line with our interviews with MPs. In the main governing parties (CDS-PP,
PS and PSD) two main criteria have been used according to the distinct selectorate. For the national quota, political experience is crucial; therefore, party leaders
evaluate the competence and the homogeneity of the pool of candidates, especially for those placed at the top of the list. On the other hand, for the regional
party bodies the link between legislators and their constituency (both voters and
local party branches) is crucial. This means that MPs are accountable to the party
organization and have to show that they care about constituency problems.

The results thus far are twofold. First, hypothesis 2a is confirmed as political
parties have enhanced their representation capacity by increasing the proportion
of MPs displaying higher civic engagement. However, if we look at partisan or
political career we find that parties have increasingly relied on their own pool of
candidates, i.e. they have not opened their political recruitment to citizens with no
relevant political background. Therefore, hypothesis 2b is not confirmed. Second,
we cannot observe any clear pattern that links the process of candidate selection to the social representation of Portuguese parties. Deputies' characteristics
seem to be more associated to the legacy of the party's genetic model, its specific

organizational culture and its ideology than to the degree of centralization or inclusiveness adopted for candidate selection.

Ideological homogeneity

To what extent has internal ideological homogeneity changed during the crisis? In order to examine this dimension, we consider the standard deviations of MPs' ideological attitudes on a left-right scale (Giannetti and Pedrazzani, 2013; Gauja and Van Haute, 2015). Taking into account data collected before the bailout, Portugal displayed average levels of internal homogeneity (Giannetti and Pedrazzani, 2013: 191). As for differences across party families, existing research suggests that green parties are more cohesive, while nationalist, ethnic or populist parties display more heterogeneous attitudes (Gauja and Van Haute, 2015, 196–197).

Our data on MPs' ideological positions confirm that distinct parties show different degrees of internal homogeneity (Figure 13.1). The orthodox communists are an outlier as the standard deviation is extremely low in all surveys. On the other hand, MPs belonging to bigger and more catch-all parties present more heterogeneous attitudes, at least as far as the left-right scale is concerned. The BE

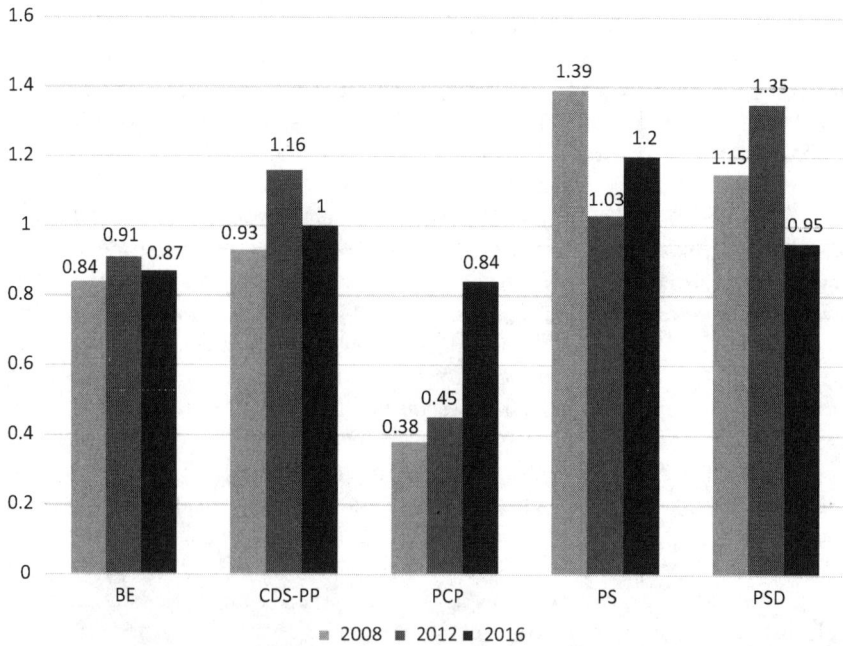

Figure 13.1 Internal ideological homogeneity before and after the crisis

Source: Freire and Viegas (2009); Freire et al. (2013); Freire et al. (2017).

Note: Data are based on standard deviation of MPs' positions on the left-right continuum (0–10).

stands between these two poles, with relatively low levels of internal homogeneity (very close to the CDS-PP).

Taking into account the longitudinal trend, there seems to be two patterns. More ideologically extreme parties – PCP and CDS-PP – show a decrease in ideological homogeneity. This trend is particularly relevant in the Communist party, which halved the level of ideological cohesion. Although we can only speculate on the causes of this effect, probably the decrease in internal homogeneity is related to the growing polarization registered during the crisis. On the other hand, the second group of parties displays no clear trend. In the case of the BE there is overall stability, whereas the PS and PSD registered ups and downs.

Even if this is a preliminary analysis and more sophisticated investigation should be conducted – i.e. considering alternative methodologies or complementary data – we can conclude that the genetic model and organizational culture matter for ideological homogeneity more than the method of candidate selection, given that all parties present the same level of inclusiveness and there are minor differences in terms of degree of centralization. In addition, we could not find any clear effect of the crisis, with the exception of the Communist party.

Conclusions

This study aimed to examine the process of candidate selection in Portugal before and after the crisis. Although there were favourable conditions for democratizing reforms during the crisis, the main political parties have displayed a remarkable stability regarding the way prospective candidates are chosen. Nevertheless, some changes have taken place within the PS, which represents the only case where we could observe some timid reforms towards more inclusive methods of candidate selection. The mechanism behind this change, however, was not related to the crisis but to internal conflicts and power struggles within party elites. Despite the pressures from new parties and challengers, party leadership has remained insulated from the environment, thus hindering the forces of change. As for the impact of candidate selection in terms of outcomes, the findings suggest that the crisis was not associated with a significant change in the socio-demographic profile of representatives, but the criteria adopted by the party leadership facilitated the recruitment of MPs with higher levels of civic engagement and political experience. More than influencing the democratization of candidate selection, the crisis seems to have strengthened the power of the party selectorate, thus confirming Pettitt's argument (2014, 206) that we cannot speak of a 'party crisis' given that 'they are the main and even the only suppliers of representatives'.

The implications of this contribution are twofold. First, candidate selection may elucidate the broader phenomenon of party change in Portugal. Party organizations have displayed a high degree of inertia and the party leadership has made it difficult to implement reforms from within (Lisi, 2015). As a consequence, party change takes place mainly in the presence of an electoral shock, and this is even more likely when this shock is combined with the passage from government to opposition. In other words, the Portuguese case shows that crisis alone is not a sufficient condition to foster party organizational changes, but it may favour democratizing reforms indirectly when associated with a deep electoral change.

Second, the Portuguese case also contributes to highlighting the importance of informal practices in candidate selection. The criteria that orientate the choice and profile of prospective candidate are decided behind closed doors but they may have relevant implications in terms of MP's representativeness and performance. In this regard qualitative research can take the discussion one step further and examine the causes and consequences of these informal practices. A second line that may be fruitful to develop is related to the use of candidate surveys, examining the perception and attitudes of individual politicians and their determinants. These strategies may contribute to illuminating the complex and often obscure process of candidate selection in Portugal and elsewhere.

Acknowledgment

This work was carried out in the framework of the project 'Crise, Representação Política e Renovação da Democracia: O caso Português no Contexto do Sul da Europa' (PTDC/IVC-CPO/3098/2014), supported by the *Fundação para a Ciência e a Tecnologia* (FCT). I am grateful to Vera Ramalhete for assistance in collecting data for this chapter.

Notes

1 We exclude from the analysis the Party of Animals and Nature (*Partido dos Animais e da Natureza*, PAN), a niche party that obtained 1.7% of the votes in the 2015 elections and was able to elect its first MP ever.
2 See the appendix for the list of interviewees.
3 For more details on the MPs' surveys see Freire et al. (2017). Data for the 2008 and 2012 surveys can be found here: http://er.cies.iscte-iul.pt/pt-pt/home
4 Besides the 'parity law' introduced in 2007 (Baum and Espírito Santo 2012), it is worth reminding that apartisan candidates – i.e. those who are not formally affiliated to any registered party – cannot run independently and must be included in one of the lists proposed by political parties.
5 See, for instance, the example of Manuela Ferreira Leite (PSD leader between 2008 and 2010) who excluded from party lists Passos Coelho (a challenger in the 2008 leadership contest), who was selected by the regional organization of Vila Real for the 2009 elections (Freire and Teixeira, 2011: 34).
6 LIVRE decided to form a coalition with the political movement *Tempo de Avançar* (TdA, Time to Move Forward) in the 2015 elections.
7 See *Expresso*, 14 January 2017 (http://expresso.sapo.pt/politica/2017-01-14-Socialistas-adiam-decisao-sobre-primarias).
8 See the appendix for complete results.

References

Barnea, S., and Hazan, R. Y. (2007). Reforming candidate selection methods. *Party Politics* 13 (3), pp. 375–394.
Baum, M., and Espírito-Santo, A. (2012). Portugal's Quota-Parity Law: An analysis of its adoption. *West European Politics* 35 (2), pp. 319–342.

Belchior, A. M., Tsatsanis, E., and Teixeira, C. P. (2016). Representation in times of crisis: Deputy – voter congruence on views of representation in Portugal. *International Political Science Review* 37 (2), pp. 277–293.

Bille, L. (2001). Democratizing a democratic procedure: Myth or reality? *Party Politics* 7 (3), pp. 363–380.

Bosco, A., and Verney, S. (2016). From electoral epidemic to government epidemic: The next level of the crisis in Southern Europe, South European society and politics. *South European Society and Politics* 21 (4), pp. 383–406.

Cancela, J., Dias, A. L., and Lisi, M. (2016). The impact of endorsements in intra-party elections: Evidence from open primaries in a new Portuguese Party. *Politics*, doi:10.1177/0263395716680125.

Chiru, M., Gherghina, S., and Rodriguez Teruel, J. (2015). Explaining change in party leadership selection rules. In Cross, W. P. and Pilet, J.-B. (Eds.), *The politics of party leadership: A cross-national perspective*. Oxford: Oxford University Press, pp. 31–49.

Cross, W. P. and Katz, R. S. (Eds.). (2013). *The challenges of intra-party democracy*. Oxford: Oxford University Press.

Della Porta, D., Andretta, M., Fernandes, T., O'Connor, F., Romanos, E., and Vogiatzoglou, M. (Eds.). (2017). *Late neoliberalism and its discontents in the economic crisis*. London: Springer.

Fernandes, T. (2017). Late Neoliberalism and Its Discontent: The Case of Portugal. In della Porta, D., Andretta, M., Fernandes, T. O'Connor, F, Romanos, E., and Vogiatzoglou, M. (Eds.), *Late neoliberalism and its discontents in the economic crisis*. Basingstoke: Palgrave, pp. 169–200

Foa, R. S., and Mounk, Y. (2017). The signs of deconsolidation. *Democratization* 28 (1), pp. 5–14.

Fonseca de Almeida, J. (2015). Recrutamento Parlamentar: O Associativismo Conta Em Tempos de Crise? In Freire, A., Lisi, M., and Viegas, J. M. Leite (Eds.) *Crise Económica, Políticas de Austeridade E Representação Política*, Lisbon: Assembleia da República, pp. 411–28

Freire, A. (Ed.). (2001). *Recrutamento Parlamentar: Os Deputados Portugueses Da Constituinte À VIII Legislatura*. Lisboa: STAPE.

Freire, A. (2016). The condition of Portuguese democracy during the Troika's intervention, 2011–15. *Portuguese Journal of Social Science* 15 (2), pp. 173–193.

Freire, A., and Lisi, M. (2016). Political parties, citizens and the economic crisis: The evolution of Southern European democracies. *Portuguese Journal of Social Science* 15 (2), pp. 153–171.

Freire, A., Lisi, M., and Tsatsanis, E. (2017a). Portuguese MPs survey: 2015 elections. Research project at CIES-IUL and IPRI-NOVA, "Crisis, Political Representation and Democratic Renewal: The Portuguese case in the Southern European context", FCT: PTDC/IVC-CPO/3098/2014. Retrieved from http://er.cies.iscte-iul.pt/

Freire, A., Lisi, M. and Tsatsanis, E. (2017b), Biographies of Portuguese MPs 2015 – Database, research project at CIES-IUL and IPRI-NOVA, "Crisis, Political Representation and Democratic Renewal: The Portuguese case in the Southern European context", FCT: PTDC/IVC-CPO/3098/2014, available online at: http://er.cies.iscte-iul.pt/

Freire, A., Lisi, M., and Viegas, J. M. L. (Eds.). (2015). *Crise Económica, Políticas de Austeridade E Representação Política*. Lisbon: Assembleia da República.

Freire, A., and Teixeira, C. P. (2011). A Escolha Antes da Escolha: A Seleção dos Candidatos a Deputados – Parte II: Teoria e Prática. *Revista de Ciências Sociais e Políticas*, 2 (September), pp. 31–48.

Freire, A., and Viegas, J. M. L. (Eds.). (2009). *A Representação Política. O Caso Português em Perspectiva Comparada*. Lisbon: Sextante.

Freire, A., Viegas, J. M. L., and Lisi, M. (2013). Portuguese MPs survey, 2012-2013: 2011 legislative election. Research project at ISCTE-IUL and CIES-IUL, Elections, Leadership, and Accountability: Political Representation in Portugal in a longitudinal and comparative perspective, FCT: PTDC/CPJ-CPO/119307/2010, available online at: http://er.cies.iscte-iul.pt/

Gauja, A., and Van Haute, E. (2015) Conclusion: Members and Activists of Political Parties in Comparative Perspective. In Van Haute, E. and Gauja, A. (Eds.), *Party Members and Activists*, Abingdon: Routledge, pp. 186–202.

Giannetti, D and Pedrazzani, A. (2013). La coesione dei partiti italiani. In Di Virgilio, A. and Segatti, P. (Eds.) *La rappresentanza politica in Italia*, Bologna: Il Mulino, pp. 179–206.

Hazan, R. Y., and Rahat, G. (2006). Candidate selection: Methods and consequences. In Katz, R. S. and Crotty, W. J. (Eds.), *Handbook of party politics*. London: Sage, pp. 109–121.

Hazan, R. Y., and Rahat, G. (2010). *Democracy within parties. Candidate selection methods and their political consequences*. Oxford: Oxford University Press.

Hobolt, S. B., and Tilley, J. (2016). Fleeing the centre: The rise of challenger parties in the aftermath of the euro crisis. *West European Politics* 39 (5), pp. 971–991.

Kittilson, M. C., and Scarrow, S. E. (2003). Political parties and the rhetoric and realities of democratization. In Cain, B. E., Dalton, R. J. and Scarrow, S. E. (Eds.), *Democracy transformed? Expanding political opportunities in advanced industrial democracies*. Oxford: Oxford University Press, pp. 59–80.

Kriesi, H. (2012). The political consequences of the financial and economic crisis in Europe: Electoral punishment and popular protest. *Swiss Political Science Review 18*(4), pp. 518–522.

Kriesi, H. (2014). The populist challenge. *West European Politics 37* (2), pp. 361–378.

Krouwel, A. (2012). *Party transformations in European democracies*. New York: SUNY Press.

Lisi, M. (2010). The democratisation of party leadership selection: The Portuguese experience. *Portuguese Journal of Social Sciences* 9 (2), pp. 127–149.

Lisi, M. (2013). Rediscovering civil society? Renewal and continuity in the Portuguese radical left. *South European Society and Politics* 18 (1), pp. 21–39.

Lisi, M. (2015). *Party change, recent democracies and Portugal. Comparative perspectives*. Lanham, MD: Lexington.

Lisi, M. and Cancela, J. (2017). Types of Party Members and Their Implications: Results from a Survey of Portuguese Party Members. *Party Politics*, https://doi.org/ DOI: 10.1177/1354068817722445.

Lisi, M., and Freire, A. (2014). The selection of party leaders in Portugal. In Cross, W. and Pilet, J.-B. (Eds.), *The selection of political party leaders in contemporary parliamentary democracies*. London: Routledge, pp. 124–140.LIVRE/Tempo de Avançar (2015). Regulamento eleitoral para as eleições primárias. Retrieved from http://tempo-deavancar.net/?page_id=916 (accessed 2 February 2016).

Mair, P. (2013). *Ruling the void: The hollowing of western democracy*. London: Verso.

March, L., and Daniel, K. (Eds.). (2016). *Europe's radical left from marginality to the mainstream?* London: Rowman and Littlefield.

Montabes, J., and Ortega, C. (1999). Candidate selection in two rigid list system. ECPR Joint Sessions. Mannheim.

Morlino, L., and Raniolo, F. (2017). *The impact of the economic crisis on South European democracies*. Basingstoke: Palgrave Macmillan.

Muro, D., and Vidal, G. (2017). Political mistrust in southern Europe since the Great Recession. *Mediterranean Politics* 22 (2), pp. 197–217.

Panebianco, A. (1988). *Political parties: Organization and power*. Oxford: Oxford University Press.

Pettitt, R. T. (2014). *Contemporary party politics*. Basingstoke: Palgrave Macmillan.

Pilet, J.-B., and Cross, W. (Eds.). (2014). *The selection of political party leaders in contemporary parliamentary democracies*. London: Routledge.

Rahat, G., and Hazan, R. Y. (2001). Candidate selection methods. *Party Politics* 7 (3), pp. 297–322.

Riera, P. (2011). Closed party list. In Colomer, J. (Ed.), *Personal representation. The neglected dimension of electoral systems*. Colchester: ECPR Press, pp. 55–80.

Sandri, G., Seddone, A. and Venturino, F. (Eds.). (2015a). *Party primaries in comparative perspective*. Farnham: Ashgate.

Sandri, G., Seddone, A., and Venturino, F. (Eds.). (2015b). Conclusion. In Sandri, G., Seddone, A. and Venturino, F. (Eds.), *Party primaries in comparative perspective*. Farnham: Ashgate.

Shomer, Y. (2012). What affects candidate selection processes? A cross-national examination. *Party Politics* 20 (4), pp. 533–546.

Streeck, W. (2014), *Buying time. The delayed crisis of democratic capitalism*. London: Verso.

Teixeira, C. P. (2009). *O Povo Semi-Soberano. Partidos Políticos E Recrutamento Parlamentar*. Coimbra: Almedina.

Teixeira, C. P., Tsatsanis, E., and Belchior, A. M. (2016). A 'Necessary Evil' even during hard times? Public support for political parties in Portugal before and after the Bailout (2008 and 2012). *Party Politics* 22 (6), pp. 719–731.

Torcal, M. (2014). The decline of political trust in Spain and Portugal: Economic performance or political responsiveness? *American Behavioral Scientist* 58 (12), pp. 1542–1567.

Van Biezen, I. (2003). *Political parties in new democracies. Party organization in Southern and East-Central Europe*. London: Palgrave Macmillan.

Van Biezen, I., and Piccio, D. (2013). Shaping intra-party democracy: On the legal regulation of internal party organizations. In Cross, W. P. and Katz, R. S. (Eds.), *The challenges of intra-party democracy*. Oxford: Oxford University Press, pp. 27–48.

Verney, S., and Bosco, A. (Eds.). (2014). *Protest elections and challenger parties: Italy and Greece in the economic crisis*. London: Routledge.

Whiteley, P. (2009). Party membership and activism in comparative perspective. In DeBardeleben, J. and Pammett, J. H. (Eds.), *Activating the citizen. Dilemmas of participation in Europe and Canada*. Basingstoke: Palgrave Macmillan, pp. 131–150.

Widfeldt, A. (1995). Party membership and party representativeness. In Klingemann, H.-D. and Fuchs, D. (Eds.), *Citizens and the state*. Oxford: Oxford University Press, pp. 134–182.

Appendix

Table 13.4 Socio-political profile of BE MPs

	2009	2011	2015
Gender (male)	62.5	50.0	68.4
Age (18–35)	31.3	12.5	31.6
Education (undergraduate)	81.3	100.0	94.8
Civic engagement	12.5	50.0	31.6
Interest groups	6.3	25.0	0.0
Political capital	43.7	50.0	78.9
Political experience	62.5	100	68.4

Source: Adapted from Freire et al. (2017b).

Table 13.5 Socio-political profile of CDS-PP MPs

	2009	2011	2015
Gender (male)	81.0	75.0	55.6
Age (18–35)	19.0	16.7	0.0
Education	94.7	85.0	94.4
Civic engagement	14.3	4.2	33.3
Interest groups	0.0	8.3	0.0
Political capital	32.9	27.5	88.9
Political experience	66.7	91.7	83.3

Table 13.6 Socio-political profile of PCP MPs

	2009	2011	2015
Gender (male)	80.0	81.3	58.8
Age (18–35)	40.0	25.0	5.9
Education	80.0	87.5	88.2
Civic engagement	13.3	12.5	35.3
Interest groups	13.3	6.3	11.8
Political capital	66.7	62.5	94.1
Political experience	86.7	100.0	94.1

Table 13.7 Socio-political profile of PS MPs

	2009	2011	2015
Gender (male)	67.0	73.0	65.1
Age (18–35)	11.3	6.8	9.3
Education	91.6	95.9	91.8
Civic engagement	17.5	4.1	26.7
Interest groups	5.2	1.4	4.7
Political capital	41.2	32.9	77.9
Political experience	81.4	97.3	86.0

Table 13.8 Socio-political profile of PSD MPs

	2009	2011	2015
Gender (male)	72.8	70.4	70.8
Age (18–35)	11.1	16.7	6.7
Education	97.4	95.2	95.4
Civic engagement	17.3	21.3	34.8
Interest groups	6.2	6.5	4.5
Political capital	25.9	25.9	49.4
Political experience	72.8	82.4	93.3

List of MP interviews:

Name	Party affiliation	Date
António Filipe	PCP	17/02/17
Joana Mortágua	BE	22/02/17
Jorge Costa	BE	31/01/17
António José Seguro	PS	18/01/17
Tiago Barbosa Ribeiro	PS	29/09/16
António Rodrigues	PSD	14/02/17
Álvaro Castelo Branco	CDS-PP	17/01/17
João Rebelo	CDS-PP	12/01/17

14 New parties and new ways of candidate selection in Spain

Antonio M. Jaime-Castillo, Xavier Coller, and Guillermo Cordero

Introduction

This chapter analyzes how candidate selection has evolved in recent times in Spain. As in other Southern European countries, Spain has witnessed a sharp decline in institutional confidence and growing political disaffection in the wake of the so-called Great Recession. In this regard, Spain represents the archetypal case of a Southern European country in which the politico-economic crisis has shaken the party system, leading to the introduction of new ways of selecting candidates. The argument we make in this chapter unfolds as follows. First, the economic crisis in Spain became also a political crisis, aggravated by several corruption scandals that amplified political discontent and criticism against political parties and elected politicians. Second, strong political discontent against the established political parties opened a window of opportunity for new parties to emerge. Finally, as these new parties adopted a discourse on political regeneration, which put intra-party democracy at the centre, the new parties introduced more participatory ways of selecting candidates. And the established parties reacted accordingly when their electoral support was threatened by the emerging parties.

The sharp decline in vote share of the two major established parties in Spain – the conservative PP (Popular Party) and the social democrat PSOE (Spanish Socialist Party) – has eroded an imperfect two-party system, giving rise to a more complex scenario in which two new parties – Podemos (*We Can*) on the left and Ciudadanos (*Citizens*) on the centre-right – compete to be pivotal players in the political process (Simón, 2016). This has had a major impact on the process of candidate selection. First, as the new parties were built on an anti-establishment discourse targeting the power of the traditional political apparatus, both Podemos and Ciudadanos have put in place more inclusive ways of selecting candidates, although with relevant nuances towards centralization and control of the elites over the outcomes of the selection process. Secondly, in an attempt to reconnect with their traditional electorates, the established parties (PP and PSOE) have moved in the direction of opening new ways of participation, as suggested by Pilet and Cross (2014). Although these changes are still in the making, the process of candidate selection in Spain is expected to change even more substantially in the years to come. Furthermore, our data show that the emergence of new ways of selecting candidates has had some (still limited) effect on descriptive representation.

The chapter is organized as follows. In the next section, we describe the scenario of politico-economic crisis in Spain in the wake of the Great Recession and how the resulting political unrest created a suitable environment for new parties to thrive. In the following section, we explain how the exclusiveness in candidate selection among established parties before the crisis was in contradiction with grassroots demand for more intra-party democracy. In the following section, we explain how this state of affairs changed dramatically after the emergence of Podemos and Ciudadanos, which introduced new participatory ways of selecting candidates, and how the established parties followed suit when their electoral support began to erode. Finally, we discuss how changes in candidate selection might have affected descriptive representation in Spanish parliament.

Political crisis and new parties

Spain has been affected by a severe economic crisis in the wake of the Great Recession, producing an economic downturn and massive unemployment. Although the official discourse of the Spanish government tried to avoid the term "bailout", as a way to differentiate from other countries where the European authorities intervened, the Spanish program of financial assistance explicitly included conditionality in economic policies and strict surveillance of the public finances. As a result, the government passed several cuts in social benefits and programs (Jordana, 2014) which, in combination with the inability of the political system to provide solutions to the endemic problems of the Spanish economy (Fishman, 2012), fuelled social protests and public demonstrations. Moreover, the economic crisis coincided with a period of serious corruption scandals, which affected all the established political parties at the national (PP and PSOE) and regional levels (CiU), but especially the Popular Party in power.

The combination of economic stagnation and high rates of unemployment with corruption scandals created the perfect milieu for social unrest and political discontent. Confidence in political institutions, and especially political parties, was already low in Spain at the time, but it plumbed historical depths. For instance, according to data from the Centro de Investigaciones Sociológicas (CIS), both confidence in political parties and confidence in the parliament dropped dramatically between 2007 and 2013, while, at the same time, Spanish citizens came to believe that politicians and corruption were two of the most important problems of the country, after the economic crisis and unemployment. Monthly data from CIS about the evaluation of the political situation in Spain (plotted in Figure 14.1) show how the public perception of politics deteriorated in Spain during the Great Recession. Between 2006 and 2008, the proportion of citizens who believe the political situation in the country was bad or very bad was typically between 30% and 40%. During 2009, the year in which the economic crisis in Spain became blatant to the public (besides attempts at denial by the PSOE government), this proportion jumped above 60%. And during the year after the 2011 general

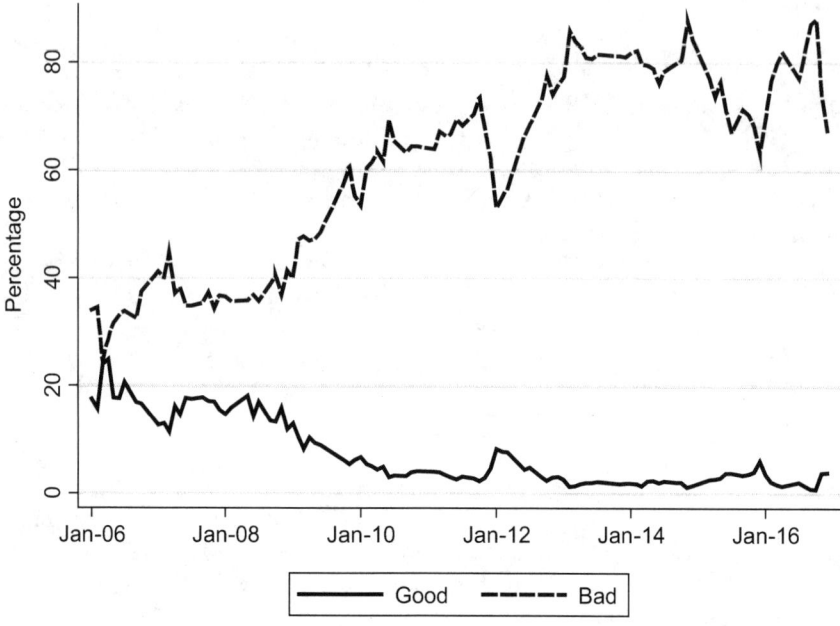

Figure 14.1 Evaluation of the political situation in Spain

Source: CIS Database, Several Studies.

election, in which the PP took over the government, the proportion grew to 80%. The proportion of people dissatisfied with the political situation only fell after an election took place during the period, but then rapidly grew to its previous level, while the proportion of individuals saying that the political situation in Spain was good or very good remained stable below 5% from 2012 onwards.

The extent of political unrest in Spain is only comparable to Greece, even though the effects of the economic crisis were less intense in Spain. Data from the European Social Survey (2017), indicates that Spain and Greece were the countries in Southern Europe where satisfaction with democracy was highest (an average slightly above 6 in both countries in 2004), while Italy and Portugal were at the rear. However, satisfaction with democracy quickly eroded in Spain (and specially Greece) during the crisis, while the decrease was more moderate in Italy and Portugal. Similarly, using data from the Eurobarometer from autumn 2007 to autumn 2011, Armingeon and Guthmann (2014) find that Spain showed the second biggest deterioration among the 26 EU member countries (after Greece) in satisfaction with democracy and trust in the national parliament.

Although political disaffection is connected to the consequences of the economic crisis (Armingeon and Guthmann, 2014; Muro and Vidal, 2017) and the economic deprivation experienced by the middle class (Polavieja, 2013), the data points to a deep crisis of representativeness as the main source of political discontent in Spain (Torcal, 2014). As in other countries, political discontent opened a window of opportunity for new parties to emerge and fill the increasing gap between citizens and established political parties (Morlino and Raniolo, 2017; Orriols and Cordero, 2016), even though, in the Spanish case, there were strong institutional and electoral barriers of entry. The Spanish electoral system belongs to the proportional party list family. However, the small size of many electoral districts has produced historically low proportionality and low levels of electoral and parliamentary fragmentation (Simón, 2016). Moreover, even though Spanish civil society has traditionally lacked dense networks of political mobilization (Fernandes, 2015; Torcal and Montero, 1998), the anti-establishment movement *Indignados* (Indignant, similar to Occupy Wall Street), as well as many others, gained rapid visibility by the end of the last term in power of the PSOE. One of its best-known slogans "*No nos representan*" (They do not represent us) refers to the established mainstream parties. In May 15th, 2011, a march was called to protest against the economic and political situation of the country by several protest movements. After the march took place, a group of demonstrators camped in Puerta del Sol in Madrid, followed by many others in the coming days and newly established camps in public squares across cities and towns all over the country, giving birth to the movement 15-M.

Although the 15-M movement declared itself apolitical, several activists of the movement, formerly linked to left-wing organizations, capitalized on the unfolding political unrest in the country to organize a political platform named Podemos, which became a political party in March 2014, just two months before the elections to the European Parliament in May 2014.[1] Against all odds, the party got 8% of the popular vote and 5 elected MEPs (Cordero and Montero, 2015). In the national election held in 2015 Podemos got 21% of the popular vote and 69 seats in the Lower Chamber (Orriols and Cordero, 2016). Even though the landslide in the Spanish party system was significant, the outcome of the election did not match electoral expectations, as many electoral surveys had predicted an even bigger share of the vote for Podemos. Podemos based its political discourse on criticisms against the inability of the political elites to solve the economic crisis, rising inequality, and the austerity measures promoted by the European institutions. In the 2016 elections, Podemos formed an electoral coalition with Izquierda Unida (the United Left, including the Spanish Communist Party).

Another political actor entered the national political arena in the centre-right. Ciudadanos appeared in the Spanish region of Catalonia in 2006 as a platform against hegemonic nationalist parties in the region. The party made some unsuccessful attempts to jump into national politics but in the elections to the European Parliament of 2014 obtained 3.2% of the popular vote and two MEPs; and in the general elections held in 2015 it won 13.9% of the popular vote and 40 seats in Congress. The ideological corpus of Ciudadanos promotes liberal values in both the economic and social realms and is also deeply rooted in a discourse about regeneration, intra-party democracy and fighting against corruption.

Even though Podemos and Ciudadanos endorse very different social and economic ideals, they both criticise strongly the political establishment. They also embrace a discourse of intra-party democracy as a way to overcome the hierarchical structure of traditional parties that had caused them to lose touch with citizens' demands and open the door for corruption. This focus on political regeneration appealed to a substantial share of the Spanish electorate which was dissatisfied with traditional parties and politicians (Orriols and Cordero, 2016) and, at the same time, increasingly interested in politics. Political interest increased substantially in Spain, from a very low level, during the years of the economic crisis.[2] Thus, it can be argued that new forms of candidate selection in Spain in the new political parties were introduced as a response to a grassroots demand for more intra-party democracy. In the next section we will focus on how the highly exclusive way of selecting candidates before the crisis was connected to the hierarchical structure of the established parties and how this was in contradiction with the grassroots demand for more intra-party democracy.

Candidate selection in Spain

The empirical evidence suggests that candidate selection within Spanish parties has been highly decentralized and exclusive (Cordero et al., 2016). The trend toward decentralization is common in multilevel government systems like Spain, in which national leaders play a limited role (Lundell, 2004). Even though a more decentralized selection process brings the decisions closer to the voters and might be an opportunity for involvement of the local affiliate (Rahat, 2007), decentralization and exclusiveness can coexist, as decentralization might only mean the transfer of the locus of control from a national oligarchy to a local oligarchy (Hazan and Rahat, 2010). However, regional parties in Spain have a more inclusive selection process than national parties, suggesting some link between decentralization and inclusiveness in the Spanish case (Cordero et al, 2016).

The lack of inclusiveness in the selection process is connected to the closed and blocked lists used in Spanish elections (except the Senate, the Upper Chamber). Closed and blocked lists encourage party discipline since MPs have incentives to follow the guidelines of party leaders to get a competitive post in the lists, and, therefore, ensure their access to the parliament (Kam, 2009; Cordero and Coller, 2015). This produces highly cohesive parliamentary groups (Jaime-Castillo and Martínez-Cousinou, 2018) and strengthens the internal power of party leaders (Royo, 2013). Furthermore, the closed and blocked lists make the representatives more accountable to the party leadership than to the voters (Carey and Shugart, 1995; Sartori, 1994).

Empirical analyses of both Lundell (2004) and Shomer (2014) point to an important regional variation in selection procedures that overcomes the variation between electoral systems. This suggests that it is not the electoral system itself which makes the difference in candidate selection, but a set of institutional arrangements that, in the Spanish case, were introduced during the transition to democracy to "strengthen the new and fragile main party organizations" (Barberà et al., 2015, 60). As a consequence, selection in traditional parties (especially the PP and PSOE) has been dominated by the party leadership with limited involvement of the rank and file and the local branches of the parties. And the most usual way of becoming a candidate has been appointment by party organs or leaders, while the proportion of candidates who nominate themselves to be in the lists has been very low (Coller et al., 2018 Jiménez-Sánchez et al., 2018).

Not surprisingly, data reported in Table 14.1 indicates that MPs have a positive view of the selection process, as they are the winners of the race. Data were collected between 2009 and 2011 (before the entrance of Podemos and Ciudadanos into the national parliament) and reveal that MPs from both PP and PSOE believe that the selection process in their respective parties was democratic, efficient and fair. However, there seems to be a trade-off between democracy and efficiency for major parties, since the PSOE scored higher in democracy than in efficiency and the opposite is true for PP, although there were no differences regarding the fairness of the process and small parties scored higher in democracy, efficiency and fairness.

Another point to note is that, in the case of PP and PSOE, personal loyalties matter more than parliamentary experience and the popularity of the candidate to become a candidate (Coller et al., 2018), which confirms that the selection process has been mainly in the hands of relevant figures within the party and personal allegiances are crucial to decide who will be in the list. Following this reasoning, we should expect that more relevant party members will be more satisfied with the selection process. We try to confirm this hypothesis by analyzing the variations in the evaluations of the selection process among MPs. In Table 14.2 we report a set of linear regressions in which the dependent variables are the degree of democracy, efficiency and fairness of the selection process as perceived by the MPs. The two most important variables affecting the perceptions of MPs about the process of candidate selection are the power within the parliamentary group and parliamentary experience. Most influential MPs perceived that the process is more democratic, efficient and fair than those who are at the bottom of the hierarchy. Moreover, and consistent with a more exclusive selection in the big parties, the selection process was evaluated as more democratic and fairer in other parties, as compared to the PP (the reference category), although some differences

Table 14.1 Evaluation of the selection process by MPs (averages on a 1–7 scale)

	PP	*PSOE*	*Other parties*	*Total*
The process is democratic	4.4	5.1	6.0	5.0
The process is efficient	5.1	4.7	5.2	5.0
The process is fair	4.4	4.4	5.1	4.5
It rests on personal loyalties	5.1	4.9	4.1	4.8
Parliamentary experience is important	4.6	4.4	4.3	4.5
Popularity is important	4.7	4.5	4.4	4.5

Source: CIS Database, Study 2827.

Table 14.2 Determinants of MPs' evaluation of the selection process OLS

	Democratic	Efficient	Fair
Power within the group	0.115***	0.131***	0.156***
	(0.035)	(0.031)	(0.032)
Ideological distance with party	0.030	0.020	0.047
	(0.050)	(0.043)	(0.045)
Terms in parliament	−0.226***	−0.118**	−0.175***
	(0.067)	(0.058)	(0.060)
PP (reference category)			
PSOE	0.696***	−0.382***	0.013
	(0.152)	(0.131)	(0.137)
Other parties	1.350***	−0.115	0.428**
	(0.190)	(0.165)	(0.171)
Congress and Senate (reference category)			
Regional Parliament	−0.041	0.219*	−0.001
	(0.146)	(0.127)	(0.133)
Female	−0.228	−0.080	−0.164
	(0.141)	(0.122)	(0.127)
Constant	4.572***	4.531***	4.038***
	(0.352)	(0.304)	(0.318)
Observations	555	554	551
R2	0.149	0.071	0.090

Source: CIS Database, Study 2827.

Notes: ***, **, and * denote significance level at 1%, 5%, and 10%, respectively. Standard errors in brackets.

between the PP and PSOE still hold in the multivariate analysis (the selection process was evaluated as more democratic in the PSOE than in the PP, but more efficient in the PP than in the PSOE). Interestingly also, parliamentary experience had a negative and significant effect, meaning that more experienced MPs thought that the process is less democratic, less efficient and less fair than new MPs, probably because they know the process better. Finally, neither gender nor the ideological distance between the MPs and the party has a significant effect on how the selection process is evaluated.

These findings are consistent with the idea that the selection process in established parties has been controlled by the party leadership and, even among those who reach the parliament, less influential MPs feel the process is less democratic, efficient and fair. This is also consistent with citizens' perceptions about the functioning of political parties in Spain. According to data from CIS (study 2930) in 2012, only 22.2% of Spaniards agree with the statement that parties take into account the opinion of the membership when decisions are made and only 7.8% agree that decisions made by political parties are transparent. Moreover, almost a half of Spaniards (43.2%) believed in 2009 that candidates should be elected by all the citizens, while only 15.5% declared that they should be selected by party organs (study 2790). Thus, both citizens and the rank and file within the parties seem to complain about lack of internal democracy, which is in line with a grassroots demand for more participatory ways of selecting candidates within the parties.

Selection models

In this section we analyze the supply side of candidate selection in Spain, or how (new and old) parties have reacted to the demand for more intra-party democracy. In what follows we draw on the analysis of regulations contained in parties' bylaws and personal interviews with party leaders when relevant information was missing. Given the large number of parties in subnational party systems in Spain, our analysis is restricted to the four national parties (PP, PSOE, Podemos and Ciudadanos). As previously argued, both Podemos and Ciudadanos introduced new selection methods as a response to the lack of intra-party democracy among established parties, although some previous attempts were made by established parties before. PSOE used primaries to select party leaders from 1998 (Barberà, Lisi and Rodríguez Teruel, 2015) and IU (now in Podemos) included the possibility of primaries to select candidates, though this never happened. Moreover, the competition of the new parties forced PP and PSOE to make some changes in the same direction. However, besides the changes, each party has its own distinctive model of candidate selection, which is the product of different organizational structures and political legacies. In fact, a key characteristic of candidate selection in the Spanish case is the variety of procedures and mechanisms between parties.

The Popular Party represents the most traditional and centralized way of selecting candidates. Formally, the selection process involves two electoral committees, at the provincial and the national level. Moreover, members of the electoral committees are appointed by the party president and approved by the executive committee of the party at each territorial level, which makes the process highly controlled by the party leadership. The selection process begins at the provincial electoral committee, which is in charge of elaborating the lists for every type of election, and the list is then sent to a national electoral committee. Formally, the national electoral committee has the power to approve the list as it is or veto it. However, the latter seldom occurs, since the party structure is highly centralized and candidates proposed at the provincial level are usually aligned with the party leadership. It is even common practice that the national leadership of the party instructs the provincial branches of the party to put some key party figures (e.g., former ministers or, less often, relevant personalities) in front-running positions in the lists. Formally, there are no previous requirements to become a candidate and both affiliates and non-affiliates can be candidates, although non-affiliates are only rarely chosen. Finally, the criteria to select candidates are inspired by the principles of equality of all affiliates, merit, capacity, evaluation of activities as representative, and whatever else is needed for the proper functioning of the parliamentary group, although incumbents usually have an advantage. However, although this party has been reluctant to change its way of selecting candidates, some signs of change have been seen in the last party conference (February 2017) when a sort of primary election to preselect candidates for leadership (at the national, regional and provincial level) was implemented. The assembly of delegates will choose then among the pre-selected candidates in the "primary" election (PP 2017, art. 35), generating a multi-stage method of selecting leaders according to Hazan and Rahat (2010, 37)

The PSOE represents the decentralized model of candidate selection. The party has two different mechanisms to select candidates. First, primaries only apply to a very limited number of posts competing for government responsibilities: the candidate for the presidency of the national government (in any case) and the candidates for the presidency of regional governments and the largest cities (only when there is more than one candidate). However, the usual mechanism for selecting candidates is a rather complex net of interactions between party organs at different territorial levels; and it is highly decentralized, given the federal structure of the party (Coller et al., 2018). The process begins at the local level, where the local chapters of the party can nominate candidates to an open list that is sent to a provincial commission. Nominations can be made at a designated meeting by either party officers at the local level or affiliates. The provincial commission then reviews the nominations and makes a proposal to be approved by the executive committee of the party at the provincial level. The proposal is then sent to a regional committee that makes a report, which is sent to a dedicated committee at the national level (*Comisión Federal de Listas*). The national commission produces a report that might include additional candidates (not proposed at lower levels) to be approved by the party's national executive committee. The national commission has veto power but has to listen to regional and provincial party organs and the speaker of the party in parliament to assess the performance of incumbent candidates.

While the national level of the party has formal veto power and a great deal of influence over the outcome, the federal structure of the organization makes room for lower (especially regional) levels to play a substantial role in the process of candidate selection. Most often, regional branches of the party with a large number of affiliates or control of the government at the regional level are very influential. In the end, candidate selection might be seen as the result of the distribution of political power between different territorial levels of the party.

Podemos represents the most inclusive model of candidate selection. The selection is made by individual vote of all the affiliates and all the posts are open for competition. Furthermore, party members and non-members can be candidates. Personal candidacies and open lists are allowed, but they must both be endorsed either by a circle (*Círculo*) or by an elected board (at the national, regional or local level), including secretariats and citizens councils (*Consejos Ciudadanos*).[3] Candidates are selected at different territorial levels depending on the election. Candidates for Congress are selected at national level. Candidates for the Senate and regional assemblies are selected at the regional level. The electoral system is the block vote, implying that each elector can use as many votes as posts to be filled and as few as he or she wishes, but only one vote to each candidate is allowed. After the election takes place, candidates are ranked according to the number of votes they receive. Then, candidates choose the list (as there is one list per district) and the post within the list for which they want to run, according to their position in the ranking. The process is regulated by the Citizen Council of the party and is overseen by two different committees (*Comisión Electoral* and *Comisión de Garantías Democráticas*). Lists are immediately enacted, requiring no further approval, and no party organ has veto power. However, the system of block voting has been used as a mechanism of control by the party elite, making primaries very uncompetitive (Pérez-Nievas et al., 2017).

Ciudadanos represents an intermediate model of inclusiveness and decentralization. List members are elected through primaries among party affiliates at the district level for each and every election, although primaries are only the rule for districts with more than 150 affiliates. Furthermore, only the first five posts in the list are chosen by primaries (the rest of the posts are filled by the executive committee). In the case of elections to Congress, the selection process involves two different elections: one for the head of the list and another one for the posts from 2 to 5. In the case of elections to the Senate, there is only one election, since the electoral system for the Spanish Senate uses open lists and candidates are, therefore, not ranked. Only individual candidacies are allowed and only party members affiliated at least six months before the election can run (although this requisite can be waived by the executive committee). In addition, to enter the race to be head of the list, candidates must be endorsed by a minimum number of affiliates, not exceeding 10% of party members in the district. The voting system for any election is the SNTV (single non-transferable vote) in which each voter only has one vote for the candidate he or she chooses. In the election to be head of the list, the candidate with most votes is appointed. In the election for the 2–5 posts, posts are filled according to the number of votes each candidate receives. After the two separate elections take place, the results are then sent to the executive committee for approval. The executive committee can break ties, complete the list and change the order, but it must provide a motive in these cases. Finally, the rests of the posts in the list (6th and onwards) are appointed by the executive committee of the party.

From these four different models of candidate selection, we can derive some common features and the main differences between parties in the Spanish case. In Table 14.3 we summarize the selection process for each party according to different relevant aspects. The selection model refers to the index proposed by Shomer (2009; 2014) and combines the dimensions of inclusiveness and decentralization (Rahat and Hazan, 2001). Furthermore, the selectorate refers specifically to the degree of inclusiveness and the selection level to the degree of centralization, while the dimension of candidacy is also taken from Rahat and Hazan (2001), although we also include specific requirements that candidates have to fulfil before entering the lists. In addition, we take into account how parties handle gender quotas in selecting candidates and how they regulate the selection process. Finally, at the bottom of the table, we summarize the key elements of primaries (scope of the selection, requirements, candidacies, voting system and corrective mechanisms) for the two parties that actually have them (Podemos and Ciudadanos).

Table 14.3 Candidate selection in Spanish political parties

	PP	PSOE	Podemos	Ciudadanos
Selection model	Provincial party delegates subject to approval of national party	Provincial party delegates subject to approval of regional and national party	Primaries	Primaries subject to approval of national party
Selectorate	Provincial electoral committees	Local chapters and provincial electoral committees	All affiliates	Affiliates within the district
Selection level	Provincial	Local and provincial	National for Congress and regional for Senate	Provincial
Candidacy	Members and non-members	Members and non-members	Members and non-members	Party members plus additional requirements
Requirements	Suitability declaration	Code of ethics and declaration of interests	Code of ethics and financial contribution commitment	Code of ethics and declaration of interests
Gender quotas	Binding by law. No mention	Zip lists	Zip lists or better for women	Binding by law. No mention
Regulation	No specific regulation	Specific regulation	Specific regulation	Specific regulation
Primaries Regulation				
Scope of the selection	–	–	Whole list	The first five posts within the list
Requirements	–	–	Endorsed by one circle or elected board	Endorsed by affiliates
Candidacies	–	–	Open lists and individual candidates	Individual candidates
Voting system	–	–	Block Vote	SNTV
Corrective mechanisms	–	–	Compliance with gender quotas	Approval by executive committee

Source: Authors' compilation.

According to the previous criteria, there are some common notes affecting the selection of candidates in every party. Firstly, although the inclusiveness of the process varies greatly between parties, selection is always restricted to party members. That is, no major party has so far adopted open primaries to design electoral lists at the regional or national level. Secondly, since the province constitutes the electoral district in most types of elections, the selection usually takes place at the provincial level (with the exception of Podemos), although the degree of centralization also varies depending on the organization of each party. Thirdly, in 2007 gender quotas in electoral lists were introduced (candidates of either sex make up at least 40 per 100 of total list members). Therefore, gender quotas are abiding by law, although the proportion of women who actually make it to the parliament varies substantially between parties (Verge and Espírito-Santo, 2016). Moreover, there are important differences in how gender quotas are introduced in the selection process, following the left-right divide. PP and Ciudadanos do not mention gender quotas (or even gender balance) in their formal regulations of the selection process, while both Podemos and PSOE use zip lists (the gender of one candidate has to be different to the previous one) and include specific clauses in their regulations about gender balance in the lists.

The main difference in the selection process can be drawn between parties using primaries (Podemos and Ciudadanos) and those who do not use primaries (PSOE and PP). In this regard, it is clear that the two newly established parties have a more inclusive way of selecting candidates as compared to the PP and PSOE. However, both Podemos and Ciudadanos introduced mechanisms for the party leadership to have some control over the outcome. Podemos requires the candidates to be endorsed by a party organ and Ciudadanos requires candidates to be affiliated to the party six months before the election (although this requirement can be waived by the executive committee of the party). In addition, the use of open lists in Podemos has a strong effect on the outcome in a newly established party in which the leadership is very charismatic (Cordero et al., 2016). This implies, in practice, that those who run in the list led by relevant and well-known figures of the party have an advantage over any challenging faction. In the case of Ciudadanos, although only individual candidacies are allowed, candidates endorsed by the party leadership have usually won the race. Moreover, in the case of Ciudadanos, the executive committee can break ties, complete the list and change the order of candidates.

In contrast, PSOE maintains a selection model that is without primaries but highly decentralized, which makes possible the nomination of party affiliates at the local level. At the same time, PSOE has introduced primaries to select some candidates competing for government responsibilities (presidents of the national and regional government and mayors of largest cities). In a few cases, these primaries have been open to the general public, not just affiliates. PP has maintained a more traditional selection model. However, it is important to note that party by-laws do not preclude the use of primaries or any other inclusive selection method by the electoral committees and some provincial branches of the party have made some innovations like candidates' hearings before nomination. Furthermore, before the last party conference in 2017 there was an internal debate about the possibility of introducing party primaries for selecting candidates, but the proposal was finally withdrawn.

Descriptive representation

A final question we try to answer in this section is whether the politico-economic crisis and the implementation of new forms of candidate selection in the Spanish parties have had a significant impact on descriptive representation. Two different mechanisms could be at work. First, the emergence of new parties with more inclusive ways of selecting candidates might have opened the parliaments to social groups that have been traditionally under-represented. Secondly, even though the formal rules for selecting candidates in the established parties did not change as much as in the new parties, as shown in the previous section, these parties might be more sensitive to informal criteria potentially affecting the representativeness of their MPs, as has happened in the case of Portugal (see chapter 13).

In Table 14.4 we provide some information about the evolution of the composition of Congress during the democratic period in Spain to find out whether changes in the selection procedures have produced substantial changes in terms of descriptive representation. We specifically focus on gender, age, education level and social extraction (measured by previous occupation) of MPs. Data reveal that there have not been major changes in the composition of the Congress in the legislatures after the politico-economic crisis. The percentage of women in Parliament increased dramatically in the period before the crisis but remain stable after 2011. The average age of MPs increased from a very young chamber in the first legislatures as many MPs were older in the next legislatures, but it did not change substantially after 2011. Something similar happened with the education level. The percentage

Table 14.4 Composition of Congress by legislature

Legislature	% Women	Average age	% College degree	% Workers and employees	% Lawyers	% Teachers
Const. (1977)	6.0	44.1	88.1	15.1	27.5	20.9
I (1979)	6.0	42.3	89.0	12.3	24.3	27.4
II (1982)	6.0	42.5	89.2	8.1	25.1	29.2
III (1986)	8.0	44.0	89.8	7.0	22.4	28.5
IV (1989)	13.7	44.5	89.6	7.3	19.2	29.1
V (1993)	13.7	46.4	90.8	8.1	20.9	28.4
VI (1996)	23.0	46.5	92.3	8.6	22.6	28.2
VII (2000)	29.4	47.3	91.5	9.4	24.1	26.5
VIII (2004)	35.4	47.9	95.0	9.5	25.5	24.6
IX (2008)	36.9	49.0	91.3	7.0	24.3	25.9
X (2011)	40.3	49.5	93.7	4.7	30.1	21.0
XI (2015)	39.7	48.4	94.0	2.2	26.3	18.4
XII (2016)	38.9	48.5	93.4	3.1	25.5	17.1
Legislature XII (2016)						
PP	39.6	51.5	95.5	2.5	35.8	13.3
PSOE	41.7	50.2	95.2	1.3	21.1	31.6
Podemos	49.3	41.6	83.6	8.1	8.1	12.9
Ciudadanos	21.9	46.2	96.9	0.0	34.4	3.1

Source: Authors' compilation after data contained in Bapolau and Bapolcon databases.

of MPs who have a college degree was already high in the first legislatures and increased slightly in subsequent legislatures, but no substantial changes have been found since 2011. Regarding the professional background of the MPs, lawyers (and other legal professions, such as judges or prosecutors) and teachers (at all levels of education, from primary school to university) have been the most frequent professions in the chamber in all the legislatures, including the last three legislatures, while, at the same time, the proportion of blue-collar workers and white-collar employees has shrunk substantially from the first legislatures to the present.

Therefore, the politico-economic crisis does not seem to have produced a substantial change in terms of descriptive representation in Spain. Does it mean that MPs from the new parties have a similar profile to MPs from established parties? The answer is no. At the bottom of Table 14.4 we report the socio-demographic profile of MPs of the last legislature by party. Overall, MPs from established parties have a very similar socio-demographic profile. The only meaningful difference between the PP and PSOE is the occupational background. There are more lawyers in the PP and more teachers in the PSOE but the sum of the two groups is about one half in both parties as is the case in all legislatures (Coller et al., 2016). However, the profile of MPs from the new parties differs in many ways. Podemos, which is the most different case with respect to the average composition of Congress, includes more women than any other party and its MPs are significantly younger than the average. At the same time, the social extraction of MPs from Podemos appears to be more open to other social strata, as the sum of lawyers and teachers is very low in comparison with any other party and the proportion of blue and white-collar workers is significantly higher. Similarly the proportion of MPs with a college degree is also lower than the average. As indicated by Kakepaki et al. (2018), Podemos introduces in Congress more social variability than its rivals. Ciudadanos looks more similar to the established parties than Podemos, but only to some extent. It includes a similar proportion of MPs with tertiary education to PP and PSOE and its MPs are only slightly younger. However, the proportion of women is significantly lower than in any other party, as well as the proportion of teachers.

All in all, it can be said that recent changes in political parties in Spain have not led yet to a significant change in the socio-demographic profile of MPs in established parties, which continue to share a very similar profile, despite the ideological differences between PP and PSOE. At the same time, the emergence of new parties has produced a limited impact on descriptive representation in Spain. MPs from the new parties are younger than average (which is consistent with their lack of political experience and will probably change in the future). In addition, new parties also include more (Podemos) or less (Ciudadanos) women than the average depending on their ideological profile, as left-wing parties have been traditionally more active in promoting women's representation (Caul Kittilson, 2006), including the case of Spain (Valiente, 2012; Santana et al., 2015). Moreover, Podemos is also more open to MPs from lower social strata.

Conclusions

Spain has been one of the Southern European countries severely hit by the economic crisis, which coincided with several corruption scandals. The inability of the traditionally mainstream parties, the PSOE and PP, to cope with the effects of the crisis has led to widespread political disaffection and a politico-economic crisis. Even though the economic situation began to improve after 2014, data on political disaffection still show strong signs of social discontent and criticism of the political establishment. Despite the strength of the imperfect two-party system, Spain has witnessed the emergence of two new political parties (Podemos and Ciudadanos) that have gained a substantial share of the popular vote in post-crisis elections. While it is difficult to anticipate whether these new parties are here to stay (Simón, 2016), they have put intra-party democracy at the centre of the political debate and produced a lasting impact on the way candidates are selected in Spain. Both Podemos and Ciudadanos use more participatory instruments of candidate selection. However, as the major parties have been challenged by the newcomers, both the PP and PSOE have reacted in different ways. Still, important differences between parties remain in the Spanish case.

The main divide in candidate selection in Spain is between the parties that use primaries (Podemos and Ciudadanos) and those that do not use them. However, both Podemos and Ciudadanos introduced different mechanisms for the party leadership to have an influence on the final outcome. The PSOE does not use primaries for candidates as the general rule, but it selects some key relevant posts using primaries and gives room for the affiliates to nominate candidates at the local level. The PP maintains a more exclusive selection model but it has introduced some changes like candidates' hearings and some sort of primaries among affiliates to select leaders following the multi-stage method, as Hazan and Rahat (2010, 37) indicate. Moreover, not all the differences in candidate selection derive from the divide between old and new parties. The ideological divide between left and right is key to explaining differences in gender balance in candidate selection. Finally, the evolution of candidate selection in the coming years will depend on the electoral resilience of the new parties. But it is unlikely that the road to more inclusive ways of candidate selection can be reversed.

Notes

1 Fernández-Albertos (2015) and Torreblanca (2015) provide excellent analyses of the origins and electoral growth of Podemos.
2 Data from ESS (2017) indicates that both trust in political parties and trust in politicians in Spain were 2.2 on average on a ten points scale in 2014 (1.9 in 2012), while the proportion of individuals who were quite or very interested in politics increased from 26% in 2006 to 41% in 2014.
3 The organizational structure of Podemos has differences with traditional parties. A citizen council (either, local, regional or national) is equivalent to an extended executive committee, while a circle is an organized group of affiliates (by territorial or sectoral level) that is not part of the organizational structure of the party.

References

Armingeon, K., and Guthmann, K. (2014). Democracy in crisis? The declining support for national democracy in European countries, 2007–2011. *European Journal of Political Research* 53 (3), pp. 423–442.

Barberà, O., Lisi, M., and Rodríguez Teruel, J. (2015). Democratising party leadership selection in Spain and Portugal. In Sandri, G., Seddone, A. and Venturino, F. (Eds.), *Party primaries in comparative perspective*. Farnham: Ashgate, pp. 59–84.

Carey, J., and Shugart, M. S. (1995). Incentives to cultivate a personal vote: A rank ordering of electoral formulas. *Electoral Studies* 14 (4), pp. 417–439.

Caul Kittilson, M. (2006). *Challenging parties, changing parliaments. Women and elected office in contemporary western Europe*. Columbus: Ohio State University Press.

Coller, X., Cordero, G., and Echavarren, J. M. (2018). Recruitment and selection. In Coller, X., Jaime-Castillo, A. M. and Mota, F. (Eds.), *Political power in Spain. The multiple divides between MPs and citizens*. Basingstoke and New York: Palgrave Macmillan, pp. 83–102.

Coller, X., Navarro, M. C., and Portillo, M. (2016). Mitos y realidades de las elites políticas. In Barreda, M. and Ruiz, L. M. (Eds.), *El análisis de la política. Enfoques y herramientas de la ciencia política*. Barcelona: Huygens, pp. 419–438.

Cordero, G., and Coller, X. (2015). Candidate selection and party discipline. *Parliamentary Affairs* 68 (3), pp. 592–615.

Cordero, G., Jaime-Castillo, A. M., and Coller, X. (2016). Candidate selection in a multilevel state: The case of Spain. *American Behavioral Scientist* 60 (7), pp. 853–868.

Cordero, G., and Montero, J. R. (2015). Against bipartyism, towards dealignment? The 2014 EP elections in Spain. *South European Society and Politics* 20 (3), pp. 357–379.

European Social Survey. (2017). *European social survey round 1–7 Data*. Bergen, Norway: Norwegian Social Science Data Services.

Fernandes, T. (2015). Rethinking pathways to democracy: Civil society in Portugal and Spain, 1960s–2000s. *Democratization* 22 (6), pp. 1074–1104.

Fernández-Albertos, J. (2015). *Los Votantes de Podemos*. Madrid: La Catarata.

Fishman, R. M. (2012). Anomalies of Spain's economy and economic policy-making. *Contributions to Political Economy* 31 (1), pp. 67–76.

Hazan, R. Y., and Rahat, G. (2010). *Democracy within parties: Candidate selection methods and their political consequences*. Oxford: Oxford University Press.

Jaime-Castillo, A. M., and Martínez-Cousinou, G. (2018). Parliamentary groups and institutional context. In Coller, X., Jaime-Castillo, A. M. and Mota, F. (Eds.), *Political power in Spain. The multiple divides between MPs and citizens*. Basingstoke and New York: Palgrave Macmillan, pp. 121–139.

Jiménez-Sánchez, M., Coller, X., Portillo, M. (2018), MPs of traditional parties' perceptions on candidate selection in times of political crisis and reform. In Cordero, G. and Coller, X. (Eds), *Democratizing Candidate Selection: New Methods, Old Receipts?*, London: Palgrave (in press).

Jordana, J. (2014). Multiple crises and policy dismantling in Spain: Political strategies and distributive implications. *Political Studies Review* 12 (2), pp. 224–238.

Kakepaki, M., Kountouri, F., Verzichelli, L., and Coller, X. (2018). The Socio-Political Profile of Parliamentary Representatives in Greece, Italy and Spain before and after the 'Eurocrisis': A Comparative Empirical Assessment. In Cordero, G. and Coller, X. (Eds), *Democratizing Candidate Selection: New Methods, Old Receipts?*, London: Palgrave (in press).

Kam, C. J. (2009). *Party discipline and parliamentary politics*. Cambridge: Cambridge University Press.

Lundell, K. (2004). Determinants of candidate selection: The degree of centralization in comparative perspective. *Party Politics* 10 (1), pp. 25–47.

Morlino, L., and Raniolo, F. (2017). *The impact of the economic crisis on South European democracies*. Basingstoke and New York: Palgrave Macmillan.

Muro, D., and Vidal, G. (2017). Political mistrust in southern Europe since the Great Recession. *Mediterranean Politics* 22 (2), pp. 197–217.

Orriols, L., and Cordero, G. (2016). The breakdown of the Spanish two-party system: The upsurge of Podemos and Ciudadanos in the 2015 General Election. *South European Society and Politics* 21 (4), pp. 469–492.

Pérez-Nievas, S., Rama, J., and Fernández-Esquer, C. (2017). New wine in old bottles? The selection of electoral candidates in general elections in Podemos. In Cordero, G. and Coller, X. (Eds.), *Democratizing candidate selection in times of crisis: New methods, old receipts?* London: Palgrave Macmillan.

Pilet, J-B., and Cross, W. P. (2014). The selection of party leaders in comparative perspective. in Pilet, J-B. and Cross, W. P. (Eds.), *The selection of political party leaders in contemporary parliamentary democracies*. London: Routledge, pp. 222–239.

Polavieja, J. (2013). Economic crisis, political legitimacy, and social cohesion. In Gallie, D. (Ed.), *Economic crisis, quality of work and social integration: The European experience*. Oxford: Oxford University Press, pp. 256–278.

PP. (2017). *Estatutos nacionales*. XVIII Congreso Nacional. Retrieved from www.pp.es/sites/default/files/documentos/estatutos_pp.pdf

Rahat, G. (2007). Candidate selection: The choice before the choice. *Journal of Democracy* 18 (1), pp. 157–170.

Rahat, G., and Hazan, R. Y. (2001). Candidate selection methods: An analytical framework. *Party Politics* 7, pp. 297–322.

Royo, S. (2013). *Lessons from the economic crisis in Spain*. Basingstoke and New York: Palgrave Macmillan.

Santana, A., Coller, X., and Aguilar, S. (2015). Las parlamentarias regionales en España: masa crítica, experiencia parlamentaria e influencia política. *Revista Española de Investigaciones Sociológicas* 149, pp. 109–128.

Sartori, G. (1994). *Comparative constitutional engineering. An inquiry into structures, incentives and outcomes*. New York: New York University Press.

Shomer, Y. (2009). Candidate selection procedures, seniority, and vote-seeking behavior: Lessons from the Israeli experience. *Comparative Political Studies* 42 (7), pp. 945–970.

Shomer, Y. (2014). What affects candidate selection processes? A cross-national examination. *Party Politics* 20 (4), pp. 533–546.

Simón, P. (2016). The challenges of the New Spanish multipartism: Government formation failure and the 2016 general election. *South European Society and Politics* 21 (4), pp. 493–517.

Torcal, M. (2014). The decline of political trust in Spain and Portugal: Economic performance or political responsiveness? *American Behavioral Scientist* 58 (12), pp. 1542–1567.

Torcal, M., and Montero, J. R. (1998). Facets of social capital in new democracies. The formation and consequences of social capital in Spain. *Working Paper #259*, Kellogg Institute for International Studies, University of Notre Dame.

Torreblanca, J. I. (2015). *Asaltar Los Cielos. Podemos y la Nueva Política*. Madrid: Editorial Debate.

Valiente, C. (2012). Spain. Women in Parliament: The effectiveness of quotas. In Tremblay, M. (Ed.), *Women and legislative representation. Electoral systems, political parties and sex quotas*. Basingstoke and New York: Palgrave Macmillan, pp. 129–139.

Verge, T., and Espírito-Santo, A. (2016). Interactions between party and legislative quotas: Candidate selection and quota compliance in Portugal and Spain. *Government and Opposition* 51 (3), pp. 416–439.

15 US politics in a post-crisis era

Populism, polarization and candidate selection

Patricia Craig

Across the Western democracies, party systems have faced upveals in the aftermath of the Great Recession. In Europe, the surge of right- wing populist parties, the success of Brexit and the declining electoral fortunes of some traditional parties have pointed to growing volatility. In the US, the unexpected triumph of Donald Trump and relative vulnerability of candidate Hillary Clinton to the challenge posed by the left-wing, independent senator Bernie Sanders raises questions about the role of parties in organizing electoral competition.

This chapter looks at the United States, whose party system has experienced similar shocks to others in the West in reaction to the global economic crisis (Schmidt, 2017; Hacker 2006): increasingly polarized electorates (Jacobson, 2016; Pisani-Ferry, 2015) a rejection of a neo-liberal agenda (Peters, 2017); anger related to cultural shifts; and the perception that traditional ways of life are disappearing (Inglehart and Norris, 2017).

However, unlike other democratic systems, there has been little in the way of outward organizational change in the US, at least in the sense of the disappearance of traditional parties or the emergence of new ones. Instead, US parties have experienced a populist wave that has been long in coming (Turney et al., 2017; Fukuyama, 2016) and has echoes in the relatively recent past (Eiermann, 2016; Oliver and Rahn, 2016). It has manifested itself though internal insurgencies in both parties, which have challenged elites, brought ideological differences out into the open and used the decentralized candidate-selection process to elect non-mainstream candidates.

This chapter is organized in the following manner. It first traces the path the US took to adopting a relatively decentralized form of candidate selection and the points at which pressure was exerted on parties to open up nomination procedures. It then examines three aspects of the party system that are specific to the US and that form the background to the response to the economic crisis: the frequency of party insurgencies, the role of money in politics, and increasing partisan polarization. The argument is that in the US the crisis was not always the cause of changes but intersected with existing institutional features of the party system in a way that now exacerbates problems of governability.

Candidate selection in the United States

The US is an example of an exceptionally decentralized and open system of candidate selection. Among the established democracies, it is often seen as an outlier (Hazan and Rahat, 2010; Gallagher & Marsh, 1988), with individual candidates having wide berth in launching electoral bids and relatively low influence on selection by parties. There are several features of the US system that make it unusual.

Unlike in many countries, candidate selection is regulated by law rather than by the parties themselves (Lundell, 2004). Primaries, where voters select candidates, are a more inclusive or democratic form of selection (Pennings and Hazan, 2001) than selection by party elites or activists. In the US, it is state law that governs the primary system, with the result that there are different models, ranging from closed primaries, where only voters registered to a particular party can vote, to completely open ones where any registered voter may cast a ballot. Two features of this system make the US stand out. Because of the openness to non-party members, the US is high on inclusiveness, even compared with other countries using a primary system (Hopkin, 2001) and parties have very little formal control over the nomination process (Ware, 1996).

The path the US took to its open and inclusive system was a winding one over the course of the 20th Century. The introduction of the primary system of candidate nomination was a product of the Progressive Era. Concerned that party bosses had a monopoly on the selection process and chose candidates who were more likely to work on behalf of the wealthy, progressive reformers pushed for a variety of measures to make candidate selection more democratic (Ahsolabehere et al., 2010). These included the secret ballot, professionalization of the civil service and state-level primary elections, which were meant to allow voters a more direct form of democracy (Ceaser, 1981).

These reforms did shift power from the parties to individual candidates, and in the decades after they were instituted, they led to more competitive elections. However, over time, this effect was attenuated (Ansolabehere et al., 2010) and by the 1960s and 1970s, the levels of incumbents being returned to office were unprecedented. Epitaphs were being written for parties (Bawn et al., 2012; Baer, 1993), which as organizations were weak (Fiorina, 2002).

The social upheaval of the 1960s, including the Vietnam War and the Civil Rights movement, influenced party activists who concluded that complacent politicians had little incentive or interest to engage with the issues of the day (Hacker, 1968). The Democratic Party in particular in the run-up to its 1968 party convention was deeply divided, with a left-leaning, insurgent anti-war contingent led by Senator Eugene McCarthy. Grassroots party activists demanded more direct democracy in the candidate-selection process; they viewed the party as seriously out of touch with popular sentiment on race and anti-war issues. They also saw a pool of convention delegates who would nominate the party's presidential candidate that did not mirror an energized base that included many African Americans and women (Walker, 1981).

A sitting but relatively unknown senator from Minnesota, McCarthy began his campaign focused on an anti-war message but quickly championed reform of the party's rules, especially around delegate selection. These rules put the McCarthy campaign at a decided disadvantage in terms of the delegate count heading into the convention. Rules for choosing delegates were not uniform across states; often convention delegates were chosen years in advance by party elites (Tichenor and Fuerstman, 2008) and in states where voters selected them, they might not be told for which candidate the delegates planned to vote (Tabach-bank and Kelly, 1975). In addition, McCarthy and his allies targeted a winner-take-all voting process on procedural questions, know as the unit rule, that existed at all levels of the party, and meant that intra-party challengers faced long odds on rule changes (Tichenor and Fuerstman, 2008).

Although McCarthy's proposals were not successful (the establishment candidate, Humphrey, won despite not having contested a single primary), the effect on candidate selection ultimately was lasting and profound. After Humphrey's defeat to Richard Nixon in the general election and in 1969, the McGovern-Fraser commission was formed. The outcome of this body was to transform candidate selection in the US. The McGovern-Fraser reforms nationalized the system (LeDuc, 2001) and transferred control from elites to the base, finally consolidating, according to Tichenor and Fuerstman (2008), the reform agenda that had been started in the Progressive Era.

Reforms led to a much more inclusive system of candidate selection and the adoption of the requirement that convention delegates be elected openly by party members (Piroth, 2000). This encouraged many state parties to drop caucuses (the deliberative in-person gatherings where party members elect candidates or delegates) in favour of primary elections (Kamarck, 2014; Pressman and Sullivan, 1974), which allowed state party officials to more easily comply with McGovern-Fraser rules (Meinke, et al. 2006). Reforms also called for explicit affirmative steps to encourage the selection of women, African Americans and young people as delegates, which increased the presence of these groups at the 1972 Democratic convention (Walker, 1981).

While 1970s era reforms were spearheaded by the Democrats, ultimately many Republican state parties followed suit. Unlike in other systems, it is state law rather than parties that govern the nomination process for presidential elections (Hazan and Rahat, 2010). Many state legislatures were controlled by Democrats in the early 1970s, which led to the adoption of similar rules across party lines (Huckshorn and Bibby, 1983).

Party insurgencies

The McGovern-Fraser reforms are rightly seen as a watershed in American politics (Kaufman et al., 2003; LeDuc, 2001; Rosenblum, 2000) in terms of ushering in the era of primaries and a candidate-centred politics (Tichenor and Fuerstman, 2008). At the same time, they highlight a recurrent feature of the institutional landscape in the US and that is the openness of parties to internal insurgencies.

In his classic treatise on parties, Key (1942) described intra-party insurgencies as a means by which disaffected voters or party activists can push a reform agenda and he saw their periodic eruption as a feature of the American political system.

The literature highlights various reasons for the prevalence of insurgencies and points to two prerequisites. Numerous authors (Oliver and Rahn, 2016; Fiorina, 2002) credit a gap between what parties are offering and what voters want as a precondition for their emergence. Fiorina (2002) describes this as an 'opening' while Oliver and Rahn (2016) contend that a 'representation gap' is apparent when such movements arise. They measure that gap by combining scores of party unity as measured by oppositional and partisan voting in the houses of Congress and polling data about how well represented voters feel by elected politicians. They find that over the past 30 years insurgent candidates have appeared when that gap is highest, including Republican presidential candidate Pat Buchanan and third party challenger Ross Perot in the mid-1990s and Republican Donald Trump and Democrat Bernie Sanders in 2016.

A second requirement for insurgencies is institutional, and many analysts point to the weakness of US parties, especially with respect to control over candidate selection. Pomper (1977) saw the parties' loss of monopoly over candidate recruitment as a key reason for successful insurgencies. More recently, the openness of candidate selection where party elites have less control over candidates has been linked to the ability of insurgent candidates and movements to prosper (Craig, 2016; Pirch, 2007).

Party weakness is also a function of their inability to control resources. Fiorina (2002) credits access to resources as critical to the success of insurgents. Resources include money and the power to control messaging and, over time, parties have seen technological changes undermine their influence on both. The advent of mass media, particularly television, encouraged the candidate-centric focus of US elections at the expense of the party (Hayes, 2009; Wattenberg, 1991) as candidates could take their message directly to voters.

The US's decentralized system of candidate selection has also made it well suited to Internet-based insurgencies. Online communities have acted as 'virtual parties' (Pirch, 2007) where partisan voters can connect with each other. Social media is a way that non-mainstream candidates can attract, communicate with and organize supporters (Herrnson et al., 2007).

Campaign finance has also been influenced by the Internet, in ways that can be especially helpful to insurgent candidates who may not have access to the large sources of cash provided by political action committees (PACs). Upstart campaigns have been able to employ new forms of fundraising and voter outreach that most notably began in 2004 when Vermont governor Howard Dean mounted a primary campaign that energized the party base. He was able to do so in part by raising large sums of money from small donors online, breaking all previous fundraising records (Cornfield, 2005).

Raising funds from small donors has been made easier by using online methods and over time has become part of the normal practice of campaigns (Squire and Moncrief, 2015) but for outsider candidates, they can still be crucial, in part because technology has removed the intermediary function of the party (Issacharoff, 2017). In recent elections, small donors, facilitated by social media and the Internet, have helped make candidacies viable without the support of mainstream party structures. In the 2016 presidential campaign, not only did Democrat Bernie Sanders take in a record $229 million from small donors during his unsuccessful primary bid (Stewart, 2016), but billionaire Republican Donald Trump raised more than $100 million in small donations, far more than any Republican candidate in history (Goldmacher, 2016).

Party financing

While the Internet and social media have provided a new platform for candidates to establish a more direct relationship with supporters without the intermediation of parties, it would be erroneous to conclude that political fundraising in the US is dominated by small donors. Over the past twenty years, the weight of small donors as a percentage of national and state-level campaign funds has declined (Mann and Corrado, 2014). At the presidential level, small donors used to provide about half of the money raised in contributions but even with the enthusiasm shown by small contributors in the last several election cycles, as Figure 15.1 shows, the importance of large donors has increased significantly.

The outsized role of money in politics in the US contributes to the weakness of the party system (La Raja, 2014) and plays an important role in candidate selection. While the openness of the candidate-selection process in theory means that anyone can run for office, in practice viable candidates have to have access to funding sources, which constrains the pool of potential candidates (Bonica, 2016).

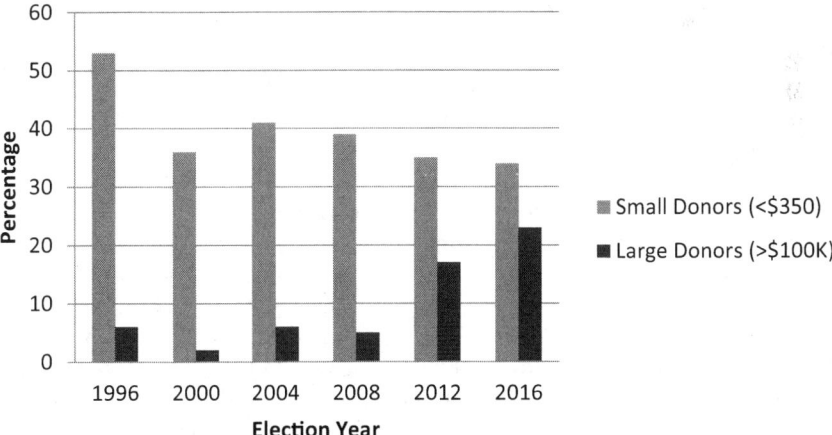

Figure 15.1 Percentage of donations to presidential campaign by source
Source: Vandewalker and Norden (2016).

It is not simply that the weight of large donors has grown over time but shifting patterns of campaign finance in the US suggest an increasing role for donor consortia, which have significant influence on the policy agenda and candidate selection (Skocpol, 2016). The landmark court decision in 2010 known as *Citizens United* struck down the law barring corporations and wealthy individuals from backing candidates and funding races on free speech grounds (Levitt, 2010).

The effect has been to double the amount of money being spent in federal races and tip the balance to outside money, such as that spent by political action committees rather than candidates themselves (Vandewalker, 2015). The legal shift in campaign finance regulations, combined with new patterns of wealth formation in the US in the tech and finance sectors have created a class of 'philanthrocapitalists' (Goss, 2016) who are increasingly pooling their money to maximize their political impact. Theda Skocpol concludes that organized donor consortia differ from past wealthy elites or lobby groups because they are well coordinated with a continuous source of funds from regular mandatory large donations from members rather than one-off donations. This allows them to focus beyond the election of candidates to more far-reaching policy change (Skocpol, 2016; Skocpol and Hertel-Fernandez, 2016c).

Organized groups of donors exist on both the left and the right; for example, the Democracy Alliance, which was founded in 2005 by former Clinton White House officials and is close to the Democratic Party (Vogel, 2014); and at the other end of the political spectrum, the network of organizations funded by the conservative billionaire Koch brothers. Yet, the donor consortia on the right appear to have been much more effective than funding groups on the left in shifting the political terrain. From the point of view of parties and candidate selection, these consortia appear to signal a new development, at least on the Republican side.

Data show that since the early 2000s, the Republican party has lost ground to extra-party organizations like think tanks and independent in terms of resources (Skocpol and Hertel-Fernandez, 2016a). In large measure, this is due to the Koch network that has been far superior to rivals on the left in raising funds, but the network operates with a 'unified political strategy' (Skocpol, 2016, 11) that puts it on a par with the two major parties. The network spent $900 million supporting candidates and legislation in the 2016 election, equalling spending by both major parties (Confessore, 2015) and plans to spend another $400 million on the 2018 midterm elections (Beavers, 2017).

There are two striking features to the growth of donor consortia on the right. First, the role of a non-party entity in effectively controlling much of the candidate-selection process is unique among developed democracies. From prominent national races to local ones, the Koch network's attempts to influence the field of candidates are notable. During the 2016 presidential campaign, the Freedom Partners Chamber of Commerce, a Koch funding organization, auditioned Republican candidates at gatherings of mega-donors, giving them the chance to compete for the millions of dollars these donors had pledged to spend on the election and to enjoy the free media exposure such appearances afford (New York

Times Editorial Board, 2015; Vogel, 2015). Federal, state, local and even school board candidates were targeted by the network as part of their $900 million investment in 2016 races (Mayer, 2016). As Skocpol and Hertel-Fernandez (2016c, p. 4) argue, "the Koch network exerts a strong gravitational pull on many Republican candidates" because of its massive scale, tight integration, ramified organizational reach, and close intertwining with the GOP at all levels.

The second question raised by the right's donor network is whether candidates are becoming less representative ideologically compared to their voters. While the candidate-selection literature typically focuses on representativeness of a demographic nature, ideological representativeness is also discussed. Hazan and Rahat (2010, 109) contend that "both kinds of representation are relevant to candidate selection because parties – in their attempts to address the electorate and to control, or at least regulate, intra-party conflicts – are likely to try to balance their lists of candidates in terms of both notions of representation." Generally, parties are assumed to follow a Downsian strategy of appealing to their median voter and see it as electorally disadvantageous for them to nominate candidates that stray too far from that mean.

Moving away from the median voter

There are few empirical studies examining the relationship between the inclusivity of candidate selection and the degree to which candidates and voters are ideologically congruent. While Hazan and Rahat (2010) suggest that inclusive selectorates would likely tend towards greater congruity, Spies and Kaiser (2012) argue that party-controlled selection processes favour an appeal to the mean voter as party leaders may be more concerned with winning elections than party members or delegates who may demand more ideological purity.

In the US, the importance of ideologically extreme donors seems to push parties away from their median voter. Barber (2015) suggests that candidates face a trade-off between trying to locate themselves at the point of the median voter and ideologically extreme donors. While both major parties have moved away from the centre, analysts argue that only in the Republican case has the push to more extreme positions been the result of donor efforts (Mann and Corrado, 2014). Skocpol and Hertel-Fernandez (2016a; 2016b; 2016c) show how across different policy realms, Republican candidates and legislators associated with the Koch network (measured by their signing pledges of the central Koch organization, Americans for Prosperity, to support certain policies) are not only far to the right of the views of the general public but also their own voters.

The US primary process and the willingness of ideologically extreme big donors to challenge more moderate incumbents within their own party in the primary (Mascaro, 2017) also discourages an appeal to the median. As Hacker and Pierson (2015) point out, under such conditions, "for these Republicans, the district median voter is less important than the Republican median voter."

Although the role of private money in US campaigns is unique in the world in its scope, an argument can be made that ideologically driven donor networks play a somewhat analogous role to political actors elsewhere who are motivated by ideological principles and who have a role in candidate selection. While some analysts (Mann and Corrado, 2014) see little distinction in practice between nominally independent political action committees or donor groups and the parties themselves, Isaacharoff (2017) argues that when parties control candidate access to money, they are more likely than external funders to 'discipline the candidates to the governance message of the party' (p. 869). In the case of the US, the pull of parties and candidates to a more extreme position than voters is part of the extremely polarized political culture and, as I will argue below, had implications for responses to the economic crisis.

Polarized politics

The third element of the party system that conditioned responses to the crisis is the level of polarization in the country. There is widespread agreement that, starting in the 1970s, the US political system has been undergoing a process of polarization (Poole and Rosenthal, 1984). The result is that both the electorate and political elites hold views that separate them from those on the other side of the ideological divide (Campbell, 2016; Abramowitz and Saunders, 2008).

Today, the major parties are far apart from each other; both parties have moved to more extreme positions, although the movement has been less than symmetric. Republican candidates and elected officials have moved sharply to the right on policy positions and moderates have largely disappeared. The leftward shift of the Democrats has been more muted and primarily driven by the replacement of conservative Democrats by Republicans, particularly in the South. This has moved the party's centre to the left (Mann and Ornstein, 2012; Barber and McCarty, 2015). The outcome is that there are fewer moderates among elected officials and very little overlap between the parties (McCarty et al., 2006).

While there are multiple explanations for increasing polarization, a growing and compelling literature examines the relationship between political polarization and income inequality, whose growth has mirrored that of polarization. McCarty, Poole and Rosenthal (2006) have argued that polarization increases during periods of higher income inequality. Garand (2010) extends this to show that state-level inequality shapes both the level of political polarization in the state and the national level voting behaviour of elected officials and that polarization is greater in states with higher levels of income inequality.

The role of political donors is also cited as a factor in polarization. Because donors may be more extreme than party members or voters (McGhee et al., 2014) their ability to recruit more extreme candidates and to focus the party's message early in a campaign helps move the party away from the centre. Campaign money, too, may play a role in polarizing the parties' elected leadership and, as a result, legislative bodies as a whole. Legislators' ideology is a reflection of their donor base as Barber (2015) has demonstrated. Heberlig et al. (2006) show that ideologically extreme politicians have come to dominate much of the Congressional leadership and are able to use their campaign funds to secure positions by redistributing those funds to colleagues who in turn vote them into more 'extended' leadership roles.

An additional mechanism has been suggested by Voorheis et al. (2015) who look at the intersection of income inequality and donor funding. They argue that income inequality moves state legislator ideology to more extreme positions but that it does so in ways that differ for Democrats and Republicans. While rising income inequality is both a cause and effect of the mean ideology of legislatures moving to the right, the authors examine inequality between and within congressional districts and conclude that for Democrats, between-district inequality pushes legislators further left, positing that demands for redistributive policies help shift their stances. For Republicans, within-district inequality is a push factor to the right because, they suggest, large donors continue to move their preferences to the right as a cycle occurs where income inequality rises because of the success of legislation that promotes increasing inequality.

The consequences of polarization are that politics have become more contentious and divisive. Iyengar and Westwood (2015) have written of the rise in 'affective' polarization over the past forty years, where partisans on one side see those on the other as members of outgroups. Today, partisanship is more predictive of ideological leaning than in the past. Over the twenty year period from 1994 to 2014, those who are politically engaged became much more likely to follow their party's lines – 70% now are closely and frequently ideologically consistent with their political parties compared with 58% of Republicans and 35% of Democrats two decades ago (Pew Research Center, 2014). Wolf et al. (2012) suggest that this greater tendency of Americans to strongly identify with one party or the other means that these partisan voters are more likely to punish politicians who seek political compromise with opponents. The result is to raise the level of incivility and further alienate less partisan voters.

The US party system after the crisis

The global economic downturn that began in 2008 has been described as having "landed in the center of American life with the force of a natural disaster" (Brownstein, 2012). In some ways, the reactions to the crisis and political fallout were the ones consistent with expected and historic patterns. As Bartels (2013) has pointed out, voters in the 2010 midterm elections following the crisis acted as voters typically do and punished the party in power. Democrats faced their worst defeat in over sixty years and lost the majority in the House of Representatives. Then, two years later, voters again behaved predictably by re-electing the incumbent President, who was helped not only by incumbency but also a slight improvement in the economy.

At the same time, the aftermath of the crisis has transformed American political life. As in other advanced capitalist democracies, the post-crisis era has experienced the wave of populism that has upended party systems across the globe. Whether the result of the increasing inability of democratic capitalist governments to ensure both free markets and welfare spending (Streeck, 2011), the rejection of a neo-liberal consensus, forged in the 1970s, that globalized trade and liberalized markets (Judis, 2016), or a cultural backlash by citizens fearing progressive changes to a traditional way of life (Inglehart and Norris, 2016), few states have been immune to the new challenges.

In the US, the rise of populism has followed an analogous trajectory to similar movements in the past. Unlike in Europe where the rise of new extremist parties, mostly on the right but also on the left, has shaken traditional party systems, the openness of US parties to insurgencies has meant that contemporary populist movements have attempted to use the political parties to advance their agenda.

The Tea Party movement was the first mass reaction to the crisis (Bartels, 2013), with an anti-tax, anti-big government agenda, coalescing around issues like opposition to an expansion of state-funded health care and bailouts of financial institutions (Love and Mattern, 2011). Started as a grassroots organization in the wake of Barack Obama's victory in the 2008 presidential election, it became a force in the Republican Party by the 2010 midterm elections.

Despite emerging from the Republican orbit, the Tea Party Movement (TPM) was not beholden to the party (Skocpol and Williamson, 2012). In particular, the TPM's extremism and unwillingness to engage in political compromise, even at the expense of electoral wins, frequently put it at odds with the Republican establishment (Bailey et al., 2012) who sought to quell the insurgency by shoring up candidates in primary races where TPM contenders presented a challenge. Organizations that acted as proxies for the Republican Party, such as the Chamber of Commerce, spent millions of dollars in 2014 Congressional and Senate races to prevent TPM activists from becoming the party's nominees (Drew, 2015; McCormick & Giroux, 2014).

It was not just at the level of elections that the Tea Party's unyielding ideological stance presented problems for Republican leadership. Its stance on issues like immigration reform and the debt ceiling complicated the GOP's legislative agenda. The biggest insult to the Republican establishment, however, came in the 2014 primaries when a Tea Party candidate defeated House Majority Leader, Eric Cantor, who had infuriated the conservative base with his support for immigration reform and opposition to the government shutdown (Martin, 2014). Never before had a sitting majority leader lost to a party challenger and this was in spite of Cantor spending over $5 million on the race compared with the $122,000 spent by his Tea Party opponent, conservative economics professor, Dave Brat (Mak & Jacobs, 2014).

In that race and others, the Tea Party cultivated an image as a grassroots organization but the success of the TPM as an insurgent force owes much to the conservative donor consortia discussed above. Mayer (2010) shows that groups like Americans for Prosperity and FreedomWorks were major funders of the Tea Party in spite of apparent attempts to keep connections between conservative funding organizations and the TPM vague. These are associated with conservative industrialists the Koch brothers; Dick Armey, a conservative, former Texas congressman; and Rupert Murdoch, the conservative media magnate.

While the Tea Party challenge burned brightly for several years and prompted many pundits to speak of the civil war it unleashed within the Republican party, by 2015, it was written off as a movement. Its popular support fell to a low of 17% (Norman, 2015) late in 2015 and never recovered. Analysts searching for a cause of its decline point to factors like its relatively unstructured organization and the weight of mobilizing conservative voters moving elsewhere like the Koch brothers' network (Berry, 2017), the Tea Party's success in shifting the Republican agenda (Geraghty, 2016) and the backlash by establishment Republicans (Mataconis, 2015). Despite the rapid decline of the Tea Party, the populist surge it represented did not fade away. The 2016 elections showed that in some ways it was just getting started.

The populist challenges of 2016

The election of 2016 produced two unexpected results: the surprising victory of Donald Trump for the presidency and the unanticipated strength of independent Senator Bernie Sanders' challenge to eventual candidate Hillary Clinton in the Democratic primary. Both Trump and Sanders defied popular wisdom and while there were clear differences in many of their positions, they both tapped a vein of deep discontent in voters dissatisfied with the status quo.

A major source of popular dissatisfaction was economic. Both candidates were economic populists, invoking Wall Street and business elites as the cause of the country's maladies (Oliver and Rahn, 2016). Trump repeatedly talked about hedge fund managers as 'getting away with murder' (Lynch, 2015) while Sanders took on Wall Street which he warned, "cannot continue to be an island unto itself, gambling trillions in risky financial instruments, making huge profits and assured that, if their schemes fail, the taxpayers will be there to bail them out" (Martens and Martens, 2016).

Trade was another area of agreement between the candidates with both showing an antipathy to free trade deals, specifically the North American Free Trade Agreement (NAFTA) and the proposed Trans Pacific Partnership (TPP). On economic issues, Judis (2016) argues that Trump and Sanders, from the right and left respectively, were taking aim at a neo-liberal consensus shared by elites of both parties that began to unravel in the minds of voters as a result of the Great Recession. He defines that consensus as one beginning in the 1970s that included trade pacts, financial deregulation, and a supply side agenda. One area of that consensus on which Trump and Sanders did not agree was immigration. While Sanders talked about a plan for 'humane' immigration reform that would set out a path to legalization and prevent the deportation of most of the undocumented immigrants (Hing, 2015), Trump famously vilified immigrants, particularly those from Mexico and Muslim nations (Lind, 2016).

The combination of the anti-elite, pro-nationalist, and backward-looking ('make America great again') discourse links Trump to other populist movements across the West and defined him as the populist candidate par excellence in the

2016 election according to Oliver and Rahn (2016). He was able to exploit the gap between the base and establishment party (Noel, 2016) and appeal to the former with a nationalist, anti-global message geared toward cultural fears (The Economist, 2016).

That Trump was able to win the US presidency with such a message underscores the role of cultural values in contemporary political life and divisions (Zakaria, 2016). Inglehart and Norris (2016) have argued that the recent upsurge of populism is less a product of the economic crisis and downturn than a reaction to long-term cultural change. They posit a new cleavage line in contemporary democracies, which is a cosmopolitan liberalism vs. populist divide that overlays the older left/right opposition.

Cosmopolitan liberalism is a stance that celebrates multiculturalism, open borders, universal human rights, egalitarian gender roles and fluid gender identity while the populist side of the cleavage is defined by protectionism, isolationism, xenophobia and traditional gender roles. In Inglehart and Norris's view, cosmopolitan liberal values are more prevalent among younger generations because they are examples of post-material values, forged during a person's formative years. Younger cohorts, who grew up during periods of relative abundance, are more likely to develop such values than older generations who came of age at a time of scarcity.

While the authors anticipate that progressive cosmopolitan liberal values will predominate over time as generational replacement occurs, they recognize that there has been a backlash against progressive values by those who feel threatened by them. In particular, older and less educated voters, will tend to support politicians and movements like Trump in the US or Brexit in the UK that "that defend traditional cultural values and emphasize nationalistic and xenophobia appeals, rejecting outsiders, and upholding old-fashioned gender roles" (Inglehart and Norris, 2016, 31).

Party selection in a populist era

While elsewhere populism has led to the emergence of new parties, the strengthening of anti-system parties and the defeat of established parties, especially on the centre-left (Kriesi & Pappas, 2015), in the US, populist tendencies have been mapped onto the existing two-party structure.

In the case of both parties, the election has laid bare deep internal divisions and posed questions about their future electoral strategies. Numerous authors (Noel, 2016; Thomsen, 2014; Mann and Ornstein, 2016) have shown that the polarization that characterized the party system is asymmetric with the Republicans having moved farther right than the Democrats have moved left. Noel (2016) suggests that while both parties have a core of ideologues, both also have members who are open to compromise. However, he argues conservative ideologues in the Republicans have generally been more successful in controlling nominations than the liberal core among the Democrats have. In 2016, though, a crowded primary field, split between candidates who were acceptable to one side but not the other, allowed Trump, a non-ideologue who was both popular among the party's activists and exploited the party's divisions on trade, to capture the nomination.

Since Trump has taken office, the strain between his populist, nationalist base and establishment, elected officials has been evident. A year after his election, Trump's overall approval rating of 37% was the lowest of any president at that point in office (Griffiths, 2017) but he remains extraordinarily popular with his base. Emboldened by Trump's victory, populist candidates who favour his 'America First' style are mounting challenges to moderate Republican incumbents (Werner et al. 2017) who may not be able to win a general election.

A number of those incumbents from swing districts chose to retire rather than run in the 2018 elections, while several high profile Republican senators who were publicly critical of Trump's extreme stances on issues like protectionism and race found their approval ratings among likely primary voters plummet. Between February and October of 2017, Tennessee Senator Bob Corker's approval among Republican voters fell from 61 per cent to 37 per cent amidst a public feud with the President, while for Senator Jeff Flake of Arizona, who had been extremely critical of Trump, September polls showed him losing the primary by more than 25 points to a Trump-supporting candidate whose primary campaign is funded by conservative super-donor Robert Mercer (Delk, 2017; Kutner, 2017). Both senators announced they would not run again.

On the left, the Democrats also exhibit a fault line between populists and establishment centrists, represented in the 2017 election by Bernie Sanders and Hillary Clinton. However, it may be simpler for them to transition to an era where the central political cleavage is one between populism and globalism. Richardson (2017) argues that the fact that Clinton won the popular vote makes it easier for the two sides to heal their rift.

The outcome of the Republican factional struggle is unknown but three possibilities suggest themselves: the party is unable to contain the factions and splinters to form a third party (Peters, 2017); establishment Republicans led by Senate Leader Mitch McConnell fight to discredit their populist challengers by casting them as white nationalists (Weigel et al. 2017); Some elements of nationalist populism like opposition to immigration reform become standard for many Republican candidates' platforms, nudging the party slightly to the right, avoiding outright schism but exacerbating problems of political polarization.

Conclusions

While the economic downturn known as the Great Recession has given way to recovery in many countries, the impact on party systems may prove to be longer lasting. In the United States, the global financial crisis unleashed a wave of populist discontent that neither the Democrats nor Republicans were able to contain.

Populist insurgents were able to take advantage of the extreme decentralization of candidate selection in the US party system to challenge elites and elect non-mainstream politicians. Especially on the right, the rise of donor consortia who are unconstrained by and unanswerable to party elites has helped drive the populist assault on the system. In doing so, these mega-funders, whose resources rival those of the parties, have exacerbated the polarization of the American electorate over the last three decades.

Organizationally, the internal strain on both parties is evident, though it appears more severe for the GOP. The populist tide that brought Donald Trump to power now presages what some Republicans and analysts are referring to as a civil war within the party (Costa, 2017; Robin, 2017; Smith, 2017). The inclusive and decentralized nomination process and the role of outside funding for candidates in the American system appears highly destabilizing when faced with such a divided party.

What the current parties' internal struggles suggest is that the emerging populist cleavage, long in the making and hastened by the global economic crisis, has given voice to those who feel excluded within the parties' ranks. Unless the parties find a way to make such voters feel there are viable solutions that offer hope for the future of their families and communities, the polarized and fractured party system will continue.

References

Abramowitz, A. I., and Saunders, K. L. (2008). Is polarization a myth? *The Journal of Politics* 70 (2), pp. 542–555.

Ansolabehere, S., Hansen, J. M., Hirano, S., and Snyder, J. M. (2010). More democracy: The direct primary and competition in US elections. *Studies in American Political Development* 24 (02), pp. 190–205.

Baer, D. L. (1993). Who has the body? Party institutionalization and theories of party organization. *American Review of Politics*, 14, pp. 1–38.

Bailey, M. A., Mummolo, J., and Noel, H. (2012). Tea party influence: A story of activists and elites. *American Politics Research* 40 (5), pp. 769–804.

Barber, M. J. (2015). Ideological donors, contribution limits, and the polarization of American legislatures. *The Journal of Politics* 78 (1), pp. 296–310.

Barber, M., and McCarty, N. (2015). Causes and consequences of polarization. In Mansbridge, J. and Martin, C. J., *Political negotiation: A handbook*. Washington, D.C: Brookings Institution Press, pp.37–90.

Bartels, L. M. (2013). Political effects of the great recession. *The ANNALS of the American Academy of Political and Social Science* 650 (1), pp. 47–76.

Bawn, K., Cohen, M., Karol, D., Masket, S., Noel, H., and Zaller, J. (2012). A theory of political parties: Groups, policy demands and nominations in American politics." *Perspectives on Politics* 10 (3), pp. 571–597.

Beavers, O. (2017). Koch brothers to spend $400 million in 2018 elections. *The Hill*. Retrieved June 25, 2017, from http://thehill.com/blogs/blog-briefing-room/news/339399-koch-brothers-to-spend-400-million-on-republican-candidates-in

Berry, J. M. (2017). Tea Party Decline. APSA 2017 Annual Meeting Paper. Retrieved from http://as.tufts.edu/politicalscience/sites/all/themes/asbase/assets/documents/berry/teaPartyDecline.pdf

Bonica, A. (2013). Ideology and interests in the political marketplace. *American Journal of Political Science* 57 (2), pp. 294–311.

Brownstein, R. (2012). What the Great Recession Wrought: The State of the U.S. in 3 Years of Polls. *The Atlantic*. Retrieved January 7, 2012, from www.theatlantic.com/business/archive/2012/01/what-the-great-recession-wrought-the-state-of-the-us-in-3-years-of-polls/251010/

Campbell, J. E. (2016). *Polarized: Making sense of a divided America*. Princeton: Princeton University Press.

Ceaser, J. W. (1981). Direct participation in politics. *Proceedings of the Academy of Political Science* 34 (2), pp. 121–137.

Corrado, A., and Mann, T. E. (2004, June). In the wake of BCRA: An early report on campaign finance in the 2004 elections. *The Forum* 2 (2).

Costa, R. (2017). With or without Trump, GOP insurgency plans for a civil war in 2018 midterms. *The Washington Post*. [September 30, 2017]. Retrieved from www.washingtonpost.com/powerpost/with-or-without-trump-gop-insurgency-plans-for-a-civil-war-in-2018-midterms/2017/09/29/11fecb6c-a47a-11e7-ade1–76d061d56efa_story.html?utm_term=.1d3c12c71a7d

Craig, P. (2016). Pressure and politics in a decentralized candidate selection system: The case of the United States. *American Behavioral Scientist*, 60(7), pp. 799–818.

Delk, J. (2017). Poll shows Flake down huge in primary and general election. *The Hill*. [September 13, 2017]. Retrieved from http://thehill.com/blogs/blog-briefing-room/350458-dem-leaning-poll-shows-flake-down-huge-in-primary-and-general

Drew, E. (2015). The Republicans: Divided & scary. *New York Review of Books* 62 (3), pp. 32–35.

The Economist. (2016). The new nationalism. *The Economist*. [November, 19, 2016]. Retrieved from www.economist.com/news/leaders/21710249-his-call-put-america-first-donald-trump-latest-recruit-dangerous

Eiermann, M. (2016). How Donald trump fits into the history of American populism. *New Perspectives Quarterly* 33 (2), pp. 29–34.

Fiorina, M. P. (2002). Parties, participation, and representation in America: Old theories face new realities. *Political science: The state of the discipline*, pp. 511–541.

Fukuyama, F. (2016). American political decay or renewal: The meaning of the 2016 election. *Foreign Affairs* 95, 58.

Gallagher, M., and Marsh, M. (Eds.). (1988). *Candidate selection in comparative perspective: The secret garden of politics*. London, UK: Sage.

Garand, J. C. (2010). Income inequality, party polarization, and roll-call voting in the US Senate. *The Journal of Politics* 72 (4), pp. 1109–1128.

Geraghty, J. (2016). The death of the Tea Party. *The National Review*. [January, 19, 2016].

Goldmacher, S. (2016). Trump shatters GOP records with small donors. *Politico*. [September 19, 2016].

Goss, K. A. (2016). Policy Plutocrats: How America's wealthy seek to influence governance. *PS: Political Science & Politics* 49 (3), pp. 442–448.

Griffiths, B. D. (2017). Poll: Trump's approval dips. *Politico*. [October 29, 2017].

Hacker, A. (1968). The McCarthy candidacy. *Commentary* 45 (2), pp. 34–39.

Hacker, J. S. (2008). *The great risk shift: The new economic insecurity and the decline of the American dream*. Oxford: Oxford University Press.

Hazan, R. Y., and Rahat, G. (2010). *Democracy within parties: Candidate selection methods and their political consequences*. Oxford, UK: Oxford University Press.

Heberlig, E., Hetherington, M., and Larson, B. (2006). The price of leadership: Campaign money and the polarization of congressional parties. *The Journal of Politics* 68 (4), pp. 992–1005.

Herrnson, P. S., Stokes-Brown, A. K., and Hindman, M. (2007). Campaign politics and the digital divide constituency characteristics, strategic considerations, and candidate internet use in state legislative elections. *Political Research Quarterly* 60, pp. 31–42.

Hertel-Fernandez, A., and Skocpol, T. (2016). *Billionaires against big business: Growing tensions in the Republican Party Coalition.* Prepared for delivery at the 2016 Midwest Political Science Association Conference April 8, 2016.

Hing, J. (2015). This Is Bernie Sanders's immigration plan. *The Nation.* [December 1, 2015]. Retrieved from www.thenation.com/article/bernie-sanders-spells-out-his-immigration-plan/

Hopkin, J. (2001). Bringing the members back in? Democratizing candidate selection in Britain and Spain. *Party Politics* 7 (3), pp. 343–361.

Huckshorn, R. J., & Bibby, J. F. (1983). National party rules and delegate selection in the Republican Party. *PS: Political Science & Politics* 16, pp. 656–666.

Inglehart Ronald, F., & Norris, P. (2016). Trump, Brexit, and the rise of populism: Economic have-nots and cultural backlash. *Harvard Kennedy School RWP16–026.*

Issacharoff, S. (2016). Outsourcing politics: The hostile takeover of our hollowed-out political parties. *Hous. L. Rev.* 54, 845.

Iyengar, S., and Westwood, S. J. (2015). Fear and loathing across party lines: New evidence on group polarization. *American Journal of Political Science* 59 (3), pp. 690–707.

Jacobson, G. C. (2009). The 2008 Presidential and Congressional elections: Anti-bush referendum and prospects for the democratic majority. *Political Science Quarterly* 124 (1), pp. 1–30.

Jacobson, G. C. (2016). Polarization, gridlock, and presidential campaign politics in 2016. *The ANNALS of the American Academy of Political and Social Science* 667 (1), pp. 226–246.

Judis, J. B. (2016). *The populist explosion: How the great recession transformed American and European politics.* Columbia Global Reports.

Kamarck, E. C. (2014). *Increasing turnout in congressional primaries.* Washington, DC: Brookings, July, 16.

Kaufmann, K. M., Gimpel, J. G., and Hoffman, A. H. (2003). A promise fulfilled? Open primaries and representation. *Journal of Politics, 65*, pp. 457–476.

Key, V. O., and Heard, A. (1949). *Southern politics in state and nation.* New York: Vintage Books.

Kriesi, H., and Pappas, T. S. (Eds.). (2015). *European populism in the shadow of the great recession.* Colchester: ECPR Press.

Kutner, M. (2017). Who is Kelli Ward, the Arizona candidate running for Jeff Flake's Senate seat? *Newsweek.* [October 24, 2017].

La Raja, R. J., and Schaffner, B. F. (2014). The effects of campaign finance spending bans on electoral outcomes: Evidence from the states about the potential impact of Citizens United v. FEC. *Electoral Studies* 33, pp. 102–114.

LeDuc, L. (2001). Democratizing party leadership selection. *Party Politics* 7 (3), 323–341.

Levitt, J. (2010). Confronting the impact of" Citizens United". *Yale Law & Policy Review* 29(1), pp. 217–234.

Lind, M. (2016). Donald Trump, the perfect populist. *Politico.* [March 9, 2016]. Retrieved from www.politico.com/magazine/story/2016/03/donald-trump-the-perfect-populist-213697

Love, N. S., and Mattern, M. (2011). The great recession: Causes, consequences, and responses. *New Political Science* 33 (4), pp. 401–411.

Lundell, K. (2004). Determinants of candidate selection the degree of centralization in comparative perspective. *Party Politics* 10, pp. 25–47.

Lynch, S. N. (2015). Trump says tax code is letting hedge funds 'get away with murder'. *Reuters*. Retrieved from www.reuters.com/article/us-election-trump-hedgefunds/trump-says-tax-code-is-letting-hedge-funds-get-away-with-murder-idUSKCN0QS0P120150823

Mak and Jacobs. (2014). How Eric Cantor sabotaged himself. *The Daily Beast*. [June 10, 2014]. Retrieved from www.thedailybeast.com/how-eric-cantor-sabotaged-himself

Mann, T. E., and Ornstein, N. J. (2016). *It's even worse than it looks: How the American constitutional system collided with the new politics of extremism*. New York, NY: Basic Books.

Martens and Martens. (2016). Key Segments of Bernie Sanders' Speech on Wall Street Reform Disappear. *Wall Street on Parade*. Retrieved from http://wallstreetonparade.com/2016/01/key-segments-of-bernie-sanders-speech-on-wall-street-reform-disappear/

Martin. (2014). Eric Cantor defeated by David Brat, Tea Party challenger, in G.O.P. primary upset. *The New York Times*. [June 11, 2014]. Retrieved from www.nytimes.com/2014/06/11/us/politics/eric-cantor-loses-gop-primary.html

Mataconis, D. (2015). Tea party support at all-time low, even among Republicans and conservatives. *Outside the Beltway*. [October 26, 2015]. Retrieved from www.outsidethebeltway.com/tea-party-support-at-all-time-low-even-among-republicans-and-conservatives/

Mataconis, D. (2010). Covert operations. *New Yorker* 30, pp. 1–10.

Mayer, J. (2016). *Dark money: The hidden history of the billionaires behind the rise of the radical right*. Anchor.

McCarty, N. M., Poole, K. T., and Rosenthal, H. (2006). *Polarized America: The dance of ideology and unequal riches*. Cambridge, MA: MIT Press.

McCormick, J., and Giroux, G. (2014, May 19). Chilling election message to Tea Party is business goal. *Bloomberg Business*. Retrieved from www.bloomberg.com/news/articles/2014-05-19/chilling-election-message-to-tea-party-is-business-goal

McGhee, E., Masket, S., Shor, B., Rogers, S., and McCarty, N. (2014). A primary cause of partisanship? Nomination systems and legislator ideology. *American Journal of Political Science* 58, pp. 337–351.

Meinke, S. R., Staton, J. K., and Wuhs, S. T. (2006). State delegate selection rules for presidential nominations, 1972–2000. *Journal of Politics* 68 (1), pp. 180–193.

Noel, Hans. (2016). Ideological factions in the Republican and democratic parties. *The ANNALS of the American Academy of Political and Social Science* 667 (1), pp. 166–188.

Norman, J. (2015). In U.S., support for Tea Party drops to new low. *Gallup*. Retrieved from:http://news.gallup.com/poll/186338/support-tea-party-drops-new-low.aspx

Oliver, J. E., and Rahn, W. M. (2016). Rise of the Trumpenvolk: Populism in the 2016 Election. *The ANNALS of the American Academy of Political and Social Science* 667 (1), pp. 189–206.

Oliver, J. E., and Rahn, W. M. (2016). Rise of the Trumpenvolk: Populism in the 2016 Election. *The ANNALS of the American Academy of Political and Social Science* 667 (1), pp. 189–206.

Pennings, P., and Hazan, R. Y. (2001). Democratizing candidate selection: causes and consequences. *Party Politics* 7 (3), pp. 267–275.

Peters, J. W. (2017). In free-range trump, many see potential for a third party. *The New York Times*. [September 11, 2017]. Retrieved from www.nytimes.com/2017/09/11/us/politics/trump-third-party-republican.html

Pew Research Center. (2014). *Political polarization in the American public*. Retrieved from: www.people-press.org/2014/06/12/section-1-growing-ideological-consistency/

Pew Research Center. (2015). *Beyond distrust: How Americans view their government*. Retrieved from: www.people-press.org/2015/11/23/1-trust-in-government-1958-2015/

Pirch, K. A. (2008). Bloggers at the gates: Ned Lamont, blogs, and the rise of insurgent candidates. *Social Science Computer Review* 26 (3), pp. 275–287.

Piroth, P. (2000). Selecting presidential nominees: The evolution of the current system and prospects for reform. *Social Education* 64, pp. 278–285.

Pisani-Ferry, J. (2015). Responding to Europe's Polarization. Project Syndicate. [December 31, 2015]. Retrieved from www.project-syndicate.org/commentary/europe-political-polarization-crisis-by-jean-pisani-ferry-2015-12?barrier=accessreg

Pomper, G. M. (1977). The decline of the party in American elections. *Political Science Quarterly* 92 (1), pp. 21–41.

Poole, K. T., and Rosenthal, H. (1984). The polarization of American politics. *The Journal of Politics* 46 (4), pp. 1061–1079.

Pressman, J., and Sullivan, D. (1974). Convention reform and conventional wisdom: An empirical assessment of democratic party reforms. *Political Science Quarterly* 89 (3), pp. 539–562. doi:10.2307/2148453

Richardson, H. C., Cohen, M., and Edlestein, J. H. (2017). Civil war has broken out inside the Democratic Party. *The Guardian*. [June 25, 2017]. Retrieved from www.theguardian.com/commentisfree/2017/jun/25/civil-war-raging-inside-democratic-party

Robin, C. (2017). Will Steve Bannon's war tear apart the Republican party? *The Guardian*. [August 22, 2017]. Retrieved from www.theguardian.com/commentisfree/2017/aug/22/steve-bannons-war-tear-republican-party

Rodrik, D. (2016). The politics of anger. *Social Europe*, *11*.

Rosenblum, N. L. (2000). Political parties as membership groups. *Columbia Law Review*, pp. 813–844.

Rosenfeld, S. H. (2014). *A choice, not an echo: Polarization and the transformation of the American party system*. Cambridge, MA: Harvard University Press.

Schmidt, V. A. (2017). Britain-out and Trump-in: A discursive institutionalist analysis of the British referendum on the EU and the US presidential election. *Review of International Political Economy* 24 (2), pp. 248–269.

Skocpol, T., and Hertel-Fernandez, A. (2016a). The Koch network and republican party extremism. *Perspectives on Politics* 14 (3), pp. 681–699.

Skocpol, T., and Hertel-Fernandez, A. (2016b). The Koch network and the rightward shift in US politics. In *Annual Meeting of the Midwest Political Science Association*, Chicago, IL.

Skocpol, T., and Williamson, V. (2014). *The tea party and the remaking of Republican conservatism*. Oxford and New York: Oxford University Press.

Smith, D. (2017). Republican civil war looms as Steve Bannon takes aim at the establishment. *The Guardian*. [September 30, 2017]. Retrieved from www.theguardian.com/us-news/2017/sep/30/republicans-steve-bannon-trump-establishment-mitch-mcconnell

Spies, D. C., and Kaiser, A. (2014). Does the mode of candidate selection affect the representativeness of parties? *Party Politics* 20, pp. 579–590.

Squire, P., and Moncrief, G. (2015). *State legislatures today: Politics under the domes*. Lanham, MD: Rowman & Littlefield.

Stewart, J. (2016). Following the money behind the nearly $500 million 2016 Democratic primary. *Sunlight Foundation*. Retrieved from https://sunlightfoundation.com/2016/06/21/following-the-money-behind-the-nearly-500-million-2016-democratic-primary/

Streeck, W. (2011). The crises of democratic capitalism. *New Left Review* 71, pp. 5–29.

Tabach-bank, B. R., and Kelly, P. D. (1975). Reform of the delegate selection process to democratic national conventions: 1964 to the present. *Sw. UL Rev.* 7, pp. 273–309.

Thomsen, D. M. (2014). Ideological moderates won't run: How party fit matters for partisan polarization in Congress. *The Journal of Politics* 76 (3), pp. 786–797.

Tichenor, D., and Fuerstman, D. (2008). Insurgency campaigns and the quest for popular democracy: Theodore Roosevelt, Eugene McCarthy, and party monopolies. *Polity* 40 (1), pp. 49–69.

Turney, S., Levy, F., Citrin, J., and O'Brian, N. (2017). Waiting for trump: The move to the right of white working-class men, 1968–2016. *California Journal of Politics & Policy*. UC Berkeley, Institute of Governmental Studies. Retrieved from http://escholarship.org/uc/item/1cq9k81z

Vandeleene, A., De Winter, L., Meulewaeter, C., and Baudewyns, P. (2013). The impact of candidate selection on mass elite ideological congruence: The case of Belgium. In *7th ECPR General Conference*.

Vandewalker, I. (2015). *Election spending 2014: Outside spending in senate races since Citizens United*. Brennan Center for Justice at New York University School of Law.

Vandewalker, I., and Norden, L. (2016). Small donors still aren't as important as wealthy ones. *The Atlantic*. [October 18, 2016]. Retrieved from www.theatlantic.com/politics/archive/2016/10/campaign-finance-fundraising-citizens-united/504425/

Vogel, K. P. (2014). The Left's secret club. *Politico*. [April 24, 2014]. Retrieved from www.politico.com/story/2014/04/democrats-democracy-alliance-liberal-donors-105972

Vogel, K. P. (2015). Koch brothers summon Bush, Cruz, Walker, Rubio to SoCal confab. *Politico*. [July 27, 2015]. Retrieved from www.politico.com/story/2015/07/koch-brothers-wealthy-donors-gop-2016-freedom-partners-seminar-california-120663

Voorheis, J., McCarty, N., and Shor, B. (2015). Unequal incomes, ideology and gridlock: How rising inequality increases political polarization.

Walker, J. (1981). Presidential campaigns: Reforming the reforms. *The Wilson Quarterly* 5 (4), pp. 88–101.

Ware, A. (2000). Anti-partism and party control of political reform in the United States: The case of the Australian ballot. *British Journal of Political Science* 30 (1), pp. 1–29.

Weigel, D., Scherer, M., and Costa, R. (2017). McConnell allies declare open warfare on Bannon. *The Washington Post*. [October 25, 2017]. Retrieved from www.washingtonpost.com/powerpost/gops-insurgents-step-up-campaign-against-mcconnell/2017/10/25/ec3a5af4-b9a0-11e7-9e58-e6288544af98_story.html?utm_term=.5b5bc9db0c6a

Wolf, M. R., Strachan, J. C., and Shea, D. M. (2012). Incivility and standing firm: A second layer of partisan division. *PS: Political Science & Politics* 45 (3), pp. 428–434. Retrieved from www.newsweek.com/who-kelli-ward-jeff-flake-arizona-senate-candidate-692088

Zakaria, F. (2016, November/December) Populism on the march. *Foreign Affairs*.

16 The effects of the Great Recession on candidate selection in America and Europe

Guillermo Cordero, Xavier Coller, and Antonio M. Jaime-Castillo

Despite the increasing attention paid to candidate selection in the recent literature, this subject can still be considered "the secret garden of politics" (Gallagher, 1988). There are at least three reasons for this. Firstly, most of the contributions on the field have analysed the formal procedures of candidate selection, forgetting the informal mechanisms behind these regulations (Ranney, 1981; Gallagher and Marsh, 1988; Hopkin, 2001; Katz, 2001; Fujimura, 2012; Cordero and Coller, 2015). As previous empirically-oriented works have shown, there are wide gaps between the internal rules (or even country regulations) and the internal practices that lead party decisions to implement and comply with formal regulations (Cordero et al., 2016). Secondly, a significant portion of the literature has focused on the selection of the candidates to prime minister or leaders of parties, forgetting how the lists for the legislative power are designed (see Sandri et al., 2015). As we know, the composition of parliamentary groups has important consequences on MPs' behaviour (Carey, 2007; Gallagher and Marsh, 1988; Hix, 2004; Hazan and Rahat, 2007; Cordero and Coller, 2015), the duration of governments (Siavelis & Morgenstern, 2008), relationships with citizens, the internal distribution of power (Katz and Mair, 2005) and, ultimately, the quality of democracy. Thirdly, the Great Recession has intensified the crisis of trust and legitimacy of parties in many countries, in which internal party life might have been put under discussion or implementation in order to reconnect with citizens, focusing especially on the way candidates are selected. The interest of this book lies in the temporal scope of the analysis, as we study how candidate selection has changed in the wake of the Great Recession.

Chapters in this book analyze the effects of the last global crisis on the formal and informal mechanisms of selection of candidates to MPs in a large sample of countries: in the American continent, US, Mexico and a chapter devoted to other Latin American countries focusing especially on Bolivia, Costa Rica, Ecuador and Venezuela have been analyzed. In Europe, Austria, Belgium, Czech Republic, Germany, Greece, Iceland, Italy, Portugal and Spain have been included to find differences and similarities in their mechanisms of candidate selection.

Why is it important to analyze how an aspect of party internal life, such as candidate selection, has changed after the global crisis? Wide attention has been devoted to political and electoral behaviour after this crisis. Voters across the globe reacted to the economic crisis by punishing governments of different ideologies, increasing the relevance of economic voting (Nadeau and Lewis-Beck, 2012; Kriesi, 2012; Brooks and Manza, 2013; Bartels and Bermeo, 2013; Hernández and Kriesi, 2016). This pattern has taken place in very different contexts, although with exceptions. However, after this first response, a wave of disaffection went through Europe (Armingeon and Guthmann, 2013; Torcal, 2014; Della Porta, 2015). Politicians and political institutions such as parties, parliaments and governments, have seen their levels of trust decrease among citizens (Cordero and Simón, 2016). One immediate effect of this lack of trust in traditional actors has been social protest (Kriesi, 2012; Della Porta, 2015; Fishman and Everson, 2016) and the electoral success of "new" political actors (Kriesi and Pappas, 2015; Rama and Cordero, 2018). Not by accident, parties such as the Movimento 5 Stelle in Italy, Alternative für Deutschland in Germany, Syriza in Greece, NEOS in Austria, Podemos in Spain and some others emerged or strengthened their electoral muscle during this economic and political crisis.

All these changes (institutional distrust, increasing social protest, electoral volatility, ideological polarization, emergence of populist discourses and new electoral competitors) provoked a political landslide in many countries. The deep economic crisis had political consequences to which traditional parties have reacted in different ways. Sometimes, in order to avoid or alleviate electoral losses, and with the goal of reconnecting with society and/or recovering power in the context of electoral defeat, some of these traditional parties have changed the way in which they organize internally. In some of them, candidate-selection procedures have been modified.

Some of the new parties that emerged during the Great Recession ran in elections implementing very participative ways of candidate selection, making use of new technologies as a way to reduce the distance between parties and citizens (Cordero and Coller, 21018). Chapters in this book analyze to what extent these practices are "new" and if these changes had a contagion effect among the "traditionally mainstream" parties in order to re-connect with their voters. The second chapter of this book offers a detailed description of the expected responses that parties may develop in a context of economic and political crisis.

Empirical analyses in chapters 3 to 15 show three different patterns in this regard. Firstly, among the countries in which "traditional" parties implemented participative ways of candidate selection (such as Spain and some Latin-American countries), these mechanisms have become more inclusive because of the emergence of new political actors. In a second set of countries, traditionally mainstream parties were able to adapt to the new situation, but without changing the way in which they implement candidate selection. In these countries, parties produced ways to connect with social movements (as in Portugal) or new ways of campaigning in the context of well-established mechanisms of selection (as in the US). Lastly, in those countries where political parties already adopted mechanisms of internal participation to select their candidates (Czech Republic and Greece) the response has been different. In fact, some new actors in these countries emerged as less internally democratic than their traditional peers. Although we were expecting a general trend towards more participative ways of candidate selection, in those countries where parties made an effort to open their internal selections to a broader selectorate before the Great Recession, the response to this economic and political crisis has been to make these mechanisms more exclusive.

Expectations

As argued before, we expected deep changes in the way traditional and new parties drive their candidate selection. To analyse the first of these changes, we have studied how these new relevant political actors, for whom the promotion of internal democracy in many cases is in their DNA, are really implementing participative ways of candidate selection and how they are (or are not) being innovative in their political environments.

However, the goal of this book has been not only to analyse empirically to what extent these new parties are implementing IPD. Following new institutionalism in sociology (DiMaggio and Powell 1991) it is reasonable to think that in political markets (as in economic markets), once an actor has introduced an innovation which is perceived as positive or successful, others will follow suit. Consequently, each chapter considers the extent to which traditionally mainstream parties are changing selection procedures to have more open and inclusive mechanisms and a more democratic way of managing their internal life. Either as a response to the crisis of legitimacy and political volatility affecting them, or because of mimetic isomorphism, we might expect a general pattern towards democratization in traditional mainstream parties. Consequently, we have analyzed to what extent the different political actors are adapting and transforming their mechanisms of selection. In order to empirically demonstrate if this is happening and its real impact, each chapter studies the scope of these changes within the general trend and its particular causes related to the context specificities.

Lastly, this book tries to make a contribution to some ongoing debates in the field about the consequences of the democratization of party life, regarding political participation and representation (Cross and Katz, 2013). Some of these debates are connected to the use of "new" technologies in candidate selection. The use of the internet and the widespread use of social networks in political campaigning has affected the way in which parties campaign, candidates are selected and citizens interact with parties (Cordero and Coller, 2018), including in countries with a long tradition of democratic institutions, such as Iceland. From primaries to internet casting, new procedures are being implemented for candidate selection to perform the representative function in parliaments. This might have also clear implications for political representation. As recent works analyze (Cross and Katz, 2013), internal democratization may become a threat to representation in territorial (decentralization), sectorial (such as the representation of Trade

Unions or civic associations) and especially gender terms. For this reason, this book pays close attention to the effects of new ways of selecting candidates on representation.

In sum, our analysis has been driven by a number of questions: How are these new ways of selecting candidates implemented? Are they so new? What does make them different? How do they really work? Are they more inclusive? What are the effects of selection procedures put in place by the new parties on other parties? Are these parties changing the way they relate to electors and society at large?

Results

Table 16.1 summarizes the findings of the book. A look at the information provided makes it possible to reach three major conclusions. Firstly, the Great Recession's *intensity* has no clear relationship with the emergence of new parties. We can see in Table 16.1 that there are countries where the intensity of the crisis is low and new parties have emerged (Germany, Austria), and countries going through intense economic hardship where no new parties do (Portugal). However, in the globalization era, the mere existence of the Great Recession, no matter the intensity with which a particular country was affected, may be considered a necessary condition for new parties to emerge, albeit not a sufficient one. Portugal, Belgium and in some respects Mexico and the US are therefore negative cases that need to be explained using country specific factors. In Portugal, traditional political elites managed to take up public unrest and incorporate it in their organizations. In Belgium, the already saturated political market and the fact that social protest was channelled through trade unions, well connected to the major parties, left little room for new parties to operate. Mexico has not seen the emergence of new parties given the "protective institutions" (electoral rules, appointment of decision makers, etc.) isolating parties from the environment's demands for participation.

Second, IPD practices for legislative candidate selection are implemented in most new actors but with some variations. In Germany, where there is legislation about the democratic nature of political parties (such as in the US), AfD selection practices have generated controversy, undermining the credibility of these practices as "democratic". In Austria, there is large variation going from the "entrepreneur" or "business" nature of some parties like Team Stronach (centralized) to the more inclusive approach of the Pirate party or NEOS, which use internet means to select their candidates following a wide inclusive approach. In the countries analyzed in Latin America IPD practices to select candidates have been implemented but more on party bases. It seems that a leftist-populist ideology, change of leadership and internal disputes may explain the case. In countries of the south of Europe (Italy, Spain, Greece) the newcomers began with an open mind towards the selection of their candidates but when they grew, had electoral success, and even began ruling important institutions (local, regional or national governments) the path toward inclusiveness was somehow reversed and the oligarchies of the parties tried to gain control, pretty much as has happened in some

Table 16.1 Summary of findings

Country	Great Recession Intensity	New Actors (or old becoming mainstream)	IPD in candidate selection in New Actors	Mimetic isomorphism	Alternative explanations for changes	Descriptive representation
Greece	High	Yes (Syriza, Golden Dawn)	Yes, but controlled by party elite	No	–	Less legal professions and family networks. More women.
Spain	High	Yes (Podemos and Ciudadanos)	Yes, but controlled by party elite	Yes	–	Diversity added
Iceland	High	Yes (Reform, Bright Future, Pirate Party)	Yes, but traditional parties were already very inclusive.	Yes	–	Some ideological congruence
Ireland	High	Yes (Social Democrats, Anti–Austerity Alliance – People Before Profit)	Yes	No	Repertoire of IPD mechanisms existed before	Better gender representation in newer parties and a wider occupational background.
Portugal	High	No	–	–	Stronger links with social protest movements.	No major changes. More women and higher civic engagement.
Italy	High	Yes (5SM)	Yes, but strongly controlled by party elite	No	–	Diversity added

Latin America	Medium	Yes	Yes, in some actors	Yes	—	Minor changes on social diversity except for the growing presence of women and young MPs.
Mexico	Medium	No	—	No	Role of regional leaders, protective institutions.	—
Czech Rep	Medium	Yes (Public Affairs, ANO and Dawn)	No. Less IPD in new actors	No	—	—
United States	Medium	No ("Insurgent" (populist) candidates in traditional parties)	—	Yes	Regulations at state level, growing party insurgencies, consortium of donors, partisan polarization.	—
Belgium	Low	No (appeared before the crisis)	—	—	Weaker crisis, trade unions role and party fragmentation	—
Austria	Low	Yes (NEOS, Pirate Party, List Pilz and Team Stronach)	Yes	No	Electoral defeats	More diversity (gender)
Germany	Low	Yes (AfD, Pirate Party)	Yes, but controversial	No	Regulations at country level.	No diversity added

Note: Countries classified by the yearly average change of country GDP–PPP[1] (World Bank) in the 2007–2012 period.

cases in Mexico. Both in Ireland and Iceland, IPD practices had entered the sedimentation phase explained in the introduction and new parties incorporated them to select their legislative candidates and sometimes went even further.

However, there is a negative case in the implementation of IPD practices. In the Czech Republic, there are new actors that have not approached the selection of their legislative candidates with more participative mechanisms. On the contrary they have followed a centralizing and exclusive approach. The explanation lies in the fact that they tend to be entrepreneur parties that by their very nature are more centralist and their functioning depends more on a centralizing oligarchy.

Third, following new institutionalism in organizational theory, mimetic isomorphism is expected among parties *qua* organizations when there is an innovation that spreads in the organizational field, especially when IPD practices as innovations are widely known and have reached the sedimentation stage. Table 16.1 suggest inconclusive results. There has been some mimetism in Spain, Iceland, Ireland, and Latin America but in the cases of Ireland and Iceland we could hardly consider IPD as innovative. The question, then, is very clear: if more inclusive and decentralized mechanisms of candidate selection are considered good insofar as they are associated to participatory democracy, why are they not more frequently incorporated into traditional mainstream parties? There are several alternative explanations. First, IPD practices may work for small and/or territorially concentrated parties but they may not be fully functional for large parties. And this is particularly the case when there are calls for early elections and parties have to create lists in a short period of time. However, the cases of Italy, Spain and Greece qualify this explanation. Second, IPD practices may work *temporarily* to solve intra-party disputes or conflicts of power but may generate other problems, such as undermining the traditional power of oligarchies, transferring to society an image of division, or finding no proper solution to technical problems like electronic voting. Third, some new parties have IPD practices embedded in their DNAs but when they achieve power or the expectation is that they will get some share of power (as, for example, indicated by opinion polls), they may feel the need to gain control over the nomination of candidates to avoid multivocality of parliamentary groups, party swapping, defections, and the like. The message sent then is that IPD practices do not work and therefore other parties may not follow. Fourth, from the microcosmic or descriptive representation point of view, IPD practices in the selection of legislative candidates may result in unintended consequences such as the under-representation of some groups (especially women) or over-representation of others (like professional politicians or party-devoted individuals). The incentive for mimetism is then sharply reduced.

Lastly, a growing social diversity in parliaments is a historical trend confirmed by the literature (Best and Cotta, 2000). Information summarized in Table 16.1 shows that wherever selection of candidates is more inclusive some social diversity is added. But this conclusion must be qualified. First, social diversity in representative chambers may be operating before new parties appear and gain some seats, as is the case of Italy, Greece, Ireland and Spain, and somehow in Latin America. Second, the presence of women has been an issue in politics for several decades now and most parties decided to incorporate quotas while others were induced by State regulation to have quotas or even generate zipper lists. As a consequence, it seems that the presence of women has increased (though still below the representation of men) in parliaments but not necessarily because new actors or the implementation of IPD practices to select candidates have resulted in a new wider proportion of women in parliament (Cordero and Coller, 2018). There are countercases, of course. AfD in Germany seems to add no diversity to the representation of society in parliaments: a situation that may be related to its ideological outlook and the position (shared by some liberal and conservative parties across the democratic world) of rejecting quotas for women in favour of, say, merits.

Following these changes, three general patterns emerge from the analyses shown in this book.

Pattern 1: Emergence of new parties with IPD and "contagion effect" on mainstream parties

There are countries where the Great Recession provided the background against which new parties emerged, introducing new means of candidate selection, and innovations were somehow replicated by traditional mainstream parties. **Spain** is a clear example of this trend. After the Great Recession and de-legitimization and electoral losses of traditional parties, Podemos and Ciudadanos, two parties in which internal democracy was a hallmark, emerged as two new electoral forces at the national level. These two new parties introduced very horizontal and inclusive mechanisms of selection with extensive use of digital technologies, although these practices evolved toward a close control of these processes by the party elites. Traditional parties, especially the social-democrat PSOE, followed a process of internal democratization, and to a lesser extent, the conservative PP, which in the last congress in 2017 adopted a mechanism to select leaderships within the party close to what Hazan and Rahat (2010:37) call "multi-stage method".

The case of Ciudadanos and Podemos (and others in this book, such as M5S in Italy and SYRIZA in Greece) should lead future research to ask why parties that began with an inclusive approach to candidate selection end up confirming Michels' Iron Law of Oligarchy. As the Spanish, Greek and Italian chapters show, recently created parties and those experiencing quick electoral growth make openness of candidate selection more challenging than it is for traditional parties. In a process of territorial implementation and growing expansion, executing a rigorous process of transparent democracy to select all candidates could erode the internal power of the elite. This threat provides incentives to these leaders to exert some influence over the process in a more or less strict way to avoid internal divisions and gain control. In some cases, internal democracy in recently created parties could hide tight control by the monolithic party elite.

Also some of the **Latin American countries** analyzed followed a pattern of internal democratization in the selection of their candidates. Despite the difficulty of drawing a broad picture for such a heterogeneous region of the world, the general trend observed in these countries is towards more inclusive ways of candidate selection. The strength of populism, the turn toward the left and new leaderships in the region have gone in parallel with the openness of the candidate selection procedures. This change has been a result of the search for stronger links with society and the mending of intra-party divisions.

The examples of **Italy**, Austria and Ireland fulfils our expectations only partially. Despite the fact that new parties emerged during the Great Recession and some of these parties used participative ways of selection, traditional parties did not implement these mechanisms as a response. In the former, while the centre-left mainstream parties implemented primaries a decade prior to the economic crisis, the newly emerged populist party M5S made this selection more inclusive, with the extensive use of new technologies for the selection of all candidates. However, as seen in Podemos, the highly inclusive mechanisms put in place by M5S ended in a process of just apparent democratization, given the exclusive and centralist control of the party elite. Four new parties emerged in recent years in **Austria**, two of them defending anti-establishment discourses and inserting highly democratic mechanisms of selection in their rules. However, the other two did not develop inclusive processes to elaborate their electoral lists. According to Jenny, this diversity of procedures has to do with its foundational moment, the type of party, as well as their expected electoral results. Furthermore, despite the Eurozone crisis being a driving force for the emergence of these new parties, the weak effects of this crisis in Austria could explain that traditional parties did not see the newcomers as a threat and did not feel the need to make significant changes in the way these parties elaborate their lists. Only the Austrian People's Party adopted changes, making more exclusive its mechanisms of selection by giving more power to its new leader. In a similar way, **Ireland** experienced an important fragmentation of its party system during the crisis. Several new parties were born in this period, although not all of them had electoral success nor did they implement democratic procedures, especially in the 2016 elections. According to the analysis of Reidy, among young parties only Anti-Austerity Alliance-People Before Profit had inclusive candidate-selection procedures in place in those elections, using the IPD repertoire of practices already operating and available in the country among traditional parties.

Pattern 2: nothing has changed. at least, apparently

The parties in this second set of countries have not experienced clear changes in line with our expectations after the Great Recession. The way in which their candidates were selected remained stable or, in some cases, were changed, although not as a result of the crisis. In the **Belgian** case, Vandeleene and De Winter show how no new parties emerged and traditional parties did not change during the crisis. Only some changes were introduced in the last decades, all of them before the Great Recession. Specifically, the Flemish Liberal Party introduced primaries, while the Socialist Party went in the opposite direction, reducing the size of the selectorate. Newer parties (that also emerged before the crisis) did not develop more participative ways of selection. On the contrary, these newly created platforms adapted their mechanisms of selection to professional structures in very centralized processes. The authors mention three reasons for the lack of relevant changes in internal party life. First, the crisis did not hit as hard in Belgium as in other countries. Second, the social protest connected to austerity was led by the Trade Unions, strongly connected with the mainstream parties. Third, the high fragmentation reached right before the economic crisis in Belgium left little room for new parties to emerge. In contrast, Belgian parties changed their mechanisms of candidate selection as a response to electoral downturns, something that happened right before the economic crisis.

Electoral volatility and defeats are also at the roots of the change in the internal life of **Portuguese** parties. However, these changes took place without a modification of either the party supply or the ways candidates are selected, as would be expected from our hypothesis. The output of these mechanisms did not generate different outputs, having the candidates selected before and after the Great Recession a similar profile. Only one aspect changed in this case, which is in fact the main reason for the exceptional strength of the *status quo* in Portuguese party life. The way which these traditional parties found to reconnect with society in a context of deep economic and political crisis was to make stronger links with social movements, giving priority to social activists in their electoral lists. This absorption or incorporation of the environment could have been perceived by the electorate as a movement of political regeneration, having as a result outstanding continuity in the Portuguese party system, despite the deep consequences of the Great Recession in the country.

As discussed in the first two chapters of the book, neither the economic and political crises nor electoral defeats are clearly the main reason behind a change in how candidates are selected. These mechanisms can also be used by party elites to legitimate their leadership and/or influence the internal distribution of power. The **Mexican** case has shown a peculiar pattern in this sense, as the three main parties of the country have changed the mechanisms to select their candidates in different directions for this reason. This changeable nature of candidate selection is the consequence of internal power battles. Parties became more (especially the PAN) or less democratic not as a result of economic crises, but as a response to internal dynamics.

The **United States** represents the last case of a country in which, at least apparently, nothing has changed. Selecting candidates in a decentralized and inclusive way has been historically one of the distinctive marks of US party life. The Great Recession did not amount to the end of these traditional mechanisms. However, Craig argues that the universal patterns towards polarization, rejection of globalization and the neo-liberal agenda as well as the anger related to cultural shifts was also reflected in American politics, impacting on its mechanisms of candidate selection. The author analyzes the frequency of party insurgencies, the role of money in politics, and increasing partisan polarization in the party supply and its interrelation with the outputs in the primaries and caucuses of Democrat and Republicans, and the exceptional success of their populist candidates.

Pattern 3: "I have been there already and it is not the solution". How the great recession made internally democratic parties more exclusive in their candidate selection

Economic crises are not the only condition nor a sufficient condition for parties to introduce IPD mechanisms of candidate selection. Some countries already developed highly democratic processes of candidate selection a long time ago and a deep crisis could lead some of these parties to go in the opposite direction, implementing exclusive ways of candidate selection. This is the case of **Iceland**, one of the most ancient democracies in the world, where their traditional parties were already implementing primaries as a mechanism of selection. However, the Great Recession made traditional and new parties introduce changes such as direct democracy or, following the opposite direction, highly personalized forms of representation. In a similar way, in the **Czech Republic** three parties emerged during the Great Recession. These new parties grew as a consequence of the economic crisis but, differently from other parties connected to social movements, internal democracy was not among their principles. On the contrary, these new parties are of the entrepreneurial type, with centralized and exclusive mechanisms of candidate selection and decision-making. In the same line, traditionally mainstream parties did not find in internal democracy a solution to their problems. On the contrary, they have tended towards more exclusive ways of candidate selection as a response to the economic crisis, considering internal democratization more a threat than a solution.

In **Greece** the electoral output of the deep crisis was not the emergence of new parties, but the advancement of traditionally fringe parties, such as Golden Dawn (radical-right populist party) and SYRIZA (left-wing populist party). In this respect, SYRIZA gained relevant electoral bases at a very fast pace. Despite internal democracy being in its DNA, the party became less democratic given this rapid and unexpected growth. Also the results of these ways of selection were evident, with candidates after the economic crisis more often male, middle-aged and belonging to "political" professions as it became a more exclusive, mainstream party, ready to rule. ND, as the traditional mainstream party, has not suffered any contagion effect. Only minor changes have been inserted, although these changes have not produced an output yet.

Germany is an exception in the field of candidate selection in Europe. The procedures of selection are regulated at the country level. This regulation establishes the mechanisms of selection for parties and so, despite some specificities, parties tend to behave similarly. However, a new party founded as a response to the refugees crisis in Germany obtained remarkable results in recent elections: Alternative for Germany. This anti-establishment party formally embraces the principle of the democratization and decentralization of its decision-making. Despite formally inclusive member conventions on the district and state level to nominate its candidates, these mechanisms are neither more inclusive nor more innovative than the mechanisms used by traditionally mainstream parties. Recently, a number of scandals and published violations of the democratic principles in these elections came out.

As these examples demonstrate, in those contexts where internal democracy was already a common practice the response of some parties to problems of delegitimization, a lack of connection with citizens and electoral defeats can be to go in the opposite direction, implementing more exclusive and vertical mechanisms of candidate selection. This is more common among recently created parties, for which implementing these complex processes is especially costly in terms of time, organization and power balance; but also among traditional parties experiencing rapid electoral success for similar reasons. When these young or recently successful parties do not implement more democratic procedures, traditional mainstream parties feel less pressure to implement these democratic changes.

Remarks and discussion

In this book we have analyzed the effects of the Great Recession on a relevant aspect of party internal life: candidate selection. We argued that the interplay between the economic and political crisis produced a demand for better political representation, affecting the way in which parties select their candidates by a wider implementation of IPD. Following this argument, parties that have emerged since the Great Recession aim to give voice to those who do not feel represented by the mainstream parties having the conception of internal democratic participation already inserted in their practices. For its part, traditionally mainstream parties would adapt their traditional ways of selection as a response to these demands of greater participation, also as a contagion effect in a process of "structural isomorphism" (DiMaggio and Powell, 1991).

The first of these arguments seems to be true for some of the cases included in this book (see Table 16.1), specifically among some of the countries most affected by the economic recession. In Greece, Iceland, Ireland, Italy and Spain new parties emerged with more inclusive mechanisms of selection. However, Austria – a country barely affected by the Great Recession— fulfils our expectations, with new parties implementing IPD. At the same time, the second argument (contagion effect among traditional parties) has been proven in Iceland, some Latin American countries and Spain. These exceptions suggest that the economic crisis is an intervening but not a determinant variable to explain institutional change. Some of the cases included in this book demonstrate that there are a series of important contextual and contingent factors, with a significant impact on the way parties select their candidates.

One of these crucial factors is party leadership. Indeed, in some other countries affected differently by the Great Recession, such as Belgium, Portugal and Mexico, the leadership of their parties took different responses to their specific context, not altering the way in which candidate selection takes place. The relevance of party leadership is even more determinant in some other scenarios. More clearly, personal leadership in entrepreneurial parties (see the case of the Czech Republic) tends to generate highly centralized and exclusive mechanisms of candidate selection which usually includes the direct control of the entire process by the party leader. Although these are the clearest and most extreme cases, party leadership also plays a determinant role among parties with overnight success. A sudden increase in the number of representatives among new parties or traditionally fringe parties (such as Podemos in Spain, SYRIZA in Greece and M5S in Italy) seems to impact candidate selection, converting internally democratic parties into organizations in which the party elite exerts a considerable degree of control on candidate selection. Also, the need to manage these new representatives could be behind these attempts to control the process in order to reduce the risk of defection and public perception of internal feud.

Thus, despite the common understanding that younger parties may develop more inclusive and horizontal internal practices in a context of crisis of representation, the empirical analyses shown in this book demonstrate that this intuitive expectation can be only partially accepted. Despite the effect of path dependency in the process and the fact that traditional institutions have incentives to maintain their practices, traditionally mainstream parties also have the economic resources, experience, territorial implementation and structures to develop participative ways of selection in a successful way. More importantly, these parties have a pool of potential candidates, some of them with experience in public positions and a certain level of proven loyalty towards the party and/or leadership. This highlights the difficulty for emerging internal democracy given that the new organizations, even if they have internal democracy embedded in their DNA, have difficulties implementing it in a context of rapid electoral success. In a party without a sufficient pool of potential candidates, in which the candidates to be representatives have only brief experience of working with the party, party leadership tends to control candidate selection in a central and exclusive way when the electoral calendar pushes.

In a similar fashion, among those countries (and parties) with established internal democratic systems to select the candidates, the common response to a crisis is not leading towards more democratic ways of selection. On the contrary, they may see democratic selection as problematic and change these inclusive mechanisms towards more professional ways of selection (see the chapters on Greece and Iceland). As the introduction of this book has pointed out, there is a pool of alternative practices for candidate selection among parties. The internally democratic parties could blame IPD as the cause of an electoral defeat or an internal dispute, implementing, as a result, more exclusive ways of selection.

However, the most significant lever of change to adopt more democratic ways of selecting candidates among mainstream parties is the threat of electoral defeat. Even more relevant than an economic or a political crisis, when traditional parties feel the threat of an electoral victory by a recently created party, mimicry of their mechanisms of selection tends to be the reaction. In doing so, traditional parties try to reduce the gap with the population and the electoral success of these new actors.

Despite parties being considered the main actors in a democracy and the fact that selecting candidates is their main attribution, these institutions are not always internally democratic. This paradox raised by Robert Michels (1962) in 1911 has been behind this book's genesis. While his "iron law" foresees the control of these mechanisms of selection, we have demonstrated that a general trend towards democratization is present in Europe and America. Although this trend is not free of the control exercised by the political elite, the empirical contributions in this book have demonstrated that internal democratization can improve the representation of traditionally poorly represented segments. However, contradictory findings have been discovered by the literature on the merits of IPD (party cohesion, electoral success or duration of governments). At the same time, while its contribution to diversity seems to be a common place among the cases studied in this monograph, the better representation achieved by women in parliaments in most of these cases has not been the result of democratizing candidate selection but the natural outcome of the adoption of quotas and the electoral growth of young parties.

In this regard, although the adoption of more democratic practices to improve representation or electoral results or solve a situation of lack of legitimacy and/ or leadership are not new, this change may make sense only if it is motivated by ideological reasons. When the democratization of party internal life is the *raison d'être* or one of the main campaign assets of a party (as for most of the recently created right and left-wing parties analyzed in this book), then the adoption of these measures make sense. Voters who care deeply about party rules are rare. In fact, empirical analysis of these cases has demonstrated that these parties tend to forget democratic practices when they (expect to) increase their size. Also, some negative cases have been shown, such as Belgium, the Czech Republic, Iceland and Greece. This reverse direction of change also demonstrates that parties already implementing democratic mechanisms of candidate selection in the past alter their internal mechanisms of decision- making towards more centralized and exclusive mechanisms in order to increase their effectiveness. As seen in this book, Michels' Iron Law seems to be alive, opening the debate about the pertinence of internal democracy as the panacea for political disaffection.

Note

1 PPP GDP is gross domestic product converted to international dollars using purchasing power parity rates. For more details, visit https://data.worldbank.org/indicator/NY.GDP. MKTP.PP.KD.

Bibliography

Armingeon, K., and Guthmann, K. (2014). Democracy in crisis? The declining support for national democracy in European countries, 2007–2011. *European Journal of Political Research* 53 (3), pp. 423–442.

Bartels, L., and Bermeo, N. (2013). *Mass politics in tough times: Opinions, votes and protest in the great recession*. Oxford: Oxford University Press.

Best, H., and Cotta, M. (Eds.). (2000). *Parliament representatives in Europe 1848–2000. Legislative recruitment and careers in Eleven European countries.* Oxford: Oxford University Press.

Brooks, C., and Manza, J. (2013). A broken public? Americans' responses to the Great Recession. *American Sociological Review* 78, pp. 727–748.

Carey, J. M. (2007). Competing principals, political institutions, and party unity in legislative voting. *American Journal of Political Science* 51, pp. 92–107.

Cordero, G., and Coller, X. (2015). Cohesion and candidate selection in parliamentary groups. *Parliamentary Affairs* 68 (3), pp. 592–615.

Cordero, G., and Coller, X. (2018). *Democratizing candidate selection: New methods, old receipts?* London: Palgrave.

Cordero, G., Jaime-Castillo, A. M., & Coller, X. (2016). Selecting candidates in multilevel democracies. *American Behavioral Scientist* 60 (7), pp. 773–780.

Cordero, G., and Simón, P. (2015). Economic crisis and support for democracy in Europe. *West European Politics* 39 (2), 305–325.

Cross, W. P., and Katz, R. S. (2013). *The challenges of intra-party democracy.* Oxford: Oxford University Press.

DiMaggio, P., and Powell, W. W. (1991). The Iron Cage revisited: Institutional isomorphism and collective rationality. In W. W. Powell and P. DiMaggio (Eds.), *The new institutionalism in organizational analysis.* Chicago: Chicago University Press, pp. 63–82.

Fishman, R. M. and D. W. Everson (2016), "Mechanisms of Social Movement Success: Conversation, Displacement and Disruption". *Revista Internacional de Sociología*, 74 (4): e045. doi: http://dx.doi.org/10.3989/ris.2016.74.4.045

Fujimura N. (2012). Electoral incentives, party discipline, and legislative organization: Manipulating legislative committees to win elections and maintain party unity. *European Political Science Review* 4, pp. 147–175.

Gallagher, M. (1988). Introduction. In M. Gallagher and M. Marsh (Eds.), *Candidate selection in comparative perspective. The secret garden of politics.* London: Sage, 1–19.

Gallagher, M., and Marsh, M. (1988). *Candidate selection in comparative perspective: The secret garden of politics.* London: Sage.

Hazan, R. Y., and Rahat, G. (2007). The Influence of Candidate Selection Methods on Legislatures and Legislators: Theoretical Propositions, Methodological Suggestions and Empirical Evidence. In Arter, D. (Ed), *Comparing and Classifying Legislatures*, London. Routledge, pp. 109–28.

Hazan, R. Y., and Rahat, G. (2010). *Democracy within parties: Candidate selection methods and their political consequences, comparative politics.* Oxford and New York: Oxford University Press.

Hernández, E., and Kriesi, H. (2016). The electoral consequences of the financial and economic crisis in Europe. *European Journal of Political Research* 55 (2), 203–224.

Hix, S. (2004). Electoral institutions and legislative behavior: Explaining voting defection in the European Parliament. *World Politics* 56, pp. 194–223.

Hopkin, J. (2001). Bringing the members back in? Democratizing candidate selection in Britain and Spain. *Party Politics* 7, pp. 343–361.

Katz, R. S. (2001). The problem of candidate selection and models of party democracy. *Party Politics* 7, pp. 277–296.

Katz, R. S., and Mair, P. (2005). Changing models of party organizations and party democracy: the emergence of the cartel party. *Party Politics* 1 (1), pp. 5–28.

Kriesi, H. (2012). The political consequences of the financial and economic crisis in Europe: Electoral punishment and popular protest. *Swiss Political Science Review* 18 (4), pp. 518–522.

Kriesi, H., and Pappas, T. S. (Eds.). (2015). *European populism in the shadow of the great recession*. Colchester: ECPR Press.

Nadeau, R., Lewis-Beck, M. S., and Bélanger, É. (2013). Economics and elections revisited. *Comparative Political Studies* 46, pp. 551–573.

Porta, D. della. (2015). *Social movements in times of austerity: Bringing capitalism back into protest analysis*. Malden, MA: Polity Press.

Rama, J., and Cordero, G. (2018). *Going populist. Explaining the vote for right-wing populist parties in Europe after the great recession*. Not published.

Ranney, A., Pennyman, H. R., & Ranney, A. (1981). Candidate selection. In Butler, D. (Ed.), *Democracy at the polls*. Washington, DC: American Enterprise Institute.

Sandri, G., Seddone, A., and Venturino, F. (2015). *Party primaries in comparative perspective*. Farnham: Ashgate.

Siavelis, P. M., and Morgenstern, S. (Eds.). (2008). *Pathways to power: political recruitment and candidate selection in Latin America*. University Park: Pennsylvania State University Press.

Torcal, M. (2014). The decline of political trust in Spain and Portugal: Economic performance or political responsiveness? *American Behavioral Scientist* 58, pp. 1542–1567.

Index

Note: Page numbers for figures are in italics, and page numbers for tables are in bold.